THE GEMSTONE LEGEND

· ·

*"...Your help is needed. Please make one, five, 10, 100 copies —
or whatever you can — and give them to friends of politicians,
groups, or media. The game is nearly up. Either the Mafia goes
— or America goes."*

— Gemstone 13:6

****

This urgent plea concludes the well-traveled but deeply mysterious *Skeleton Key to the Gemstone Files,* and to a large extent this report is responding to the above request 18 years after it was first circulated.

However, the legendary "Gemstone thesis" has never been seriously researched and confirmed through independent, objective means. Very little information has been uncovered and released concerning the purported author of the Gemstone Files, Bruce Roberts. These circumstances made it necessary to push *Project Seek* to a successful conclusion — and encourage open debate about these important, historic questions:

What motivated Roberts to issue forth his elaborate theories about Aristotle Onassis, Howard Hughes, the Kennedy family and Watergate? What has happened since? What does the future hold? How does it all tie in?

Find out in *Project Seek.*

PROJECT
SEEK

Onassis, Kennedy and
the Gemstone Thesis

Gerald A. Carroll

For permissions, serializations, condensations, adaptations, or for our catalog of other publications, write the Publisher at the address below.

Library of Congress Cataloging-in-Publication Data

Carroll, Gerald A., 1954-
    Project Seek: Onassis, Kennedy and the Gemstone Thesis
    by Gerald A. Carroll
       p.   cm.
    Includes index.
    ISBN 0-9640104-0-2   13 digit: 978-0964010406
    1. United States – Politics and government – 1945-1989.
    2. Kennedy, John F. (John Fitzgerald,) 1917-1963. 3. Onassis, Aristotle Socrates, 1906-1975. 4. Hughes, Howard, 1905-1976. 5. Kennedy family. 6. World politics – 1945-. 7. Political corruption – History – 20th century. 8. Conspiracies – History – 20th century. I. Title.
E839.5.C35 1994
973.92-dc20
for Library of Congress

                           94-2937
                             CIP

Published By:
Bridger House Publishers, Inc.
PO Box 599, Hayden ID, 83835
1-800-729-4131

Cover Design: Julie Melton, The Right Type, USA therighttype.com
Printed in the United States of America
10 9 8 7 6 5 4 3 2

DEDICATION

· · · · · · · · · · · · ·

F or those unfamiliar with the Gemstone thesis, this report will come as a shock.

For those who have cursory knowledge of this material, this report will provide a provocative introduction to an alternate history of the 20th century as described in the Gemstone Files and the Skeleton Key *to the Gemstone Files, including their origins and a candid appraisal of their historical significance.*

Finally, for veteran "Gemstoners," the more intrepid minds who have endured the challenges and dangers of verifying this type of information, this report will help serve as vindication of those efforts and a lasting memorial to fearless researchers such as Don Bolles, Danny Casolaro and Paul Wilcher — all of whom died pursuing a more enlightened ideal for us all.

It is to this hardy breed of probing, investigative journalist — the "seeker" of truth in a free but often hostile society — that Project Seek *is dedicated.*

— GAC

TABLE OF CONTENTS

. . . .

INTRODUCTION

. . . .

Our initiation to the Gemstone thesis took place on a clear spring day in April of 1976 on the campus of California State University-Sacramento.

Howard Pine was a fellow student and reporter/editor for the campus newspaper, the *State Hornet*. He was also half Native American and had a slightly different slant on politics than did the average career student at the time. The bearded, pony-tailed Pine was enigmatic, his thirtysomething demeanor always crinkled in thought.

On this particularly memorable afternoon, Pine handed us a 22-page mimeographed document. We skimmed through its contents, and were aghast at what was being stated. We asked Pine if any mainstream media had followed up on any of the allegations, and he responded: "Nobody important has run any of this, except I think *Hustler* magazine has." We didn't check this at the time, but Pine apparently had information enough to successfully forecast the future: *The heavily edited* Hustler *version of Gemstone did not run until February of 1979.*

Still, at that time in 1976, we were young and preparing for graduation and the rude world beyond. We had little interest in the apparent nonsense Pine's document presented.

But little did we realize this scene was being repeated hundreds, maybe even thousands, of times across the nation and even the world. This information was being passed from person to person, in strictly clandestine fashion, with great discretion, almost fearfully.

And with good reason. Only a year old was the awful symbolism of the fall of Saigon. The Vietnam War was over, and the United States was enduring international humiliation. Watergate had penetrated the very essence of Americans as a nation, and a President had resigned in disgrace only two years before. The nation was in a state of almost moribund depression. That is why these papers were handled as carefully as they were; some of the information proved to be deadly to its owners.

The copies were well-worn; that is, it was easy to tell they were copies of copies of copies — to the extent that some of the typed characters were considerably blurred. Yet, it was easy to make out what was being written.

The ideas presented were, in our estimation at the time, the most far-fetched fantasies imaginable. Following is a brief synopsis of the rambling document, which carried the title *A Skeleton Key to the Gemstone Files*:

- Aristotle Onassis, the famed yet mysterious Greek shipping magnate, had deep business ties (legal and otherwise) with Joseph Kennedy in the early part of this century. The relationship earned huge war-related profits for both men over the years.
- Onassis, deeply involved in both the legal opium and illegal narcotics trades internationally, ordered the kidnap of billionaire Howard Hughes in 1957 in Nassau, the Bahamas. The real Hughes was drugged and transported to Onassis' island of Skorpios, while a double was inserted in Hughes' place. The double was always surrounded by heavy security and never seen in public. Kidnap motive: To enable Onassis to control Hughes' massive defense-industry and aviation empire. *The Hughes double is identified in the* Skeleton Key.
- Joseph Kennedy's two sons, John and Robert — who became President and Attorney General of the United States in 1960-61 — uncovered details of the old links

between Joseph Kennedy and Onassis and sought to dissolve them by arresting many alleged associates of Onassis. Most of this activity occurred after Joseph Kennedy suffered a stroke in January, 1961 — after which Joseph Kennedy lost control over the activities of his sons. The ensuing arrest of organized-crime figures, like Teamsters boss Jimmy Hoffa, enraged Onassis.

- The resulting turmoil was chaotic, historic and violent. Onassis allegedly started a series of well-planned counter-assaults to the younger Kennedy's Camelot-style crusade. His first move was to woo Jacqueline Kennedy, wife of the President. Onassis did so by inviting the First Lady on an excursion in the Mediterranean Sea aboard his luxury yacht, the *Christina*. There, in October of 1963 just before the assassination of President Kennedy, *Onassis became romantically involved with Jackie.* Witnesses aboard the yacht — who have since written separate testimonies to that fateful trip after the Gemstone report was circulated — confirm the romantic tie, and the ensuing love triangle which ended up being one of several motivational factors in the JFK assassination plot.

- Onassis allegedly ordered the assassination of Kennedy, using a well-trained Mafia team that had earlier tried and failed to assassinate Cuban President Fidel Castro. Onassis wanted Castro erased because Cuba's Communist revolution had wiped out casino profits for organized crime figures, including Onassis. The failed Bay of Pigs invasion and JFK's lack of enthusiasm for the project (and lack of promised air support) angered Onassis to the point of switching targets from Castro to Kennedy.

- Lee Harvey Oswald was part of the JFK hit squad, but his instructions were to shoot Texas Gov. John Connally, which he did. The Gemstone report identifies the remaining assassins, their firing techniques and sophisticated strategies in Dallas, their complicity with the Dallas police department, and how they were rewarded for their efforts.

- Gerald Ford, later to be rewarded with a non-elected Presidency following the Watergate scandal, successfully covered up much of the JFK assassination evidence as head of the Warren Commission. Anything remotely attaching Onassis or his alleged subordinates to the assassination plot was cleanly swept away.
- His brother's death motivating him, Robert Kennedy foolishly ran for President in 1968 in a continued attempt to fight Onassis and his organization. This ended in yet another Onassis-ordered hit, this one on RFK. With both primary Kennedy brothers out of the picture and kid brother Ted Kennedy now capitulating to Onassis' every wish, Onassis was free to marry Jackie, which he did. The marriage was nightmarish for the entire Kennedy family, and a final gloating symbol of Onassis' clear victory in the "gang war" between himself and the Kennedys.
- Soon thereafter, Mary Jo Kopechne, a key organizer in the RFK presidential campaign, reportedly "read too much" as she was packing RFK's files in California and uncovered evidence of the Onassis-Kennedy connection. She made the mistake of publicly proclaiming this knowledge during a party at the Kennedy compound near Chappaquiddick, and soon after died in a watery car crash involving Ted Kennedy. The Gemstone report's version of events at Chappaquiddick differs much from the established record, but much has since been confirmed by a later series of books on the subject. The *Hustler* magazine version of the *Skeleton Key* in 1979 *heavily edits the original segments pertaining to Chappaquiddick. **We have that missing material.***
- In 1972, the Watergate break-ins were engineered by President Richard M. Nixon's associates, many of whom were involved in the Bay of Pigs invasion and Kennedy assassination in the early 1960s. Nixon's top security

advisors were convinced that the Democratic National Committee had come into possession of material connecting the Kennedys to Onassis. There was no apparent motive for this political espionage, since Sen. George McGovern was a ridiculously easy pushover for Nixon in the upcoming election. Still, two break-ins were ordered into the Democratic National Headquarters at the Watergate Hotel. Electronic bugs were planted during the first break-in, which proceeded without incident. The second break-in was ordered not only to remove the bugs, but to *photograph all DNC files,* something the conspirators thought unreasonable and dangerous. They were right. The sheer volume of the task was a causative factor in the burglars being discovered and arrested.

• Earlier, *Washington Post* publisher Katharine Meyer Graham, whose late husband Philip had been a strong ally of the Kennedys in the struggle against Onassis, had monitored the activities of Nixon's associates long before Watergate. When the two burglaries took place, her own private investigator monitored and recorded all events. After the first break-in, it was Graham and her private investigator, *who is identified in the Gemstone report,* who set the trap for the second anticipated break-in, and the ensuing arrest. It was this investigator, dressed as a mailman, who *taped the door a second time in the Watergate Hotel,* tipping the security guard who then called police. Graham, in possession of all Watergate-related materials first-hand, became her own "Deep Throat," feeding information to a pair of obscure reporters, Bob Woodward and Carl Bernstein, who "broke" the series of Watergate stories that led to Nixon's eventual resignation in August, 1974. In this way, Graham protected herself from any direct confrontation with Onassis.

• After Nixon's resignation, Ford was the logical successor, having full knowledge stretching from his successful efforts through the phony Warren Commission to cover up the true story behind the JFK assassination, all the way through the Watergate controversy as the non-elected vice presidential successor to the corrupt, resigned and disgraced Spiro T. Agnew. Ford would serve Nixon, and Onassis, quite well, as it turned out.

****

That is the essence of *A Skeleton Key to the Gemstone Files*, which are not to be confused with G. Gordon Liddy's "Gemstone Plan" that led to Watergate (although he could have borrowed that designation from his knowledge of the *real* Gemstone files).

The reputed author of these Gemstone files was identified as an American man named Bruce Roberts, who allegedly penned them over many years — using an interconnected network of international sources. *Hustler* magazine's edited Gemstone version in 1979 carried the by-line of "Bruce Roberts" but was vague on exactly who Bruce Roberts was, and his background.

Was "Bruce Roberts" a pseudonym? We have discovered that it was not; that Bruce Roberts did exist, that his claims of an international intelligence network carried some merit; and that much of the material contained within his Gemstone thesis can be cross-checked and verified through other means.

Since 1976 when copies of *A Skeleton Key to the Gemstone Files* were distributed, much of what the files reveal has been confirmed by other authors on a number of different fronts, although any direct link between Onassis and the JFK-RFK assassinations has yet to be publicly scrutinized as a viable conspiracy theory. Further, any direct links between Onassis and Joseph Kennedy early in this century have yet to be adequately researched.

But we have uncovered evidence of such connections. We have also been able to verify much of what the *Skeleton Key* reveals. Our historical perspective of these seemingly unrelated events goes far deeper than many of the fragmented conspiracy theories bandied about through various print, broadcast and cinema over the past 30 years since the JFK assassination stunned the world.

It is not the purpose of this book to falsely accuse anyone. Bruce Roberts makes the allegations; we are simply determining if they have any merit. Indeed, we have found that much of the Gemstone material and its major points, despite their sensational nature, are based upon kernels of truth.

That is why we will approach this explosive topic in the following way:

- In the first three chapters — and for the first time ever — we will reproduce and make fully public a complete transcript of *A Skeleton Key to the Gemstone Files*, with each portion numbered and cross-referenced, so that the document can be referred to as it pertains to its ensuing narrative and analysis.
- The passages will then be objectively evaluated, with a goal of supporting or refuting the information by way of credible, independent sources.

The reader is then free to make a choice as to the veracity of this material. This historic account provides an absorbing rewrite of 20th-century history. It has been 18 years since the *Skeleton Key* has been circulated. To date, nobody has actively tackled its merits — until now.

We are changing that, through *Project Seek*.

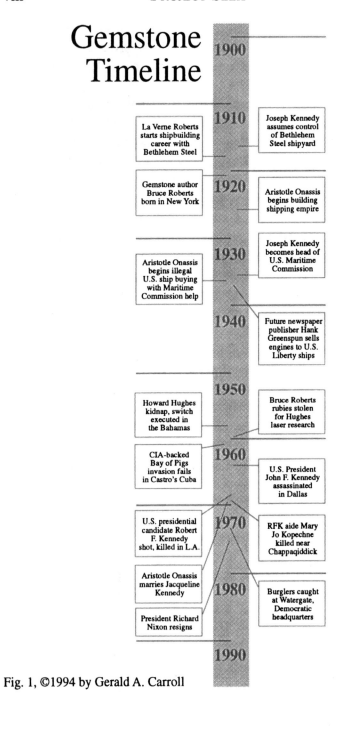

Gemstone Timeline

1900

1910

La Verne Roberts starts shipbuilding career with Bethlehem Steel

Joseph Kennedy assumes control of Bethlehem Steel shipyard

1920

Gemstone author Bruce Roberts born in New York

Aristotle Onassis begins building shipping empire

1930

Aristotle Onassis begins illegal U.S. ship buying with Maritime Commission help

Joseph Kennedy becomes head of U.S. Maritime Commission

1940

Future newspaper publisher Hank Greenspun sells engines to U.S. Liberty ships

1950

Howard Hughes kidnap, switch executed in the Bahamas

Bruce Roberts rubies stolen for Hughes laser research

1960

CIA-backed Bay of Pigs invasion fails in Castro's Cuba

U.S. President John F. Kennedy assassinated in Dallas

1970

U.S. presidential candidate Robert F. Kennedy shot, killed in L.A.

RFK aide Mary Jo Kopechne killed near Chappaqiddick

Aristotle Onassis marries Jacqueline Kennedy

1980

Burglers caught at Watergate, Democratic headquarters

President Richard Nixon resigns

1990

Fig. 1, ©1994 by Gerald A. Carroll

CHAPTER 1

. . . .

The Skeleton Key: Part I

The *Skeleton Key to the Gemstone Files* was pieced together by an unnamed individual who claims to have accessed much of Gemstone Files author Bruce Roberts' work. Despite its second-hand nature, and despite its enormous complexity, the *Skeleton Key* does present claims and circumstances which can be independently traced and corroborated, and indeed many researchers have done just that in books and articles which have appeared long after the *Skeleton Key* was circulated.

The *Key* also contains plenty of names — many of which were simply deleted when the *Key* ran in the February, 1979, edition of *Hustler* magazine. Had it not been for *Hustler* publisher Larry Flynt's almost crazed dedication to revealing all that he and his magazine could relating to the assassination of John F. Kennedy, this later record would carry little meaning. For, despite Flynt's devil-may-care attitude, he and his editors still watered down the *Skeleton Key* tremendously. We won't make the same mistake. The *Key* appears here, for the first time, in annotated form, so that readers can see how the published *Hustler* version stacks up to the original. It also will go far in explaining why Flynt sat on this story for over three years before finally going to press with it; the fact that someone tried to shoot him to death might have had something to do with the delay as well.

Flynt offered a reward of $1 million to "anyone who can solve" the "conspiracy" surrounding the Kennedy assassination. The reward was offered in January of 1978, just over 15 years after the November 22, 1963, killing of the President. Two months later, on March 5, Flynt was shot by an unknown assailant, who had pulled up in a car right after Flynt and his attorney left a Lawrenceville, GA, courtroom where the publisher was on trial for obscenity charges. The shooting left Flynt paralyzed from the waist down.

The shooting was blamed on overzealous, right-wing Christians who were reportedly enraged at Flynt's lengthy history of "smut" publishing. However, the timing of the shooting soon after his pronouncement of the $1 million JFK conspiracy reward leaves some doubt as to the assassin's true motives.

Regardless of the circumstances surrounding the first public disclosure of the *Skeleton Key*, the facts as presented certainly provide some valuable material from which a coherent investigation of these facts can be conducted. *Hustler* might not have published the entire *Key* script as circulated at that time, but it did print the most critical passages — those connecting Aristotle Onassis with the assassinations of JFK, RFK and the Watergate scandal. Further, the editors at *Hustler* also added some information that was *not* in the original *Skeleton Key*. This information, including astounding facts on the organized-crime background of Gerald Ford's real father, lends further credibility to whatever passages in the Gemstone Files that could be construed as Bruce Roberts' private fantasies.

Biographical information on Roberts himself is sprinkled throughout the original *Key*. However, *Hustler* deleted much of this material. We decided to include the missing fragments pertaining to Roberts, and even uncovered a few more on our own — just to show that Roberts was who he claimed to be, and that he was indeed author of the Gemstone thesis (see Chapter 8).

It is easy to see why the mainstream media in the United States and around the world failed to pick up on *Hustler's* lead in reporting any connection between the Kennedy assassinations and Onassis. A magazine which so blatantly exploits women and that contains such outrageous fiction and other sordid content can hardly be credible enough to carry a story of this magnitude with any seriousness. The cover art on the story showed the "Kennedy boys" and Onassis, among others, dressed in pinstripe, gangster-style suits. The whole package was difficult to take seriously, and it wasn't.

But that was before the **real** *Skeleton Key* started showing up again on college campuses and among certain individuals who could finally compare the original with the sanitized *Hustler* version. For the first time anywhere, we will produce a hybrid copy of the *Key* which will vividly show the original *Key* alongside the *Hustler* version. Readers can then decide for themselves what has transpired — and what motivated Flynt's editors to do what they did.

Now what of Bruce Roberts himself? Here is how *Hustler* magazine described the author of the "article" entitled "The Gemstone File":

"The author of this article is deceased. How he died is not known. What is known is that he was a man trained as a crystallographer who claimed to have stumbled onto dark and murky, but nonetheless discernible, interconnections between the aberrant world of Howard Hughes, the Mafia, the Central Intelligence Agency and the United States government...

"His name was Bruce Roberts. In the 1950s he lived in the Sunset District of San Francisco and began to preach to all who would listen about the evil conspiracies he had discovered..."

Hustler's prologue of this issue (February, 1979) cited that the "Gemstone File" was "presented to us with the following warning: 'Everyone else who has this information is now dead' — including its author, Bruce Roberts." *Hustler* admitted in its introduction that it did not know how Roberts died. But we found out how, along with some other facts about his life which are pretty hard to come by.

Bruce Porter Roberts was born Oct. 27, 1919, in the state of New York, and died July 30, 1976, in San Francisco of "respiratory failure (due to) metastatic carcinoma of lung (adenocarcinoma);" in other words, lung cancer. However, as we will discover, Roberts wrote his Gemstone papers nearly up to the day he died — and had a strange explanation for his development of the "cancer." But more on Roberts' background in Chapter 8. Now it is time to present the *Skeleton Key*, with the following preamble:

First, the *Hustler* report is not the actual "Gemstone File" as the title might suggest. It is only the *Skeleton Key*, quoted virtually verbatim except for passages which were either left out or added on. Further, the magazine's editors changed the tenses from the predominantly past tense (that the original *Key* uses), into a present tense that is more newswriting style. That will make the following annotated document somewhat confusing to read straight through, but it is not necessarily designed to be a literary masterpiece. It is designed as a reference upon which the rest of this volume is based.

Following is a key for the better understanding of *A Skeleton Key to the Gemstone Files* which follows:

- All <u>underlined</u> passages are those included in the original *Key* and not presented in the February, 1979, issue of *Hustler*.
- All **bold-faced** passages, which are comparably few, are *Hustler's* additions which are not included in the original *Key*.
- In areas where *Hustler* rewrote or rephrased passages, or changed individual words, from the original *Key*, brackets ([ ]) will set apart *Hustler's* rewrite — and it will immediately follow the original phrase.
- Passages in the *Key* will be numbered, just as books of the Bible have each verse numbered. In this way, when text of the book refers to the *Key*, the reader can easily refer back to that particular passage without compromising continuity. And now, without further delay, we present the annotated *Skeleton Key to the Gemstone Files* as circulated in 1976, with *Hustler's* 1979 version included:

A SKELETON KEY TO THE GEMSTONE FILES

Introduction: The Gemstone files were written in many segments over a period of years — by an American man named Bruce Roberts. Parts of the files were released to certain Americans beginning in 1969. The number of hand-written pages is well over a thousand, which I have read about four hundred. I have been able to verify some of the statements made in the files, but I do not have the time or the research facilities to verify the entire story. Perhaps others can help.

Since the scope of the work is so large, and the events described so complex and interlocking, it may be more easily understood with this skeleton outline of the Gemstone thesis. Individual papers can then be read with greater comprehension.

THE GEMSTONE FILE: JFK'S KILLERS REVEALED
By Bruce Roberts

This magazine has an abiding interest in shedding light on those concerts of evil that are known by the name of conspiracies. It is not just because our publisher was shot down by an unknown gunman in a small Southern town and will bear the physical evidence of that cowardly act for too long. Unseen fingers, pulling unspottable triggers, with silent eyes framing invisible cross hairs, are not strangers to those in public life in this country. The forces of evil that foster such things are far too evident to be a figment of paranoid imagination. There are conspiracies; just ask Jimmy Hoffa's son or Medgar Evers' brother or any of the Kennedy family. Or you could ask Larry or Althea Flynt.

Throughout history, wherever new voices become powerful and commanding, there is a traceable pattern of violent response. Whether from the right or the left, there is a stealthy, savage reaction, like a shaft of ramrod steel. From Jesus Christ to Chile's Salvador Allende, the markings are clear. Action calls forth reaction, and nowhere is this more clear than in the savage history of our own country: Abraham Lincoln, Huey Long, John Fitzgerald Kennedy, Robert Kennedy and all the others whose cries for justice have been stilled by the staccato burst of a gun. These are the facts of our political life. Sudden death is not just an overtime in professional football.

The article that follows, *The Gemstone File* — a condensation of a thousand-page manuscript — may be considered by many to be a work of madness. But remember, through all the ages all innovative work of genius has thought to be a product of insanity. One need only reflect on the spectacle of Galileo recanting before the church. It was madness — they said — for him to advance the notion that the earth moved around the sun. And they were right: It was madness, even though he was correct. The astronomer's thinking was madness because it upset the settled scheme of things and could be demonstrably proven for all to see. For that reason, Galileo's idea had to be dismissed and done away with — perhaps, just the *The Gemstone File*.

No doubt reasonable men will say that the factual assertions of *The Gemstone File* are simply preposterous — because they go too far and encompass too much. That may be true, but it should never be overlooked that the hellish vision the article contains may well bear the germs of truth, virulent though they may be.

The author of this article is deceased. How he died is not known. What is known is that he was a man trained as a crystallographer who claimed to have stumbled onto the dark and murky, but nonetheless discernible, interconnections between the aberrant world of Howard Hughes, the Mafia, the Central Intelligence Agency and the United States government.

He claims that through his inventions in the field of artificial-gemstone technology (the cornerstone of laser-beam application), he had penetrated into the heart of the beast:

that he became privy to worlds that can just barely be imagined, let alone glimpsed by ordinary mortals. His wisdom (if such it was) led, he claimed, to the death of his father at the hands of these malignant forces.

His name was Bruce Roberts. In the 1950s, he lived in the Sunset District of San Francisco and began to preach to all who would listen about the evil conspiracies he had discovered. This was well before the madness that eventually took place in Dealey Plaza and Vietnam.

You, then, will be the judge of Roberts' jarring legacy. Is there a connection between the deaths of popes and the flow of oil and heroin? Do the forces that applaud death and disintegration over life and human progress really exist? And do they take the forms Roberts postulates? Is this an incredible web of paranoid lunacy or a searing glimpse into the fourth dimension of history?

We do not presume to judge the material that follows — material we have obtained as a result of our advertisements calling for information about the JFK assassination. Nor do we intent to maliciously cast ill toward anyone by publishing this article. We consider only this: *The Gemstone File* is a cry that needs to be heard. Whether or not your ears are deaf is a matter for you alone to decide. — John G. Clancy.

****

(Gemstone 1:1) 1932: [Aristotle] Onassis, a Greek drug pusher and shipowner who made his first million selling "Turkish tobacco" (opium) in Argentina, worked [works] out a profitable deal with Joseph [P.] Kennedy, Eugene Meyer and Meyer Lansky: Onassis was [is] to ship booze directly into Boston for Joseph Kennedy. Also involved was a heroin deal with Franklin D. and Elliott Roosevelt.

(1:2) 1934: Onassis, [John D.] Rockefeller [Jr.] and the Seven Sisters (major oil companies) signed an agreement outlined in an oil cartel memo: F--- the Arabs out of their oil, ship it [transport it] on Onassis' ships [and get richer]; <u>Rockefeller and the Seven Sisters to get rich.</u> All this was [is] done.

(**1:3**) <u>Roberts, studying journalism at the University of Wisconsin, learned these things via personal contacts. His special interest was in crystallography — and the creation of synthetic rubies, the original Gemstone experiment.</u>

(**1:4**) 1936-1940: Eugene Meyer buys the *Washington Post* to get control of [the] news media; other Mafia [figures] buy newspapers, broadcasting [radio stations], <u>TV,</u> etc. News censorship of all <u>other</u> major news media goes into effect.

(**1:5**) 1941-1945: World War II very profitable for Onassis, Rockefeller [and the Rockefellers], Kennedys, [and the] Roosevelts, <u>I.G. Farben, etc., etc.</u> Onassis — selling oil, arms and dope to both sides — went [goes] through the war without losing a single ship or man.

(**1:6**) 1949: Onassis buys [U.S.] war surplus "Liberty Ships" in questionable (illegal) purchase. <u>Lawyer Burke Marshall helps him.</u>

(**1:7**) 1956: Howard Hughes, Texas billionaire, is meanwhile buying his way toward control of the U.S. electoral process — <u>with a view toward personal gain.</u> He buys senators, governors, etc. He finally buys his first politician — newly elected [re-elected] V.P. [Vice President Richard] Nixon, via a quarter-million-dollar [$205,000] non-repayable loan to Nixon's brother, Donald.

(**1:8**) Early 1957: <u>V.P. Nixon repays the favor by having IRS-Treasury grant tax-free status (refused twice before) to "Hughes Medical Foundation," sole owner of Hughes Aircraft, creating a tax-free, non-accountable money funnel or laundry, for whatever Hughes wanted to do. U.S. government also shelved antitrust suits against Hughes TWA, etc.</u>

(**1:9**) March, 1957: Onassis carries out a carefully planned event: he has Hughes kidnapped from his bungalow at the Beverly Hills Hotel, using Hughes' own men <u>(Chester Davis, born Cesare in Sicily, et al). Hughes' men either quit, get fired</u>

or stay on in the news Onassis organization. A few days later, Mayor Cannon of Nevada (now Senator Cannon) arranges a fake "marriage" to Jean Peters, to explain Hughes' sudden loss of interest in chasing movie stars. [A fake marriage between starlet Jean Peters and Hughes is arranged.] Hughes, battered and brain-damaged in the scuffle [during the kidnapping], is taken to the Emerald Isle (Beach) Hotel in the Bahamas where the entire top floor has been rented for the "Hughes party." There he is shot full of heroin for thirty [30] days and later dragged off to a cell on Onassis' island, Skorpios. Onassis now has a much larger power base in the U.S. (the Hughes empire), as well as control over V.P. Nixon and other Hughes-purchased politicians. L. Wayne Rector, "Hughes'" double since 1955, becomes Hughes. [A Hughes double becomes "Hughes."]

(2:1) September, 1957: Onassis calls the Apalachin [, New York, organized-crime] meeting to announce to U.S. Mafia heads his grab of Hughes and his adoption of Hughes' game plan for acquiring power: buying U.S. senators, congressmen, governors, [and] judges, en masse, to take control "legally" of the U.S. government. Onassis' radio message to Apalachin from a remote farmhouse [is] intercepted (reluctantly) by the FBI's J. Edgar Hoover, on the basis of a tip-off from some Army intelligence guys who weren't in on the plan.

(2:2) Also in 1957: Joseph [Joe] Kennedy takes [his son], John F., and Jackie to see Onassis on his yacht, [the *Christina*, to] introduce John, and [to] remind Onassis of an old Mafia promise: the Presidency for a Kennedy. Onassis agrees.

(2:3) 1958: Hordes of Mafia-selected, [Mafia-] purchased and [Mafia-] supported "grass roots" candidates sweep into office. [!]

(2:4) 1959: [Fidel] Castro takes over from dictator [Fulgencio] Batista, thereby destroying [the] cozy and lucrative Mafia gambling empire run for Onassis by Meyer Lansky. Castro scoops up $8 million in Mafia casino receipts. Onassis is furious. V.P. Nixon becomes operations chief [White House

Action Officer] for CIA-planned Bay of Pigs invasion, using CIA Hunt, McCord, etc. [E. Howard Hunt as political officer for the operation, James McCord, etc.] and Cuban ex-Batista strong-arm cops (Cuban freedom fighters) [Eugenio] Martinez, [Virgilio] Gonzales, etc., as well as winners like Frank Sturgis ([alias Frank] Fiorini) [, a gunrunner with a gambling background].

(2:5) [Also] 1959: Stirring election battle between [John F.] Kennedy and Nixon [begins]. Either way, Onassis wins, since he has control over both candidates.

(2:6) JFK elected. American people happy. Rose Kennedy happy. Onassis happy. Mafia ecstatic.

(2:7) Roberts brings his synthetic rubies — the original "Gemstones" — to Hughes Aircraft in Los Angeles. They steal his rubies, the basis for laser-beam research, laser bombs, etc., because of the optical quality of the rubies. One of eleven possible sources for one of the ingredients involved in the Gemstone experiment was the Golden Triangle area. Roberts was married to the daughter of the former French consul in Indochina. In that region, Onassis' involvement in the Golden Triangle dope trade was no secret. Roberts' investigation revealed the Onassis-Hughes connection, kidnap and switch.

(2:8) "Gemstones" — synthetic rubies and sapphires with accompanying "histories," otherwise known as Gemstone papers — were sold or given away to foreign consular officials in return for information. A worldwide information network was gradually developed, a trade of the intelligence activities of many countries. This intelligence network is the source for much of the information in the Gemstone files.

(2:9a) January, 1961: Joseph Kennedy had [has] a stroke, ending his [personal] control over [sons] John and Bobby. The boys decided [decide] to rebel against Onassis' control. Why? Inter-Mafia struggle? Perhaps a dim hope of restoring this country to its mythical integrity?

(2:9b) They began committing Mafia no-nos: Arrested Wally Bird, owner of Air Thailand, who has been shipping Onassis' heroin out of the Golden Triangle (Laos, Cambodia, Vietnam), under contract with the CIA (Air Opium), arrested [They arrest and jail] Teamster Mafia Jimmy Hoffa and put him in jail. Declared [and declare] the $73 million in forged "Hughes" land liens, deposited with San Francisco's Bank of America, as "security" for the TWA judgment against Hughes, to what they are: forgeries.

(3:0) April, 1961: CIA Bay of Pigs fiasco. Hunt, McCord, CIA, Batista's Cubans [Cuban exiles] and Mafia angry about JFK's lack of enthusiasm. Mafia Onassis and his U.S. right-hand man, [CIA hires] "Hughes'" top aide, former FBI and CIA [man] Robert Maheu (nicknamed "IBM" for "Iron Bob Maheu") [to act as go-between for its Mafia contacts to put together a team to get Castro] hire and train a Mafia assassination team to get Castro. The team of a dozen or so includes John Roselli and Jimmy "The Weasel" Fratianno, expert Mafia hit men [an expert Mafia hit man], assisted by CIA's Hunt, [and] McCord and others. This was reported at the time by Jack Anderson, who gets a lot of his "tips" from his friend, Frank (Fiorini) Sturgis, who was also on the Castro assassination team. The team tries five times to kill Castro with everything from long-range rifles to apple pie with sodium morphate in it. **They nearly succeed, but some are caught and executed in Havana the day of the invasion.** Castro survives.

(3:1) 1963: Members of the Castro assassination [anti-Castro Cuban-exile training] team [are] arrested at Lake Pontchartrain, La., by Bobby Kennedy's Justice boys. Angered, Onassis changes targets and goes for the head: JFK, who — according to Onassis — "welched" ["welches"] on a Mafia deal. JFK sets up "Group of 40" [(advisors)] to fight Onassis.

(3:2a) August, 1962: Two murders had [have] to occur before the murder of JFK; of people who would understand the situation and [who] might squawk:

(3:2b) Senator Estes Kefauver, whose Crime Commission investigations had uncovered the 1932 [Onassis] deal between

Onassis, Kennedy, Eugene Meyer, Lansky, Roosevelt, et al. Kefauver planned [plans] a speech on the Senate floor denouncing Mafia operations. Instead, he ate [eats] a piece of apple pie laced with sodium morphate [(allegedly a poison)] (used in rat poison), and has [had] a sodium-morphate-induced "heart attack" on the Senate floor.

(3:2c) Philip Graham, editor [publisher] of the *Washington Post*. Philip had married Katharine Graham, Eugene Meyer's daughter who had inherited the *Washington Post* and allied media empire. Graham [Phil] put [puts] together [media empire as well as] the Kennedy-Johnson ticket and was [is] Kennedy's friend in the struggle with Onassis. According to Gemstone, Katharine Meyer Graham bribed some psychiatrist [a psychiatrist is bribed] to certify that Phil was insane. He was [is] allowed out of the nuthouse for the [one] weekend and died [dies] of a shotgun wound to the head, in the Graham home in Washington; [his] death [is] ruled [a] "suicide."

(3:3a) November 1, 1963: The hit on JFK was [is] to take place in true Mafia style: a triple execution, together with [at the same time as South Vietnam's Ngo Dinh Diem and Ngo Dinh Nhu] Diem and Nhu in Vietnam. Diem and Nhu got theirs, as scheduled. Onassis had invited [invites] Jackie for a cruise on the *Christina*, where she was [is] when JFK got [is] tipped off that big O [Big-O] planned [plans] to wipe him out. JFK called [calls] Jackie on the yacht from the White House, hysterical [telling her]: "Get off that yacht [even] if you have to swim," and canceled [cancels] his appearance at a [Chicago] football stadium in Chicago where the CIA-Mafia assassination team was [is] poised for the kill. Jackie stays on board [the *Christina*], descended the gangplank a few days later on Onassis' arm, in Turkey, to impress the Turkish boy, Mustapha. Madame Nhu, in the United States, bitterly remarked, "Whatever happened in Vietnam will see its counterpart in the United States."

(3:3b) One of the assassination team (Tom Wallace, a double for Oswald) was picked up in Chicago, with a rifle, and quickly released by police).

(3:3c) Three weeks later, the Mafia's alternate [backup] and carefully arranged execution plan went [goes] into effect: JFK was [is] assassinated in Dallas. A witness who recognized pictures of some people arrested in Dealey Plaza as having been in Chicago three weeks earlier told Black Panthers Hampton and Clark.

(3:4a) The JFK murder: Onassis "Hughes" man Robert Maheu reassigned [reassigns] the Mafia-CIA Castro assassination team to the murder of JFK, adding [adds] Eugene Brading, a third Mafia hit man [gunsel] from the Denver Mafia Smalldones "family." Two months earlier, Brading, on parole after a series of crimes, applied for a new driver's license, explaining to the California DMV (Department of Motor Vehicles) that he had decided to change his name to "Jim Braden." Brading got [gets] his California parole officer's permission for two trips to Dallas; in November, on "oil business" — the first time to look things over; and the second time, when JFK was [is] scheduled for [to make] his Dallas trip.

(3:4b) Lee Harvey Oswald, [of the] CIA, with carefully planned links to both the ultra-right and to the Communists, was [is] designated as the patsy. He was [is] supposed to shoot at [Texas] Gov. [John] Connally, and he did [does so].

(3:4c) Each of the four shooters [gunmen] — Oswald, Brading, Fratianno and Roselli — had [has] a timer and a backup man. [Timers give the signal to shoot.] Backup men were [are] supposed to pick up the spent shells, and get rid of the guns. Timers would give the signal to shoot. Hunt and McCord were there to help. Sturgis was in Miami.

Fratianno [, considered an excellent shot] shot [fires] from a second-story window in the Dal-Tex Building, across the street [kitty-corner] from the Texas School Book Depository. He apparently used a handgun; he is an excellent shot with a pistol. Fratianno hit Kennedy twice, in the back and in the head. Fratianno and his backup man were [are] "arrested," driven away from the Dal-Tex Building in a police car, and released (without being booked). (The Dallas police office is [was] located in the Dal-Tex Building).

(3:4d) Roselli shot Kennedy once, hitting the right side of his head and blowing his brains out, with a rifle, from behind a fence in the grassy knoll area. [From behind a fence on the grassy-knoll area, Roselli — armed with a rifle — gets Kennedy once, hitting the right side of his head and blowing his brains out.] Roselli and his timer went [go] down a manhole behind the fence and followed [follow] the sewer line away from Dealey Plaza.

(3:4e) The third point of the triangulated [Kennedy] ambush was supplied by Eugene Brading, shooting from Kennedy's left, from a small pagoda (sic, pergola) at Dealey Plaza, across the street from the grassy knoll. (Brading missed [misses], because Roselli's and Fratianno's shots had just hit Kennedy from the right and rear, nearly simultaneously). Brading's shot hits the curb and ricocheted [ricochets] off. Brading was [is] photographed on the scene, stuffing his gun under his coat. he wore [wears] a big leather hat, its hatband marked with large, conspicuous X's. (Police had been instructed to let anyone with an X-marked hatband through the police lines; some may have been told they were Secret Service).

(3:4f) After his shot, Brading ditched [ditches] his gun <u>with his backup man</u> and walked [walks] up the street [with his backup man] toward the Dal-Tex building. Roger Craig, a deputy sheriff, rushed [rushes] up to Brading, assuming [assumes] he is Secret Service and tells him he has just seen a man come out of the Book Depository and jump into a **Rambler** station wagon. Brading was [is] uninterested. Instead, he [Brading] walks into the Dal-Tex building to "make a phone call." <u>There he was arrested</u> [He is picked up for questioning] by another deputy sheriff, showed [shows] his "Jim Braden" driver's license and was [is] quickly released — without being booked.

(3:4g) Oswald shot [shoots] Connally twice from the Texas School Book Depository. he split [splits] from [through] the front door. His backup man was [is] supposed to take the rifle out of the building (or so Oswald thought [thinks]); instead, he "hid" [hides] it behind some boxes, where it would be found later [where it will later be found].

(3:4h) Three men dressed as "tramps" picked [pick] up the spent shells from Dealey Plaza. <u>One of them was Howard Hunt.</u> [Then] They drifted [drift] over to am empty boxcar sitting on the railway spur behind the grassy-knoll area and waited [wait]. A Dallas police officer ordered [orders] two Dallas cops to "go over to the boxcar and pick up the tramps." The three tramps paraded [parade] around Dealey Plaza to the police department, in the Dal-Tex Building. They were held there until the alarm went out to pick up Oswald; then they were [are] released, without being booked. In all, 10 men were [are] arrested [questioned] immediately after the shooting. All were [are] released soon after. None were [are] booked. Not a word of [about] their existence is mentioned in the Warren [Commission] Report.

(3:4i) Regarding Lee Harvey Oswald: Officer [J.D.] Tippit is dispatched in his police <u>radio</u> car to the Oak Cliff section, where Oswald had [has] rented a room. Tippit may have met Oswald on the street. He may have been supposed to kill Oswald, but something went [goes] wrong. Tippit was shot by two men, using two revolvers [Tippit is shot by two men armed with revolvers]. <u>The "witness," Domingo Benavides, who used Tippit's police car radio to report "we've had a shooting here,"</u> <u>may have been one of the men who shot him.</u> [A witness, Domingo Benavides, uses Tippit's police-car radio to report, "We've had a shooting here."] (A "Domingo Benevides" [also] appears in connection with the Martin Luther King shooting [shooting of Dr. Martin Luther King] <u>also.</u>

(3:4j) Oswald went [goes] to the movies. A "shoe store manager" told [tells] the theatre [theater] cashier that a suspicious-looking man had sneaked in without paying. <u>Fifteen assorted cops and FBI</u> [Sixteen police] charged [charge] out to the movie theatre [Texas Theater] to look for the guy who had [who's] sneaked in.

(3:4k) Oswald had [been given] a pistol that wouldn't [doesn't] fire. It may have been anticipated [Others anticipated] that the police would [will] shoot the "cop killer" for "resisting arrest." But since that doesn't happen, <u>the Dallas police brought Oswald out for small-time Mafia Jack Ruby to kill two days later</u> [small-time Mafioso Jack Ruby kills Oswald two days later].

(3:5) <u>Brading stayed at the Teamster-Mafia-Hoffa-financed "Cabana Motel" in Dallas. Ruby had gone to the Cabana the night before the murder, says the Warren Report.</u>

(3:6a) The rest, as they say, is history. Onassis was [is] so confident of his control over police, media, FBI, CIA, Secret Service and the U.S. judicial system that he had [has] JFK murdered before the eyes of the nation — then systematically bought [buys] off, killed [kills] off, or frightened [frightens] off all witnesses, and had [has] the evidence destroyed; <u>then put a 75-year seal of secrecy over the entire matter.</u>

(3:6b) [Unwitting] Cover-up participants include, among many: Gerald Ford, on the Warren Commission (a Nixon recommendation); <u>CIA attorney</u> Leon Jaworski, <u>of the CIA-front Anderson Foundation, representing Texas before the Commission to see that the fair name of Texas was not besmirched by the investigation</u> [(just off the Texas assassination commission, who keeps the fact that Oswald had operative status with the FBI secret from the Warren Commission)]; CIA <u>Dallas</u> chief John McCone; his assistant [CIA Deputy Director] Richard Helms; and a passle of police, FBI, news media, etc.

(3:7a) Where are they now? Johnny Roselli received [receives] part of his payoff for <u>the head shot on JFK</u> [shooting at JFK] in the form of a $250,000 "finder's fee" <u>for bringing "Hughes" (Onassis) to Las Vegas in 1967</u> [when the Desert Inn is sold to Hughes in 1966]. **When Roselli fails to collect mob money from a Las Vegas casino owner, he is asphyxiated in 1976.**

(3:7b) Jimmy Fratianno's payoff included [includes]

$109,000 in "non-repayable loans" from the San Francisco National Bank (President: Joe Alioto). Credit authorization for the series of loans, from 1964 to 1965, came from Joe Alioto and a high Teamster official. Dunn & Bradstreet noted this transaction in amazement, listing the loans in their 1964-65 monthly reports, and wondering how Fratianno could obtain so much "credit," as his only known title (listed in D&B) was "Mafia Executioner." Fratianno went around for years bragging about it: "Hi there. I'm Jimmy Fratianno, Mafia Executioner..." A bank V.P. told the whole story to the California Crime Commission, where Al Harris heard it, and it was hidden in a file folder there. Al Harris, who later shot off his mouth a little too much, "heart attacked."

(3:7c) When last seen (March, 1975), Fratianno was testifying before a San Francisco grand jury in regard to his participation, with East Coast Mafia Tony Romano, in the Sunol Golf Course swindle (which cost San Francisco somewhere between $100,000 and $500,000), with the active help of Mayor Joe Alioto.

(3:7d) In between, Fratianno used his $109,000 in "non-repayable loans" to start a trucking company in the Imperial Valley, where he engaged in a lot more swindling — involving U.S. government construction contracts. As one California Crime Commission member explained: "The Mafia is doing business directly with the U.S. government now."

(3:8a) [Eugene] Brading was [is] questioned by the FBI two months after his arrest [interrogation] — and release — in Dallas, as part of the Warren Commission's determination to "leave no stone unturned" in its quest for the truth about the JFK assassination. In spite of the fact that Brading was [is] a known criminal with an arrest record dating back about 20 years [a long arrest record], the FBI reported [reports] that Brading knew [knows] nothing whatsoever [whatever] about the assassination, **and Brading is not called to testify before the Warren Commission.**

(**3:8b**) Brading became [becomes] a charter member of the La Costa Country Club, Mafia heaven [a country club] down near San Clemente [, a reputed Mafia haven].

(**3:9**) **A group of bankers, headed by a Bank of America official, picked Gerald Ford for Congress at the beginning of his career. The reason for the selection was his real father: Leslie King Sr. Almost everyone knows the touching story of Ford's adoption as an infant, and he reappearance of his real father, Leslie King Sr., driving a Cadillac when Ford was a college football hero. Almost no one knows that Leslie King Sr. was a minor member of the Denver Smalldones "family" — engaged in minor swindles and scams in Montana. The Smalldones "family" does a few favors for King Sr. They pick his son Leslie King Jr. (a.k.a. Gerald Ford and Mr. Clean) for Congress. After the JFK murder the time comes for the Denver Smalldones to ask for their return favor. They have Representative "Gerry Ford" put on the Warren Commission.**

(**3:9a**) Gerald Ford, of the Warren Commission, went on to become President — by appointment of Nixon, then in danger of even further and more serious exposure — from which position of trust Ford pardoned Nixon one month later for "any and all crimes he may have committed." That covers quite a lot — but Ford is good at covering things up.

CHAPTER 2

The Skeleton Key: Part II

The following is a continuation of the annotated *Skeleton Key to the Gemstone Files* comparing two versions: One distributed through an underground network in 1976, and another published in the February, 1979, edition of *Hustler* magazine. To reiterate, the following key to the text applies:

- All <u>underlined</u> passages are those included in the original *Key* and not presented in the February, 1979, issue of *Hustler*.
- All **bold-faced** passages are *Hustler's* additions which are not included in the original *Key*.
- In areas where *Hustler* rewrote of rephrased passages, or changed individual words, from the original *Key*, brackets ([ ]) will set apart *Hustler's* rewrite — and it will immediately follow the original phrase.
- Passages in the *Key* will be numbered, just as books of the Bible have each verse numbered. In this way, when text of the book refers to the *Key*, the reader can easily refer back to that particular passage without interrupting continuity.

And now, the *Skeleton Key* continues:

(Gemstone 4:0) [John] McCone, head of CIA-Dallas [head of the CIA], went [goes] on to become a member of the ITT Board of Directors [Board of Directors of ITT] — sitting right next to Francis L. Dale, <u>then</u> head of CREEP (<u>the</u> Committee to Re-Elect the President).

(4:1) Richard Helms, McCone's assistant in [at] Dallas,

ultimately was [is] rewarded with the post of CIA Director. Leon Jaworski, <u>CIA attorney,</u> became [becomes] the Watergate prosecutor, replacing Archibald Cox, who was getting too warm. Jaworski turned [turns] in a sterling performance <u>in our "government-as-theater"</u> — <u>the honest, conscientious investigator who "uncovered" not a bit more then he had to</u> — <u>and managed to steer everybody away from the underlying truth.</u>

(4:2) Dr. "Red" Duke, the man who dug two bullets out of Connally and saved his life, was shipped off to a hospital in Afghanistan by a grateful CIA.

(4:3) Jim Garrison, New Orleans D.A. [Jim Garrison] who tried [tries] to get Eugene Brading out of L.A. [Los Angeles to be questioned by his commission of inquiry], but used [uses] one of Brading's other aliases, <u>Eugene Bradley,</u> by mistake, had his witnesses shot out from under him <u>and was framed on charges of bribery and extortion</u> [and his case is discredited in an interminable press controversy launched by James Phelan, who collaborates with Bob Maheu on a book about Hughes].

(4:4) <u>FBI officers "confiscated" photos of Brading taken on the scene. Et cetera.</u>

****

(4:5a) After JFK's death,[:] Onassis quickly established [establishes] control over Lyndon Johnson through fear. On the trip back to Washington, Johnson was [is] warned by radio, relayed from an Air Force base: "There was [is] no conspiracy. Oswald was a lone nut assassin. Get it, Lyndon? Otherwise, Air Force 1 [One] might have an unfortunate accident on the [its] flight back to Washington."

(4:5b) Onassis filled (fills) all important government posts with his own men. All government agencies become <u>a</u> means to accomplish an end: Rifle the American treasury, steal as much as possible; keep the people confused, disorganized and leaderless; pursue world domination. JFK's original "Group of 40" was [is] turned over to Rockefeller and his man, <u>Henry</u> Kissinger, so that they could more effectively f--- over South America.

(4:5c) Onassis was one of the first to console Jackie when she got back from Dallas with JFK's body.

(4:6) Silva, a San Francisco private detective hired by Angelina Alioto to get the goods on philandering Joe, followed Joe Alioto to Vacaville to the Nut Tree Restaurant, where Joe held a private meeting with other Mafioso to arrange the details of the JFK assassination payoff to Fratianno.

(4:7) 1967: Onassis had always enjoyed the fast piles of money to be made through gambling (in Monaco, in the '50s, and in Cuba, under Batista). Onassis took over Las Vegas in 1967, via the "Hughes" cover. U.S. government officials explained that it was all right because "at least Hughes isn't the Mafia." (ha, ha).

(4:8) Note: L. Wayne Rector was hired around 1955 by the Carl Byoir P.R. agency (Hughes' L.A. public relations firm) at act as Hughes' double. In 1957, when Onassis grabbed Hughes, Rector continued to act as his stand-in. Rector was the Hughes surrogate in Las Vegas; Robert Maheu actually ran the show. Maheu got his orders from Onassis. The six "nursemaids," called the "Mormon Mafia," kept Rector sealed off from prying eyes.

(4:9a) June 17, 1968: Bobby Kennedy knew [knows] who killed his brother; he wrote about it in his unpublished book, *The Enemy Within*. When he foolishly tried [tries] to run for President, Onassis had him offed, using a sophisticated new technique: Hypnotizing Sirhan Sirhan shooting from the front, "security guard" Thane Cesar (from Lockheed Aircraft) shooting from two or three inches away from Bobby's head — from the rear. Sirhan's shots all missed; Cesar's couldn't possibly miss. Evelle Younger, then the Los Angeles D.A., covered it all up, including the squawks of L.A. coroner Thomas Noguchi. Younger was rewarded with the post of California Attorney General later. His son, Eric Younger, got a second-generation Mafia reward: A judge-ship at age 30 (see Ted Charach, L.A., author and director of *The Second Gun*, a documentary film on the RFK murder, bought and suppressed by Warner Brothers, for more details).

(4:9b) After Bobby's death, Teddy knew who did it, he ran to Onassis, afraid for his life, and swore total obedience. In return, Onassis granted him his life and said he could be President, too, just like his big brother, if he would just behave himself and follow orders.

(5:0a) Sept. 16, 1968: Hit-and-run accident on Roberts' car, parked in front of the Soviet consulate in San Francisco (the Soviets routinely take pictures of everything that goes on in front of the consulate). Their photos showed the license plate of the hit-and-run car: UKT-264, on a blue Cadillac belonging to Mia Angela Alioto, Joe's daughter, being driven by Tom Alioto, Joe's son, whose driver's license, and the car's license, were both fraudulent. To cover up the hit-and-run circumstances, the Presidio quickly staged a few more hit-and-runs on the same corner — all duly filmed by the Soviets. Kathryn Hollister, the Alioto family nurse, was "persuaded" to take the rap for the hit-and-run. Roberts threatened to spill the whole story in court with photos.

(5:0b) Next evening, Brading and Fratianno showed up in the Black Magic Bar — Brading wearing his X-marked hat from Dallas — to see whether Roberts recognized it, how much he knew, etc. A military policeman from the Presidio piped up from the end of the bar: "I heard they let everyone with an X-marked hatband through the police lines in Dallas."

(5:0c) Cover-up support for Alioto in the hit-and-run was complete.

(5:1) Mafia Joe Alioto had Presidential ambitions, shored up by his participation in the Dallas payoff. Everyone who helped kill JFK got a piece of the U.S. pie. But J. Edgar Hoover, FBI head, blew his cover by releasing some of the raw FBI files on Alioto at the Democratic National Convention. Joe was out of the running for V.P., and Hubert H. Humphrey had to settle for

Edmund Muskie. Humphrey planned to come to S.F. for a final pre-election rally, sparked by Joe Alioto; Roberts threatened to blow the hit-and-run story plus its Mafia ramifications wide open if Humphrey came to S.F. Humphrey didn't come. Humphrey lost San Francisco, California and the election.

(5:2) October, 1968: Jackie Kennedy was now "free" to marry Onassis. [According to] An old Mafia rule: If someone welches on a deal, kill him and take his girl and his gun; in this case, Jackie and the Pentagon.

(5:3a) July, 1969: Mary Jo Kopechne, devoted JFK girl and later one of Bobby's trusted aides [a former secretary of Robert Kennedy], was [is] in charge of packing up his [Bobby's] files after his assassination in L.A. She read [reads] too much — learned [learns] of the [about] the Kennedy-Mafia involvement and [among] other things. She said to friends: "This isn't Camelot, this is murder." She was an idealistic American Catholic. She didn't like murdering hypocrites. She died [dies] trying to get off Chappaquiddick Island[.] ,where she had overheard (along with everyone else in the cottage) Teddy Kennedy's end of the D.H. Lawrence cottage telephone calls from John Tunney, and to Joe Alioto and Democratic bigwigs Swig, Shorenstein, Schumann and Bechtel.

(5:3b) Teddy's good friend Tunney called to complain that Alioto's friend Cyril Magnin and others had tried to bribe Jess Unruh to switch from the Governor's race to run for the Senate — for the seat Tunney wanted — so that Alioto would have an easier run for Governor. Teddy called Alioto, who told him to go to hell; then Teddy called the rest to arrange for yet another Mafia murder.

(5:3c) Mary Jo, suddenly up to there in Mafia s---, ran screaming out of the cottage on her way to see Nader. Drunken Teddy offered [offers] to drive her to the ferry. Trying to get away from the curious Sheriff Look, Teddy sped [speeds] off toward the bridge, busted Mary Jo's nose when she tried to grab his arm while sitting in the back seat, and bailed [bails] out of the car as it went [goes] off the bridge. Mary Jo, with a busted nose, breathed in an air bubble in the car for more than two hours, waiting for help [waits for help — her nose is badly broken —] while Teddy, Assuming she was [is] dead, ran [runs] off to set up an alibi. Mary Jo finally suffocated [suffocates] in the air bubble, which was [is] diluted with carbon dioxide from her exhalations. It took her two hours, 37 minutes to suffocate while Teddy had Joseph Kennedy II steal a boat and ferry him across to Edgartown.

(5:3d) Mary Jo was still pounding on the upturned floor-boards of Teddy's car while Teddy called Jackie and Onassis on the *Christina*. Teddy also called Katharine Meyer Graham, lawyers, etc. On Teddy's behalf, Jackie called [calls] the Pope, who assigned [assigns] Cardinal Cushing to help. [The Cardinal assigns priests, who appear before the Kopechnes "direct from God," with personal instructions from Him that Mary Jo's broken nose is patched up.] The next morning, the first person Teddy tried to call after deciding he'd have to take the rap himself was lawyer Burke Marshall, Onassis' friend in the U.S. Liberty Ships deal back in the '40s, also the designated custodian of JFK's brains after Dallas (the brains have since disappeared). [He (Teddy) also calls Ted Sorenson.]

(5:4) Cover-up of the Chappaquiddick murder required the help of the following:

- The Massachusetts Highway Patrol, which "confiscated" the plates from Teddy's car after it was fished out of the pond.
- The Massachusetts Legislature, which changed a 150-year-old law requiring an autopsy (which would have revealed the suffocation and broken nose).
- Coroner Mills, who let Kennedy's aide, K. Dun Gifford, supply him with a death certificate, already prepared, for Mills' signature, listing the cause of death as "drowning."
- Police Chief Arenas, and Cardinal Cushing's priests, who appeared before the Kopechnes "direct from God" with

personal instructions from Him that Mary Jo was not to be disturbed.

- A Pennsylvania mortuary where Mary Jo's broken nose was patched up.
- East and West Coast phone companies, which clamped maximum security on records of calls to and from the cottage (S.F. Police Chief Cahill was reassigned to a new job: Security Chief for Pacific Telephone).
- And the rest: The U.S. Senate, which never said a word about Teddy's (required equipment) plug-in phone; the judge who presided over the mock hearing; James Reston, editor of Martha's Vineyard's only newspaper, who never heard a word about Teddy's phone at the cottage, though residents called in to tell the newspaper; the *New York Times, Washington Post,* etc., etc.

(5:5a) John Tunney's sister Joan heard her brother's end of the phone call, made from her house in Tiburon to the Chappaquiddick cottage. The next day, after Mary Jo died, Joan ran away to Norway, where she was kidnapped by Mafia hoods Mari and Adamo. They locked her up in a Marseilles heroin factory for 60 days, where the heroin fumes turned her into a junkie (no needle marks). Then they turned her loose outside the factory.

(5:5b) Joan's husband complained, so she chopped his head off with an ax and was subsequently locked up in a nuthouse belonging to the Marquess of Blandford, then Tina Livanos Onassis' husband.

(5:5c) Mari and Adamo got pressed into scrap metal in a New Jersey auto junkyard.

(5:6) In the panic of trying to cover up Teddy's guilt at Chappaquiddick, many things became unglued. The JFK murder threatened to come out of the woodwork again. Black Panthers Hampton and Clark were murdered (the Chicago cops fired over attorney Charles Garry's [unreadable garble]) because of what they knew about the JFK murder squad's presence in Chicago on Nov. 1, 1963.

(5:7) September, 1969: "Gemstones," with histories, had been released around the globe for several years. In 1969, Roberts gave a Gemstone, with history, to Mack, head of California's CREEP, for Nixon, with the proposition: The Presidency in return for wiping out the Mafia. The "history" included: Teddy's phone calls to and from the Lawrence cottage on Chappaquiddick, billed to Teddy's home phone in Hyannis Port. Nixon, being Mafia himself, wasn't interested, but kept the information to use on Teddy whenever it seemed advantageous.

(5:8) May 4, 1970: Charlotte Ford Niarchos called her ex-husband, Stavros, worried about the Ford Foundation's involvement in the Chappaquiddick cover-up. Eugene Livanos Niarchos, in bed with her husband, overheard the conversation. Stavros was forced to beat her to death; he ruptured her spleen and broke the cartilage in her throat. Cause of death was listed as "overdose of barbituates," though autopsy showed these injuries.

(5:9a) End of 1970: Howard Hughes' presence on earth was [is] no longer required. His handwriting could [can] be duplicated by computer. His biography — all the known facts about his life — had [have] been compiled, and a [the] computerized version [biography is] issued to top Hughes executives. And Hughes was ill.

(5:9b) Clifford Irving, author of *Hoax*, [a book] about an art forger, became [becomes] interested in "Hughes." Living on Ibiza, he heard the Mediterranean gossip that "Hughes" was [is] a hoax, too. He went [goes] to "Hughes'" so-called "Mormon Mafia," the six "nursemaids," for information. One of them — Merryman — perhaps tired of the game — gives Irving the computerized Hughes biography, and from it, Irving wrote [writes] his "autobiography."

(5:9c) Hughes' death was expected shortly. Preparations were being made so that it would not interfere with the orderly continuation of his empire.

(5:9d) Irving wrote [writes] his book — and the publishers

announced [announce] it. Onassis knew [knows] someone had [has] given Irving the information. He thought it was Maheu [Thinking it was Maheu], he fired [fires] him in November, 1970. On Thanksgiving Eve, 1970, in the middle of the night, "Hughes" (Rector) made [makes] a well-publicized "secret departure" from Las Vegas to the Bahamas.

(5:9e) December, 1970: Onassis discovered [discovers] his mistake, and had Merryman killed [and has the nursemaid responsible for leaking the information to Irving killed].

(6:0a) Robert Maheu, accidentally deprived of his half-million dollars annual salary, sued "Hughes" for millions — mentioning "Hughes'" game plan for the purchase of presidents, governors, senators, judges, etc. Onassis pays off — cheap to the price — to maintain his custodianship of "American democracy" and the "free world[.]" — and keep from hanging for multiple murders.

(6:0b) The "Hughes" Mormon Mafia party, plus Rector, fled [flees] around the world — from Bermuda, where they murdered an uncooperative governor and police chief, to Nicaragua, where they shot [shoot] the U.S. Ambassador between the eyes for noticing that there wasn't [isn't] really any Hughes; and thence to Canada, where Mormon Mafia nursemaid [Howard] Eckersley looted [loots] a goodly sum in a swindle of the Canadian Stock Exchange; and on to London, to [the] Rothchild's Inn of the Park.

(6:1a) April 18, 1971: Howard Hughes, a human vegetable as the result of serious brain damage during his 1957 hustle — plus 14 years of heroin — grew sicker and sicker. A final overdose of heroin did [does] him [Hughes] in. His coffin is lowered into the sea from a rocky headland off the coast of Skorpios. Present at the funeral were: Jackie Kennedy Onassis, Teddy Kennedy, Francis L. Dale, director of CREEP and on the ITT board of directors; Tom Pappas, also of CREEP; and a South Vietnamese cardinal named Thuc. Onassis allowed some pictures to be taken from a distance; he himself did not appear.

The pictures were published in *Midnight,* a Canadian tabloid.

(6:1b) Albanian frogmen, tipped off, were [are] waiting under [in] the water. They seized [seize] the coffin and took [take] the corpse off to Yugoslavia, thence to China and the Soviet Union [Russia], and then, perhaps to Boston in a footlocker. The corpse's dental work was compared to Hughes' own dental records, and they matched [match]. News of Hughes's death, the U.S. Ambassador by Onassis [the U.S. takeover by Onassis], and the facts surrounding the murders of JFK, RFK, Martin Luther King Jr., Mary Jo Kopechne, and many more, and the subsequent cover-ups (involving still more murders) has been circulating around the globe for several years. Any country with this information can blackmail the U.S. government, which has no choice but to pay up.

(6:1c) The alternative: Be exposed as a bunch of treasonous [treasonable] murderers. This is why China-hating, red-baiting Nixon was [is] forced to "recognize" China (which he has since claimed [now claims] as [is] his greatest accomplishment); and why the USSR walks off with such good deals in the U.S. loans, grains [grain] and whatever else it wants. All they have to do is mention those magic words: "Hughes," JFK, RFK, Mary Jo — words to conjure by — and the U.S. Mafia government crawls into a hole.

(6:2a) Information once leaked can't be unleaked. The only way to end the dilemma is through a nuclear war — and that wouldn't be one-sided. The other way would be to throw the Mafia out of the United States. Starting at the top — with Ford, Rockefeller and Kissinger. Super-patriots please note: No one — not all the radicals and subversives hounded by the U.S. domestic intelligence put together — has done one fraction of he damage done to the U.S. economy, morality, power and prestige than has been accomplished by the thieves at the top.

(6:2b) On the day Hughes was buried, Clifford Irving's wife presented a publisher's check made out to "H. Hughes" to

Onassis' Swiss bank for payment. Onassis paid off — cheap at the price.

****

(6:3) "Gemstone" papers rolling around the world here and aboard kept the situation hot. Everyone was nervous. Rockefeller gave Kissinger $50,000 for Carlson and Brisson to write their "expose" for *Look* magazine entitled *The Alioto Mafia Web.* Their mission: Find out everything that was public record about Alioto's connection with the JFK murder (his payoffs to Fratianno, listed in D&B) and explain it away — in any way that didn't lead back to Dallas. The idea was to get Alioto to quickly go away but still keep the lid on everything.

(6:4) May, 1971: Tina Livanos Onassis Blandford married Stavros Niarchos, her former brother-in-law until he killed her sister Eugenie.

(6:5a) May, 1971: "Folk hero" Daniel Ellsberg, a well-known hawk from the Rand Corporation who had designed the missile ring around the "Iron Curtain" countries (how many missiles to aim at which cities), [releases] was told to release the faked-up "Pentagon Papers" to help [which helps] distract people from Hughes, JFK, RFK, MLK [King], etc. The papers were carefully designed by Ellsberg and his boss, Rand chief and later World Bank chief Robert McNamara to make the Vietnam War look like "just one of those incredibly dumb mistakes." This helped [helps] to cover up the real purpose of the war: Continued control, for Onassis and his friends, of the Golden Triangle dope trade (Vietnam, Laos, Cambodia); and the same kind of control [and for] Onassis and the oil people, [control] of Eastern oil sources. The war also had the effect of controlling [— to say nothing of control over] huge Federal [federal] monies [sums], which could [can] be siphoned off in profitable arms contracts, or [made to] conveniently "disappear" in the war effort.

(6:5b) McNamara's "World Bank" [International banking

circles] — handing out American money to "starving nations" — actually set up huge private bank accounts [for various dictators] in Onassis-controlled Swiss banks, payoffs for various dictators. This [The] money could [can] be used as needed to support and extend Mafia operations. Example: $8 billion in World Bank funds for "starving Ethiopians" wound [winds] up in [Emperor] Haile Selassie's personal Swiss bank accounts. This would make him the richest individual in the world at the time — but other dictators have Swiss accounts, too. Maybe even larger. The money drained from America and other captive Mafia nations to feed a greed that can never be satisfied.

(6:6) Rand Corp. [Corporation], one of our major "think tanks," had [has] another goody in store for the public: "Project Star," Rand's cover-up fallback version of the JFK murder — held in reserve should public restlessness over the Warren Commission Report cover-up ever threaten to get out of hand. **This version is "leaking" out now, in the Rockefeller Commission's "hints" that JFK was behind the CIA-Mafia attempts on Castro and that Castro retaliated by having JFK shot.**

(6:7a) Notes in passing: The dope routes are: Golden Triangle to Taiwan to San Francisco. Heroin coming from the Golden Triangle was sometimes smuggled into S.F. inside the bodies of American GIs who died in battle in Vietnam. One body can hold up to 40 pounds of heroin, crammed in where the organs would normally be.

(6:7b) Some dope gets pressed into dinner plates, and painted with pretty patterns. One dope bust in San Francisco alone yielded $6 billion in heroin "China plates" — the largest dope bust in history — quickly and completely hushed up by the S.F. press Mafia. The dope sat in S.F.P.D. for a while, then was removed by FBI men and probably sent on its way — to American veins. All this dope processing and shipping is controlled and supervised by the Mafia for the Mafia. Dope arrests and murders are aimed at independent pushers and maverick peddlers and smugglers who are competing with, or holding out on, the Mafia. While Nixon was conducting his noisy campaign against dope smuggling across the Mexican border, his dope officer in charge of protecting the Mafia dope trade was E. Howard Hunt.

(6:7c) Lots of heroin gets processed in a Pepsi Cola factory in Laos. So far, it hasn't produced a single bottle of Pepsi Cola.

(6:7d) Some dope gets processed in heroin factories in Marseilles (see the movie, *The French Connection*).

(6:7e) Still more dope comes from South America — cocaine, and now heroin. U.S. aid went to build a highway across Paraguay (Uruguay?). Useless to the natives, who have no cars; they use it for sunbathing during the day. All night, airplanes loaded with cocaine take off from the longest landing strip in the world — financed by U.S. tax money for the benefit of international Mafia dope pushers. And then there is opium from Turkey — morphine, the starting point of Onassis' fortune.

(6:8) In case one is still wondering whether the Mafia can actually get away with such things, consider the benefits derived from controlling the stock market, the courts, the police, etc., in one swindle alone: The 1970 "acquisition" by "Hughes" of "Air West," which involved swindling Air West stockholders of $45 million. Indicted for this swindle by the S.E.C. (in a civil suit) were "Howard Hughes" and Jimmy "The Greek" Snyder (not usually associated with the Hughes crowd) and others.

(6:9) June [13], 1971: The *New York Times* began [starts] publishing the Pentagon Papers[.], Rand Corp.'s prepared cover-up of the real reasons for the Vietnam War.

(7:0a) Nixon had gotten a copy of the first Gemstone papers circulated in the U.S. back in 1969. He was now wondering how much information Democratic Chairman Larry O'Brien had received about Hughes, Onassis, JFK, RFK, et al, and how much of the dirt the Democrats planned to use.

(7:0b) Nixon set [sets] up the "plumbers" unit[.] to "stop security leaks, investigate other security matters." Ehrlichman, Krogh, Liddy, Hunt, Young, etc. were the core members. [E.

Howard] Hunt, as "White House consultant," worked [works] for the [CIA-front] Mullen Corp., a CIA cover [— after he resigns from the CIA]. Mullen's chief client was [is] "Howard Hughes." Robert Bennett was head of the Mullen Corp.

(7:1) June 28, 1971 [Dec. 29, 1971]: Ellsberg indicted for leaking the Pentagon Papers.

(7:2) Sept. 3, 1971: The Watergate team broke into Ellsberg's doctor's (Fielding's) office [into the office of Ellsberg's doctor (Lewis Fielding)] to get Ellsberg's psychiatric records. Team members: CIA [CIA's] Hunt, and [G. Gordon] Liddy [plan it]; Cuban "freedom fighters" [Felipe] DeDiego, [Eugenio] Martinez, and [Bernard] Barker take part. All except Liddy had worked together at the Bay of Pigs.

(7:3) Question: Why the intense battle between Mafia forces? Answer: While Onassis was the recognized crowned head of the Mafia, intense no-holds-barred scuffling for the lucrative second spot (control of the U.S. Presidency, government and so on) was permissible and encouraged under the Mafia code of rules. The only stipulation: Outsiders must not know about it. "Hughes" contributed liberally — and equally — to both Democratic and Republican parties for the 1972 election. The winner would get even more money from "Hughes."

(7:4) Sept. 23, 1971: E. Howard Hunt spliced up the phony cables implicating JFK's administration in the Diem assassination.

(7:5) October, 1971: *Look* magazine apologized to Alioto for their "Alioto Mafia Webb" article — and folded. The sticking point: They couldn't prove Alioto's Nut Tree meeting back in 1963 related to the JFK murder.

(7:6) November, 1971: Alioto re-elected S.F. mayor.

(7:7) December, 1971: Roberts applied for a "Gemstone" visa from the Soviet consulate — on a tapped phone. Phone was tapped by Hal Lipset, S.F. private investigator, who worked for Katharine Meyer Graham, and others, and routinely monitored consulate phone calls.

(7:8) January, 1972: The Watergate team shows up at the S.F. Drift Inn, a CIA-FBI safe-house hangout bar [in San Francisco] where Roberts conducted a nightly Gemstone rap for benefit of any CIA, FBI or anyone who wandered in for a beer. James McCord, Martinez, Bernard Barker, Garcia and Frank Sturgis showed up — along with a San Francisco dentist named Fuller. James McCord remarked: "Sand and oil with hydrogen heat makes glass brick" — threat of war to Arab nations. The event, like any other nightly rap, is taped by [the] Drift Inn bartender Al Strom, who was paid to do so by his old friend, Katharine Meyer Graham — but [who] told [tells] his other friend, Roberts, about it. The bar was [is] also wired for sound by Arabs, Soviets [Russians] and Chinese.

(7:9) January 27, 1972: Liddy and Dean met in Mitchell's office, with Liddy's charts of his $1 million "plan" of spying, kidnapping, etc. The plans included breaking into Hank Greenspun's Las Vegas office safe in hopes of recovering Greenspun's files on the Hughes kidnapping and Onassis' Vegas operations, which Greenspun had successfully used to blackmail Onassis out of $4 million or so. A "Hughes" getaway plane would stand by to take the White House burglars to Mexico.

(8:0) February, 1972: Liddy and Hunt traveled around a lot, using "Hughes Tool Co." calling cards and aliases from Hunt's spy novels.

(8:1a) Liddy, Hunt and other Watergaters dropped by for a beer at the Drift Inn, where they were photographed while sitting on bar stools; the photos were for Katharine Graham and were later used in the *Washington Post* when Liddy, Hunt and the others were arrested at Watergate — because CIA men like Liddy and Hunt aren't usually photographed.

(8:1b) Roberts quoted to Liddy the "Chinese stock market in ears" — the price on Onassis' head, by the ear — in retaliation for a few things Onassis had done; on Wayne Rector, the Hughes double; Eugene Wyman, California Democratic Party Chairman and Mafia JFK payoff bag man; and on Lyndon

Johnson: "Four bodies twisting in the breeze."

(8:1c) Roberts: "Quoting the prices to Liddy at the Drift Inn made their deaths a mortal cinch. Liddy's like that — and that's why the murdering slob was picked by the Mafia... Gemstones rolling around the Drift Inn in February inspired Liddy's 'Gemstone Plan' that became Watergate."

(8:2) February, 1972: Francis L. Dale, head of CREEP and ITT board of directors member, pushed Magruder to push Liddy into Watergate.

(8:3a) In a Mafia-style effort to shut Roberts up, his father was murdered by "plumbers" team members Liz Dale (Francis L. Dale's ex-wife), Martinez, Gonzales and Barker; in Hahnemann's Hospital in San Francisco — where the senior Roberts had been taken after swallowing a sodium morphate "pill" slipped into his medicine bottle at home by Watergate locksmith Gonzales (from Miami's "Missing Link" locksmith shop). The pill didn't kill him; he had weak digestion and vomited up enough of the sodium morphate (it burned his lips and tongue on the way out). But the senior Roberts also had emphysema and went to the hospital.

(8:3b) In the hospital, "nurse" Liz Dale and "doctor" Martinez assisted the senior Roberts to sniff a quadruple-strength can of aerosol medicine — enough to kill him the next day.

****

(8:4a) The day before, Tisseront, head of the [Sacred] College of Cardinals at the Vatican, was [is] pushed out of a Vatican window. Tisseront [He] had followed the career of the present pope, Montini [of Montini, then Pope Paul VI] (whose mother was Jewish). Montini sodium-morphate-murdered Pope Pius XI; was banished from Rome for it by Pius XII; became Pope in 1963 [and returned home to become Pope Paul VI in 1963]. Tisseront wrote it all down; calling [called] the Pope [the] "Deputy of Christ at Auschwitz" and the fulfillment of the Fatima 3 prophecy: That the "Antichrist shall rise to become the head of the church."

(**8:4b**) Tisseront <u>also</u> wrote about all the suppressed secrets of the Roman Catholic Church, i.e., that Jesus Christ was an Arab, born <u>April 16, 6 B.C.</u>, at the rare conjunction of Saturn and Jupiter. Arab (Persian) astronomers (the Magi) came to Bethlehem to look for *their* king — an Arab baby — and found him in a stable[.], <u>because the Jews wouldn't let Arabs Mary and Joseph into their nice clean inns even then.</u>

(**8:4c**) <u>When Jesus overturned the tables of the moneylenders at the Temple, the Jews had the Romans nail him to a cross. He died on the cross when the Roman soldiers stuck a spear in his side, pulled out his liver and ate it. Tacitus, the Roman historian, described it all in a chunk of history deleted by the Church.</u>

(**8:4d**) <u>Nero burned Rome — but that didn't stop the spreading of Jesus' teachings by the early Christians (Arabs). So the Romans decided to adopt the religion, clean it up, make Christ a Jew and Mary a virgin, and work out a church-state deal to fuck the people in the name of God and country which has been in operation ever since.</u>

(**8:4e**) <u>Around 300 A.D., at the Council of Nicaea, the Christian Orthodoxy was established; a dissenting bishop had his hands chopped off; another bishop was assigned to round up all the old copies of the Bible and destroy them, in favor of the "revised" de-Arabized version. Cleaned-up Matthew, Mark, Luke and John were declared "it," the other Gospels were declared Aprocryphal and heretical. Roman emperor Constantine became the first "Christian" emperor. Later, during the "Holy Crusades," the Bible was again rewritten — to include Jesus' warning against the "yellow race."</u>

****

(**8:5**) <u>"Twenty-seven Gemstones, with histories, to 27 countries, brought Red China into the U.N. and threw Taiwan out."</u>

(**8:6**) April, 1972: Money pours into CREEP: "Gulf Resources and Chemicals Corp., Houston, Texas" [Gulf Oil Corporation] contributes $100,000. [Ashland Oil, $100,000; Braniff Airways, $40,000; American Airlines, $55,000. Financier] Robert Vesco gives Maurice Stans [and John Mitchell a] $200,000 "campaign contribution," etc., etc. Liddy gives McCord $76,000 [, etc.] McCord buys $58,000 worth of bugging equipment, cameras, etc.

(8:7) May, 1972: J. Edgar Hoover had [has] the Gemstone file [File]; [and] threatened [threatens] to expose Dallas-JFK in an "anonymous" book, *The Texas Mafia.* Instead, someone put sodium morphate in his apple pie. The corpse was carted away from his home in the back seat of a Volkswagen — [and] his files were burned, but some of them got away [although some are retrieved].

(8:8a) May 28, 1972: First break-in at [the] Watergate. McCord, Barker, Martinez, Garcia, Gonzales and Sturgis were involved. DeDiego and Pico stood guard outside. Hunt and Liddy directed the operation from a (safe?) distance — across the street. The object was [is] to check on Onassis' two men at the Democratic Party headquarters: Larry O'Brien and [R.] Spencer Oliver. (O'Brien's chief "public relations" client had [has] been "Hughes;" Oliver's father worked for Onassis). [James W.] McCord wiretapped [wiretaps] their [the Democratic National Committee's] phones. [Oliver's phone is tapped.]

(8:8b) But! Little did [does] McCord know [that] the "plumbers" were [are] being observed by Hal Lipset, Katharine Graham's S.F. detective, who had followed two of the plumbers from Liz Dale's side in San Francisco to Watergate. [a detective, who reports his operations by radio-phone.] Lipset "watched in amazement" as the plumbers broke in and bugged the phones; then he reported back to his boss, Graham. Lipset and Graham set the trap [and the trap is set] for the Watergaters when they returned [return] to remove their bugs and equipment.

(8:9a) June 17, 1972: Bernard Barker was wearing his Sears, Roebuck deliveryman costume — the same one he wore at the

Dr. Fielding break-in and at the Hahnemann's Hospital murder of the senior Roberts.

(8:9b) Hal Lipset, Graham's spy, was dressed as a mailman. He left his mailsack behind when he taped the door at Watergate [The detective tapes the door lock at the Watergate], watched [watches as] security guard Frank Wills remove [removes the tape] it and walks on, retaped the door [; he *retapes* the lock, Wills sees the door taped again] and, as a result, Frank Wills went [goes] across the street and called [to call] the police — and McCord, Martinez, Sturgis, Barker and Gonzales were [are] caught in the act. Graham had them on tape and film, too, every minute of the time. Liddy and Hunt, across the street supervising via walkie-talkie, were not [are not caught].

(8:9c) Time to burn files. Liddy shredded [has his secretary, Sally Harmony, shred] the Gemstone files [File] at CREEP headquarters.

(8:9d) [John] Dean cleaned [cleans] out Hunt's safe at the White House and gave Hunt's copy of the Gemstone file (File) to L. Patrick Gray, acting FBI head, saying: "Deep-six this — in the interest of national security. This should never see the light of day." Gray burned the file.

(9:0) June 20, 1972: DNC Chairman Larry O'Brien filed [files] a $1 million suit against CREEP — naming Francis L. Dale, the head of CREEP. This was [is] a big Mafia mistake — for Dale led directly back to Onassis.

(9:1) June 21, 1972: The 18 1/2-minutes of accidentally erased White House tape: [Eighteen-and-half minutes of White House tape is "accidentally" erased.] Nixon [is], furious over the Watergate plumbers' arrests, couldn't figure out who had [has] done it to him: Who taped the door at [the] Watergate that led to the arrests? Hal Lipset, whose primary employer at the time was Katharine Graham, couldn't tell him [The detective won't tell him]. Nixon figured [figures] that it had [has] to do somehow with Roberts' running around Vancouver tracing the "Hughes" Mormon Mafia nursemaid (Eckersley's) swindle of the Canadian Stock Exchange; and Trudeau. The 18 1/2 minutes was [is] of Nixon raving about Canada's "a--hole Trudeau," "a--hole Roberts," Onassis, "Hughes" and Francis L. Dale. It simply couldn't [can't] be released.

(9:2) Stephen Bull's secretary, Beverly Kaye, later heard the "erased" tape, stored in a locked room in the White House. She was horrified. She sent out some depressed Christmas cards and notes to friends, and sodium-morphate "heart-attacked" at age 40 in a White House elevator outside the locked room where the tapes were stored.

CHAPTER 3

. . . .

The Skeleton Key: Conclusion

B efore we conclude the actual text of *A Skeleton Key to the Gemstone Files*, a few words of explanation are in order.

First, the conclusions drawn by Gemstone author Bruce Roberts are his own. We do not pretend to submit this material as purely factual. However, Roberts has certain basis for making some of these statements, and a great deal of his points can be logically supported by circumstantial and other evidence. That is, by definition, what this book is about, and further examination of the *Key* will reveal that aspect of this research.

However, we also feel the *Key* must be presented in its entirety, even though some of the material appears highly suspect as to its truthful content. The comparison to the only widely published version of the *Key* in the February, 1979, edition of *Hustler* magazine is also valuable; assertions can be made as to why *Hustler* decided to suppress some of this material.

The violence which characterized world politics in the period from 1957 to 1972 can be more easily understood if it is presented in the framework of an old-fashioned gang war, which is what Roberts is attempting to do. As the final episode of the *Key* is presented here, it will make the preceding two chapters more readily understood.

In short, it might be easy to laugh off this material as a cruel hoax — until all of it is fully presented and analyzed. It was our view that much of Roberts' material was bogus in the context of the mid-1970s. However, events since that time have confirmed much of what the *Key* asserts. Therefore, patience is required to absorb fully the profound impact on 20th century history the *Key* could represent if it is analyzed based upon fact, not fiction. That analysis begins in Chapter 4. In the meantime, the final annotated segment of the *Skeleton Key* follows, using the same key as presented in the prior two chapters:

(Gemstone 9:3) January, 1973: Tisseront was dead — but as the Church rushed to destroy every copy of his papers, Roberts received one, and wrote a few of his own, released over New Year's:

1. "The Cover-up and Murder of Christ."
2. "The Yellow Race Is Not China — The Yellow Race Dead-F---ed Mary Jo Kopechne."
3. "Mrs. Giannini's Bank of America Financed the Murder of JFK at Dallas Via Alioto's Fratianno, Brading and Roselli."
4. "Vietnam — Fatima 3 — Holy Crusade."

"Four documents — four bodies twisting slowly in the breeze."

(9:4) Lyndon Johnson: [has a] sodium-morphate "heart attack" at his ranch on the Pedernales River. Among his last words: "You know, fellows, it really was a conspiracy..."

(9:5) Alexander Onassis' plane crash at the "1,000-foot Walter Reuther level," via a fixed altimeter, at Athens Airport.

(9:6) Eugene Wyman, California Democratic Party Chairman and JFK assassination payoff bag man: Heart attack.

(9:7) L. Wayne Rector, Hughes' double: Killed at Rothchild's Inn of the Park in London.

(9:7a) "Started the shattering of the Mafia economy."

****

(9:8) March 18, 1973: Roberts called Hal Lipset, discussing these matters publicly — over a tapped phone. Lipset reported to Dean, who had hired him away from Graham after they figured out who had taped the door at Watergate (Mitchell: "Katie Graham's liable to get her tit caught in a wringer.")

(9:9) March 19, 1973: Dean, to Nixon, nervously: "There is

a cancer growing on the Presidency."

(10:0) March 21, 1973: Nixon said that on this date, he "received new evidence" on Watergate. Lipset later bragged on TV that he had been the one to bring the "new evidence" to Nixon.

(10:1) Meanwhile, back at the *Washington Post*, Katharine Meyer "Deep Throat" Graham had been feeding Woodward and Bernstein information for their articles.

(10:2) May 10, 1973: The first witness at the Watergate hearing, running down the names on the CREEP organizational chart, mentioned the name at the top: Francis L. Dale, Chairman. Dale was never mentioned again during the rest of the trial.

(10:3) July 9, 1973: Roberts had used Al Strom's Drift Inn bay as an "open lecture forum" for any and all — and Al Strom taped it, for his boss, Katharine Graham. But "Al was fair" — and told Roberts he was doing it — for which he was murdered on this date.

(10:4a) August, 1973: Murder of Chile, by "Group of 40:" Rockefeller and his man Kissinger, working with the CIA, and $8 million, accomplished this task. Allende's Chile had nationalized ITT. Rockefeller had copper mines in Chile. Admiral Noel Gayler, Naval Intelligence, told Roberts 1-1/2 years earlier that Chile would get it; Roberts warned the Chilean consul in advance: Allegria, who later "taught" at Stanford.

(10:4b) ITT has now exacted $125 million payment for its Chilean plants — a good return on their $8 million investment. Mafia-controlled Chile's annual inflation rate had set a world record. The whole deal was arranged in the style of the old Holy Roman Empire: A slave nation paying tribute to the conqueror.

(10:5) October, 1973: Another "Holy War" — Israelis vs. Arabs.

(10:6) January, 1974: Joe Alioto grants Sunol Golf Course lease to Mafioso Romano, Fratianno, Muniz, Madeiros, Abe Chapman and Neil Neilsen. Alioto sets up the Dallas murder squad in San Francisco for more murders.

(10:7) Jan. 26, 1974: "Hughes" extradition trial canceled in Reno by "Alioto Mafia Webb" Mafia Judge Thomson, after Moses Lasky — from Mafia Alioto's California Crime Commission — waves the forged "Howard Hughes" signature under his nose.

(10:8) Maheu "wins" his damage suit against "Hughes" — his blackmail payoff — after discussing Hughes' "game plan" for buying politicians: Governors, judges, senators and even Presidents.

(10:9) February, 1974: Mafia Hearst's daughter Patty "kidnapped" by Lipset's SLA — in a fake terrorist action.

(11:0) [June 30, 1974:] Martin Luther King's mother was [is] murdered — by a black student, a self-declared "Israelite" [follower of Hananiah Israel] — "acting alone," who had a list of other mothers as targets [who is escorted to church by someone and who has a list of other black women as targets]. Next day, the real target, Shirley Chisholm, got the message, and rushed to sign off on the DNC suit against CREEP, naming Francis L. Dale; she had been the final holdout.

(11:1) April 4, 1974: Mary McCarthy, a writer who had been given a copy of the Gemstone file, said in an article in the *New York Review of Books* that the key to the formation of Liddy's Gemstone plan lay in the whereabouts and activities of the plumbers between December, 1971, and February, 1972. Answer: They were at the Drift Inn, watching Gemstones rolling around on the bar top.

(11:2) Aug. 6, 1974: Nixon and Ford signed [sign] a paper [an agreement] at the White House. It was an agreement: Ford could be President; Nixon got to burn his tapes and files and murder anyone he needed in order to cover it all up.

(11:3a) Aug. 7, 1974: Roberts passed information to Pavlov at the S.F. Soviet consulate which led directly to Nixon's resignation: The *More* journalism review's story about Denny Walsh's "Reopening of the Alioto Mafia Web" story for the *New York Times*, a story killed in a panic; plus a long, taped discussion about who and what the Mafia is. Hal Lipset, listening to the conversation in the bugged consulate room, had phone lines open to Rockefeller and Kissinger, who listened, too. Rockefeller sent Kissinger running to the White House with Nixon's marching orders: "Resign. Right now."

(11:3b) Nixon and Julie cried. But there was still some hope, if Nixon resigned immediately, of drawing the line somewhere — before it got back to the King of the Mountain himself: Onassis. Nixon, on trial, would blurt out those names to save himself: Onassis, Dale, "Hughes," even "JFK."

(11:4) Aug. 8, 1974: Nixon stepped [steps] down and Ford stepped [steps] up, to keep the cover-up going.

(11:5) Aug. 23, 1974: Fratianno was in and around San Francisco, staying at the nearby Sunol Golf Course. More murders were scheduled pertaining to the Gemstone cover-up.

(11:6) Aug. 30, 1974: Ford hires Mafia lawyer Becker to work out a pardon deal for Nixon, who might otherwise name Onassis, Graham and the Pope (Montini) to save himself.

(11:7) San Francisco "Zebra" Murders: A series of "random" killings, dubbed "Zebra Murders" by the police because, supposedly, blacks were killing whites. The real target was Silva, the witness to Alioto's Mafia Nut Tree meeting. Silva was shot to death in an alley. Careful Mafia planning went into this series, to kill several birds with one stone: 1. Get witness Silva out of the way, without being "obvious" about it; 2. Spread fear of "black terrorists" and convince people that the police department needed more money and more repressive power; 3. Blame — and frame — Black Muslims, knocking off leaders of the opposition.

(11:8) Sept. 7, 1974: Roberts had made an agreement with a friend, Harp, of Kish Realty, over a bugged phone. Harp was to buy a Gemstone, with history, for $500 — the price of a trip to Canada for Roberts to check into the "Hughes" Mormon Mafia Canadian stock market swindle, and other matters. But Harp was sodium-morphate poisoned on this date, before the deal could go through.

(11:9) Note: Sodium morphate is a favorite Mafia poison used for centuries. It smells like apple pie and is sometimes served up in one, as to J. Edgar Hoover. Sometimes it is placed in a pill or capsule. Symptoms: Lethargy, sleep, sometimes vomiting. Once ingested, there is a heart attack — and no trace of the chemical is left in the body. Proof is in the vomit, which is usually not analyzed. It is not mentioned in your standard medical books on poisons, etc., yet is a common ingredient in rat poison.

(12:0) Sept. 8, 1974: Ford [— from his position of trust —] pardons Nixon for "all crimes committed from June 20, 1969 (oops, make that January) through August, 1974." [pardons Nixon for all crimes that he committed, or that he may have committed or was involved in "from July (i.e. January) 20, 1969, through August 9, 1974." (Ford makes a verbal error).]

(12:1) Gemstone papers are still floating around the world. Indira Gandhi talks about the "U.S.'s bloody deeds."

(12:2) October, 1974: Ford drops "extradition" of Hughes from the Bahamas. Explanation: "We dropped it because we knew he wouldn't come." That's for sure! [Also 1974: Indictment against Hughes dropped when U.S. Attorney Devoe Heaton is told by the Justice Department to back off. Heaton proceeds anyway, and his second indictment is thrown out. Bahamas refuses to allow extradition of Hughes when the Securities and Exchange Commission tries again.]

(12:3) Oct. 3, 1974: The Watergate trial — the cover-up of the cover-up — got under way, starring Montini's Ben Veniste, Onassis' Nel, Graham's Jill Volner. In the White House, Mafia mayors Alioto, Daley and Beame met with the "truth squad" — Ford, Scott and Griffin — and Mike Mansfield, in secret.

(12:4) Oct. 10, 1974: Tina Livanos Onassis Blandford Niarchos was sodium-morphate-poisoned by husband Stavros: She puked, slept and died of a "heart attack."

(12:5) Losing his son, Alexander, took all the fun out of

killing for Onassis. Who was there to inherit the world empire he had dreamed of handing over to his son?

****

(12:6a) December, 1974: Four targets are chosen by the international Mafia: Chou En-Lai, Leonid Brezhnev, Bruce Roberts and Saudi Arabia's King Faisal. Chou En-Lai has a heart attack. Soviet leader Leonid Brezhnev had scheduled [schedules] a meeting with [Egypt's] Anwar Sadat of Egypt. The outcome would not help the U.S. — no matter how many trips Kissinger made to the Middle East with clean socks and blank checks. A new U.S. "secret weapon" was [is] apparently used — a tiny speck of metal [nickel dust], somehow introduced [introduced somehow] into Brezhnev's lymph system. It lodged [lodges] in the cluster of lymph nodes over his heart, and there it was [becomes] coated with layers of phlegm — much as an oyster creates a pearl around an irritating grain of sand. Brezhnev's lymph system clogged up [Brezhnev's lymphatic system cancels out]; he got [gets] the "flu" and the meeting with Sadat is canceled. Russian doctors X-rayed [X-ray] him him and found [find] a huge lump in his chest. Then, they put him before a Kirlian camera and checked [check] his "aura" for cancer. No cancer.

(12:7) Note: [()Kirlian photography [—] was the latest Russian diagnostic tool. [—] It reveals the presence of disease — physical or moral (it also detects lies) [It purportedly detects lies as well a cancer.] Brezhnev's "lump" had to be [is] treated with radiation therapy — hence rumors [that] he had [has] cancer.

(12:8) March, 1975: Onassis died [dies]. The Mafia organization regrouped [regroups] itself. Prince Faisal watched his uncle, King Faisal, silently watch the shift in Mafia power — and couldn't stand it any more. He shot his uncle, the spiritual leader of 400,000,000 Moslems, an individual who had played ball with Onassis all along.

(12:9) South Vietnam's Thieu [Nguyen Van Thieu], dubious about which way the Mafia cookie would crumble now that Onassis was [is] dead, decided [decides] the time was [is] right to quit [split]. He abandoned [abandons] the war effort, cursed [curses] the U.S. and split [splits] for Taiwan. His plane was so overloaded with gold bullion that he had [has] to dump some of it overboard.

(13:0) March 15, 1975: Roberts got [gets] the "Brezhnev flu" and spent [spends] two weeks in [at] a U.C. [University of California] hospital [Hospital in San Francisco]. Doctors there, without the [Russian] Kirlian photography diagnostic technique, assumed [assume] the softball-sized lump over his heart was [is] cancer [and attempt to treat it with radiation]. It wasn't.

(13:1) The Cambodian domino was no fun at all; fell right over [falls over]. Premier Lon Nol fled [flees] to exile in a Hawaiian suburb.

(13:2a) CIA Chief [William] Colby, in a fit of spite, "leaked" the "stolen" story of the CIA-"Hughes" *Glomar Explorer's* raising of the bodies of drowned Russian sailors from their sunken nuclear submarine. Purpose: To bug the Russians and also halt criticism of the CIA by pointing out how noble, brave and self-sacrificing they are in their efforts to save us [distract the public from Onassis' death and the reshuffling of Mafia ownership].

(13:2b) The Russians are funny about their dead. They bitterly resented Colby's game. They quietly went through a massive "war game" — the rehearsal of a nuclear attack on the United States.

(13:3) Which brings us to 1975. Ford, Kissinger and Rockefeller were squatting like toads on the corpse of America. By the time of the Bicentennial, the stink should have been unbearable, but it wasn't — not yet, anyway.

(13:4) Ford planned a propaganda movie version of his book, *Portrait of an Assassin*, which was to have reiterated the cock-and-bull notion that Oswald was JFK's "lone assassin." With singularly inept misunderstanding of the times, he seems to think Americans would take his word for it and be "reassured" in the face of those "crackpot conspiracy theories." He didn't seem to realize that he would be reminding, or informing, Americans of his role on the infamous Warren Commission.

(13:5a) May 5, 1975: An assassination attempt is made on Marshal Tito of Yugoslavia, who has recently received a Gemstone letter. Egypt's Sadat schedules a special meeting with Tito for May 29-30 in Belgrade to discuss the matter — just before Sadat's scheduled meeting in Austria with U.S. President Ford. A CIA kill team is in Belgrade, with instructions to assassinate Tito and Sadat should certain events take place.

(13:5b) June 1, 1975: President Ford falls down Air Force One's landing ramp on his way to meet Sadat — landing on all fours in a "perfect Moslem salute." He stumbles again. Sadat holds him up. Ford is scared. He knows — and Sadat knows — that Sadat had been the CIA target two days earlier. Sadat — and Egypt — get millions out of the meeting.

(13:5c) Tito cancels his meeting with Ford and goes hunting instead. Back in the States, the Rockefeller Commission winds up its investigation of the CIA's illicit attempts on foreign heads of state, saying, "They may have made a few mistakes, but basically they're OK."

(13:6) I hope this outline will make individual Gemstone papers easier to understand. If you found this outline interesting: You won't be reading it in newspapers. At present, the only way to spread this information here in America is via hand-to-hand. Your help is needed. Please make one, five, 10, 100 copies — or whatever you can — and give them to friends of politicians, groups, or media. The game is nearly up. Either the Mafia goes — or America goes.

— **End of Skeleton Key** —

CHAPTER 4

. . . .

The Early Years

The first questions about this material should appear obvi. ous: *Is any of it true?* If so, why has it been buried and ignored by mainstream media for so long? And just how credible is Bruce Roberts as a solitary researcher and reporter of this information?

Claims that an early liaison between Joseph P. Kennedy, patriarch of the Kennedy political dynasty, and Aristotle Onassis appear to set the tone for the rest of the Gemstone thesis. Further, Onassis is painted as a dreaded enemy from the very beginning. In Gemstone 1:1, Onassis is openly accused of dealing drugs and transporting opium, and portrayed as a villain from his very early beginnings in Argentina. To review the *Skeleton Key*:

(Gemstone 1:1) 1932: [Aristotle] Onassis, a Greek drug pusher and shipowner who made his first million selling "Turkish tobacco" (opium) in Argentina, worked [works] out a profitable deal with Joseph [P.] Kennedy, Eugene Meyer and Meyer Lansky: Onassis was [is] to ship booze directly into Boston for Joseph Kennedy. Also involved was a heroin deal with Franklin D. and Elliott Roosevelt.

Drug pusher? This is quite a serious charge, especially in the early part of this century when the international opium trade was still legal in much of the world. And the alliance with Eugene Meyer, then the publisher of the *Washington Post* and father of Katharine Meyer Graham, and gangster leader Meyer Lansky? Is there really anything to that?

Let's take a closer look at the very beginning of the Onassis era to see if any evidence of the circumstances described in 1:1 actually exists.

Most of the biographical information contained about Onassis reflects a similar line of reasoning; in fact, all the biographies echo each other and appear to have drawn upon the same source of tightly controlled information.

The Associated Press Biographical Service offered the following scenario on Feb. 1, 1969:

"...The Onassis story began Jan 15, 1906, when he was born in Smyrna, Turkey, the son of Homer Socrates and Penelope (Dologlou) Onassis. His father was a wealthy and influential Greek tobacco merchant whose family had lived in the city for generations.

"In 1922, the year Onassis graduated from the Evangelical High School there, Turkish nationalists captured the city from Greek occupying troops, driving Greek residents out. The Onassis family eventually reached Athens in drastically reduced circumstances. It was decided that Aristotle should recoup the family fortune. In 1923 the 17-year-old youth sailed for Argentina, arriving in Buenos Aires with $60 in his pocket.

"...His first job was as a telephone operator, working nights. He used daytime hours to set up a modest tobacco importing industry. From money saved he expanded trading to grains, hides and whale oil. By the time he was 25 he had made his first $1 million."[1]

This rags-to-riches tale is dependably repeated, without variation, in virtually every news account of Onassis' life. There is only one problem: The numbers simply do not add up. Onassis only had menial jobs on the surface — telephone operator,

---

1. Sketch 4364, The Associated Press Biographical Service, Feb. 1, 1969.

tobacco salesman making only five percent commission, electrician at $25 per week, and cigarette vendor. Parlaying those occupations, and on his own initiative, he is supposed to have transformed his $60 into over $1 million in a mere eight years. Actually, the bulk of that $1 million would have to have been made in only six years. One of the more thorough biographies ever written on Onassis states that he started his own cigarette manufacturing business in 1925, "financed by the $25,000 Onassis had saved and a loan of $25,000."[2] In the 1920s, with economics the way they were, $1 million was a huge amount of money. It is inconceivable that Onassis could have made it on tobacco and his side jobs alone.

However, the lucrative opium trade was quite another story. For starters, it was legal at that time in many nations of the world. Secondly, Onassis' family had been based for generations in the city of Smyrna, also known as Izmir, and a major port for the export of Turkey's major cash commodity — opium.

Almost all Turkish and Greek farmers grew opium in its heyday entering the 20th century. In fact, Turkish opium was the most potent of all:

"At one time Turkey was able to produce, without let or hindrance, opium of excellent quality much valued for its high morphine content, which might be as much as fifteen percent (in most other producer countries the morphine content does not exceed nine or ten percent)...

"...The poppy has been cultivated in Turkey from time immemorial. In the museum at Pergamum near *Izmir* (emphasis ours), the flower may be seen in Greek bas-reliefs dating back two thousand years.

"...Under the Ottoman Empire — that is, until Kemal Ataturk's accession to power and the advent of a republican

---

2. *Aristotle Onassis*, by Nicholas Fraser, Philip Jacobson, Mark Ottaway and Lewis Chester, 1977, J.B. Lippincott Co., p.31.

government in *1923* (emphasis ours) — opium could be *exported from Turkey virtually without restriction* (emphasis ours)."[3]

Opium was the ideal consumer product. It is non-perishable. It has been known to be kept in storage for 100 years or more without deteriorating. Hoarding opium was a form of health insurance for Turks of that time and deeply woven into their culture. And, of course, the drug *"never depreciates in value, at least on the black market* (emphasis ours)."[4]

It would be impossible for the family of Aristotle Onassis not to know of opium and its value. And it would by foolhardy for Onassis to not take advantage of the lucrative overseas market for opium — especially in a major New World port city like Buenos Aires.

Now, with opium going for upwards of $100 per pound, compared to the paltry 20 to 25 cents per pound that premium imported tobacco would draw, it is then easy to see that Onassis could have "made his first million selling 'Turkish tobacco' (opium) in Argentina" as Gemstone 1:1 bluntly asserts.

Further, Greek shippers were being increasingly blamed for expansion of the opium trade, which began infesting other nations, including the United States. Just as they are today with such illegal commodities as cocaine, law enforcement bodies of the early century were overwhelmed by the tide of opium, and Greeks were openly accused of drug-dealing.

During one 1915 drug bust in San Francisco, in which the Pacific Mail steamer *City of Para* was stopped and boarded by police on March 31, 22 tins of opium were confiscated. The Surveyor of Customs, Justus S. Wardell, complained: "We have good reason to believe that many Greek seamen connect themselves with the steamers solely for the purpose of smuggling

---

3. *The International Connection: Opium from Growers to Pushers*, Catherine Lamour and Michael R. Lamberti, Pantheon Books, 1974, p. 201.

4. *Ibid.*, p. 202-203.

(opium)."[5]

The reasons were clear. Turkish opium was prized for its high morphine content, which in the early 20th century was as much as 15 percent. Opium from most other producers has, at best, nine to 10 percent morphine content. The poppy was "Turkey's oil."

And the actual role Onassis would play, simply that of transporter and middleman, was not that risky. It was highly unlikely Onassis actually dealt dope openly on the streets of Buenos Aires, although he could well have been a dealer at the very start of his business; to get his foot in the door. But as a mere transporter, and later providing ships for such transport, he would spend as little as a few hours per month actually attending to the business. His strategy was to simply skim some profit off the transport, quietly, without raising suspicions.

The larger drug operations have "world-wide contacts, political protection and vast financial resources. And their ingenuity is inexhaustible."[6] Such a profile fits Onassis seamlessly.

And the market was just beginning to boom. World War I brought with it, along with the general misery of people around the world and especially Europe, a widespread addiction to morphine, which was liberally used to treat war wounded. Just as succeeding wars would do, World War I triggered a human avalanche of drug addiction that quickly spread to all lands and cultures. The market was huge.

Indeed, the idea that Onassis could be completely clean of opium-dealing operations in South America is unlikely, but what is even more significant is his choosing of vocation in the early days. As a telephone operator, he was easily able to listen in on conversations of others. Onassis not only knew his native tongue, but learned Spanish quite quickly, and several other

---

5. *San Francisco Chronicle*, "Opium Hidden on Coast Steamer," April 1, 1915.

6. *Op. cit.* Lamour and Lamberti, p. 20.

foreign languages. Using these tools, it would be relatively easy for him to set up his own network of contacts to enhance his business enterprises, illegal or otherwise.

And Onassis was not hesitant to engage in illegal activities, even if they had nothing to do with opium. He pirated the trade name of one of Argentina's best-selling cigarettes of the day, Bis — placing that trademark on his own cigarette packages, passing them off as Bis, but selling them at far below the normal price of Bis. The company eventually caught Onassis, sued and forced him to settle out of court for "a few thousand pesos."[7]

In fact, Onassis cigarette-making enterprise ended up being a money-loser in the long run, which is yet another reason why he could never have made his first $1 million so soon after settling in Argentina without engaging in the sale or distribution of contraband substances.

When Onassis decided to extend his enterprises beyond the mere sale of tobacco, according to one of his biographies, he became more active in governmental activity in Argentina and was appointed extraordinary deputy consul in Buenos Aires. This put him in position to swindle the citizens from this position of authority by obtaining "substantial sums of currency at official rates, which he then resold on a flourishing black market."[8] It appears that Onassis' life of crime began at an early age.

Even this, his age, was in question. His passport in 1932 claimed he was born on Jan. 7, 1900, when his real birthdate was six years later. In later life, he would claim he had to say he was older in order to get work in Buenos Aires. The pattern, however, was clear — Aristotle Onassis was setting himself up for a life which did not have to answer to the laws of man.

****

Now what of the connection with Joseph P. Kennedy men-

7. *Op. cit.* Fraser, p.33.
8. *Ibid.*, p.38.

tioned in Gemstone 1:1? And of the alleged narcotics deals cooked up with the Roosevelt boys?

In none of the Onassis biographies is there any mention of an early knowledge of or alliance with Joe Kennedy. On the surface, then, that would be the logical conclusion, that no relationship of any consequence existed between the two men, and that Onassis did not "ship booze directly into Boston for Joseph Kennedy" as 1:1 stipulates.

But that is not entirely true, and early connections between the two men — and of other key names which are intertwined in the *Skeleton Key*, can be found, mainly through the early-century maritime network and the shipbuilding trade.

First, Kennedy was the assistant general manager of Bethlehem Steel's booming Fore River shipyard in Quincy, Mass., from 1917 until the end of World War I. Another long-time employee of Bethlehem Steel was a youthful, strapping 28-year-old shipyard worker in 1917: <u>LaVerne Dayle Roberts, father of Bruce Roberts — author of the Gemstone Files</u>. Bruce Roberts describes a sequence of events (Gemstone 8:3) in which he asserts his aging father was killed by the Watergate plumbers. In any event, the connection of Roberts' father with Bethlehem Steel during that early period of time would give the younger Roberts a channel through which first-hand information on the more unseemly side of international shipping would be more easily accessed (please note Gemstone 1:3 in which it is stated Roberts used "personal contacts" — probably including his maritime-connected father — to "learn these things").

Twenty years later, in 1937, with great aplomb, Kennedy was named chairman of the new Maritime Commission, which had been formed to revive American commerce on the high seas, Instead, many unscrupulous shippers—including Aristotle Onassis and future newspaper publisher Hank Greenspun—used the Commission and Kennedy's position to set themselves up for profitable, yet shady, deals on used American ships. That proves at least a cursory Onassis-Kennedy connection in the early days.

At least three instances of documented reports connect Kennedy with maritime decisions which helped Onassis, directly or indirectly. The first instance can be found on June 30, 1937, soon after Kennedy was named chairman of the Maritime Commission. On that date, hidden as an addendum to some seemingly routine subsidies handed down to 16 U.S. shipping lines to help prop them up against foreign competition, the following was reported:

"...In only one instance is the direct subsidy higher than the mail pay subsidy. This is for the *Pacific-Argentina-Brazil Line* (emphasis ours), operating from San Francisco to Los Angeles and *Argentina* (emphasis ours)."[9] That would be a direct link between Onassis and Joe Kennedy, since Onassis was very much involved in the Argentine shipping industry at that point. It would also give some credence to Gemstone 1:1, where it is stated that a "profitable deal" had been worked out between Onassis and Kennedy. Indeed, this kind of subsidy would in effect help underwrite Onassis' shipping operations to and from the U.S.

The second major proof of an Onassis-Kennedy collaboration during Kennedy's brief stint as chairman of the Maritime Commission occurred on Oct. 21, 1937. On that date, the Commission announced the acceptance of bids totaling $991,111.93 for the purchase of 22 of the 25 "obsolete vessels in the commission's laid up fleet...Four of the old ships were bid in by a *New York concern for a Greek customer* (emphasis ours) who will use them with the pledge that they will not be operated in competition with American shipping.

"...Boyd, Weir and Sewell of New York City, who placed the kid *for the Greek customer* (emphasis ours), offered $367,536.93 for the four ships to be placed in foreign operation."[10]

---

9. *San Francisco Examiner*, "U.S. Grants 16 Ship Lines New Subsidies," July 1, 1937.

10. *San Francisco Examiner*, "U.S. Sells Old Ships," Oct. 22, 1937.

Indeed, of the 22 ships purchased, 18 were bought only for scrap metal. The other four, broken-down as they were, nonetheless were placed into operation. There was only one "Greek customer" doing that at the time in this country — Aristotle Onassis. Again, the Commission, while Joseph P. Kennedy was its chairman, assisted Onassis in the building and expansion of his shipping empire.

The third case of a decision by the Commission greatly enhancing Onassis' position in international shipping circles also came in 1937, when Kennedy was still chairman. This time, a third name entered the picture — that of a small-in-stature Jewish business entrepreneur named Hank Greenspun, much later to become a Las Vegas newspaper publisher and focal point in the controversy swirling around reclusive billionaire Howard Hughes (Gemstone 7:9).

Greenspun had been tipped off in 1937 that the Nagle Engine Works in Erie, Pa., was up for sale. Closed by the depression, it had an asking price of $500,000, but was worth many times that. One report stated that:

"...Although Hank had saved up only $1,000, he secured an option to buy it (Nagle). Then he went to the Maritime Commission in Washington, D.C., and *secured a $2,486,000 contract for reciprocating engines, to be installed in Liberty Ships* (emphasis ours)."[11]

Please refer to Gemstone 1:6. Exactly what kind of ships does Onassis end up buying from the U.S. in yet another big transaction that, this time, turned out to be illegal? Liberty ships! The involvement of Greenspun also deeply connects the *Las Vegas Sun* publisher to Onassis in the early days, while Kennedy was still in a position to help individuals like Onassis, Greenspun and others swing these massive, government-backed shipping deals that would later come back to haunt the U.S. It

---

11. *San Francisco Examiner*, Jan. 3, 1976, "Herman M. Greenspun: Shirt-Sleeve Publisher," by Jim Scott.

would also provide some foundation for Greenspun knowing about some of Onassis' more sordid activities as pointed out in Gemstone 7:9. It is too bad Greenspun went to his grave at the age of 79 on July 22, 1989, without ever divulging the secrets hidden inside his office safe concerning the Onassis-Hughes-Kennedy connection.

****

What about Eugene Meyer, Jr. and his alleged association with Onassis as implied in Gemstone 1:1? Indeed, the time frame certainly seemed to fit. It was Meyer who bought the down-and-out *Washington Post* in 1932 (the year the *Skeleton Key* indicates a relationship was struck between Meyer and the Greek shipper) and turned it into one of the world's great newspapers. Daughter Katharine Meyer also caught the news bug, and she started in the business in San Francisco as a waterfront reporter for the old *San Francisco News* in 1938. It is interesting that the *Skeleton Key* talks of Ms. Graham's connections with San Francisco — connections which, according to the *Key*, were instrumental in monitoring the activities of the so-called "plumbers" long before the Watergate break-in. It could well be that during these early days, Katharine Meyer — who would soon become Katharine Meyer Graham after marrying Philip Graham — educated herself quite thoroughly on the nuances of finance and crime, and how they are used to manipulate the capitalist system and make certain individuals wealthy beyond imagination. Ms. Graham might be many things, but "Kay" was and still is fundamentally a seeker of truth, an oasis of reason and journalistic pulchritude amid a vast desert of print-media corruption and sordid mob connections.

It would be foolhardy to assume that Ms. Graham, during her early days under her father's direct influence before his death in 1959, would not be aware of such newsworthy topics as the opium trade, which was still quite alive and well in the post-depression 1930s, and which generated more than its fair share of lively copy along the waterfront beat Ms. Graham supposedly prowled. Further, she worked in a Pacific Rim metroplex whose dealings with overseas shippers always carried with it the cloud of illicit contraband dealings as each and every suspect freighter steamed into San Francisco Bay.

Was the senior Meyer involved in the drug trade with Onassis, as Gemstone 1:1 asserts? That would be difficult to prove directly — but indirectly, Mr. Meyer's connections with big-time financiers and low-level Mafia types is inescapable. In 1944, the *Post* bought WINN, a minor radio station which had been used by numbers racketeers to calculate daily winning numbers. Meyer had the station's staff change to a classical music format, but the mob association was nonetheless there.

Don't forget that the *Post* simply served as Mr. Meyer's plaything and second career. This man was busy in earlier life. As a money manager, Meyer was involved in plenty of shady, big-bucks deals in the early '30s. He was named head of the Federal Reserve Board in early 1931 as the nation was trying to extract itself from the depths of the Great Depression.

But Meyer was blamed by many for the very circumstances in elite financial circles which helped trigger the Depression in the first place. His selection to the Reserve Board was disputed bitterly. As Aristotle Onassis was busy building his maritime fleet, Meyer was assembling his own monetary firepower. A Senate subcommittee in the mid-1920s investigated charges that Meyer got a "rake-off" on the bond stabilization operations of the War Finance Corp. during and just after World War I.[12]

This high involvement in multinational finance, related to the war industry, could well have placed Meyer on an inevitable collision course with Onassis. He was not only the managing director of the War Finance Corp., he also served on the War Industries Board, National Committee on War Savings, Federal

12. *San Francisco Examiner*, Jan. 28, 1931, "McFadden Says J.P. Morgan Co. Backed Meyer" (Universal Service).

Farm Loan Commission, Reconstruction Finance Corp. as its chairman — and, finally, governor of the Federal Reserve Board. Mr. Meyer was long in a prime seat of monetary power and authority long before his little excursion into publishing. However, this enormous influence cut both ways: His tenure with the Federal Reserve came during the much-maligned administration of Herbert Hoover, and it was easy to target Meyer as a prime cause of the misery endured by the general population as a result of the Hoover administration's abject misunderstanding of economic realities.

And, like Onassis (see Gemstone 1:5), Meyer was a huge backer of war, and profited handsomely from it. In the late 1930s, Meyer was all but shoving the United States into World War II long before the general population accepted the idea as even remotely palatable. Even the conservative, even reactionary, *San Francisco Examiner* of William Randolph Hearst pointed this out, stating in an April 14, 1939 editorial: "...Mr. Meyer's newspaper, the *Washington Post*, usually represents the attitude of big business and the banks, and usually attacks President Roosevelt. Tuesday morning, however, Mr. Meyer's newspaper printed an editorial asserting that *American involvement in the impending war is inevitable, and even desirable* (emphasis ours)."[13]

Gemstone 1:4 implies that Meyer bought the *Post* specifically to "gain control" of news media, and that "other Mafia buy other papers, broadcasting, TV, etc." Even if Meyer had no connection with organized crime, his monopolization of large amounts of capital largely targeted for war-related expenses, and his alleged role in the triggering of the Great Depression, provide plenty of impetus to buy the *Post* and effectively shield him from any real criticism concerning his past and present activities.

---

13. *San Francisco Examiner*, April 14, 1939, "Keep America Out of War."

****

We now arrive at another key name in Gemstone 1:1 — that of well-known gangster Meyer Lansky. Did this notorious crime boss actually connect with Onassis, and if so, for what purpose? One thing is certain: If Onassis was involved in the opium trade, then business with Lansky would have been not only possible, but necessary, for Onassis to make any inroads on the U.S. and Caribbean markets for illicit drugs. Timing is again crucial in this scenario, for Lansky became one of the early drug lords — right at the time, the early 1930s, when Onassis' shipping empire started to take hold on the world economic scene, as Nicholas Gage of the *Wall Street Journal* astutely reported in 1969:

"...But during the 1930s, there was little time for reflection. With the repeal of prohibition, activities such as prostitution, hijacking, gambling, narcotics and extortion became more important to the mob. Lansky, Siegel, Luciano and Lepke set up a factory to process drugs. Lepke founded a group of paid killers who replaced the Bugs and Meyer mob and became the syndicate's enforcement arm. The group was dubbed Murder Incorporated and killed over 800 persons before racketbusters Burton Turkus and Thomas E. Dewey put it out of business and sent Lepke to the electric chair."[14]

No drug trade, however, could survive long without an extensive distribution network, and Onassis could not have been in a better position. His ships were already plying waters around the globe, and the Caribbean and southern U.S. were on his itinerary. Interaction between Onassis' forces and the legions of Lansky is certainly a believable state of affairs.

And do not forget the so-called "Murder Incorporated," which operated over a wide area. Some of these trained assas-

---

14. *Wall Street Journal*, Nov. 19, 1969, "How One Gang Leader Thrives While Others Fall by the Wayside," Nicholas Gage.

sins, according to the *Skeleton Key*, were recruited not only for routine rub-outs, but for political assassinations as well. Fidel Castro and John F. Kennedy were likely mob targets for a variety of well-chronicled reasons. Castro survived, but JFK did not.

****

The advent and spread of an even more potent, concentrated version of morphine, a substance called heroin, took the already lucrative drug trade to still new heights. The infamous I.G. Farben Co. — mentioned in Gemstone 1:5 but glaringly edited out of the *Hustler* rendition — perfected development of heroin in between the two World Wars as a prelude to its even more insidious product: The death gas used in Nazi concentration camps during World War II.

In somewhat gratuitous fashion, the *Key* mentions in 1:1 that a "heroin deal" was also involved between Onassis and two Roosevelts: Franklin D., the President, and his somewhat prodigal son, Elliott. It would be fantasy to find any evidence that connects FDR with a direct narcotics network engineered by Onassis, but Elliott is another story entirely.

The President's son, a heavily decorated veteran flier in World War II whose specialty was aerial photography, was involved in more than one brush with organized crime, and pulled some fast ones on his own — using the power of his father's high office in abusive fashion. One major flap occurred in 1936, when Elliott was accused of pocketing a $500,000 "fee" for assisting German warplane manufacturer Anthony H.S. Fokker in supplying military planes to the Russian military.[15]

In a far more glaring incident, and one which connects Elliott directly to a mob-related activity and to a possible connection with Lansky and even Onassis, Elliott Roosevelt was implicated in an assassination plot of the Prime Minister of the

---

15. *San Francisco Examiner*, Oct. 7, 1936, Associated Press report: "Soviet Deal Laid to Elliott."

Bahamas. One news account put it this way:

"A convicted stock swindler said today he was offered $100,000 by Elliott Roosevelt and an asserted mobster frontman to assassinate Bahamian Prime Minister Lynder O. Pindling.

"Louis P. Mastriana, now in the federal penitentiary at Texarkana, Tex., said the assassination contract was offered because of Pindling's failure to grant a gambling license to mobster Meyer Lansky.

"...'They came to me and offered me $100,000 to kill, to whack Pindling,' Mastriana told the (Senate permanent) committee (on investigations). Who are 'they'? asked Sen. Charles Percy (R-Ill.). Mastriana replied, 'Roosevelt and (reputed mobster Mike) McClaney.'

"'They brought the contract to Roosevelt and Roosevelt came to me,' he said.

"Mastriana said he was paid $10,000 immediately. Of that sum, $2,500 came in a check from McClaney to Roosevelt. A staff member said *the check had been endorsed by Roosevelt over to Mastriana* (emphasis ours)."[16] The damaging effect is to link Elliott Roosevelt in any way to these mobsters, who probably enjoyed more than a cursory association to Mr. Onassis himself.

Elliott also allowed himself to be indulged by none other than billionaire Howard Hughes, who figures heavily in the *Skeleton Key*. One embarrassing list leaked to the press in 1947 showed that Hughes' publicist John Meyer spent $5,083.79 entertaining Elliott Roosevelt and his friends at posh hotels all across the United States from 1941 through 1946. These expenditures included money for "girls at hotel (late)" and other unseemly activities.[17]

---

16. *San Francisco Examiner*, Sept. 18, 1973, "A Con Names a Roosevelt," Associated Press.

17. *San Francisco Examiner*, Aug. 3, 1947, "Expense Account of John Meyer Gives Details of Cash Spent on Elliott Roosevelt," Associated Press.

The mention of Elliott in Gemstone 1:1 is also left off the *Hustler* version.

And yet another of the Roosevelt clan, Franklin Roosevelt Jr., spent quite a bit of time on Onassis' luxury yacht, the *Christina*, and was photographed at least once while on the vessel in October of 1963 — accompanied by Jackie Kennedy, widow of the President, and Onassis himself. On the surface, it certainly appeared to be a cozy group, and the mainstream media never really paid it much attention.

In short, it is not easy to casually dismiss the *Skeleton Key*, at least this early segment, as totally unfounded as actual facts and circumstances are studied. Actual hard proof of these early connections might be difficult to come by, but plenty of circumstantial evidence, and questionable alliances between the individuals mentioned, leave enough in doubt as to prevent the *Key* from being dismissed as a total fabrication.

And we have but scratched the surface.

CHAPTER 5

· · · · · · · · · · · ·

Liberty Ships, Oil and
Howard Hughes

For much of the Gemstone thesis to be understood, the early 20th-century historical background provided by Gemstone 1:1 through 1:6 is vitally important, and an aspect of modern history which is largely misrepresented. Many times in various biographical sketches regarding Onassis, it is mentioned that he and his organization actually paid large sums to *keep his name out of encyclopedias and history books*. It might be hard to fathom, but even the most highly recognized information sources, such as the complete 1982 Funk & Wagnalls Encyclopedia, do not mention Onassis at all — not even a cursory reference to his marriage to the former Jacqueline Kennedy, or even a listing in the encyclopedia's master index.

It is not that Onassis shunned the limelight; on the contrary, he was Topic A on many a gossip columnist's list. However, most stories were restricted to the "lives of the rich and famous" genre, the "fabulous Greeks" and so forth. Onassis would also grant interviews to female journalists only, another curiosity. His hermit-like existence, primarily on the luxurious decks of the *Christina* and away from the prying eyes of the general public, kept his mysterious ways secretive right up until his death in 1975.

Yet, even if the negative side of Onassis' life is edited out of the equation, there is no question his business life alone had an enormous impact on the international business and social scene.

Information about Onassis and his activities, though, is restricted to a handful of carefully controlled and approved biographies, and has seldom been subjected to the scrutiny of the international press.

Consider these things as this material continues to unfold.

****

(Gemstone 1:5) 1941-1945: World War II very profitable for Onassis, Rockefeller [and the Rockefellers], Kennedys, [and the] Roosevelts, I.G. Farben, etc. Onassis — selling oil, arms and dope to both sides — went [goes] through the war without losing a single ship or man.

(1:6) 1949: Onassis buys [U.S.] war surplus "Liberty Ships" in questionable (illegal) purchase. Lawyer Burke Marshall helps him.

Aristotle Onassis quickly discovered an even more profitable product than opium to be transported on his ships — petroleum, oceans of which were being extracted from the Middle East to feed the Western world's heavy appetite for it. But it needed transportation, and the gigantic oil tankers were the answer.

Onassis knew who held the reigns to power in the oil industry, and the Rockefellers were a good place to start. John D. Rockefeller, in the mid- and late 19th century, monopolized the domestic oil industry before the U.S. government broke it up in 1911. Still, the Rockefeller involvement in big oil would continue until the present day.

However, in order for Onassis to expand into the tanker business, he needed more ships, and needed them quickly, to build his capital reserves in anticipation of the petroleum windfall to come. He found a solution in the so-called "Liberty ships," which were for sale in the late 1940s — but only to American citizens, or businesses owned by Americans. Since Onassis was not an American citizen, he tried to dance his way around the regulations by setting up dummy companies "based" in the United States, and making illegal Liberty ship purchases through those dummy companies.

Onassis accomplished this goal through his usual channels in Massachusetts, where he used one of Joseph Kennedy's longtime associates, former Rep. Joseph E. Casey, to help him defraud the U.S. government related to the illegal purchase of these vessels. The scheme, set and executed during the late 1940s as Gemstone 1:6 relates, started becoming unraveled in the early 1950s when the U.S. government caught wind of the swindle and decided to take legal action. The consequences would be terrible. Onassis, in his own slippery way, would never admit to any wrongdoing, and would pay substantial fines, but he would forever hold a deep bitterness inside his soul for the United States and its leaders — and later, if the *Skeleton Key* is any indication, would adopt an old Mafia custom: "If someone welches on a deal, kill him and take his gun and his girl — in this case, (JFK), Jackie and the Pentagon (Gemstone 5:2)."

As it turned out, the investigation of the Liberty ships deal by Attorney General Brownell's office in 1951-52 disclosed that Casey and "a group of prominent public figures" scored enormous profits from the ships deal. As Gemstone 1:6 accurately states, the ship-buying contracts were executed during the Truman administration (1945-53). Total monetary figure was reportedly $18 million, and all ships were sold by the "old Maritime Commission, which has since been abolished."[1] Along with some prominent lawyers and business executives who were implicated, six corporations were also named in the U.S. indictment against Onassis — including Victory Carriers. Remember that name. It will surface again.

During the next several years, into the late 1950s, the ship-buying issue would be kicked around the halls of the U.S.

---

1. *San Francisco Examiner*, Feb. 9, 1954, "Surplus Ships Deal Indicts 9," Associated Press.

judicial system and Congress until the inevitable settlement, which involved a fine of $7 million paid by Onassis. It was a cheap way out, and provided more profiteering opportunities for the wily Greek.

But first, he would infiltrate the American legal system in his own nefarious way — meeting with then-Assistant Attorney General Warren Burger in a series of "10 to 12 conferences," then recalling one sharp-witted comment he made to Mr. Burger: "I said, 'Mr. Burger, if I'd done that (buy the ships) in some other country, England, I'd been knighted. Here, I was indicted.'"[2]

Then, the invariable twist that would make Onassis famous time and time again: He turned right around and soaked the U.S. Maritime Administration for a whopping $8 million windfall in a deal that allowed for the construction of three large oil super-tankers at a cost of $51.3 million — with *87.5 percent of the cost to be guaranteed by U.S. government aid.* Graciously, Onassis agreed to have these tankers built in an American shipyard as his part of the transaction. Which shipyard? None other than the Bethlehem Steel shipbuilding plant in Quincy, Mass., the same one that Joe Kennedy ran during World War I. If not a strange coincidence, then what?

As oil became a profound profit-producer that began to dwarf even international drug trafficking, Onassis turned his attention to various attempts at monopolizing Middle East oil transportation. Among the most famous of his swindles was one in which Onassis is accused of signing a document in disappearing ink in order to defraud a Greek ship broker, Spyridon Catapodis. As this scheme came to light, the international press began to close in, and Onassis' true nature began to leak out:

"...Spyridon Catapodis, a Greek ship broker...claims that the Greek-born, Argentine-naturalized Onassis swindled him to the tune of 200,000 pounds sterling ($560,000) in the disappear-

---

2. *San Francisco Examiner,* June 6, 1958, "Onassis' Jokes Parry House Ship Queries," Associated Press.

ing ink deal...

"Ramifications of the (Catapodis) suit reach Washington, New York and other centers of international finance and 'oil diplomacy,' and allegedly involve *a host of shadowy and strange figures, including one-time Nazi Finance Minister Hjalmar Schacht*" (emphasis ours).[3] (This would lend great credence to Gemstone 1:5 concerning profiteering during World War II, a scenario that would have to involve a cozy relationship to Nazi Germany for Onassis to go "through the war without losing a single ship or man," and make enormous profits to boot.)

The *Skeleton Key's* further accuracy (Gemstone 1:2) is further confirmed later in this same news account:

"...Catapodis charged in his damage suit that he was in the middle man in obtaining the disputed agreement signed last January whereby Onassis' tanker fleet *obtained priority* (i.e., take unfair advantage, Gemstone 1:2) in transporting oil produced in Saudi Arabia by the Arabian American Oil Company (Aramco).

"(Aramco is made up of four American oil companies — the Texas Company, Standard Oil of California, the Socony-Vacuum Oil Co., and the (sic) Standard Oil of New Jersey.)"[4] Indeed, Aramco is a combine containing four of the so-called "Seven Sisters" further described in Gemstone 1:2.

That isn't the end of Onassis' apparent wrongdoing in this naked attempt at monopolizing Saudi oil transport:

"...Catapodis accused Onassis of getting the agreement by bribing Saudi Arabia's foreign minister, Mohammed Ali Reza, with payments that would *go over a million dollars.* (emphasis ours)."[5] The methods of Onassis knew no bounds, according to those who worked and dealt with him. In this and other docu-

---

3. *San Francisco Examiner*, Nov. 21, 1954, "Mystery Man Accused of Big Oil Deal Fraud," International News Service.

4. *Ibid.*

5. *bid.*

mented incidents, it would appear the *Skeleton Key* does not stand alone when detailing these activities.

Further attempts at monopolizing the transport of oil from Saudi Arabia kept Onassis busy during the mid-'50s. Jack Lotto, a reporter for the old International News Service, was best at wrapping up this expansive era for Onassis in the following widely published account:

"For its breath-taking daring, nothing could stop the bombshell dropped on the oil and shipping industry in 1954 by independent tanker operator Aristotle Onassis.

"In the ensuing uproar, nine governments, including the United States, vigorously protested the explosive secret deal (Note: Gemstone 1:2 might be in reference to this, although the timing, 1934, is slightly off; it could have been that Onassis was dabbling in oil transport even then).

"An agreement between Onassis and the Saudi government would have given the tanker man a priority and eventually a monopoly on the hauling of Saudi Arabia's oil, which amounts to 40,000,000 tons per year or seven percent of the world's production.

"The deal would have shut down scores of other independent shippers — including Onassis' brother-in-law Stavros Niarchos — and could have opened up to a possible rate squeeze (of) the four American oil companies which, as the Arabian American Oil Company (Aramco) operate the fabulously rich oil concessions.

"...In return, Onassis agreed to operate for the Arabian government a 600,000-ton tanker fleet and *pay a royalty on all oil he moved* (emphasis ours). This meant the Saudis, if they chose to nationalize their oil as the Iranians had, could sell and ship to anyone they pleased."[6]

To understand the impact of Onassis' early oil dealings, and

---

6. *San Francisco Examiner*, Jan. 31, 1957, "Oil Contract a Bombshell," Jack Lotto, International News Service.

how the fallout from those early agreements would bring him into repeated, bitter entanglements with the U.S. government, these pacts need to be objectively evaluated. It is easy to see that Onassis would become an arch-enemy of the United States, developing a brutal and stormy relationship which would give the Greek shipper more than enough reason to precipitate political turmoil in the United States.

In February of 1954, the true dimensions of Onassis' attempts at monopolizing the oil transportation business were brought to light by the mainstream press, but virtually ignored by the many Onassis biographers who were to follow. This material is critical in linking Onassis to the names in Gemstone 1:1 and 1:2. Terms of that original Saudi deal follow:

"**1.** The Saudi Arabian government would authorize Onassis to use his tankers to transport all oil not carried in tankers owned by the four American companies united in Aramco...

"**2.** In return, Onassis would pay Saudi Arabia a royalty per ton (amount not known) for all oil carried in his tankers.

"**3.** Onassis would register the tankers under the Saudi Arabian flag. *Government officials said this sort of arrangement was unprecedented in modern shipping usage and practices* (emphasis ours)."[7]

The United States government, clearly seeing the threat to U.S. oil profiteers in Onassis' pact with Saudi Arabia, then decided to use the Liberty ships deal as a legal roadblock — indicting 18 people on Feb. 23, 1954, including Casey (the former Massachusetts congressman and Joe Kennedy associate); Julius C. Holmes, former U.S. Minister to London; and Greek shipper Stavros Niarchos, Onassis' brother-in-law and bitter business rival.

It was alleged in the indictment that Casey and a group of "prominent public figures" made huge profits in the transac-

---

7. *San Francisco News*, Feb. 12, 1954, "Greek's Deal Hits Arabian Oil Pact," Jack Steele, Scripps-Howard News Service.

tions involving sale of the surplus ships in the late 1940s. Casey and Holmes were alleged to have sold stock in the shipbuyers' purchasing company to others without the approval of the Maritime Commission. Onassis is mentioned as one of the buyers, but he had already been indicted along with Casey on Feb. 9 in the same scandal.

As this issue played itself out, other political issues in the United States did not escape Onassis' notice. It was easy to forecast that the U.S. would become the largest consumer of petroleum and petroleum-based products in the years to come. A next logical step would be to gain control of the defense industry in the U.S., and Onassis would see to that (Gemstone 1:7, 1:8), according to the *Skeleton Key*:

(Gemstone 1:7) 1956: Howard Hughes, Texas millionaire (actually, by this time he was quite the billionaire), is meanwhile buying his way toward control of the U.S. electoral process — with a view toward his own personal gain. He buys senators, governors, etc. he finally buys his last politician — newly elected Vice President Richard M. Nixon, via a $250,000 (it was actually $205,000) non-repayable loan to Nixon's brother, Donald.

(1:8) Early 1957: V.P. Nixon repays the favor by having IRS-Treasury grant tax-free status (refused twice before) to "Hughes Medical Foundation," sole owner of Hughes Aircraft, creating a tax-free, non-accountable money funnel or laundry, for whatever Hughes wanted to do. U.S. government also shelved antitrust suits against Hughes' TWA, etc.

(1:9) March, 1957: Onassis carries out a carefully planned event: He has Hughes kidnapped from his bungalow at the Beverly Hills Hotel, using Hughes' own men (Chester Davis, born Cesare in Sicily, et al). Hughes' men either quit, get fired, or stay on in the new Onassis organization. A few days later, Mayor Cannon of Nevada (now Senator Cannon), arranges a fake "marriage" to Jean Peters, to explain Hughes' sudden loss of interest in chasing movie stars. [A fake marriage between starlet Jean Peters and Hughes is arranged.] Hughes, battered and brain-damaged in the scuffle [during the kidnapping], is taken to the Emerald Isle Hotel in the Bahamas where the entire top floor has been rented for the "Hughes party." There he is shot full of heroin for thirty [30] days and later dragged off to a cell on Onassis' island, Skorpios. Onassis now has a much larger power base in the U.S. (the Hughes empire), as well as control over V.P. Nixon and other Hughes-purchased politicians. L. Wayne Rector, "Hughes' double since 1955, becomes Hughes. [A Hughes double becomes "Hughes."]...

Of all the material contained within the *Skeleton Key*, none is as far-fetched as this segment about Howard Hughes, and the seemingly fanciful (and impossible) tale of his kidnapping. Even so, such an event would go far to explaining many mysterious aspects of Mr. Hughes, and would help explain some other mysteries the *Key* does not even touch upon, but are quite directly related to the above passages. It would also explain some of the abrupt foreign policy about-faces the U.S. government made during the late 1950s and early 1960s.

The allegation in Gemstone 1:7 concerning Hughes' "buying" of government officials appears to have some merit. After all, it is clear that Hughes and his various companies and manufacturing interests had their hands deep into the pockets of U.S. taxpayers, and had the financial clout to buy just about anything and anybody they wanted. More than one U.S. journalist went after the roots of the vast Hughes empire as its influence spread far and wide, and the newspapers courageous enough to make these efforts realized quickly that Hughes' life was simply too enigmatic and too isolated to be understood:

"...No one really knows, of course, just what life is like for Howard Hughes. Only one thing is certain: Before the sun sets on an average day, Howard Hughes, *secreted away* (emphasis ours) in a two-story suite atop the Xanadu Princess Hotel on

Grand Bahama Island, will have collected nearly $1.7 million more from the United States Treasury than he had when the sun rose in the morning.

"That has been the Hughes empire's average daily take from America's taxpayers for 10 years now. Since 1965, Hughes companies have received more than $6 billion in contracts from nearly a dozen different departments and agencies of the federal government...

"...Howard Hughes' Washington is a place of intricate deals, shadowy alliances and quiet understandings, a place from which the millions of dollars flow forth in a never-ending stream — and a place where even the *law itself has been suspended, and none of the usual requirements of accountability or perfor-mance or competition seem to hold sway* (emphasis ours).

"...All this takes place against a shadowy backdrop of occur-rences that include: *secret political contributions, business deal-ings punctuated by suicides, stated campaigns to buy and control politicians,* sharply inflated markups on government contracts; and the *failure of both the Watergate special prosecutor's office and the Senate Watergate Committee to investigate the full range of Hughes' ties to the administrative associates of former President Richard M. Nixon* (emphasis ours)."[8]

Indeed, Gemstone 1:7 can hardly be termed the blabberings of a madman; instead, it is nothing less than a consensus of underlying truth which could give Hughes the basis from which to hold virtually unlimited power over the U.S. public and private sectors. Gemstone 1:7 also makes mention of the large $205,000 "loan" to F. Donald Nixon, the President's brother. That was alleged to have taken place in 1956 and was duly reported by noted columnist Drew Pearson:

"...Pearson wrote that 'the family of Richard M. Nixon' had

---

8. *Philadelphia Inquirer*, Dec. 14-20, 1975, "The Silent Partner of Howard Hughes," special investigative series by Donald J. Barlett and James B. Steele.

received a $205,000 loan on Dec. 10, 1956, from the Hughes Tool Company, owned by industrialist Howard Hughes, and that Hughes' problems with various Government agencies had *improved after this* (emphasis ours)."[9]

Still, Donald Nixon's relationship with Hughes continued to flourish, and the resulting press was visibly impacting Richard Nixon's credibility. Years later, this aspect of that case would also receive notice from a U.S. media already electrically charged by the Watergate break-in and the crumbling of the Nixon presidency overall. According to a Feb. 4, 1974, report from United Press International:

"...The White House got the Secret Service to investigate business activities of the President's brother, F. Donald Nixon, and put him under electronic surveillance at a time when aides were worried that Donald's affairs would hurt Nixon's 1972 reelection chances.

"The President told a news conference last fall he authorized electronic surveillance of his brother because of a national security matter.

"But government sources report that administration concern about Donald began with his dealings with an *associate of billionaire Howard Hughes and later included trips to the Dominican Republic, Switzerland, Italy, Greece and Hawaii* (emphasis ours)."[10] What possible business could Donald Nixon have in places like Italy and Greece, Onassis' home turf? Interestingly, the initial news of Donald's business connection with Hughes was publicly disclosed right before the 1960 general election, as brother Richard and John. F. Kennedy were locked in mortal political combat on the campaign trail. Such a disclo-

---

9. *San Francisco Examiner*, Oct. 27, 1960, "Nixon Aide Rips 'Smear' on Loan" (kicker reads "$205,000 to Kin"), by Associated Press and United Press International.

10. *San Francisco Examiner*, Feb. 4, 1974, "The Probes of Donald Nixon," by Clay F. Richards, United Press International.

sure could not have come at a worse time for Nixon, and may well have had an impact on voters before they went to the polls — pushing the narrow advantage in Kennedy's favor.

It is also interesting to note that *Las Vegas Sun* publisher Herman "Hank" Greenspun, who spent much of his early life involved in building engines for Liberty ships that Onassis would soon illegally buy (see Chapter 4), was right on top of the 1964 addendum to the Donald Nixon saga:

"...For more than a year, the investigation centered on the brother's (Donald's) business deals with John Meier, a Hughes scientific advisor for mining claims now under indictment for income tax evasion.

"Herman Greenspun, owner of the *Las Vegas Sun*, said that '(Nixon aide John) Ehrlichman sent (Nixon's personal lawyer) Herbert W. Kalmbach to see me in late 1971 to find out what Don Nixon was doing with Meier.'

"Greenspun said that he could tell Kalmbach little because he had rarely seen Don Nixon in Las Vegas. But he said he has since begun to believe that Kalmbach thought he was *holding something back*, and this 'may have inspired' the *plan by the Watergate burglars to break into his safe* (emphasis ours). The burglary was never carried out."[11]

This would be but one of many links between Greenspun and the several aspects of the *Skeleton Key* which are to come to light as this report continues to unfold. Hank Greenspun was a solid reporter, but knew when and how to use the information he possessed — and when to sit on an unbelievably big story, for profit or otherwise. According to the *Key*, Greenspun was one newspaperman with the story of the century — that of Onassis' involvement with the disappearance of Howard Hughes and his supportive role in the premeditated assassination of JFK — sitting quietly in his office safe. It would later pull in some blackmail cash (Gemstone 7:9) from Onassis, says the *Key*, but

---

11. *Ibid.*

that informational legacy would later die along with Greenspun himself in 1989.

Greenspun, as a seeming linchpin in information access to, from and about Howard Hughes, received plenty of attention from the U.S. government and legal system because of his interaction with the reclusive billionaire. Just as Clark Kent was one of the few people who could track down and locate Superman (indeed, he was one in the same), Hank Greenspun was one of very few journalists who could access the murky world of Howard Hughes. Bruce Roberts was not the only researcher to make these assertions about Greenspun and the information he possessed and largely kept to himself. Even Roberts' blackmail assertion in Gemstone 7:9 is backed by a mountain of circumstantial evidence. More about this issue will be taken up later.

Now, however, Roberts' claim of Hughes' kidnapping needs to be addressed. Of all the *Skeleton Key* assertions, Gemstone 1:9 appears, on the surface, to be completely devoid of truth or backing. But just under the surface, doubts emerge. No matter what precisely happened on the Bahamas in the summer of 1957, it was mysterious, for that is when Howard Hughes ended his high-profile existence and went into "seclusion" — not for a week, a month, a year, but for the rest of his life.

This sudden reclusiveness has never been explained in any coherent manner. It is clear that Hughes' affairs were run not by him, but his associates, *after* this mystery-shrouded 1957 trip to the Bahamas. It is clear his behavior radically changed. And, some people around Hughes changed, for in 1957, former FBI agent Robert Aime Maheu, also known as "Iron Bob Maheu" (IBM), started "working" for "Hughes." It was 1957 that the so-called "Mystery Mormons" began "nursemaiding" Hughes, or what people thought was Hughes. Needles to say, something happened in the Bahamas that has not been fully divulged, but that Bruce Roberts claims was a kidnapping and switch of the billionaire.

Could a kidnapping have happened? Input from some of the

people near Hughes at that time would be of value. Let's start with Carter Burgess, president of Hughes' airline, TWA, and Noah Dietrich, Hughes' long-time financial director. It was Dietrich through whom Hughes trusted for many of the complex financial deals that had to be pieced together to keep the Hughes empire running smoothly. The two men were inseparable — until March of 1957, according to Burgess, who related the following story about a mysterious phone call he received from Hughes:

"...Hughes added a few more compliments and then got to the point. 'I'm up in Montreal. Mr. Dietrich and I have come to a parting of the ways and I wanted you to know that. The sole reason for my call this evening is that I want to find out if you can be loyal to me.'

"That Dietrich and Hughes had parted company *came as a complete surprise to Burgess* (emphasis ours). In his autobiography, Dietrich said the break occurred March 17, 1957. Either Dietrich was mistaken in the date, or Hughes managed to keep it a secret for several months. The consensus of those interviewed on the reason for their estrangement was that Dietrich demanded a greater financial reward for his work and Hughes thought he was being greedy...

"Startled by the question and the news that Dietrich was out, Burgess still didn't hesitate.

"'Mr. Hughes, I can be loyal to the airline.'"[12]

That ambiguous response indicated that Burgess was astonished and mystified, almost as though he were not even talking to the real Howard Hughes. The changes in Hughes' character and approach were to become more drastic. Soon thereafter, Hughes appropriated one of his TWA 1649 aircraft and kept it himself from June until December of 1957. This infuriated Burgess, and later led to the airline president's resignation.[13]

---

12. *Howard Hughes' Airline, an Informal History of TWA*, by Robert Serling, St. Martin's/Marek, 1983, p. 220

13. *Ibid.*, p. 221

The aircraft was used to transport Hughes from Burbank, Calif., to Montreal, Canada, and later to Nassau, the Bahamas, in August. Gemstone 1:9 indicates that the kidnapping actually occurred in March of 1957 (when Hughes allegedly fired Dietrich and when all the turmoil within his company hierarchy began to erupt), so Burgess's recollection of these incidents merges closely with the *Skeleton Key's* timetable of when Hughes' behavior began to change radically. However, the *Key* also might be simply indicating, via the March date, when the kidnapping and switch sequence *started*. It might have taken a long time to complete, and that time was certainly made available by Hughes absconding his own company's airplane for six months.

According to Burgess and other sources, Hughes piloted the first leg of the trip in the 1649 from Burbank to Montreal, along with TWA Capt. Ted Moffitt as co-pilot; Hughes was quite the aviator himself. Long-time Hughes aides Bill Gay and Johnny Meyer were also aboard. Joining Hughes in Montreal were another aide, Bob Rummel, and actress Jean Peters, whom Hughes had just married.[14] This "marriage" was termed a fake in Gemstone 1:9, and is discussed later. Regardless of circumstances, the Hughes entourage stayed in Montreal for a month.

This is where is gets sticky once again:

"Moffitt and his flight engineer returned to Los Angeles almost immediately and Hughes *wanted another TWA crew sent to Montreal* (emphasis ours).

"The replacements were Capt. Jim Rappatoni and flight engineer Bill Bushey...

"'You'd be gone about three days,' the chief pilot assured them. He finally chose Bushey who accompanied Rappatoni to Canada, where they reported to Hughes. They were checked in at the Ritz Carlton told to be on call at all times, and to charge everything to Hughes. Their main job was to *accompany Hughes on a number of 1649 test flights* (emphasis ours). On one occa-

---

sion, they flew to Ottawa, where Hughes shot landings all night long.

"Rappatoni tired of all this and asked Gay and Rummel if he could go home. They called Bushey, wanting to know whether he'd be willing to fly with Hughes alone. Bushey, who was thoroughly enjoying himself, said 'Sure.' He had no idea of what was going to happen. On August 1, Bushey was informed they were going to fly to an unnamed destination about 1,500 miles from Montreal. Bill guessed Houston, but he was way off — they went to Nassau."[15]

If there was a plot to kidnap Hughes and replace him with a double as Gemstone 1:9 asserts, then these would be the first stages: Isolate Hughes, preferably aboard one of his own TWA airplanes, for as long as possible, make the switch, shift the accompanying pilots around so that nobody would be in a position to see anything they weren't supposed to see, keep the airplane moving around to various destinations, and above all keep Hughes sealed off from outside exposure. The pilot eventually chosen to accompany Hughes to Nassau, Bushey, was relatively young, and probably not very familiar with Hughes, his demeanor, habits and other personality traits. Hughes was an experienced pilot and could easily fly any of TWA's airplanes without all this "assistance" from other pilots. However, if the real Hughes was replaced with a double, he would *have* to have at least one pilot at his disposal to actually fly the aircraft.

Upon arrival in Nassau, the following was alleged to have taken place:

"...They stayed in Nassau for three months. Bushey's chief duty was to accompany Howard when he wanted to fly the Connie (another Hughes-owned aircraft), parked at Oates Field *under 24-hour guard by special security men* (emphasis ours). Bushey got a day's notice before every trip. Gay would tell him, 'The boss wants to go flying tomorrow,' but otherwise his time

---

15. *Ibid.*

was his own. *The whole party, not more than eight or nine persons as Bushey remembers, was quartered at the Emerald Beach Hotel where Hughes had leased the entire fifth floor* (emphasis ours). When the hotel management wanted to shut down for some pre-winter remodeling, Hughes *refused to move* (emphasis ours). He was paying about $8,000 a day just for rooms and meals. he even charged the plane's gas to his room.

"Exactly what he was doing in Nassau, why he went there in the first place and the reason he stayed so long was never explained..." (emphasis ours).[16]

Hughes did quite a bit of flying while on this extended stay in the Bahamas, but Bushey was always with him. Bushey considered him "an above-average pilot — 'good, although not in the same class as an airline pilot.'"[17] Interesting statement, but the truth of the matter was that Hughes was an expert pilot — at least the *real* Howard Hughes was. Furthermore, any exposure of Bushey to "Hughes" was restricted to the cockpit. It was obvious that the crowd of people surrounding Hughes had something to hide, and they were very successful at hiding it.

If anyone could shed light upon the possibility of Howard Hughes being kidnapped, it would have been Robert Maheu. The former FBI agent was hired by Hughes in 1957, ostensibly to run the Hughes empire which had expanded into Las Vegas. In reality, he was an efficient intelligence operative capable of keeping a lid on the terrible secret of the true identity of "Hughes," and the *Skeleton Key* states that he actually worked for Onassis, not Hughes (Gemstone 3:0). Maheu was an expert in keeping sensitive information away from prying eyes and ears. He was as hard-nosed a counter-espionage man as ever lived. However, even Maheu broke character after he was reportedly "fired" by

---

16. *Ibid.*, p. 222.

17. *San Francisco Examiner*, Jan. 24, 1972, "Hughes Asks Total Power" (kicker: "Maheu Talks"), by Ron Laytner, excerpts from *Howard Hughes, the Maheu Files*, by Ron Laytner, Quadrangle Books.

Hughes in December of 1990. The dismissal was abrupt, and took Maheu completely by surprise. He then sued Hughes for $50 million after losing his $500,000 a year job.

The *Skeleton Key* states that Maheu was fired because of a leak from inside the Hughes organization that enabled author Clifford Irving to access a computer printout of information pertaining to Hughes' life, which had previously been available only to Hughes insiders (Gemstone 5:9; implications of Irving's "biography" of Hughes and the controversy it generated will be discussed at length later). The *Key* also states that it was Onassis, not "Hughes," who did the firing. Maheu, having plenty of common sense along with plenty of cash that Onassis spilled on him during 15 years' lucrative employment, knew when to keep his mouth shut. But the firing embittered him. He then proceeded to put together a book on the subject of his days with "Hughes," entitled *Howard Hughes: The Maheu Files*, which carefully ducks any mention of Onassis. The 1972 book, which author Ron Laytner helped Maheu write, is not widely available, but it contained statements by Maheu which inevitably back the *Skeleton Key's* interpretation of events relating to Hughes:

"Howard Hughes wants total power. I don't think he feels he has enough power," Laytner quoted Maheu as saying. "He wants power over everyone. he craves power. There is no doubt in my mind that he feels he is more powerful than the President. he wishes to control history."[18] Replace the name "Hughes" with "Onassis," and Maheu's tirade would make more sense. It was not in the flamboyant personality of Howard Hughes to be preoccupied with his place in history. He wanted to chase movie stars and fly airplanes, and everything else was secondary — until late 1957 in the Bahamas.

Maheu revealed crucial insight into the world of Howard Hughes, or at least the person who was supposed to be Hughes:

---

18. *Ibid.*

"...What all Hughes watchers have in common is this: None of them has seen Howard Hughes in nearly 18 years.

"Robert Maheu is an exception. During the 15 years he worked for the man he saw him twice, once in 1955 in Nassau's Emerald Beach Hotel, once in 1967 when Hughes arrived in Las Vegas aboard a special train from Houston. *On both occasions, Hughes did not speak to Maheu,* nor did Maheu speak to Hughes (emphasis ours)."[19] The 1967 incident is worth relating, because it is supposedly the only time another human being outside of Hughes' inner circle actually saw Hughes between 1957 and the time "Hughes" died in 1976. The sighting occurred in Ogden, Utah, as Hughes was being transported "secretly" to Las Vegas. According to Maheu:

"...By the time I got back from checking a street barrier, Hughes had already stepped down from the train and was about to get into the back of the truck. He asked how long the trip would take to the hotel, *called for a special driver* (emphasis ours) and ordered him to drive slowly.

"'It was a very dark hour and I couldn't get a good look at Hughes,' Maheu said. 'He was wearing a dark coat. I'd been working for him since 1955 at this point and yet it was only the second time I'd ever seen him."* (emphasis ours)[20]

This incident more than anything points to a concentrated conspiracy to keep the identity of "Hughes" completely concealed at all times. Here was a close employee of Hughes, indeed one that was not only paid an exorbitant salary, but who was entrusted with some of the company's most closely held secrets, and even he was never given a chance to see his boss in person.

Maheu also admitted himself that, in the back of his mind, the person who was supposed to be Howard Hughes might

---

19. *Ibid.*

20. *San Francisco Examiner,* Jan. 26, 1972, "Maheu Reveals Hughes' Fears" (kicker: "Kidnap Try Hinted"), by Ron Laytner, excerpts from *Howard Hughes: The Maheu Files,* by Ron Laytner, Quadrangle Books.

indeed be a double. According to Laytner:

"...Maheu said there always was the possibility someone might have *impersonated Hughes* (emphasis ours) and that this is something, if true, that the United States government deserves to know. He said he had listened to recordings made of Hughes' voice made at the 1947 Brewster hearings and that the man he had spoken to (over the phone) sounded the same."

Maheu also addressed the concerns about the alleged kidnapping of Hughes, an issue which had long been rumored but not proven. Again, Laytner wrote about this, even mentioning the Bahamas stay in 1957 in the same passage:

(Under the subheading "Kidnap Attempt?":) "...When it was suggested that no kidnapper could ever get near Hughes, the man (Maheu) replied emphatically: *'Don't you believe they wouldn't try.'*

"Had they ever tried? He (Maheu) remained silent for a long time, and said, *'I don't know* (emphasis ours).'

"In the middle Fifties, said Maheu, Hughes lived in the Los Angeles area, usually in the Beverly Hills Hotel. He had various accommodations including several cottages and a suite or two in the hotel.

"In 1957 he went to Montreal, Maheu continued. Then he traveled to the Bahamas where he stayed six or seven weeks on the fifth floor of the Emerald Beach Hotel in Nassau before returning to Los Angeles."[21]

Anyone reading these passages knows what kind of tightrope Maheu was walking, if indeed any of the *Skeleton Key* material relating to this alleged Hughes kidnapping in 1957 has a kernel of truth to it. But you don't have to take Bruce Roberts' word for it. Other intriguing connections add further to the case that the real Hughes was sold out by his own people during that turbulent period in 1957, and that some connections with Onassis, Maheu and the Mafia in general could also be made.

---

21. *Ibid.*

First, the reference to Hughes aide Chester Davis as being a Sicilian by nationality (Gemstone 1:9), and changing his surname from Cesare to Davis in order to conceal his true identity, has been confirmed through a variety of sources. And the crucial insiders in the Hughes organization under Davis included mostly former heavy hitters from the FBI, IRS, CIA and Justice Department. Examples: Richard Danner, general manager of the Hughes-owned Sands Hotel and Casino in Las Vegas, who testified before Congress that he delivered $100,000 in campaign contributions to the Republican campaign in 1970, was a former FBI agent. Walter Fitzpatrick, one-time manager of the Hughes-owned Desert Inn, was a former IRS agent. Ralph Winte, director of security for Hughes' Summa Corp., was also a former FBI agent. Henry Schwinn, managing director of the Frontier Hotel soon after Hughes acquired it, was a former IRS official. Dean Elson, a former FBI agent, was employed in Hughes' Nevada operations. Edward P. Morgan, a former FBI agent, a Truman administration official and chief counsel to the Senate subcommittee on foreign relations, represented Hughes on many occasions. Robert D. Peloquin, president of International Intelligence Inc. (Intel), supervised security at Hughes' Las Vegas casinos.

So, frankly, it is not far-fetched that Hughes organization, as stated in Gemstone 1:7, was "...buying his way toward control of the U.S. electoral process, with a view toward his own personal gain."

But what of Onassis, and the reference to his hiring of Maheu, with the Hughes organization simply a front for the move? There is a connection, and it involved Maheu's role in helping derail the Greek shipper's attempts at monopolizing the oil-transportation trade out of Saudi Arabia. To wit:

"...The Case of the Greedy Greek was a classic tragedy. At least for Aristotle Onassis. In his hubris, the tycoon had made a secret deal with the dying king of Saudi Arabia that gave him a virtual monopoly on shipping oil from the Persian Gulf. It was

Maheu's mission to scuttle that contract. Ostensibly he was working for Onassis' blood rival Stavros Niarchos. But the CIA was definitely in on it and so was then-Vice President Richard Nixon, and while not even the players seemed to be sure who was using whom on whose behalf, Big Oil was probably pulling the strings to make the world safe for Aramco. Still, it was Maheu's show. He bugged Onassis' offices in New York, Paris, and London, got proof that the contract has been bought with a bribe, exposed the scandal in a Rome newspaper secretly owned by the CIA, and finally journeyed to Jidda, where he personally presented this evidence to the Saudi royal family and killed the whole deal. Not bad for a private peeper on his first big job."[22]

The implications for Onassis are ominous because of this earlier clash with Maheu. If indeed Maheu bugged Onassis' phone lines, he would have obtained information about the entire Onassis organization. This sequence took place in the early 1950s, when Onassis was on the bubble with the U.S. government regarding the illegal purchase of the Liberty ships. The information gathered by Maheu was enormously crucial. It can readily be seen that Onassis probably admired this man's efficient intelligence-gathering methods, and instead of getting rid of him, it would be much more effective for Onassis to simply hire him to his side. With Maheu in hand, he would have the knowledgeable operative required to pull off the Hughes switch and build the necessary organization to cover it all up. Plus, with Maheu, he could further his ambitions for such targets as Castro and JFK as outlined in these early passages of the *Skeleton Key*.

A final element to this Hughes kidnapping scenario: What of L. Wayne Rector, the person who allegedly took the place of Hughes after the kidnapping? And what of the Carl Byoir public relations agency, the group who supposedly hired Rector for this task? Gemstone 4:8 refers to the set-up involving Rector:

---

22. *Citizen Hughes,* ©1985, by Michael Drosnin, Holt, Reinhart and Winston, p. 66.

(Gemstone 4:8) <u>Note: L. Wayne Rector was hired around 1955 by the Carl Byoir P.R. agency (Hughes' L.A. public relations firm) to act as Hughes' double. In 1957, when Onassis grabbed Hughes, Rector continued to act as his stand-in. Rector was the Hughes surrogate in Las Vegas; Robert Maheu actually ran the show. Maheu got his orders from Onassis. The six "nursemaids," called the "Mormon Mafia," kept Rector sealed off from prying eyes.</u>

The sequence is underlined because it was contained within the original *Skeleton Key* outline, but not published in the *Hustler* version. The sensitivity of this passage is probably the reason why *Hustler* backed off, because to identify the Hughes surrogate would be to further enhance a case in favor of an actual Hughes kidnap and switch.

Another footnote *not* contained within the *Skeleton Key:* Carl Byoir himself, founder of the firm, died on Feb. 4, 1957 — only months before Hughes made his fateful trip to Nassau. The cause of death was not disclosed, according to an obituary that ran in the *San Francisco Examiner* that same day. Could it have been that Byoir knew a little too much about the events to come, and of Rector's role? Byoir was also a veteran war propagandist, and published newspapers and had deep business connections in Cuba in the late 1930s and early '40s. Because of that involvement, and because of Onassis' future plans for Cuba has outlined in the *Skeleton Key*, it could well have been that Byoir became an obstacle to the destiny of Hughes, Cuba and the ensuing events which were to unfold with all their horror in the United States — events duly noted in the *Skeleton Key*.

Oh, and a few words about the "faked" marriage to Jean Peters — that's exactly what it was, according to more than one source. Donald Neuhaus, a member of Hughes' personal staff at Hughes headquarters in Southern California, told us in a Dec. 5, 1993, interview that he was responsible for guarding Ms. Peters' bungalow at the posh Beverly Hills Hotel in the late summer of 1957:

"...I recall all this quite vividly. At that time, Walter Winchell (a Hearst Newspapers syndicated columnist) 'broke' the story about the Hughes marriage to Jean Peters. But there was only one problem — Howard was out of town somewhere, nobody knew exactly where, although it was rumored he was either still in Montreal or out of the country (according to pilot Bushey, he was in the Bahamas), and we had no way of knowing where he was.

"But the marriage was impossible, because *I was guarding Jean Peters' bungalow* (emphasis ours). She was in Bungalow No. 6, and Hughes always stayed in Bungalow No. 8 when he was at the hotel. This is easy to remember because I was responsible for her not being disturbed. Howard would call her every night, and talk to her for two, three hours at a time... I recall one night that they talked over five hours on the phone."

The involvement in Sen. Howard Cannon is also confirmed by sources other than the *Key,* It was gossip columnist Louella Parsons who, along with Winchell, broke the story in her column, "announcing" the wedding. Reporters combed Nevada, unable to find any evidence of a marriage. Stanton O'Keefe, in his book *The Real Howard Hughes*, described the marriage scenario:

"...It (marriage) took place in Tonopah, Nevada. Senator Howard Cannon, who was then the city attorney of Las Vegas and a personal friend of Hughes, took care of all the legal arrangements — including the trick maneuver that protected the validity of the marriage contract while allowing the couple to register under *assumed names* (emphasis ours).[23]

Hughes expert and conspiracy theorist Mae Brussell and co-writer Stephanie Caruana — who has admitted to penning at least one version of the *Skeleton Key* under the direct tutelage of Bruce Roberts — developed this topic further in an article for the November, 1974, edition of *Playgirl* magazine entitled *Is Howard*

---

23. *Playgirl*, November, 1974, "Is Howard Hughes Dead and Buried Off a Greek Island?" by Mae Brussell and Stephanie Caruana.

Hughes Dead and Buried Off a Greek Island? The article states that Hughes and Jean Peters were supposed to be living in a Bel Air mansion for several years after their "marriage," but the home's owner never saw the "husband." The couple was never seen in public together in over 13 years of marriage, and there is no record of their ever having been photographed with each other. This strange union ended in 1971 — with Peters getting a quick $2 million divorced settlement. Coincidentally, this came about at the time the story started circulating that Hughes had died, and that a double, or doubles, had taken his place.

Neuhaus, presented with a copy of the *Skeleton Key* in 1987, made the following observations in a letter to us, dated Nov. 29, 1993, concerning the sudden, jolting changes the Hughes company underwent in that fateful first week of August, 1957:

"...I was called at home at around 1 or 1:30 a.m. one day during that summer of 1957, and told to report to the office immediately because of an emergency, and when I arrived, it was explained to me and some of the other staff members that Noah Dietrich had been fired and we were to seal all entrances and exits to the Romaine Street building. Shortly after this episode, I noticed a complete change in the way operations were conducted but at the time gave it very little thought... It was not until 1987 that I stumbled across a poorly copied 24-page memo titled *The Gemstone Abstract*, which hit me like a thunderbolt. The peculiar, contradictory and downright weird events that occurred in 1957 started to become clear to me and I have spent a part of my time during the past six years trying to find the balance of the Gemstone papers."

Neuhaus is convinced that Dietrich misled people in his written accounting of his leaving the company. Dietrich wrote in his book that he left the Hughes company in March of 1957, but that could be a deception. Neuhaus is firm in recalling the announcement of Dietrich's departure as coming the first week of August.

Furthermore, Neuhaus offers the first firm evidence of an

Onassis link to the Hughes organization — a link that cannot be ignored and that is invariably a key ingredient to all this. Neuhaus has long been good friends with a man named Jack Egger, who is now director of security at Warner Brothers Studios in North Hollywood. Egger was captain of the Beverly Hills Police Department in 1957 — and was handed direct orders from the CIA to keep an eye on "Hughes" and keep him bottled up inside the Beverly Hills Hotel when he returned from his Bahamas excursion.

"Jack knew a ton of CIA guys," sand Neuhaus. "They were all over the place. Bob Maheu, formerly of the FBI, was also with the Hughes company at that time and had just joined, but there were CIA and FBI men all over."

But it was Jack Egger's father, Frank, who possessed the explosive link to Onassis and his maritime fleet, which at that time was nearing its zenith in power, money and productivity.

"Frank Egger was a major partner in the insurance firm of Bailey, Martin and Faye," Neuhaus said. "Frank ran the division of that company that was one of the *largest brokerage firms in the world that dealt almost exclusively with insurance for tanker hulls. Onassis was a very big customer, and so was Exxon and a lot of other tanker companies* (emphasis ours)." With that kind of enormous financial leverage — oil tanker insurance has never been cheap, especially for a fleet of such vessels — it would be easy to see that Onassis would be calling the shots behind the scenes.

And was Maheu part of Onassis' team at that time, as the *Skeleton Key* asserts? Neuhaus could not recall if Maheu and Onassis ever got together during this period, "although it's a distinct possibility because of Frank Egger and his son Jack. Anything is possible in a situation like that."

Frank Egger was also big behind the scenes in Los Angeles politics. He was a Democrat, and supported Los Angeles Mayor Sam Yorty when Yorty was still in the Demos' camp before he turned right and became a Republican. Frank Egger routinely ran major fund-raising drives for Yorty. It should be emphasized that Yorty became a central figure in the alleged cover-up of the Robert Kennedy assassination in 1968. That is another reason why these connections as outlined by Neuhaus should be considered as much more than just quaint coincidences.

Another Onassis link is John Meyer, who according to Neuhaus started in the Hughes organization as a driver. Hughes insisted that his personal staff travel in company cars with their own drivers, so that full attention could be paid to guests who would also be passengers in the cars. This was appropriate, Neuhaus said, because of the volume of movie stars and starlets that Hughes entertained. During this time, Meyer got really close to Hughes, and the billionaire trusted him enough to appoint him as a key public-relations man in the company.

However, as of 1974, Brussell and Caruana write that John Meyer defected over to the Onassis camp, stating: "...In 1942, he (Hughes) hired John Meyer to curry favor with politicians, generals and the like. (John Meyer is now *press aide to Aristotle Onassis; one of his responsibilities is watching over Jackie.*) (emphasis ours)"[24] As stated earlier, Meyer was a key player in getting Elliott Roosevelt, President Franklin D. Roosevelt's son, entangled in more than a few wild parties thrown by Hughes. The parties included girls and everything associated with having a grand old time. The connections are inescapable, and lend all the more credence to Bruce Roberts' main Gemstone thesis as outlined in the *Skeleton Key.*

****

(Gemstone 5:9a) End of 1970: Howard Hughes' presence on earth was [is] no longer required. His handwriting could [can] be duplicated by computer. His biography — all the known facts about his life — had [have] been compiled, and a [the] computerized version [biography is] issued to top Hughes

---

24. *Ibid.*

executives. <u>And Hughes was ill.</u>

We jump ahead because the *Skeleton Key* does not mention anything further about Hughes until this point. This is the start of material which seemed outrageous when the *Key* was being circulated in the mid-1970s, but has become more and more plausible as material leaks out from former Hughes associates and others close to the situation.

It was first disclosed that Howard Hughes' existence had been reduced to a computer program in the Jan. 28, 1971, edition of the *Los Angeles Times*. A photo accompanying that story clearly showed the computer duplicating Hughes' handwriting, and his signature. It was rough, but handwriting experts and computer experts of the day agreed that duplicating Hughes' signature would eventually be a cinch. Today's technology could turn the trick in very short order, but 23 years ago, such technology was in its infancy. Still, it was representative of the cutting edge that Hughes had over the rest of the world in high-tech solutions to many problems. Hughes was also beginning to take control of industries — such as satellite communications — which would later revolutionize the media industry. And we cannot forget the huge advances in laser technology, one of the driving forces behind Bruce Roberts' entire Gemstone thesis.

****

(**Gemstone 5:9b**) Clifford Irving, author of *Hoax*, [a book] about an art forger, became [becomes] interested in "Hughes." Living on Ibiza, he heard the Mediterranean gossip that "Hughes" was [is] a hoax, too. He went [goes] to "Hughes'" so-called "Mormon Mafia," the six "nursemaids," for information. One of them — <u>Merryman</u> — perhaps tired of the game — gives Irving the computerized Hughes biography, and from it, Irving wrote [writes] his "autobiography."

(**5:9c**) <u>Hughes' death was expected shortly. Preparations were being made so that it would not interfere with the orderly continuation of his empire.</u>

(5:9d) Irving wrote [writes] his book — and the publishers announced [announce] it. Onassis knew [knows] someone had [has] given Irving the information. He thought it was Maheu [Thinking it was Maheu], he fired [fires] him in November, 1970. On Thanksgiving Eve, 1970, in the middle of the night, "Hughes" (Rector) made [makes] a well-publicized "secret departure" from Las Vegas to the Bahamas.

(5:9e) December, 1970: Onassis discovered [discovers] his mistake, and had Merryman killed [and has the nursemaid responsible for leaking the information to Irving killed].

(6:0a) Robert Maheu, accidentally deprived of his half-million dollars annual salary, sued "Hughes" for millions — mentioning "Hughes'" game plan for the purchase of presidents, governors, senators, judges, etc. Onassis pays off — cheap to the price — to maintain his custodianship of "American democracy" and the "free world[.]" — and keep from hanging for multiple murders.

The whole wild episode about Clifford Irving's sensational "faked" biography of Howard Hughes is a prime example of just how monolithic and unreasonable the New York-centered literary society can be. It is interesting that, in 1989, Irving's only existing copy of the 989-page typed manuscript was sold at an auction in Houston for $5,000. The name of the buyer was never disclosed, although some entertainment reporters used the manuscript's sale as a footnote to their weekly columns, indicating that it was surprising that the Hughes memorabilia collection would find any value at all in such a "faked" biography.

But the trouble with that story is that everything in Irving's book was true, if Gemstone 5:9b has any merit. If indeed Irving used a computer printout to manufacture the biography, it is a good bet that the facts were right. The biggest factor was that the printout was leaked and not intended to be published. It evidently carried hints of Hughes' background which elements of organized crime and the U.S. intelligence community wanted squelched, at least for the time being. So McGraw-Hill, the publishing firm that paid $750,000 to Irving and Hughes for the manuscript, was pressured into backing off the book, which was well into production by January of 1972 and scheduled for a March 27 release.

Still, the New York pressures were too great and McGraw-Hill knuckled under and never published the book. Irving became famous for all the wrong reasons. It was not so much that he was writing fabrications; it was just that he used the wrong methods — saying that he had met with Hughes for "close to 100 taping sessions" and that these interviews were done live, one-on-one, with the reclusive billionaire. In reality, Irving had never met Hughes face-to-face.

Anyway, a person describing himself as Hughes addressed a group of seven reporters on Jan. 11, 1972, by way of a voice box attached to a telephone in New York, saying that the biography was a fake and Irving a fraud. The publishing of such a book was unthinkable with the major source, Hughes, pulling the plug. *Life* magazine, which had purchased serial rights, was equally distraught.

One of those seven reporters was Frank McCulloch of *Time* magazine, later the editor of the *Sacramento Bee* and *San Francisco Examiner.* He was credited with making the contact with Hughes that exposed the book as a "fake." There are a couple versions of this story, both interesting. In the book *Hoax*, which tells the story about the Irving biography of Hughes, the episode surrounding McCulloch is treated as follows:

"...The first questions he (McCulloch) addressed to Hughes were technical: Could he tape the call, and was the conversation on the record? The reply was in a nasal, raspy voice, and it was 'No' to both. McCulloch knew that it could only be Hughes. At the other end of the phone, Howard Hughes launched into a tirade that lasted half an hour. The book was a phony, he said, and he had never met Clifford Irving, who was also a phony..."[25]

---

25. *Hoax*, by Stephen Fay, Lewis Chester and Magnus Linklatter, Viking Press, 1972, ©1972 Times Newspapers Inc., pp. 125-126.

However, there was only one problem: McCulloch could not make himself believe the book was a fake. He read the manuscript in question the next day; the first half of a copy was supplied by the Time-Life management:

"...McCulloch read it that evening and found it a revelation. The style, the pace, the earthiness of the language all sounded so true to Hughes' form that when he went into the office the next day he was able to inform *Life* editor Ralph Graves that *he was a convert* (emphasis ours)... He (McCulloch) had seen enough to persuade him that the *tone was right and the facts, so far as he could see, were accurate*" (emphasis ours).[26]

Then why all the fuss? It was obvious that blocking publication of the biography could easily be used to muzzle certain elements of U.S. media that were beginning to get wise to the falsehoods of the military-industrial complex and the heavy illegal drug-trade burden it carried with it. Still, it is ugly to see naked censorship of this magnitude successfully executed against any writer, no matter how controversial the material.

Irving found himself in quite a predicament, if the *Skeleton Key's* points have any merit. He had drawn the material for his biography from the disenchanted Hughes' Mormon aide, Merryman (the name is stricken from the *Hustler* version of the *Skeleton Key*), who according to the *Key* supplied Irving with the detailed computer readout (which apparently included a comprehensive clip file of virtually every story written about Hughes by the mainstream press to that point). Like any reasonable journalist, Irving would have considered that material accurate — especially with the clip file that went with it. The only problem would be to convince the public that he actually met with Hughes personally; none of the computerized information would have any value as it stood. So, fabricating the story that he had met with Hughes and "interviewed" him would be the only cheating he would have to do in order to produce an

---

26. *Ibid.*, p. 128.

otherwise sensational book, because there was no way to challenge authenticity of the information itself.

The stakes were enormous in one of the most brutal battles in American literary history. Clifford Irving had a huge story. McGraw-Hill agreed to publish it. Irving was paid the $750,000 advance. Advance orders totaled 400,000, and total sales were expected to top four million.[27] But it was a story that *could not be allowed* because of some obvious connections that could be drawn from it; i.e. the possible connections leading to Onassis. So it was discredited in a bruising struggle that ended up keeping the true nature of "Hughes" from being uncovered. Plenty of firepower from the New York literary elite kept Irving's version from being published, and it came from all sides.

Unexplained incidents rippled through the controversy. Soon after McGraw-Hill announced it would publish the book, severe opposition erupted. On New Year's Day, 1972, McGraw-Hill announced it was convinced that Irving's material was authentic. Irving added that the publisher had "incontrovertible proof from several sources of the authenticity of the book." Associated Press reported that:

"...Various individuals close to the project said Hughes had sent an 11-page handwritten letter to a high official of McGraw-Hill attesting to the manuscript's authenticity.

"The sources said leading handwriting experts had examined the letter and concluded it was written by the same man who wrote a letter to Hughes Tool Co. officials *ordering them to fire Robert Maheu, the man Hughes had hired to run his estimated $300 million Nevada gambling empire* (emphasis ours).

"The earlier letter was accepted as evidence last year in a judicial determination that Hughes meant to fire Maheu."[28]

Gemstone 6:0a talks about the Maheu firing, but does not

---

27. *San Francisco Examiner,* Jan. 2, 1972, "Hughes Hoax or Real Life: A Mysterious New Book," By James R. Nesman, Associated Press.

28. *Ibid.*

connect its documentation to the early stages of the Irving "hoax." It was evident from the very start that Irving's material was genuine, and that it would have some damaging effects on not only the Hughes empire, but other powerful people as well. It had to be censored. The battle was on.

A reporter from the *Los Angeles Times* was given access to Irving's material and gave it a thorough analysis, and the *Times'* news service came out with a follow-up published on Jan. 10 in most major newspapers across the nation — including the *San Francisco Examiner.* Remember, this is before McGraw-Hill got its arms twisted, and before the Hughes people opened up with both legal barrels to stage an all-out effort to derail the Irving biography. The story was datelined Ibiza, Spain:

"...I came with a reviewer's skepticism to this island to interview Clifford Irving, the writer who reportedly had persuaded billionaire Howard Hughes to tell his own story.

"I leave strongly convinced that *The Autobiography of Howard Hughes*, to be published by McGraw-Hill Book Co. March 27, is *completely authentic* (emphasis ours).

"This is not only because I have heard Irving's detailed account of the way the book was initiated, researched, written and edited, but also more importantly because Irving gave me *complete access to the manuscript, the transcripts and notes, the file of letters, affidavits and documents involved in the negotiations* (emphasis ours).

"...I agreed not to quote from the material itself.

"...What is described in these pages is bound to surprise even those who have speculated as to their source.

"It is not only the world of *look-alikes* (Gemstone 1:9, 4:8, 9:7), codes, secret phone calls, disguises and *stand-ins* (Gemstone 4:8) which is evoked in this work..."[29]

It is critical to understand that a few select writers and

---

29. *San Francisco Chronicle*, Jan. 10, 1972, "Hughes Autobiography Dispute: 'The Book Is Authentic,' Los Angeles Times Service.

analysts accessed Irving's raw manuscript before anyone linked with the Hughes organization could censor any of it. After this brief window of opportunity, all hope of getting to the truth of the work was essentially lost. Even the "only copy" of the Irving manuscript that was preserved long enough to be auctioned off in 1989 is probably not a clean original. The critical factor is to remember that every expert exposed to the material — Frank McCulloch, a long-time Hughes expert, the Los Angeles Times Service and the McGraw-Hill braintrust — was *convinced* that Irving's work was genuine.

Irving then unleashed a bombshell on Jan. 16, 1972, that confirmed Gemstone 1:8 and 1:9 concerning the Hughes pay-offs to Donald Nixon, Richard Nixon's brother, back in 1956. In a leaked portion of his manuscript, it was reported that former Secretary of State Clark Clifford asked Hughes for a $205,000 loan for Donald Nixon.[30] Clifford was later pegged in the early 1990s as being a point man in the nefarious Bank of Commerce and Credit International (BCCI) scandal which has cast an ongoing pall on the entire U.S. banking industry.

Amid all this chaos, other Hughes books were being "released" by other publishers and authors close to Hughes. These releases — and excerpts from them that hit most major newspapers at the same time the Irving fiasco was still in a turbulent phase — confused the U.S. media establishment, and hence the American public, even more. The selection includes:

- Rosemont Enterprises Inc., which sued McGraw-Hill, Time-Life, Dell Publishing Co. and Irving in a Manhattan court on Jan. 13, 1972, claiming they had secured "rights" to the Hughes biography by as early as 1965.
- Noah Dietrich, the chief executive for Hughes Tool Co. who suddenly resigned in 1957 right as the reclusive billionaire dropped from sight. Dietrich made an aston-

---

30. *San Francisco Examiner*, Jan. 17, 1992, "Hughes Loan to Nixon Kin," Associated Press.

ishing statement on Jan. 10, 1972, concerning Irving's biography, saying: "I think his (Hughes') attorneys got hold of the manuscript and they discovered *he had labeled several parties* (emphasis ours) and they considered this could be very, very serious."[31] To write his book, Dietrich apparently used the same computer printout (it was available to Hughes' executives according to Gemstone 5:9a) that was leaked to Irving. Former Hughes insider Donald Neuhaus, quoted earlier in this chapter, told us he thinks Dietrich was paid a large sum to write his version of the book (assisted by James Phelan), editing out any sensitive portions of the original computer printout.

• James Phelan, a Los Angeles freelance writer, apparently had access to the same computer printout, and claimed to have ghost-written Dietrich's book just before Irving wrote his version — and that Irving somehow copied it. Phelan's announcement was made on Feb. 11, 1972, but it is obvious to anyone with an ounce of common sense that he was used as a belated "plant" to help further discredit Irving. At long last, McGraw-Hill and Time-Life Inc. had the firepower needed to unload Irving. On that same day, the two publishing firms "declared that the 230,000-word (Irving) manuscript was a fraudulent and manufactured document."[32] They trumpeted the announcement and the big media companies quickly fell in line. But the circumstances behind Phelan's claim are questionable to say the least:

"...Phelan, a former reporter for the *Saturday Evening Post*, flew to New York early yesterday from California at the urging of Frank McCulloch, a Time-Life editor who has known Hughes for years and who has worked hard in

---

31. *San Francisco Examiner*, Jan. 11, 1972, "Hughes Trapped, Says Former Top Aide," CDN Service.

32. *San Francisco Chronicle*, Feb. 12, 1972, "Irving Book Fraudulent." L.A. Times News Service.

recent weeks to solve the Irving case.

"Phelan and an editor at McGraw-Hill compared the two manuscripts — Irving's and Phelan's. The Californian (Phelan) had written material for a still-unpublished book on Hughes by Noah Dietrich, a former advisor and confidant of Hughes for 32 years. Hughes fired the 83-year-old Dietrich several years ago.

"...Irving learned of the Phelan project from McCulloch late Thursday night. Irving's comment was, 'Wow.' It was perhaps one of the shortest literary comments in the whole battle of the book."[33]

Life magazine, which had excerpt rights to the Irving book, cancelled its plans to use the material the next day. McGraw-Hill said it was "reconsidering" the contract; it was later to rescind it altogether. The behind-the-scenes maneuvering during the entire Irving episode is nauseating to anyone who favors an open and honest literary establishment. The delay in Phelan's announcement only meant that it took nearly a month to get him a copy of the computer printout so he could quickly fabricate a manuscript to present as "proof" that Irving's effort was fraudulent.

- *True* magazine, which announced Jan. 17, 1992, that it would publish its own version of the Dietrich story.[34]
- Ron Laytner, whose book *Howard Hughes: The Maheu Files* was excerpted in major newspapers Jan. 24-26. The book, obviously derived from the same computer printout everyone else had, was also written from additional information supplied by Robert Maheu, who had been cut loose by "Hughes" by that time and who had a lawsuit pending against the billionaire as a result of that dismissal.[35]

---

33. *Ibid.*
34. *San Francisco Examiner*, Jan. 18, 1972, "3rd Publisher Joins Hughes Derby," Associated Press.
35. *San Francisco Examiner*, Jan. 24-26, 1972, excerpts from *Howard Hughes: The Maheu Files*, by Ron Laytner.

****

(**Gemstone 6:0b**) The "Hughes" <u>Mormon Mafia</u> party, plus <u>Rector</u>, fled [flees] around the world — from Bermuda, where they murdered an uncooperative governor and police chief, to Nicaragua, where they shot [shoot] the U.S. Ambassador between the eyes for noticing that there wasn't [isn't] really any Hughes; and thence to Canada, where <u>Mormon Mafia</u> nursemaid [Howard] Eckersley looted [loots] a goodly sum in a swindle of the Canadian Stock Exchange; and on to London, to [the] <u>Rothchild's</u> Inn of the Park.

The *Skeleton Key's* effort at chronology turns out to be confusing in this case, for the *Key* broke off briefly from telling the end-game of the Irving story to point out these obscure movements by "Hughes" and his group which have never received widespread attention. It was clear, however, with Clifford Irving threatening to blow open the entire Hughes story, which would have intensified the questions about "Hughes'" existence in the first place, that the Hughes group had to make itself scarce for a while. It turned out to be almost a year on the run, harassed by international media almost the entire way.

Regarding the first reference to Bermuda, we were unable to find any firm information on the alleged killings, but it was clear the Nassau government did not want the group there and eventually forced it to fly to Nicaragua.

In a match of Gemstone 6:0b, Hughes and his party were reported in the Nicaraguan capital of Managua in February of 1972, for alleged "business" reasons, but it was plain that getting away from the Irving mess was a top priority. And suspicion was starting to set in regarding the true nature of Hughes. It started in December of 1970, when the Hughes party bolted from Las Vegas to the Bahamas where it stayed until the Managua trip in February of 1972. "Hughes" and his people were forced out of the Bahamas when the government there finally "made an issue of his staff's working permits, and deported four top aides."[36]

However, it is appropriate to mention that Hank Greenspun, publisher of the *Las Vegas Sun* and "No. 1 Authority on Hughes,"[37] told the *Chicago Sun-Times* on Dec. 7, 1970, that Hughes "literally was 'kidnapped' from his Las Vegas penthouse by his Hughes Tool Co. group and flown to the Bahama Islands:

"This was made possible, according to Las Vegas sources, by decoying Robert Maheu, head of the Nevada faction, to a cocktail party during which Hughes was moved out of his Desert Inn apartment and spirited to a waiting plane.

"Hughes' health, contrary to the report yesterday from Nevada Gov. Paul Laxalt and Dist. Atty. George Franklin, has been deteriorating at a rapid pace...

"...Meanwhile, Hughes and his 'constant companions' are ensconced in the Britannia Hotel on Paradise Island in the Bahamas, far removed from the battle scene physically and mentally. The 'six constant companions' are his hand-picked secretaries and nursemaids, living with him in eight-hour shifts on a round-the clock basis to protect his passion for privacy."[38]

It was easy to see that "Hughes" was running out of excuses for never appearing in public, and it looked like his attendants were also running out of patience. That would carry through in the Bahamas, where government officials finally pressured them into leaving for Managua in February of 1972 as the Irving situation threatened to blow "Hughes'" cover completely.

"Hughes" would be welcomed with open arms to Nicaragua, a country under the rule of iron-fisted dictator Anastasio Somoza,

---

36. *San Francisco Examiner*, Feb. 18, 1972, "Hughes in $400-a-Day Hideout," United Press International.

37. *San Francisco Examiner*, Dec. 9, 1970, "Claim His Health Is Deteriorating," by Irv Kupcinet, Chicago Sun-Times.

38. *Ibid.*

who was later to be deposed and eventually assassinated via car bomb in South America. U.S. Ambassador Turner Shelton was also available to render assistance and extend the "Hughes" cover, for Shelton knew Hughes from the days they were both involved in the motion picture business in Hollywood.[39]

The press would not let up on the Hughes group, leading to conflicting stories coming out of Nicaragua as to why "Hughes" was there to begin with. On Feb. 18, 1972, it was reported that Hughes Tool Co., executives has been visiting Managua regularly, seeking possible sites for a gambling casino.[40] Three days later, Associated Press reported that "Hughes" was in Nicaragua to discuss the sale of airplanes, but that he would not be seeing Somoza in person.

"If he ('Hughes') wants to do business in Nicaragua, I don't have to see him," Somoza was quoted as saying.[40] On March 4, it was reported that Hughes planned to stay in Nicaragua for an indefinite period of time, and that "aides of the billionaire have bought six luxury autos."[41] Money had never been an object to the "Hughes" entourage.

Finally, as Gemstone 6:0b states, the Hughes party flew to London, where the British press was ready:

"...The Lockheed Jetstar of the fabulous hermit touched down at London's Gatwick Airport around midnight last night. It can carry 10 passengers and came via Gander, Newfoundland and Shannon, Ireland.

"Awaiting the jet were four Rolls Royces. Even the Queen, on official trips with her staff, normally uses two Rolls...Hughes' private jet was wheeled into the shadows, away from the flood-lit area used for personal planes.

39. *San Francisco Examiner*, Feb. 18, 1972, "Hughes in $400-a-Day Hideout," United Press International.

40. *Ibid.*

41. *San Francisco Examiner*, Feb. 21, 1972, "Hughes in Nicaragua to Discuss Plane Sales," Associated Press.

"One of the four limousines, curtains drawn on the windows, whizzed away to a destination unknown a few minutes after midnight.

"...What he will do in Britain and for how long he remains is, of course, the usual Hughes mystery."[42]

Gemstone 6:0b is confirmed once again with this report, which specifies that the jet had stopped in Newfoundland (Canada) before flying across the Atlantic. This matches the mention in Gemstone 6:0b concerning "nursemaid" Howard Eckersley's alleged Canadian stock-market swindle. However, the mention of the U.S. official's murder is slightly out of sequence, although such a shooting actually did happen in January of 1973:

U.S. NICARAGUA CONSUL DIES OF BULLET WOUND

PANAMA (AP) — James Z. Hargrove, the U.S. consul in Managua, Nicaragua, died of a bullet wound yesterday in the Canal Zone's Gorgas Hospital. An official statement said the head wound was the result "of an apparent accidental discharge of a small-caliber automatic weapon."

The U.S. Embassy in Nicaragua issued the statement, which said Hargrove, 44, was found in critical condition Friday in Managua and was flown to he Canal Zone, where he died.

...The statement said Hargrove was found at 8 p.m. Friday, but did not say where and gave no other details on the shooting.[43]

This incident would go far in explaining why the Hughes group had to split Nicaragua in such haste, and why they decided to get as far away as possible, to London. If, indeed, this luckless U.S. official did see something he was not supposed to

---

42. *San Francisco Examiner*, Dec. 27, 1972, "S-h-h, Hughes Is in London," by Seymour Freidlin.

43. *San Francisco Examiner*, Jan. 7, 1973, "U.S. Nicaraguan Consul Dies of Bullet Wound," Associated Press.

see while the Hughes entourage was in Nicaragua, then he would most certainly have to be eliminated. However, there would be nothing to stop one of Hughes' people from staying in Nicaragua and handle the "unfinished business" of disposing of the witness.

In any event, Gemstone 6:0b provides yet another example of the *Skeleton Key* author having access to facts which are generally correct. This is amazing, since as we will see in Chapter 8, the author did not have a lot of time to piece together Robert's letters into a coherent outline.

****

(Gemstone 6:1a) April 18, 1971: Howard Hughes, a human vegetable as the result of serious brain damage during his 1857 hustle — plus 14 years of heroin — grew sicker and sicker. A final overdose of heroin did [does] him [Hughes] in. His coffin is lowered into the sea from a rocky headland off the coast of Skorpios. Present at the funeral were: Jackie Kennedy Onassis, Teddy Kennedy, Francis L. Dale, director of CREEP and on the ITT board of directors; Tom Pappas, also of CREEP; and a South Vietnamese cardinal named Thuc. Onassis allowed some pictures to be taken from a distance; he himself did not appear. The pictures were published in *Midnight*, a Canadian tabloid.

(6:1b) Albanian frogmen, tipped off, were [are] waiting under [in] the water. They seized [seize] the coffin and took [take] the corpse off to Yugoslavia, thence to China and the Soviet Union [Russia], and then, perhaps to Boston in a foot-locker. The corpse's dental work was compared to Hughes' own dental records, and they matched [match]. News of Hughes' death, the U.S. Ambassador by Onassis [the U.S. takeover by Onassis], and the facts surrounding the murders of JFK, RFK, Martin Luther King Jr., Mary Jo Kopechne, and many more, and the subsequent cover-ups (involving still more murders) has been circulating around the globe for several years. Any country with this information can blackmail the U.S. government, which has no choice but to pay up.

The entire sequence of Hughes' "death" is drawn from the obscure Canadian tabloid, *Midnight*, which claimed in an Oct. 18, 1971 story with photographs that an invalid, wheelchair-bound man was being kept on the Greek island of Skorpios, and photos of him were snapped by a visiting tourist.

"I took the pictures from the cruise ship *Oriana*, on which my wife and I were enjoying a 10-day holiday," explained (George) Duncastle. "We passed close to Skorpios, and the guide on board called our attention to the island."[44]

One of the two photographs published showed a feeble-looking man seated in a wheelchair, his head covered with what looks like a swimming or shower cap. He is attended by two men and a woman; the woman, according to *Midnight*, resembled Jacqueline Kennedy Onassis. The second photograph shows the two male attendants helping the feeble man walk.

This was not the first story about a feeble, withered man who had taken up residence on the island of Skorpios, normally a well-guarded enclave of the Onassis family that seldom gets any outside exposure. *Midnight* published an earlier account in its Aug. 30, 1971 edition that featured eyewitness reports about a mysterious, crippled old man on Skorpios. *Midnight* speculated the man was John F. Kennedy, who survived the assassination attempt on Nov. 22, 1963, and who was taken to the island by Aristotle Onassis. The critical point here is that U.S. tabloids picked up on that story, stating that JFK was alive and living on a Greek island. *Could it have been that Onassis knew the story about a feeble old man on a Greek island would break sooner or later, and that this "cutout" was planted to cover for the fact that this old man was in reality Howard Hughes?*

One thing is certain: Gemstone 6:1a stands confirmed as to the sightings of a male invalid on the nearby island of Tenos on

---

44. *Midnight*, Oct. 18, 1971.

more than one occasion; it could have been the Bruce Roberts used the *Midnight* stories as source material for this passage.

Included in the Aug. 30, 1971 *Midnight* story is a block of quotes from a Greek nurse named Koula Markopolis, who stated she had been in the service of the Onassis family on the nearby island of Tenos from November, 1968, until January, 1969. Her story follows:

"I was hired because I have a good knowledge of English. Mr. Onassis told me that the patient I would be taking care of was an Englishman. The job was on the island of Tenos. I was paid a very high salary to go there...(and told) that people who talk about Mr. Onassis' personal business do not work for him long.

"There were three nurses and two doctors at Mr. Onassis' private hospital on Tenos, but there was only one patient. I thought at the time that he was about 50, but he could have been older or younger (Hughes would have been 63 in 1968). We had to feed him, bathe him, clean up after him. Sometimes he seemed to listen to us talk, but there was seldom any sign that he understood. Mostly he stared.

"He was quite tall, probably well over six feet tall before he was injured (Hughes was 6-foot-3). He weighed practically nothing, just skin and bones, no muscles. He was helpless, like a baby. His body was wasted away."[45]

Markopolis stated that the man was called simply "Mr. Smith," and that he showed evidence of severe injuries:

"One of the worst I've ever seen... The entire back of his head was a scarred mess. It had been operated on several times. There was a metal plate under the skin to protect the brain where the bone was broken away. I was told that part of the brain was removed years ago. From the condition of the man I could only assume that it was true..."[46]

---

45. *Ibid.*
46. *Ibid.*

It is this passage more than any other that would give the U.S. tabloid press enough reason to echo *Midnight's* guess that this was JFK instead of Howard Hughes. However, if the Greek nurse's report has any truth to it, it would match well with the *Skeleton Key's* version (Gemstone 1:9), where it states that Hughes was "battered and brain-damaged in the scuffle" during his alleged kidnap and transport to Skorpios. It also matches Gemstone 5:9a and 5:9c, which indicate Hughes was increasingly ill. Gemstone 6:1b also refers to brain damage.

But what the *Key* author and Bruce Roberts might not have known at that time was that Howard Hughes was seriously injured in an airplane crash on July 7, 1946. Noah Dietrich states in his book (drawn apparently from the infamous computer printout Irving used for his maligned biography) that Hughes suffered nine broken ribs, bad burns on his left hand and a collapsed left lung. Other accounts say that Hughes' face had been burned, his skull fractured and cheekbone crushed. Facial scars were noticeable and his hearing impaired. It could well have been that Hughes was still suffering from the lingering effects of the crash when he was spirited off to Skorpios from the Bahamas as Gemstone 1:9 states.

Midnight also published a version of the Howard Hughes "funeral" on a Greek island that quoted a U.S. Army Major David Cordrey, who claimed to have witnessed a burial at sea on April 18, 1971 — the date noted in Gemstone 6:1a:

"Two high-powered speedboats (came) out from Skorpios and started clearing the waters around a rocky point at one end of the island... Later in the day, people gathered on the rocky point. I was curious and watched through my binoculars. *One was a priest. One was Jackie Onassis, and one was Ted Kennedy* (emphasis ours). They and the others went through a ceremony over a coffin, and then watched while it was lowered into the sea."[47]

---

47. *Ibid.*

This is one confirmation of Gemstone 6:1a that leaves some doubt that Bruce Roberts accessed *Midnight* as a source for his report. Reason: *Midnight* fails to identify the "priest," and further does not distinguish what type of religion the "priest" espoused. It would not fall into the realm of knowledge of a U.S. Army officer, perhaps, to specify through binoculars exactly who this "priest" might have been. The *Skeleton Key* states flatly that the "priest" was a "South Vietnamese cardinal named Thuc." Had Roberts used *Midnight* as his source, he must have secured the identity of the "priest" from yet another source.

In any event, these alleged sightings of an old man on Skorpios and Tenos only enhance the credibility of the *Skeleton Key to the Gemstone Files.*

CHAPTER 6

· · · · · · · · · · ·

Setting the Stage for JFK's Murder

O rganized crime and the United States government have had a cozy coexistence which dates back to the formation of this country. According to the *Skeleton Key to the Gemstone Files*, the super-rich and super-influential people of the early and mid-20th century exploited these longstanding relationships. Howard Hughes, and later Aristotle Onassis, positioned themselves to gain the absolute most from these sordid deals. The biggest payoffs in all of crime history have come from the U.S. Treasury, and the biggest victims are U.S. taxpayers. Tapping into this vast reserve of wealth was Howard Hughes, and he protected it by placing most of his vast fortunes under the umbrella of the "non-profit" Hughes Medical Foundation (Gemstone 1:8). This arrangement allowed Hughes not only to monopolize many U.S. defense contracts and extract the ensuing wealth from them, it allowed him to collect this bonanza virtually tax-free.

Aristotle Onassis hated taxes. That is one reason why he probably saw the Hughes empire as a valuable acquisition, and a seat from which power could be exercised over most of the Western world along with a way in which to tap the veins of the world's richest wealth — tax money from U.S. citizens. The easy way to this vast power base would be to control Hughes himself (Gemstone 1:9). A logical next step would be to set up the network necessary to sustain the initial power grab:

(**Gemstone 2:1**) September, 1957: Onassis calls for the Apalachin [, New York, organized-crime] meeting to announce to U.S. Mafia heads his grab of Hughes and his adoption of Hughes's game plan for acquiring power: buying U.S. senators, congressmen, governors, [and] judges, en masse, to take control "legally" of the U.S. government. Onassis' radio message to Apalachin from a remote farmhouse [is] intercepted (reluctantly) by the FBI's J. Edgar Hoover, on the basis of a tip-off from some Army intelligence guys who weren't in on the plan.

(**2:2**) Also in 1957: Joseph [Joe] Kennedy takes [his son], John F., and Jackie to see Onassis on his yacht, [the *Christina*, to] introduce John, and [to] remind Onassis of an old Mafia promise: the Presidency for a Kennedy. Onassis agrees.

(**2:3**) 1958: Hordes of Mafia-selected, [Mafia-] purchased and [Mafia-] supported "grass roots" candidates sweep into office. [!]

(**2:4**) 1959: [Fidel] Castro takes over from dictator [Fulgencio] Batista, thereby destroying [the] cozy and lucrative Mafia gambling empire run for Onassis by Meyer Lansky. Castro scoops up $8 million in Mafia casino receipts. Onassis is furious. V.P. Nixon becomes operations chief [White House Action Officer] for CIA-planned Bay of Pigs invasion, using CIA Hunt, McCord, etc. [E. Howard Hunt as political officer for the operation, James McCord, etc.] and Cuban ex-Batista strong-arm cops (Cuban freedom fighters) [Eugenio] Martinez, [Virgilio] Gonzales, etc., as well as winners like Frank Sturgis ([alias Frank] Fiorini) [, a gunrunner with a gambling background].

(**2:5**) [Also] 1959: Stirring election battle between [John F.] Kennedy and Nixon [begins]. Either way, Onassis wins, since he has control over both candidates.

(**2:6**) JFK elected. American people happy. Rose Kennedy happy. Onassis happy. Mafia ecstatic.

****

(**2:9a**) January, 1961: Joseph Kennedy had [has] a stroke, ending his [personal] control over [sons] John and Bobby. The boys decided [decide] to rebel against Onassis' control. <u>Why?</u> <u>Inter-Mafia struggle?</u> <u>Perhaps a dim hope of restoring this coun-</u> <u>try to its mythical integrity?</u>

(**2:9b**) <u>They began committing Mafia no-nos: Arrested Wally</u> <u>Bird, owner of Air Thailand, who has been shipping Onassis'</u> <u>heroin out of the Golden Triangle (Laos, Cambodia, Vietnam),</u> <u>under contract with the CIA (Air Opium), arrested</u> [They arrest and jail] Teamster Mafia Jimmy Hoffa <u>and put him in jail.</u> Declared [and declare] the $73 million in <u>forged "Hughes"</u> land liens, deposited with San Francisco's Ban of America, as "security" for the TWA judgment against Hughes, to what they are: forgeries.

(**3:0**) April, 1961: CIA Bay of Pigs fiasco. Hunt, McCord, CIA, Batista's Cubans [Cuban exiles] and Mafia angry about JFK's lack of enthusiasm. <u>Mafia Onassis and his U.S. right-</u> <u>hand man,</u> [CIA hires] "Hughes's" top aide, former FBI <u>and</u> <u>CIA</u> [man] Robert Maheu (nicknamed "IBM" for "Iron Bob Maheu") [to act as go-between for its Mafia contacts to put together a team to get Castro] <u>hire and train a Mafia assassina-</u> <u>tion team to get Castro.</u> The team of a dozen or so includes John Roselli <u>and Jimmy "The Weasel" Fratianno, expert Mafia hit</u> <u>men</u> [an expert Mafia hit man], assisted by CIA's Hunt, [and] McCord and others. This was reported <u>at the time</u> by Jack Anderson, who gets a lot of his "tips" from his friend, Frank (Fiorini) Sturgis, <u>who was</u> also on the Castro assassination team. The team tries five times to kill Castro <u>with everything</u> <u>from long-range rifles to apple pie with sodium morphate in it.</u> **They nearly succeed, but some are caught and executed in Havana the day of the invasion.** Castro survives.

(**3:1**) 1963: Members of the <u>Castro assassination</u> [anti-Castro Cuban-exile training] team [are] arrested at Lake Pontchartrain, La., by Bobby Kennedy's Justice boys. Angered, Onassis changes targets and goes for <u>the head:</u> JFK, who — according to Onassis — "welched" ["welches"] on a Mafia deal. JFK sets up "Group of 40" [(advisors)] to fight Onassis.

The above segments of the *Skeleton Key* are critical to clearly understanding the historical pressures which eventually led to the assassination of President John F. Kennedy. With the enormous resources of the Hughes empire now at his disposal, Onassis could be virtually assured that his agenda of world domination could not only be realized, but sustained. However, with Joe Kennedy's offspring maturing quickly, and one newly elected to the Presidency, it was time for Onassis to unleash the firepower at his disposal and gear up for what would be a full-blown gang war against his old friend's sons.

The methodology was extremely crucial. Onassis had to avoid detection as the ultimate source of the upheavals to come. According to the *Key*, he would employ the services of the most ruthless criminals in existence. The support would be wide-spread. Along with the Kennedy boys, though, stood Fidel Castro as a prime source of irritation for Onassis. Cuba would be the next target, since Onassis still believed he would make amends with the Kennedy clan in the long term.

Castro was another story. His revolution was complete, and the lucrative gambling empire run by Meyer Lansky's trustees — with Onassis the eventual beneficiary — was crushed thoroughly in 1959. Actually, Roberts' statement that $8 million in casino receipts were taken by the revolutionaries during the sacking of the casinos and overthrow of Cuban dictator Fulgencio Batista appears to be vastly underestimated. Castro's troops not only stormed and commandeered the casinos, they took sledge-hammers to the slot machines while stealing their millions. Total United States investment in Cuba topped $1 billion[1] at the time, incredible money for that period. Fueling the revolution

---

1. *San Francisco Examiner*, "Castro Leader Hints at Seizure of U.S. Firms," by Associated Press and United Press International, Jan. 30, 1959.

was the fact that American banks had been siphoning large amounts of cash from the Cuban economy for many years, with the casinos being the biggest exploiters. Corruption was rampant. It was an ugly scene for most Cubans under Batista:

"...Rebels hated legalized gambling because it made Cubans poorer, rich American racketeers richer and added millions to Batista's vast fortune. That fortune has been estimated at $200,000,000 stashed away in foreign banks... The play in casinos often ran between $1,000,000 and $2,000,000 a night."[2]

Organized crime would not sit still for this damaging insurgence. It all happened very quickly. There was no time to react. But there would be ample opportunity to assemble a measured response; an invasion of Cuba, preceded by the assassination of Castro and fully supported by the United States. Onassis, if Gemstone has any merit, had enough control of the U.S. arsenal to make it happen no matter what the American people wanted. Since he figured to have control of the Presidency no matter who won the 1960 election (Gemstone 2:5), he would bide his time. What he did not figure on was the reluctance by Kennedy to help carry out this nefarious plan.

Gemstone 2:4 is critical, too, in pointing out Richard Nixon's early role in the Onassis organization; i.e. willing and hard-nosed enforcer of operations. Had Nixon been elected president in 1960, there is little doubt that the Bay of Pigs invasion would have been a full-blown attack on Cuba — not a watered-down CIA foulup with a tentative Kennedy looking the other way when the hammer came down on the luckless invaders. Onassis would not forget this loyalty. Nixon would have his day in the presidential sun — after the Kennedys were out of the picture.

Compounding Onassis' eventual plans for Cuba was the complication of Joe Kennedy's stroke, soon after John Kennedy was inaugurated in January of 1961. Joe had an iron grip on his

---

2. *San Francisco Examiner*, "Gambling Industry Doomed by Castro," by Larry Allen, Associated Press, Jan. 4, 1959.

boys, who had long been aware of their father's relationship to Onassis. However, with Joe in a wheelchair an unable to function, John and his brother and newly appointed attorney general, Robert F. Kennedy, decided to double-cross Onassis and thereby trigger the biggest political bloodbath in United States history.

With the mob blown out of Cuba, the Kennedys turned their attention to Onassis' big profit center — the drug trade. They interfered with Golden Triangle operations (Gemstone 2:9b, a passage conveniently omitted from the *Hustler* version of the *Key*), jailed big-league Onassis deputy Jimmy Hoffa and even started to tangle up Onassis' newly won Hughes empire in governmental probes. The battle was heating up.

Plans to eliminate Castro and get Cuba back into mob hands were accelerated, but with all the rush, they were botched — this despite one of the more talented paramilitary and espionage teams ever assembled. E. Howard Hunt, who was later to become a very big name during the Watergate scandal, was a major organizer of the Bay of Pigs operation along with other familiar names (Gemstone 2:4), but as the situation developed leading up to the Bay of Pigs, President Kennedy played it very, very cool. During the election campaign against the pit-bull Nixon, Kennedy denounced communism even more vehemently than his opponent — swaying, for the moment, the Cuban exile community in the United States in his direction. This confused Onassis and many other organized-crime figures. Once JFK was elected, however, and once Joe Kennedy's health collapsed, the whole picture changed.

Gemstone 3:0 condenses the Bay of Pigs incident and clearly points the finger at JFK's "lack of enthusiasm," which manifested itself in lack of promised air support for the CIA-trained invasion force. Hunt himself figured out JFK's true motives even before the Bay of Pigs invasion:

"...He (Hunt) must have known even then (spring and summer of 1960, during the Kennedy-Nixon campaign) that JFK was a communist at heart because his chief support came from the pinko elements of the land...

"...But the Bay of Pigs was a disaster for the free world and H.H. (Howard Hunt) uses the word 'betrayal.' As the sun set on the beachhead which he never saw, 'only vultures moved.' Although safe in Washington, 'I was sick of lying and deception, heartsick over political compromise and military defeat.' Fortunately, H.H.'s sickness with lying and deception was only temporary. Ten years later Camelot would be replaced by Watergate and H.H. would at last be able to hit the beach in freedom's name..."[3]

The gloves came off after the Bay of Pigs fiasco, and the same bunch who ran that ill-fated invasion attempt on April 17, 1961, gave up hope for any military victory by going for Castro himself. They tried six times, according to reports by maverick American syndicated columnist Jack Anderson, who would later be used by Onassis to plant disinformation about the *real* reasons for JFK's assassination in the late 1970s when the Rockefeller Commission reopened the case in the face of new evidence that clearly discredited the bogus Warren Commission findings. Anderson planted that thought as early as Jan. 18, 1971, with the following phrase:

"...Among those privy to the CIA conspiracy (to kill Castro), there is still a nagging suspicion — unsupported by the Warren Commission's findings — that Castro became aware of the U.S. plot on his life and somehow recruited (Lee Harvey) Oswald to retaliate against President Kennedy."[4] This is precisely the disinformation needed to deflect the American public's perception of exactly why JFK was assassinated — the so-called "Project Star" drummed up by Rand Corp. and described in Gemstone 6:6. The *Hustler* version adds more to this subject

---

3. *New York Review*, "The Art and Arts of E. Howard Hunt," by Gore Vidal, 1973.

4. *Miami Herald*, Jan. 18, 1971, "Six CIA Attempts to Kill Castro Failed — Plot Hushed," by Jack Anderson.

than does Roberts (in bold-face):

(**Gemstone 6:6**) Rand Corp. [Corporation]<u>, one of our ma-</u>
<u>jor "think tanks,"</u> had [has] another goody in store <u>for the</u>
<u>public:</u> "Project Star," Rand's cover-up fallback version of the
JFK murder — held in reserve should public restlessness over
the Warren Commission <u>Report</u> cover-up ever threaten to get
out of hand. **This version is "leaking" out now, in the**
Rockefeller Commission's "hints" that JFK was behind the
CIA-Mafia attempts on Castro and that Castro retaliated by
having JFK shot.

Still, Anderson's main reason for writing that same column
on Jan. 18 was to blow the lid off the Castro conspiracy and
make the United States citizenry aware that its own intelligence
apparatus was treasonous. Just as Roberts described in Gemstone 3:0, Anderson did with even more detail, especially with
regard to hired killer John Roselli:

"...For the first try, the CIA furnished Roselli with special
poison capsules to slip into Castro's food. The poison was
supposed to take three days to act. By the time Castro died, his
system would throw off all traces of the poison so he would
appear to be the victim of a natural if mysterious ailment."[5]

Anderson provided even more detail about the assassination
attempts on the Cuban leader, but the critical factor here is the
method attempted through poisoning — specifically using a
substance called sodium morphate. The *Skeleton Key* describes
exactly what sodium morphate is (see page 339) and how it is
used to silence those who would otherwise be an information leak
that would threaten the mob:

(**Gemstone 11:9**) <u>Note: Sodium morphate is a favorite Ma-</u>
<u>fia poison used for centuries. It smells like apple pie and is</u>

---

5. *Miami Herald*, Jan. 18, 1971, "Six CIA Attempts to Kill Castro Failed
   — Plot Hushed," by Jack Anderson.

sometimes served up in one, as to J. Edgar Hoover. Sometimes it is placed in a pill or capsule. Symptoms: Lethargy, sleep, sometimes vomiting. Once ingested, there is a heart attack — and no trace of the chemical is left in the body. Proof is in the vomit, which is usually not analyzed. It is not mentioned in your standard medical books on poisons, etc., yet is a common ingredient in rat poison.

But just as Gemstone 6:6 includes a *Hustler* addendum that clearly points to a tired and misdirected, but widely accepted, belief that Castro had it out for JFK and wanted him dead, Gemstone 3:0 has another disturbing tag concerning the eventual fate of the assassination team: **"...They** (assassination team members) **nearly succeed** (in killing Castro)**, but some are caught and executed in Havana the day of the invasion."** It is a very subtle tactic, but whoever transcribed the *Hustler* version felt it necessary to eliminate at least a portion of the Castro assassination squad so that a connection to JFK and Dallas would be less plausible. In fact, virtually all the would-be Castro assassins survived to team up in Dallas, if the *Skeleton Key* has any merit. Whatever the circumstances, it is clear that Anderson led the way for many columnists to write about a totally bogus version of the assassination — that Castro was behind it — so that if evidence about the real reason behind JFK's death started to leak out, this convenient fall-back position would already be on the table, ready-made for American consumption.

In 1978, when the Rockefeller Commission revisited the assassination scenario, the whole idea behind the astonishingly stupid "lone nut assassin" and "single-bullet theory" smoke-screens concocted by Gerald Ford and the Warren Commission were readily discarded. However, taking their place was the Cuban theory, pushed by Anderson himself in a television documentary on the subject. The media was again duped into believing something that was just as false, if not more so, than the Warren Commission's findings.

Indeed, if the Bay of Pigs disaster led to Onassis turning against the Kennedy family once and for all, it would be Attorney General Robert F. Kennedy, the president's brother, who would finally provoke the actual assassination of JFK. The *Key* states:

(Gemstone 3:1) 1963: Members of the <u>Castro assassination</u> [anti-Castro Cuban-exile training] team [are] arrested at Lake Pontchartrain, La., by Bobby Kennedy's Justice boys. Angered, Onassis changes targets and goes for <u>the head:</u> JFK, who — according to Onassis — "welched" ["welches"] on a Mafia deal. JFK sets up "Group of 40" [(advisors)] to fight Onassis.

Again, notice *Hustler's* editing of the original *Key* (inside brackets), attempting again to separate personnel from the Castro assassination team, calling them instead members of an "anti-Castro Cuban-exile training" team! This backs the false Rand fallback explanation of the JFK killing and helps to obscure the real culprits. This is also the crucial point in which Onassis finally realizes that the Kennedy boys are not going to revert to the Joe Kennedy pre-stroke days of compliance; that they have definitely turned against Onassis and effectively "welched" on the long-lasting "deal" with Joe Kennedy spanning much of the 20th century. The time for open warfare had arrived.

It is at this point that Katharine Graham and the *Washington Post* take an active role in the proceedings, for the *Skeleton Key* places doubt about the husband Philip Graham's "suicide" and the sudden, unexpected death of Sen. Estes Kefauver, the nation's foremost crime-fighting elected official at the time and proverbial thorn in the side of the Mafia:

(Gemstone 3:2a) August, 1962: Two murders had [have] to occur before the murder of   JFK; of people who would understand the situation and [who] might squawk:
(3:2b) Senator Estes Kefauver, whose Crime Commission investigations had uncovered the 1932 [Onassis] deal <u>between</u>

Onassis, Kennedy, Eugene Meyer, Lansky, Roosevelt, et al.
Kefauver planned [plans] a speech on the Senate floor denouncing Mafia operations. Instead, he ate [eats] a piece of apple pie
laced with sodium morphate [(allegedly a poison)] (used in rat
poison), and has [has] a sodium-morphate-induced "heart attack" on the Senate floor.

(3:2c) Philip Graham, editor [publisher] of the *Washington
Post.* Philip had married Katharine Graham, Eugene Meyer's
daughter who had inherited the *Washington Post* and allied
media empire. Graham [Phil] put [puts] together [media empire
as well as] the Kennedy-Johnson ticket and was [is] Kennedy's
friend in the struggle with Onassis. According to Gemstone,
Katharine Meyer Graham bribed some psychiatrist [a psychiatrist is bribed] to certify that Phil was insane. He was [is]
allowed out of the nuthouse for the [one] weekend and died
[dies] of a shotgun wound to the head, in the Graham home in
Washington; [his] death [is] ruled [a] "suicide."

Taking the Kefauver death first, it is obvious from news
reports that a sodium morphate-style poisoning was a distinct
possibility. Once of the symptoms of sodium morphate poisoning are sudden rupturing of heart vessels; it will be shown that
the deaths Roberts attributes to such poisoning throughout the
Skeleton Key indeed are matched by medical facts, and information contained on death certificates. In Kefauver's case, he was
a strapping, healthy 60-year-old who had few health problems
until Aug. 10, 1963:

"...He (Kefauver) had left the Senate floor Thursday evening
feeling ill. He thought it was acute indigestion. Doctors said he
had suffered a 'mild heart attack'... Death came unexpectedly
but quietly as doctors were preparing to operate on an aneurysm
(ballooning) of the aorta, main blood vessel through which the
heart pumps blood into the body. The artery broke before preparations for the operation were completed.

"In typical fashion, Kefauver had spent an active day on the

Senate floor Thursday, fighting what he considered a "give-away" of national resources to private interests in establishment of the Communications Satellite Corporation as a privately owned firm and what he called free access to nationally financed satellite developments."[6]

It was Kefauver who first uncovered the extent of organized crime in the United States by way of the famous 1950-51 hearings of the Senate crime investigating committee, which had given Americans their first look at the country's top racketeers and hoodlums. His book, *Crime in America*, would become a painful spear in the side of organized crime for years to come. Through these connections, it would be easy to see that Kefauver might have already known of links between American crime syndicates and the Cuban situation, including Onassis' ties.

Regarding Philip Graham, the *Skeleton Key* insinuation that Katharine set up her husband is dubious at best. They were a good team for the *Post* and for the liberal politics of the day, including the surge of the Democrats with the days of Camelot in their full glory. Still, something happened with Philip Graham which has long been difficult for political writers to describe. His background could well have made him a target.

For one, Graham served in the U.S. Army Air Force during World War II, was commissioned in 1943 and served with *military intelligence*, where it would be easy to obtain sensitive information related to foreign trade, shipping and illegal drug trafficking. In another little-known fact, Graham was connected with Rand Corp., the masters of deception mentioned in Gemstone 6:6 and the birthplace of Pentagon Papers conspirator Daniel Ellsberg (Gemstone 6:5a). But Graham refused to be part of the media cover-up game, and instead became a robust supporter of the Kennedy clan. This support might have cost him his life.

CHAPTER 7

. . . .

The Perfect Crime of JFK's Murder

One refreshing aspect of the *Skeleton Key* is that it handles the bulk of information relating to the assassination of President John F. Kennedy with a far-reaching perspective. JFK's death has been the subject of much debate, but the shameful fact is that much of the controversy centers around the events in Dallas on the day of the assassination, Nov. 22, 1963, and the picking apart of physical and circumstantial evidence at the moment the actual shooting occurred. Even the most viable, rational conspiracy theories become tedious after a while; some of the wild-goose chases undergone by conspiracy theorists border on the ludicrous.

So it would seem with the *Skeleton Key*, which outlines a rather blunt and chillingly candid version of the events at Dealey Plaza, stripped of any emotion or analysis. Whether the *Key* is even remotely accurate along these lines, one thing is certain: Information revealed in the years since 1976 when the *Key* first came to light have done nothing to discredit the *Key's* version of events. If anything, the new revelations have confirmed much of what the *Key* states about the assassination.

The first major element of the *Key* which lends credence to its assassination scenario is the root motive for such an act — a blood feud between two powerful families. Assassinating a president is something that takes enormous planning, flawless execution and astonishing resources. What force, political or otherwise, would have the savvy to pull it off? Most conjecture surrounding motives of JFK's assassination is focused on some simplistic explanations, such as "Castro's Cuba wanted it to happen" or "the CIA did it." The huge flaw in all the material written about the assassination — aside from concentrating too much on the shooting itself — is that no compelling motive has materialized. Only the *Skeleton Key to the Gemstone Files* offers a plausible motive, names the personnel needed to accomplish the task, appropriately links the assassination with other historical events, and injects some common sense into the equation.

Some of the more popularly accepted theories behind the assassination of President Kennedy, and who planned and finally perpetrated the act on Nov. 22, 1963, include the following:

- Lee Harvey Oswald acted alone, firing three shots from an Italian rifle into the Kennedy motorcade while perched at an open window on the sixth floor of the Texas School Book Depository. One shot missed, the other two found their mark. One of the bullets entered Kennedy's body through his upper back, exited through his neck, then struck Texas Gov. John Connally in his back, penetrated his torso, then struck his right wrist and thigh. The third bullet blew the right side of Kennedy's head off, killing the president. This version was confirmed through the Warren Commission's findings, and enjoyed a resurgence of popularity by way of a PBS special 1993 edition of *Frontline* which uses sophisticated computer models to reenact conditions surrounding the assassination. In that show, entitled *Who Was Lee Harvey Oswald?*, all the so-called "evidence" is repackaged in a way that makes it more palatable and "reasonable." Other conspiracy theories are also slammed by the presentation of this "evidence."

- Lee Harvey Oswald alone fired the fatal shots, but was tied to organized crime figures, anti-Castro Cuban exiles, the Central Intelligence Agency (CIA), Soviet KGB and other such groups, and was acting on the behalf of someone other than himself. This is the linchpin behind many conspiracy theories.

- Lee Harvey Oswald was part of a multiple-gunman assassination team consisting of three to six members, depending on the conspiracy theory. It was determined in advance that he would be the person to take the full blame, covering for the other assassins and burying any further evidence of a more widespread conspiracy. It was his job to shoot Gov. Connally, whom he hated for ignoring his request for a reinstated honorable discharge from the U.S. Marines. Writer James Reston Jr. makes this case in a 1988 book. The *Skeleton Key* also points out that it was Oswald's role to take out Connally. Other snipers were aiming at the president.

- Lee Harvey Oswald was a stooge set up to take the blame while a well-coordinated and well-equipped team of professional shooters did the job. These shooters, depending upon the conspiracy theory, were either French nationals or Mafia gunmen hired for the hit by a mysterious, unknown power.

- Secret Service Agent William Greer blew Kennedy's head away with a point-blank shot from a .45 caliber pistol from inside the presidential limousine. This appears unlikely, mainly because practically all Secret Service people on the scene had weapons drawn by that time. But conspiracy advocates indicate that photographic evidence exists to show that Greer was not only holding the weapon, but got off the fatal shot amid the bedlam triggered by Oswald's initial shots from the Depository perch.

- Zionists hired an assassination team to kill Kennedy, with Clay Shaw — the major target of New Orleans District Attorney Jim Garrison's investigation several years later

— a major contact person in the conspiracy network. The entire operation was bankrolled by British intelligence.[1]

- Cuban revolutionary leader Fidel Castro, angered over U.S. intelligence attempts to assassinate him, authorized a counterstrike and sent a team of assassins to kill Kennedy. This scenario, pushed by columnist Jack Anderson, among others, is by far the most ludicrous. It was Kennedy who stopped a full-scale invasion of Cuba during the Bay of Pigs incident and instead let the smaller invasion force be defeated handily by Cuban revolutionaries. Castro should have been happy about that, not mad. And it was almost certain that Castro realized it was the U.S. intelligence community — and its associated mob goons — that wanted him dead just after the revolution, since gambling and drug money quickly dried up in Cuba following the overthrow of the Batista dictatorship.

- The Soviet Union wanted to eliminate Kennedy as a prelude to a nuclear attack, using defector-sympathizer Oswald as its agent of destruction. This is a highly suspect theory, made popular at that time because of the Cuban missile crisis the year before, and because the Cold War had reached fever pitch.

There can be no denying that Lee Harvey Oswald did get off three shots at the presidential motorcade in Dallas. That much evidence is clear. He did shoot from the Texas School Book Depository. The real hard questions, though, surface when considering exactly where the bullets struck Kennedy. Extensive photographic evidence from various angles indicates more than one gunman was involved. One stretch of movie film shot by Abraham Zapruder shows the president being struck from a bullet shot from an angle to the right and in front of Kennedy. A

---

1. *Secrets of the Kennedy Assassination Revealed*, essay by Dr. John Coleman, 1993.

Polaroid photo from the opposite side taken by Mary Ann Moorman shows the exact moment when Kennedy's head is struck by that right-front shot — and the shadowy figure of a gunman and a discharging firearm. The photographic evidence seems to contradict the Warren Commission version, and all the PBS *Frontline* propaganda in the world cannot refute that.

However, the Gemstone version of the assassination carries with it a ring of truth in many respects, and at least it deals with the situation as a small part of a much larger picture. That is why we will not bother with rehashing the many versions of the complex conspiracy theories of the Kennedy case; rather, we will present the *Key's* blunt version and decide whether it has any merit:

(Gemstone 3:3a) November 1, 1963: The hit on JFK was [is] to take place in true Mafia style: a triple execution, together with [at the same time as South Vietnam's Ngo Dinh Diem and Ngo Dinh Nhu] Diem and Nhu in Vietnam. Diem and Nhu got theirs, as scheduled. Onassis had invited [invites] Jackie for a cruise on the *Christina*, where she was [is] when JFK got [is] tipped off that big O [Big-O] planned [plans] to wipe him out. JFK called [calls] Jackie on the yacht from the White House, hysterical [telling her]: "Get off that yacht [even] if you have to swim," and canceled [cancels] his appearance at a [Chicago] football stadium in Chicago where the CIA-Mafia assassination team was [is] poised for the kill. Jackie stays on board [the *Christina*], descended the gangplank a few days later on Onassis' arm, in Turkey, to impress the Turkish boy, Mustapha. Madame Nhu, in the United States, bitterly remarked, "Whatever happened in Vietnam will see its counterpart in the United States."

The above passage is a compact summary of a huge picture, one that gets to the foundation of the entire Gemstone thesis. Point No. 1: The "real reason" for the Vietnam War (Gemstone 6:5a) was clearly preservation and expansion of the drug trade. That is why explaining the timing of the Ngo Dinh Diem and Ngo

Dinh Nhu shootings leading up to the JFK assassination itself is so critical, and so damning to the perpetrators. Think about it:

"The build-up of the American presence in south-east Asia, the course of the Second Indo-China War from the sixties onwards and the arrival in Vietnam of American troops in 1965 — *all these were to revolutionize the nature of the (drug) traffic, which now expanded at a dizzy rate* (emphasis ours)."[2]

The Corsican drug traders knew the business end of the trade, and freely admitted the following credo: "You can't buy, stock or transport drugs unless you have *protection in political and administrative circles* (emphasis ours)."[3] It was clear that Diem, then president of South Vietnam, and his brother Nhu were not going to rubber-stamp the status quo. A major policy shift was about to be attempted in Vietnam in the early 1960s, and it directly involved drug trafficking. The JFK presidency, with enforcer Bobby Kennedy the driving force, was already cleaning house with regard to domestic drug trafficking, going after well-known mobsters who had enjoyed, until that point, tacit approval from most law enforcement, which was paid off with dirty drug money to keep the lines of commerce open.

That was not the case with the Kennedy administration. It was on the verge of going after the illegal narcotics trade at its source — the Golden Triangle — and organized crime would have no part of that. The major immediate impact would be to cut into the profits of major transporters of drugs, namely the maritime networks, including Onassis' ships, which by the 1960s numbered in the hundreds and were transporting cargo — legal and otherwise — to and from most major seaports in the world. We will present more about how the Vietnam War was carefully designed and extended to protect and expand illegal narcotics

---

2. *The International Connection: Opium from Growers to Pushers*, by Catherine Lamour and Michael R. Lamberti, p. 135, ©1974, Pantheon Books.

3. *Ibid.*

traffic, making the United States the largest-ever cash market for illegal drugs.

But now, suffice it to say that Kennedy, with his allies Diem and Nhu in Vietnam, were about to de-emphasize Vietnam as a military consideration. This was intolerable to organized crime. It is interesting that nobody of any consequence has questioned the timing of the Diem and Nhu slayings, which occurred on Nov. 1, 1963, in relation to the JFK assassination, or pursued any possible connections. The circumstances of the slayings were quite mysterious. Both leaders were executed by gunshot from point-blank range, but when the story first broke, the deaths were called "suicides." However, the American media already had strong presence throughout Vietnam as the military aspects of the Vietnam conflict came into greater focus, and the press did not buy the suicide story.[4] A day later, it was reported the two were "...murdered by trigger-happy revolutionary soldiers."

But one Associated Press reporter penetrated the smokescreen. Roy Essoyan was on the inside at the time in Saigon, and saw photographs of the bodies of Diem and Nhu. Diem's body was riddled with bullets, and there was evidence of a gunshot wound to the head. Nhu's body bore bruises, as if it was beaten, and there was evidence of stab wounds.

The JFK administration desperately tried to save Diem through attempts by U.S. Ambassador Henry Cabot Lodge, but Diem opted to fight to the last on his own. High U.S. officials who refused to be identified bitterly regretted the slayings — realizing it could lead to a rapid escalation of the war, regardless of who was in the White House.

One thing was certain: With Diem and Nhu out of the way, South Vietnam's government would look more favorably on two major items of interest: Expanding the Vietnam War by leaps and bounds, and inviting as many thousands of U.S. troops over for the party as the American people would permit. That is

---

4. *San Francisco Examiner*, Nov. 2, 1963, "A Pro-U.S. Junta in Power."

exactly what happened. Instead of short-term involvement with mostly military advisors, the U.S. ended up sending waves of combat troops into the war. These troops, whose terms of duty were religiously rotated annually, insured a regular flow of drug addicts back to the United States following their military stints in Southeast Asia. Addiction usually meant direct involvement in the drug trade as a dealer at home; there was no alternate way of financially supporting a heroin habit short of robbery. So a wave of drug dealers was born and nurtured for 11 long years — from the time JFK was assassinated in 1963, to the time U.S. troops were finally withdrawn "with honor" shortly before the resignation of President Richard M. Nixon in 1974. Without the extraordinary protraction of the Vietnam War, drug addiction, abuse and its associated social ills would have never reached the fever pitch it eventually did, and it certainly would not be the huge social bane it is today.

A footnote: Madame Nhu, mentioned in Gemstone 3:3a (a passage left out of the *Hustler* version, for whatever reason) as being bitter about her husband's death, was not fooling anyone within the U.S. military intelligence network. In earlier years, she was known as "Saigon's opium queen" and openly did business with her counterparts in Laos.

Then there is the reference in Gemstone 3:3a (a loaded passage if there ever was one in this document) to Jacqueline Kennedy's little excursion on Aristotle Onassis' yacht, the *Christina*, a monumental floating palace to the excesses of the illegal narcotics trade. The *Christina* had every luxury imaginable, including a dance floor that would sink and convert itself into a swimming pool. Incredible artwork and sculpture, including an Indiana Jones-style "golden Buddha" clearly from the Golden Triangle region, decorated every room. There was no guessing as to its worth; where William Randolph Hearst had his castle, Aristotle Onassis had the *Christina*. Among Onassis' regular guests aboard the ship was Sir Winston Churchill, a member of the so-called "Committee of 300" and one former head of state with whom Onassis communicated his deepest philosophical feelings.

It was October of 1963 when Jackie took a two-week cruise on the *Christina*, a cruise in which ship servants observed that the first lady was falling in love with the Greek shipping baron.[5] There was extreme nervousness on the part of President Kennedy about the wisdom of letting Jackie on the yacht in the first place; having known of his father's connections with Onassis in the early part of the century, he undoubtedly hated the way the Greek could literally sweep his wife off her feet and dazzle her with the astonishing opulence of the *Christina*; the "dark side of the force" to use a *Star Wars* metaphor.

During this cruise, largely unpublicized events transpired which could be construed as having major importance as the days counted down toward Dallas and Dealey Plaza. For one, there was a stretch of several days in which the actual physical safety of the first lady was in question. Associated Press reported the situation in the following manner:

JACKIE YACHT MYSTERY

LAVKAS ISLAND (Greece) — (AP) — The whereabouts of the luxury yacht *Christina*, carrying Mrs. John F. Kennedy on a vacation cruise, remained a mystery today.

There had been reports the vessel would come to this Ionian Sea island yesterday afternoon, but it did not appear.

Authorities on various islands between Lavkas and Crete, where Mrs. Kennedy spent Tuesday, said they had not sighted the vessel.

Rainstorms and heavy seas plagues the Greek islands Wednesday. It was possible the *Christina* waited amid smaller islands to wait out the storm, maritime authorities said.

---

5. *Onassis: The Inside Story*, by Christian Cafarakis, as told to Jacques Harvey, ©1972.

At the same time the White House, queried on the yacht's whereabouts, offered a "no comment" response.

The 400-mile voyage from Crete to Lavkas should take about 24 hours on the yacht, which Greek shipping magnate Aristotle Onassis has put at Mrs. Kennedy's disposal...

...The *Christina*, a converted destroyer carrying modern communications equipment, is considered sturdy enough to weather any ordinary storm.

The lack of news, however, touched off speculation that the vessel might be heading out of Greek waters, *to Italy and even Tangier, Morocco or Cairo* (emphasis ours).

U.S. Undersecretary of Commerce Franklin D. Roosevelt Jr. (Gemstone 1:1), who had been aboard the yacht until leaving it Tuesday at Crete, said Mrs. Kennedy was *making up her mind about ports of call as she went along*...(emphasis ours).[6]

Needless to say, there are considerable unexplained aspects of this journey which border on the incredible. How could the U.S. government, particularly the Secret Service, allow the wife of the president of the United States to go on such a high-risk cruise? Alone on the waters on the open sea, a vessel such as the *Christina*, however seaworthy it might have been, is vulnerable to attack — a virtual sitting duck. If Onassis had ulterior motives, such as using the first lady as a hostage in negotiations with the young, hawkish administration bent upon "cleaning up" America (and the free world at large), he would be able to exert tremendous leverage on JFK and the Kennedy family overall.

Was the United States government concerned? Extensive proof exists that the entire U.S. military intelligence operation was prepared to move forward aggressively to "rescue" Jackie if that drastic step turned out to be necessary. Underscoring this concern was at least one documented move to withhold "pay-

---

6. *San Francisco Chronicle*, Oct. 10, 1963, "Jackie Yacht Mystery."

ments" due Onassis from the U.S. Treasury until Jacqueline Kennedy's safety could be guaranteed:

A BLAST AT U.S. NEWS SECRECY

WASHINGTON — (UPI) — A Washington newsman protested yesterday that agriculture department officials held back data on government payments to Greek shipping magnate Aristotle Onassis *until Mrs. Jacqueline Kennedy had ended a Mediterranean tour on his yacht.* (emphasis ours).

James V. Mathis, White House correspondent for the advance news service of the Newhouse newspapers, testified at the opening hearing by a Senate judiciary sub-committee of information.[7]

This tiny story appeared in some major newspapers and largely escaped notice by the general public, and it was only written and distributed by United Press International after a reporter squawked about the obvious suppression of news out of the federal bureaucracy in reference to dealings with Onassis. It is also an indication that Onassis had his hand in the U.S. Treasury through a number of lucrative channels:

- Howard Hughes' company, if indeed he had taken control of the reclusive billionaire's assets through the kidnapping alleged in Gemstone 1:9.
- Generous contracts to ship legitimate U.S. cargo, such as grain (i.e. U.S. agricultural department).
- Equally generous shipbuilding arrangements through which Onassis would be able to expand his tanker fleet at U.S. taxpayer expense, as long as the ships were built in U.S. shipyards (i.e. Bethlehem Steel).

It should be no surprise that President Kennedy would have concerns for his wife's safety, and that Gemstone 3:3a does have

---

7. *San Francisco Examiner*, "A Blast at U.S. News Secrecy," Oct. 29, 1963.

some merit. Could JFK call the yacht by telephone as mentioned in the same passage? Yes, he could. The *Christina* had its own radio telephone system that had a worldwide reach; in fact, Onassis would often work late into the night on business by phone from various parts of the world while he was on the *Christina*. His telephone bills ran into the thousands of dollars per month; into the hundreds of thousands annually, according to many of his biographical accounts.

As for the canceled speaking trip to the football stadium in Chicago in Gemstone 3:3a, it leads to the next passage, which has some intrigue all its own:

(Gemstone 3:3b) <u>One of the assassination team (Tom Wallace, a double for Oswald) was picked up in Chicago, with a rifle, and quickly released by police).</u>

In some other published versions of the *Skeleton Key*, this passage carries a different name for the "Oswald double." For example, in a vanity-press rendition of the *Skeleton Key* by Peter Renzo, entitled *Beyond the Gemstone Files* (Vantage Press), identified the man as "Tom Vallee" instead of Tom Wallace. Naturally, Gemstone 3:3b was stricken from the *Hustler* version. In Jim Keith's *The Gemstone File,* the Oswald "double" is identified as "Tom Mallee." The Chicago connection continues in the next passage:

(Gemstone 3:3c) Three weeks later, the Mafia's alternate [backup] and carefully arranged execution plan went [goes] into effect: JFK was [is] assassinated in Dallas. <u>A witness who recognized pictures of some people arrested in Dealey Plaza as having been in Chicago three weeks earlier told Black Panthers Hampton and Clark.</u>

Again, *Hustler* sees fit to delete the Chicago reference. This is curious; in fact, *Hustler* appears to delete most references to such groups as the Black Panthers, or the so-called "Zebra killings" in the San Francisco Bay Area (more on those eye-opening slayings later in this book). Perhaps the passages were edited due to space restrictions; perhaps they were edited to cover up even more possible leads.

(Gemstone 3:4a) The JFK murder: Onassis "Hughes" man <u>Robert Maheu</u> reassigned [reassigns] the Mafia-CIA Castro assassination team to the murder of JFK, adding [adds] Eugene Brading, a third Mafia hit man [gunsel] from the Denver Mafia Smalldones "family." Two months earlier, Brading, on parole after a series of crimes, applied for a new driver's license, explaining to the California DMV (Department of Motor Vehicles) that he had decided to change his name to "Jim Braden." Brading got [gets] his California parole officer's permission for two trips to Dallas; in November, on "oil business" — the first time to look things over; and the second time, when JFK was [is] scheduled for [to make] his Dallas trip.

The most glaring deletion is the name of "Robert Maheu" from the *Hustler* version, which refers to simply "Onassis 'Hughes' man." Everything checks out regarding Brading in this passage, but *Hustler* leaves out Gemstone 3:5, which refers to Brading staying at the Cabana Hotel, where Jack Ruby hung out the night before the assassination. The reference to a "Eugene Bradley," one of Brading's aliases and a target of New Orleans District Attorney Jim Garrison's conspiracy probe, is also deleted from Gemstone 4:3 by *Hustler*. Apparently, Mr. Brading's involvement in most of this was regarded as too sensitive to go to press with. The final deletion is the entire phrase of Gemstone 4:4, which mentions the famous FBI photos of Brading taken at the scene of the assassination where he is wearing a hat marked with conspicuous "Xs."

(Gemstone 3:4b) Lee Harvey Oswald, [of the] CIA, with carefully planned links to both the ultra-right and <u>to</u> the Communists, was [is] designated as the patsy. He was [is] supposed to shoot at [Texas] Gov. [John] Connally, and he did [does so].

Amazingly, this angle on Oswald's involvement and his intelligence connections are greatly amplified by a 1988 book written by James Reston Jr., *The Great Expectations of John Connally*, in which it is pointed out quite accurately that Oswald hated Connally because of a sequence of events that led to Connally effectively blocking Oswald from getting an honorable discharge from the U.S. Marine Corps. The book is interesting, as it also points out that Oswald also expressed admiration for President Kennedy while bitterly criticizing Connally. If an assassination team needed a patsy, Oswald was perfect. He was not bright enough to see that he was being used, and he was also part of a major-league conspiracy in which he would be one of the shooters. The fact that he was going to get Connally made it more personally satisfying for him, if Reston's analysis has any merit.

Reston's thesis mentions Oswald's acquaintance George De Mohrenschildt, who has an astonishing intelligence background on which Reston failed to fully elaborate in his book. However, we have uncovered documentation that connects De Mohrenschildt, a Russian emigre, with the U.S. intelligence community — and specifically to mind-control experimentation by the U.S. government.

Oswald's Russian-born wife Marina was reportedly "befriended" by Alexandra De Mohrenschildt, George's daughter, in early 1962 when Marina and her baby left the then-unemployed and despondent Lee Harvey and went separate ways. Father George De Mohrenschildt was only termed "a flamboyant loudmouth" who "toyed with Oswald in uneven intellectual games," according to Reston's thin narrative. But Mr. De Mohrenschildt was more than that. Much more.

De Mohrenschildt was a "White Russian" and aristocrat and had connections with the Nobel oil family which prospered under the czar, as his father managed the Baku oil fields for the Nobel family. This relationship would invariably connect De Mohrenschildt's family to Onassis, since the Greek shipper was deeply connected with all major petroleum producers, including those in Russia, then part of the Soviet Union. Another reason why De Mohrenschildt might have deeper knowledge of Onassis and his operations was his role as a Nazi spy during World War II. He remained an intelligence agent after the war, which would have placed him in a position of knowing more about people like Philip Graham, the future *Washington Post* publisher who also happened to be an intelligence officer for the United States military during World War II. Naturally, Bruce Roberts could well have knowledge of these activities (as we will read later in Chapter 8) because of his military connections with friends who would later retire from military service, yet remain a part of his own intelligence network which generated most of the information contained in his Gemstone files, from which the *Skeleton Key* is derived.

De Mohrenschildt himself also had a more direct role with the Oswald family than Reston and others would have us all believe. It might have been daughter Alexandra who actually did testify to the Warren Commission as to the background of Lee Harvey Oswald, but George De Mohrenschildt was brought up before the House Select Committee on Assassinations (a.k.a. the Rockefeller Commission) because of a tip by a professor, Wilhelm Oltmans, who told the committee in 1977 that De Mohrenschildt held the key to the JFK assassination, as De Mohrenschildt had privately confessed to him prior to the assassination that he was aware of a *conspiracy to murder the president in Dallas.* According to our sources, Oltmans further reported that De Mohrenschildt was ready to have a book published which would reveal these conspiracy details.

The Select Committee then agreed to further investigate Oltmans' claims and track down De Mohrenschildt if the situation called for such a move. However, any such move was too late. A week later, George De Mohrenschildt was found dead of a shotgun blast to the head (the same fate that befell Philip Graham in 1963) in Palm Beach, Fla. Local officials termed the death "suicide," but indications are that some kind of mind control was at work to coerce De Mohrenschildt, under certain circumstances, to take his own life. A curious fact surrounding the death was that De Mohrenschildt, again according to documentation we have received, was on that day in late March of 1977, he was in the middle of being interviewed by Edward J. Epstein, who was penning a new book, *The Legend of Lee Harvey Oswald.* The two broke for lunch at around 1 p.m. and agreed to resume the session at 3 p.m. When De Mohrenschildt failed to show at that time, Epstein called his hotel room and was informed by a distraught maid that De Mohrenshildt had taken his own life.

De Mohrenschildt's attorney, Pat Russell, backed Oltmans' testimony and verified that De Mohrenschildt told him before he died that persons other than Oswald had participated in the JFK assassination. Russell claimed to have in his possession taped interviews with De Mohrenschildt, a book-length manuscript and a photograph. Then Oltmans resurfaced with some quotes from De Mohrenschildt that were given to him before De Mohrenschildt died.

In an interview dated Feb. 23, 1977, De Mohrenschildt told Oltmans that in June of 1976, "I completed a manuscript. That's when disaster struck. You see, in that book I played the devil's advocate. Without directly implicating myself as an accomplice in the John F. Kennedy assassination, I still mentioned a number of names — particularly of FBI and CIA agents who apparently may *not* be exposed under *any* circumstances. I was drugged surreptitiously and, as a result, I was committed to a mental hospital. I was there eight weeks and was given electric shocks and, as a consequence, I sometimes forget details...temporarily."

Oswald remained unaffected by any of this; it was obvious he would need full use of his mental capacity to pull off what would later be termed the murder of the century. Needless to say, much remains unexplained about the mixed company the Warren Commission's model assassin kept prior to the JFK shooting itself.

****

(**Gemstone 3:4c**) Each of the four shooters [gunmen] — Oswald, Brading, Fratianno and Roselli — had [has] a timer and a backup man. [Timers give the signal to shoot.] Backup men were [are] supposed to pick up the spent shells, and get rid of the guns. <u>Timers would give the signal to shoot. Hunt and McCord were there to help. Sturgis was in Miami</u>.

Notice again the underlined portion of Gemstone 3:4c. It was yet another deletion in the *Hustler* version. Before the assassination team's tactics can be discussed, let us deal with the issue of E. Howard Hunt and Frank Sturgis, both of whom are accused by conspiracy theorists of being involved with the assassination in some way.

But were either of these men in Dallas that day? The *Skeleton Key* states that Frank Sturgis was in Miami, and he was. However, Hunt is a different story. He cannot confirm he was *not* in Dallas on Nov. 22, 1963. He claims to have been in Washington, D.C. that day on family business, saying his children would confirm that. However, his son, who was nine years old in 1963, could not confirm that his father was in Washington that day. The younger son was not yet born. And Mrs. Hunt was killed in a mysterious plane crash before the Rockefeller Commission started its work in 1975. Therefore, E. Howard Hunt could well have been in Dallas.

As for the tactics described in Gemstone 3:4c, it was clear what the roles were for the people involved. Motion picture director Oliver Stone, in the controversial movie *JFK*, has stressed that he believes a "paramilitary operation" took place in Dallas involving "a dozen or so men." Indeed, this is what the *Key* implies here. If four shooters are involved, and each has a backup man and timer (for most Mafia-style political hits, the timer and backup would be one person), that would be eight people on the scene for starters. Counting support personnel and drivers (in the JFK case, complicity with the Dallas police department is implied), the number could easily be "a dozen or so."

The element of a timer is crucial here. At least one witness did report more than one person in the open sixth-floor window of the Texas School Book Depository; it could well have been that Oswald had his backup/timer with him as did the three others. The existence of timers as part of the assassination team would explain the multiple hits Kennedy took inside of a split-second as the Abraham Zapruder assassination film shows. It would also explain the curious twists and turns the president's body exhibited when hit by the head shot later in the sequence. Timers are critical; synchronized firing sequences can wreak havoc with any forensic pathology analysis of a particular shooting. Such is perhaps why doctors who performed the autopsies and wrote their preliminary and final reports appeared so confused as to the number and direction of shots that actually struck the president's body — and felt obliged to change those reports later.

(Gemstone 3:4c continued) Fratianno [, considered an excellent shot] shot [fires] from a second-story window in the Dal-Tex Building, across the street [kitty-corner] from the Texas School Book Depository. He apparently used a handgun; he is an excellent shot with a pistol. Fratianno hit Kennedy twice, in the back and in the head. Fratianno and his backup man were [are] "arrested," driven away from the Dal-Tex Building in a police car, and released (without being booked). (The Dallas police office is [was] located in the Dal-Tex Building).

(3:4d) Roselli shot Kennedy once, hitting the right side of his head and blowing his brains out, with a rifle, from behind a fence in the grassy knoll area. [From behind a fence on the grassy-knoll area, Roselli — armed with a rifle — gets Kennedy once, hitting the right side of his head and blowing his brains out.] Roselli and his timer went [go] down a manhole behind the fence and followed [follow] the sewer line away from Dealey Plaza.

Alleged Dal-Tex Building sniper Jimmy "The Weasel" Fratianno was short-changed in the *Hustler* version of Gemstone 3:4c. Note the underlined passage — included in the original *Skeleton Key* but stricken by *Hustler* — referring to the type weapon Fratianno used, his reputation with that particular type of firearm, and the location where his shots actually struck the President. Why would *Hustler* choose to run Gemstone 3:4c without that sentence? That answer should be obvious: To offer no viable alternative to the Warren Commission's one-gunman, three-shot, two-hit theory. As it stands, *Hustler's* version of Gemstone 3:4c without that singular sentence becomes meaningless; it is a tease. It becomes entertaining speculation about a second gunman, and even if such a gunman existed, and even if shots were fired, if they did not strike the President, then the Warren Report still remains unscathed as to the "explanation" of the fatal shots. Certainly, the original *Skeleton Key* language gives a gunman other than Oswald credit for at least two hits. Where does that leave Oswald? To keep that sentence crosses the line from speculation into the "forbidden" area of getting away from Oswald entirely.

And what of these two gunmen, Fratianno and John Roselli? Were they really there in Dallas that day? Did they participate in the actual assassination? There is no questioning their ability to shoot well enough to be part of a team such as this. Another factor is clear: Fratianno and Roselli worked well as a team, and such camaraderie is freely expressed in a book on Fratianno's life, *The Last Mafioso*. The book's author, Ovid Demaris, mixes much of the narrative with actual conversations between Fratianno and Roselli. It is clear these conversational passages were designed to skirt the JFK situation for the most part, and offer sufficient mob "confirmation" that Fidel Castro was behind the "conspiracy" to assassinate the president:

One of these "discussions" between Fratianno and Roselli follows:

"...You know, Johnny (Roselli)," he (Fratianno) had said, "the more of this bulls--- (rumors of a mob connection to the JFK assassination) I read, the more I'm convinced that we've become *scapegoats for every unsolved crime committed in this century* (emphasis ours). What's this mob the papers are always talking about, for Christ's sake? It's against the f---ing rules (apparently an unwritten Mafia code) to kill a cop, so now *we're going to kill the President* (emphasis ours)...

...Roselli sighed. "Jimmy, what're you going to do? I'll bet you any amount of money the CIA never tells the Warren Commission about their little deal with us (hired as part of the Castro assassination unit)

"I hope not (Fratianno responds), or *you'll be dragged right into the middle of this thing* (JFK conspiracy, emphasis ours). You think maybe Castro is behind the hit?"

"*No question in my mind* (emphasis ours)," Roselli said. "But it's got *nothing to do with us* (emphasis ours). I think he hit Kennedy because of the Bay of Pigs invasion. I don't think he's even aware of our deal..."

...(Fratianno:) "Maybe if you had clipped him (Castro), Kennedy would still be alive."[8]

This book, like many on the mob, cleared many hurdles through the research process and was thoroughly laundered before it went to press. That is why Fratianno and Roselli are portrayed as "talking" about the JFK issue, with the words carefully selected as to preclude any direct involvement. Still, in studying these quotes (note the italicized passages), it is easy to see that they drop subtle clues that they *could* have done it if they wanted to. They certainly have no hesitation about discuss-

---

8. *The Last Mafioso*, by Ovid Demaris, New York Times Books, ©1981, p. 193.

ing the conspiracy aspect of the assassination — in print. Finally, the final wistful mention by Fratianno, in an openly corny patriotic vein, that "maybe if you (Roselli) had clipped him (Castro), Kennedy would still be alive," is an absolute dead giveaway (no pun intended), and a quote specifically designed to paint these Mafia hoods as "good guys" because they at least tried to get Castro, who was vilified by the U.S. press from the infancy of his revolution.

Another thing about Fratianno: He lived the good life for much of the period between JFK's assassination in 1963 and when he died at the age of 79 on July 2, 1993. The *Skeleton Key* accurately reports his financial relationships with such luminaries as former San Francisco mayor, attorney and financier Joseph L. Alioto, as does the Demaris book (in fact, Demaris relates a conversation, replete with direct quotes, between Fratianno and Alioto in a meeting that concerned possible loans between Alioto's newly founded San Francisco bank and the Mafia gunman — loans allegedly connected to a payoff from the JFK assassination, according to the *Skeleton Key*).

Further, Fratianno received rare treatment from the U.S. government, including generous payoffs, as part of a so-called "witness protection program." This looks every bit like a thinly veiled cover for Fratianno's possible role in the JFK assassination. The mobster continued his associations with Mafia gangsters despite this "witness protection" program. But was the U.S. government protecting Fratianno for the information he possessed on the mob overall, or the information he might have harbored about the JFK assassination? The actual mobsters Fratianno helped the government nail in court included Carmine "Junior" Persico, chief of the Columbo family, and Frank "Funzi" Tieri, chief of the Genovese family — both largely unconnected with the usual mob kingpins mentioned as possible JFK conspirators: Carlos Marcello and Santo Trafficante.

It has also never been explained why Fratianno was paid and protected as part of this "witness protection program" for 10 years — from 1977 to 1987. It is curious, too, why he decided to "rat" on his Mafia brethren when he had achieved top-dog status inside the Los Angeles-area Mafia organization in the years following the JFK murder.

Fratianno was also stunned when the "witness protection" program ended.

"How in the hell can they take you off the program after you have been in it for 10 years?" Fratianno rhetorically asked *San Francisco Examiner* reporter Seth Rosenfeld. "I'm on my way to another country. No use telling you where."[9]

Roselli, meanwhile, had connections everywhere in Mafia operations, and was a key reason why Howard Hughes managed to wedge his way into Las Vegas (Gemstone 3:7a). Note, however, that *Hustler's* version updates 3:7a with news of Roselli's death in 1976. Curiously, *Hustler* states that Roselli was "asphyxiated in 1976." Actually, Roselli's body was found strangled, stabbed and stuffed into a 55-gallon drum that was found floating on Biscayne Bay near Miami, Fla. The previous year, 1975, was when Roselli started to squawk openly to the Senate Intelligence Committee, which was gathering information to precede the Rockefeller Commission's revisiting of the JFK case. It was at that time that Roselli started yapping more and more about his role in the Castro assassination attempts, that he was recruited by former FBI agent and Howard Hughes strongman Robert Maheu. It could have been that Roselli was about to say a little too much about his role in the JFK assassination.

Another observation to be made about Gemstone 3:4d is the alleged location of Fratianno's sniper nest — on the second floor of the Dal-Tex Building, which housed the Dallas Police Department offices and an apparel shop owned by amateur film shooter Abraham Zapruder (interesting coincidence). A recently published book by Harrison Edward Livingstone, *Killing the*

---

9. *San Francisco Examiner*, Aug. 27, 1987, "Mobster-turned-informant leaving U.S.," by Seth Rosenfeld.

Truth, points out the excellent vantage point — illustrated by photos — that the second-floor stairs give a shooter looking straight down Elm Street at the Houston Street intersection along the route taken by the JFK motorcade.

Regarding the more graphic descriptions of Gemstone 3:4d, the infamous Zapruder film shows the right side of Kennedy's head being blown away from a shot or combination of shots; many of the film's analysts have trouble pinpointing exactly when Kennedy knew he was first struck by a bullet, when Gov. Connally was wounded and, finally, when the fatal head shot to JFK occurred. Some versions of the Zapruder film have frames missing. Because of these gaps, it could well have been that JFK was hit by a smaller-caliber bullet much earlier, as the limousine had made its turn from Houston to Elm. This would explain some of the Zapruder anomalies, and give credence to a Dal-Tex gunman.

Going back to fresh assassination news reports, right after the murder occurred and before doctors were coerced into changing their stories, can also confirm this version of the assassination. *The New York Times* reported on Dec. 18, 1963, that the bullet that struck the President in the right shoulder several inches below the collar line had *lodged in the body*. One doctor on the scene at Parkland Hospital stated that the wound in question was a few inches deep, and that he could stick his finger inside it and feel where the wound stopped; that the bullet had not penetrated all the way through Kennedy's body as the so-called "single-bullet theory" had proposed. If true, the bullet could not have also caused the wounds on Gov. Connally's body as asserted by the Warren Commission report.

The *Times* was not the only newspaper to report this development. The *Washington Post* also ran a story on May 29, 1966, stating that many newspapers, including the *Post*, ran accounts stating that the first bullet to enter the President's body "was found deep in his shoulder." The report was confirmed prior to publication by the FBI. In any event, such a version of the first bullet striking Kennedy in the upper back-right shoulder area correspond with Gemstone 3:4d.

The multiple, nearly simultaneous hits described in Gemstone 3:4b also have the Zapruder film to back that assessment. In frames 312 and 313, Kennedy's body appears to jerk slightly forward, as if struck by a projectile, before being blown backward violently with the head shot. This would indicate the distinct possibility of a double-hit.[10]

As for the whole concept of Gemstone 3:4d regarding a shooter on the grassy knoll, it has long been established a gunman was there, and that shots were fired. The nonsense being spilled forth in Gerald Posner's recently published JFK propaganda book, *Case Closed*, includes systematic attacks on witnesses who saw shots being fired from that direction, and the gunman himself. It is no secret that Posner is part of a well-calibrated attack on any and all conspiracy theories that was launched in late 1993 in conjunction with the 30th anniversary of the assassination. Dan Rather of CBS and PBS's *Frontline* also made sure that the Warren Report's assessment of Oswald was a "proven fact."

But that does not silence the testimony of at least 32 people who heard shots from the grassy knoll area, many of whom testified to that fact to the Warren Commission, which turned a deaf ear to it all. And it does not stop the 1988 analysis by photography experts Jack White and Gary Mack, who used computer-enhanced enlargements of a photograph taken of the assassination to prove that a gunman and backup man were on the grassy knoll.

Those enlargements appeared on the video program, *The Forces of Darkness*, part of a larger series, *The Men Who Killed Kennedy*, which contained mostly speculative material surrounding the most popular JFK conspiracy theories. However, in the

---

10. *A Note on the fatal Shot, As Depicted on the Zapruder Film*, by David S. Lifton.

case of this photo, a black-and-white Polaroid snapped by Mary Ann Moorman, speculation is hardly the operative word. The photo clearly shows a gunman, backup man, smoke from a muzzle blast — and, in the foreground, President Kennedy's head jerking back and his hair flying up as the bullet strikes the right side of his head.

Greatly strengthening this case was the discovery of a uniformed military man who was filming the President's motorcade from just in front and to the right of the gunman, who was situated behind him. This witness, Gordon Arnold, is shown in the photo enlargement shying away from the sound of a gunshot just behind him. Arnold, in a petrifying state of fear and near-panic, never disclosed he was in that area for years after the assassination, and only recently came forward. When White and Mack showed him the enhanced enlargements, Arnold broke out into tears and could barely hold back his pent-up emotions. It was a convincing display of sincerity.[11]

****

(Gemstone 3:4e) The third point of the triangulated [Kennedy] ambush was supplied by Eugene Brading, shooting from Kennedy's left, from a small pagoda (sic, pergola) at Dealey Plaza, across the street from the grassy knoll. (Brading missed [misses], because Roselli's and Fratianno's shots had just hit Kennedy from the right and rear, nearly simultaneously). Brading's shot hits the curb and ricocheted [ricochets] off. Brading was [is] photographed on the scene, stuffing his gun under his coat. he wore [wears] a big leather hat, its hatband marked with large, conspicuous X's. (Police had been instructed to let anyone with an X-marked hatband through the police lines; some may have been told they were Secret Service).

---

11. *The Forces of Darkness: The Men Who Killed Kennedy*, video documentary, 1988, Time-Life Co.

The bullets from missed shots were seen striking the pavement by several witnesses, confirming this observation in Gemstone 3:4e. One witness, known only as Mrs. Baker by the Warren Commission, stated a bullet struck the Elm Street pavement near a street sign. Royce Skelton, another witness, said he also saw a bullet strike the pavement at the left front of the presidential limousine. A bystander standing near the overpass where the motorcade was headed was struck by a bullet or bullet fragment that ricocheted off a curbstone.[12] These reports confirm misses, and by more bullets than could have been fired from the Texas School Book Depository alone.

As for Brading being photographed with his weapon, it must be pointed out that any Secret Service personnel in Dallas would have weapons at the ready in case they were needed. It would appear that at the time Brading was photographed, it was some seconds after the initial shots rang out, and that he was thought to be simply one of many Secret Service people going for his weapon during an obvious sign of big trouble. The *Skeleton Key* inserts a speculative note about people who saw Brading being told he was a Secret Service agent because of the X-marked hat.

****

(Gemstone 3:4f) After his shot, Brading ditched [ditches] his gun with his backup man and walked [walks] up the street [with his backup man] toward the Dal-Tex Building. Roger Craig, a deputy sheriff, rushed [rushes] up to Brading, assuming [assumes] he is Secret Service and tells him he has just seen a man come out of the Book Depository and jump into a **Rambler** station wagon. Brading was [is] uninterested. Instead, he [Brading] walks into the Dal-Tex Building to "make a phone call." There he was arrested [He is picked up for questioning] by

---

12. *Accessories to the Fact*, by Sylvia Meagher, ©1967, Bobbs-Merrill Co. Inc.

another deputy sheriff, showed [shows] his "Jim Braden" driver's license and was [is] quickly released — without being booked.

(3:4g) Oswald shot [shoots] Connally twice from the Texas School Book Depository. he split [splits] from [through] the front door. His backup man was [is] supposed to take the rifle out of the building (or so Oswald thought [thinks]); instead, he "hid" [hides] it behind some boxes, where it would be found later [where it will later be found].

(3:4h) Three men dressed as "tramps" picked [pick] up the spent shells from Dealey Plaza. <u>One of them was Howard Hunt.</u> [Then] They drifted [drift] over to am empty boxcar sitting on the railway spur behind the grassy-knoll area and waited [wait]. A Dallas police officer ordered [orders] two Dallas cops to "go over to the boxcar and pick up the tramps." The three tramps paraded [parade] around Dealey Plaza to the police department, in the Dal-Tex Building. They were held there until the alarm went out to pick up Oswald; then they were [are] released, without being booked. In all, 10 men were [are] arrested [questioned] immediately after the shooting. All were [are] released soon after. None were [are] booked. Not a word of [about] their existence is mentioned in the Warren [Commission] Report.

Possible complicity with some members of the Dallas police department (or of some men dressed as police officers who appeared to blend into the crowd) is indicated in Gemstone 3:4f, and has always been a source of lively speculation among assassination conspiracy researchers. At the very least, the Dallas police department's handling of the situation before, during and after the shots were fired — not to mention the incredible lack of security when Oswald was shot quite easily by the charging Jack Ruby some 36 hours later — was so disjointed and terribly managed, it almost seems as if some of this carelessness was planned. At least this segment of the *Key* tries to make sense out of the lack of substantial, documented arrests of people even remotely considered to be security risks immediately after the assassination. It also appears that suspicious characters were isolated and held for a brief period of time before simply being released.

This is highly irregular police procedure. Even if these people had nothing to do with the assassination, they might have at least been held a little longer for routine questioning; perhaps they could be material witnesses to the crime. These breakdowns are difficult to explain. Police are trained how to conduct themselves under such pressures. Their security screens are usually tighter than ever for something as big as a Presidential visit. This systemic failure of police to apprehend and hold possible suspects and key witnesses has never been explained. It is certainly brought out quite clearly in this segment of the *Key*.

Next, the entire episode concerning the rifle allegedly used by Oswald to fire the fatal shots (Gemstone 3:4g) has always been subject of heated debate. It is almost believable that Oswald was not the shooter on the sixth floor of the Texas School Book Depository; rather, he was the backup man and timer, as described in Gemstone 3:4c that describes the assassination team. One of the fascinating aspects of the entire Oswald story is that he was hilariously miscast as a crack shot and diehard communist when he was neither. He might have been a former United States Marine, but he was also a below-average shot with a rifle. Sure, he was carrying an oblong package to work the day of the assassination, but that would be the case even if he were simply the weapons handler on the team.

But the more likely scenario would be for the Oswald backup to be the crucial part of a set-up, if there was one. The backup man and timer would be in a unique position to leave evidence conveniently located for police to find later. The shooter's job is simply to aim, pull the trigger, hand the weapon over to someone else, and look casual while calmly leaving the scene. This scenario was also described to White and Mack in *The Forces of Darkness*, with a deaf-mute providing corroborating testimony regarding the day of the assassination. This deaf-mute confirmed the existence of a grassy-knoll shooter and his backup man.[13]

****

(**Gemstone 3:4i**) Regarding Lee Harvey Oswald: Officer [J.D.] Tippit is dispatched in his police <u>radio</u> car to the Oak Cliff section, where Oswald had [has] rented a room. Tippit may have met Oswald on the street. he may have been supposed to kill Oswald, but something went [goes] wrong. Tippit was shot by two men, using two revolvers [Tippit is shot by two men armed with revolvers]. <u>The "witness," Domingo Benavides, who used Tippit's police car radio to report "we've had a shooting here," may have been one of the men who shot him.</u> [A witness, Domingo Benavides, uses Tippit's police-car radio to report, "We've had a shooting here."] (A "Domingo Benevides" [also] appears in connection with the Martin Luther King shooting [shooting of Dr. Martin Luther King] <u>also.</u>

The shooting of police officer J.D. Tippit and its circumstances provide the most firm evidence yet of a conspiracy to assassinate President Kennedy. From the first day the Warren Commission convened to the actual issuance of the Warren Report, everything associated with this incident points to outright deception on the part of the Dallas police, fraudulent "evidence" gathered at the scene, and a reluctance by the Commission of dealing with the actual killers of Tippit, since it can be shown that Oswald is a highly unlikely suspect.

And a closer look at the Tippit incident will prove beyond a doubt that Gemstone 3:4i is a basically accurate rendition of what transpired, based upon an investigation of available evidence, and the outright fabrications included in the Warren Report regarding this killing. Just as the incident at Chappa-

---

13. *The Forces of Darkness: The Men Who Killed Kennedy*, video documentary, 1988, Time-Life Co.

quiddick seriously implicated Ted Kennedy and threatened to blow the Gemstone scenario wide open in 1969, the Tippit incident threatened to blow open the entire JFK setup — and remains a spear in the side of those people who still choose to believe there was no widespread conspiracy.

First, Gemstone 3:4i states that Tippit was *dispatched* to the Oak Cliff area of suburban Dallas, and did not wander over there on his own volition. This is true, and the Dallas police department tried to cover it up. The Commission received three different transcripts of the Dallas police radio log. The first version was an edited one prepared by the Dallas police on Dec. 3, 1963 (Sawyer exhibits "A" and "B"). This version excludes a 12:45 p.m. transmission instructing Tippit to move into the Oak Cliff area (Tippit was shot between 1 p.m. and 1:15 p.m. on Nov. 22, soon after JFK was assassinated). The nature of this transmission, and at least three others directed at Tippit from the dispatcher between 12:45 and 1:08 p.m., is extraordinary, because the President had just been shot, and most of the dispatch language was directing police officers to congregate in the area of the Texas School Book Depository.

But as late as April of 1964, the Warren Commission sought a reason for Tippit's location at the time he was shot. Officers Sgt. Calvin Bud Owens, Lt. Rio S. Pierce and Sgt. James A. Putnam all speculated to the Commission that Tippit had started in the direction of the downtown area from his normal beat, and that took him to the general area where he was shot. Not one of these men offered the true explanation that he was ordered there by a dispatcher request.

Not satisfied with this explanation, the Commission requested and received a verbatim radio log transcript which included the 12:45 request for officer No. 78 (Tippit) to move into central Oak Cliff. This was the first disclosure of the dispatcher's instruction, and the question was raised as to why it was not included in the first edited transcript in December. Dallas Police Chief Jesse Curry was asked that question by the

Commission during testimony April 22, 1964:

"...His (Curry's) reply was confused and incoherent. Curry, one of the key officials responsible for the President's safety in Dallas, was distraught and seemed merely to improvise his answers — at one point seeming to suggest that *Tippit had moved out of his assigned district to search for his own murderer.*" [14]

Curry also could not justify leaving out the 12:45 command to Tippit in the first version of the radio log presented to the Commission. It should be emphasized that the police department prepared its own versions of the logs, and officers were appointed to listen to the dispatcher tapes and provide the written transcriptions. At all times was the material under the control of the Dallas police. Only when the Commission pressed for a verbatim transcript did this information come forth.

Another question looms, if the 12:45 directive is authentic: Why was Tippit ordered to Oak Cliff? The area was quiet at the time; no disturbance was evident. At the same time, the President has just been shot, and the entire city — especially law enforcement personnel — was being mobilized to respond to the assassination, primarily at the Texas School Book Depository and Parkland Hospital. Why would the dispatcher bother to send an officer into this area at this particular time? That has never been suitably explained. And there was one more incredible "coincidence:" Lee Harvey Oswald lived in a furnished room in *central Oak Cliff.*

And although Oswald would soon become a suspect in the assassination, nobody was a firm suspect at 12:45 p.m. on Nov. 22, 1963. Oswald's absence from the Texas School Book Depository had not yet been noticed, and his Oak Cliff address was known only to a few close friends.

Soon after Tippit was asked to report to central Oak Cliff, at 12:54 p.m., the dispatcher reportedly told him to *"be at large for*

---

14. *Accessories After the Fact,* by Sylvia Meagher, ©1967, Bobbs-Merrill Co.

any emergency that comes in." Could it have been that Dallas police had prior knowledge that Oswald would be a shooter in the JFK assassination, and that he would probably head home soon after the shots rang out in Dealey Plaza? Why would the dispatcher give Tippit this warning if trouble was not expected?

Gemstone 3:4i reports Tippit "may have been supposed to kill Oswald." It certainly looks like Tippit was out looking for a particular individual, and may have found him, but ran into resistance and ended up losing his life — especially if Oswald suddenly realized that, having fired the shots at the presidential motorcade, he would now be "expendable."

At 1 p.m., the dispatcher tried again to raise Tippit, but there was no response. It was at that exact time that Earlene Roberts, a housekeeper at the rooming house where Oswald was a tenant, spotted a police cruiser pulling up to the house, stopping, blowing its horn, then slowly driving away. Mrs. Roberts reporter she thought two police officers were in the car; at least, a police officer and one other occupant. She sketchily recalled two numerals on the car as "1" and "0." The car Tippit drove was No. 10. Again, this is a firm indication that Tippit was looking for a specific person, Lee Harvey Oswald, despite the fact that Oswald had not yet been announced as a suspect in the JFK assassination.

Eight minutes later, at 1:08, Tippit twice signaled the police dispatcher, but received no response. It was right about this time that the officer became involved in the altercation that led to his being shot. Why did he not receive a response from the dispatcher at this time?

The next assertion by Gemstone 3:4i is that two men, using two revolvers, actually shot Tippit. It is curious that the *Hustler* version rewrites the phrase to read simply "two men armed with revolvers," which makes it appear the guns were the same type. The original Gemstone 3:4i implies that the guns were two different types.

Witnesses who were in that area of central Oak Cliff during

the shooting reported different versions of the sequence — and different people fleeing the scene, which is a clear indication that Gemstone 3:4i is correct on this matter. The major witness to the shooting and aftermath was Mrs. Helen Markham, who claims to have seen how the meeting between Tippit "a pedestrian," which she insists was Oswald, began:

"The man stopped...I saw the man come over to the car very slow, leaned and put his arms out just like this, he leaned over this window and looked in this window...The window was down...Well, I didn't think nothing about it; you know, the police are nice and friendly and I thought (this was) friendly conversation. Well, I looked, and there was cars coming, so I had to wait...This man, like I told you, put his arms up, leaned over, he — just a minute, and he drew back and he stepped back about two steps...The policeman calmly opened the door, very slowly, wasn't angry or nothing, he calmly crawled out of his car, and I still just thought (it was) a friendly conversation."[15]

Markham's testimony indicates that neither the pedestrian nor Tippit exhibited signs of alarm, tension or hostility, and yet this was supposedly seconds before a violent shooting. The pedestrian also did not look overly tired from his "escape" from Dealey Plaza. Another unusual factor was that Tippit left his vehicle; had he located a suspect in the JFK assassination, which happened only 45 or so minutes before, he would have requested assistance before attempting an arrest on his own. It could only be that officer Tippit was up to something else, something different, at that time.

Did two gunmen (other than Oswald) really execute Tippit? That also seems likely due to eyewitness accounts. The major stumbling block with blaming Oswald alone for that shooting is the varied descriptions given to an armed man fleeing the scene of the killing:

---

15. Warren Commission testimony, 3H 307.

- The aforementioned Mrs. Markham gave this description of the killer on the afternoon of the Tippit murder: "White male, about 18, black hair, red complexion, and dark trousers."
- R.W. Walker, a Dallas police officer on the scene soon afterward, reported this description of the killer: "...He's a white male, about 30, 5 feet, 8 inches, black hair, slender, wearing a white jacket and dark slacks."
- Mrs. Barbara Jeanette Davis gave a description to an officer J.M. Poe of the Dallas police, indicating the killer wore a "dark coat."
- H.W. Summers, another Dallas police officer, reports this description from the scene between 1:33 and 1:40 p.m.: "I got an eyeball witness to the getaway man...He is a white male, 27, 5 feet, 11 inches, 165, black wavy hair, fair complected, wearing light gray Eisenhower-type jacket, dark trousers and a white shirt...and was apparently armed with a .32, dark finish, automatic pistol which he had in his right hand."
- Domingo Benavides (more on him later), the man named in Gemstone 3:4i as the one using the police radio to call in the actual shooting, said the killer wore a "light beige zipper-type jacket."
- William Scoggins, reportedly saw a man who looked like Oswald running toward him, carrying a gun, right after the shooting. However, when shown a gray zipper jacket found near the area by police, said that the jacket worn by the man he saw running was "a little darker."
- Ted Calloway said the man he saw wore "a light tannish gray windbreaker jacket," but when he was shown the gray jacket found by police in the area, he said it was the same type of jacket but "actually, I thought there was a little more tan to it."

The common thread running through all these comments is that people in the area of the Tippit shooting probably saw different people fleeing the scene. It could well have been the Oswald was there, but that he did not actually fire the gun that killed Tippit. As we will see in the examination of the bullets and shell casings on the scene — and the type revolver Oswald had in his possession when he was finally arrested a little later — also favor the multiple-gunmen scenario regarding Tippet.

But what of Domingo Benavides, mentioned in Gemstone 3:4i? This "truck driver" was also mentioned prominently by investigators, and the Warren Commission as well. He was the closest to the actual shooting, an estimated 15 to 25 feet. Yet, Benavides *did not identify Oswald at that time.* And he did not identify Oswald when shown a photograph of him months later during his testimony to the Commission. If the witness closest to the shooting could not identify Oswald, then who could? Witness William Scoggins was also close to the scene, yet he did not see the actual shooting because a tree obscured the actual gunfire.

The verbatim radio log also confirms that, at 1:16 p.m., "a citizen" broke in on the police radio to report the shooting of a policeman at 404 East 10th Street. This confirms Gemstone 3:4i, and Benavides would be the likely "citizen," being so close to the scene, although the Commission does not identify this "citizen." If this is not amazing enough, the dispatcher's immediate reaction was to call No. 78, Tippit, again — *before* there was any reason whatsoever to link Tippit with the slain officer.

What would motivate Benavides to stick around, and even go so far as to warn police on heir own radio? *If there were a conspiracy, it would be prudent of all co-conspirators to get as many Dallas police on Oswald's tail, as soon as possible, to get not only a JFK patsy in hand, but someone who could also take the blame for the Tippit killing.* It was a matter of covering all tracks and keeping a lid on the essence of any conspiracy. Despite what might have gone wrong on the part of Tippit's role, the conspirators were largely successful in isolating Oswald.

Finally, the forensics evidence indicates more than one

weapon could have been involved. The Warren Report says that six live cartridges were found in Oswald's .38-caliber handgun — three Western .38 Specials and three Remington-Peters .38 Specials. Five live cartridges were found in his pocket, all Western .38s. Four expanded cartridge casings were found near the Tippit scene — two Western .38s and 2 Remington-Peters .38s. Four bullets were recovered from Tippit's body — three Western-Winchesters and one Remington-Peters. There is a discrepancy between the spent casings found at the scene — two Westerns and two Remington-Peters — and those found in Tippit's body — three Westerns and one Remington-Peters. But that is only the beginning of this glaring problem.

Two different brands of shells were found in Oswald's gun and at the scene of the shooting. However, none of these shells were found in Oswald's room. He had to purchase a box of each type of ammunition some time before the day of the assassination, but no record of such a purchase has been found. The lack of leftover ammunition also is cause for consternation.

There is an answer, however. The ammunition was planted on Oswald by the Dallas police, and similar shells inserted into his gun. Two different gunmen using two different revolvers — and, of course, different ammunition — killed Tippit before fleeing the scene.

Did Oswald know Tippit beforehand? According to some witnesses, including a waitress named Mary Dowling, who spotted Oswald at her restaurant, Dobbs House. On that day, 10 a.m. Wednesday, Nov. 10, Dallas police officer J.D. Tippit was also in the restaurant. When Oswald bawled out Dowling for giving him a wrong order of cooked eggs, Tippit "shot a glance at Oswald." [16] This information was given to the FBI in December of 1963, but the FBI failed to forward it on to the Warren Commission. Such an incident might have been crucial to the

---

16. *Op. cit.,* Meagher.

entire Tippit investigation.

(Gemstone 3:4j) Oswald went [goes] to the movies. A "shoe store manager" told [tells] the theatre [theater] cashier that a suspicious-looking man had sneaked in without paying. Fifteen assorted cops and FBI [Sixteen police] charged [charge] out to the movie theatre [Texas Theater] to look for the guy who had [who's] sneaked in.

(3:4k) Oswald had [been given] a pistol that wouldn't [doesn't] fire. It may have been anticipated [Others anticipated] that the police would [will] shoot the "cop killer" for "resisting arrest." But since that doesn't happen, the Dallas police brought Oswald out for small-time Mafia Jack Ruby to kill two days later [small-time Mafioso Jack Ruby kills Oswald two days later].

Notice that *Hustler* leaves off any reference to the FBI in Gemstone 3:4j, saying the 16 police took part in the final assault on the Texas Theater, not "15 assorted cops and FBI." This is interesting, because the FBI was not supposed to be involved in post-assassination activity until the JFK autopsy, and they were on top of that from the start.

(Gemstone 3:5) Brading stayed at the Teamster-Mafia-Hoffa-financed "Cabana Motel" in Dallas. Ruby had gone to the Cabana the night before the murder, says the Warren Report.

(3:6a) The rest, as they say, is history. Onassis was [is] so confident of his control over police, media, FBI, CIA, Secret Service and the U.S. judicial system that he had [has] JFK murdered before the eyes of the nation — then systematically bought [buys] off, killed [kills] off, or frightened [frightens] off all witnesses, and had [has] the evidence destroyed; then put a 75-year seal of secrecy over the entire matter.

Once again, the *Hustler* version saw fit to censor yet another crucial circumstantial fact that one of the named assassins was linked beforehand to Jack Ruby, the nightclub owner who shot Oswald. *Hustler* also edited the reference about Ruby's shooting of Oswald to exonerate the Dallas police, although it has been clear from the start that security surrounding Oswald was lax from the very beginning of his arrest and interrogation.

Hustler then decided to downplay the 75-year period the Warren Commission placed on document releases concerning the JFK assassination — a lid that has recently been pried open by insistent assassination researchers. The autopsy photos obtained by Robert Groden, for example, were part and parcel of that suppression order, but they surfaced, and Oliver Stone made the controversial film *JFK* as a result. More documents are forthcoming.

In the meantime, the JFK assassination aftermath, which led directly to the assassination of brother Robert Kennedy, provides a vivid paper trail that the *Skeleton Key* relentlessly follows. We will follow that trail after we take a closer look at Gemstone Files author Bruce Roberts.

PHOTOGRAPHS

. . . .

*T*he following photographs are a composite collection from the author's own files and submissions from sources who have agreed to supply the photographs on the condition of anonymity.

We have independently confirmed that these photographs are genuine, and that they were taken in the year stated.

The photos were selected based upon their ability to better illustrate the Gemstone thesis.

Some may be familiar and have been published over a wide area. Others, however, are rare and, if published at all, were available only to a limited viewing audience at the time they were taken and processed.

— *GAC*

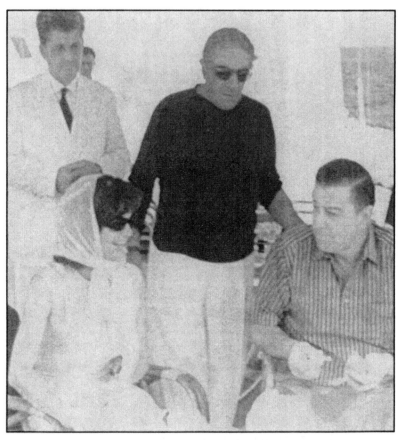

This is a photo of Jacqueline Kennedy (left), Aristotle Onassis (center) and Franklin Roosevelt Jr. (right) aboard Onassis' yacht, the *Christina*. The waiter at left is unidentified, but some years later these servants would go public with much of what went on aboard the yacht. The caption is misleading, saying that the photo was taken during a Mediterranean cruise "a couple of years ago" from its 1968 release. In reality, this photo was taken in October of 1963, only weeks before President John F. Kennedy was assassinated. Roosevelt Jr. is prominently mentioned as an Onassis business associate in the early portion of the *Skeleton Key to the Gemstone Files*. This also confirms that Jacqueline Kennedy was with Onassis in November of 1963, just prior to the assassination. Some *Christina* staff people confirm that the first lady and Onassis were romantically tied prior to the assassination. In fact, multiple sources confirm the *Key's* account of Onassis being the first to console Jackie upon her return to Washington, D.C. on Air Force One.

Onassis (left) and his attorney Edward J. Ross pose before a
fourth day of testimony before the House Merchant Marine
Subcommittee in June of 1958. Onassis was in continual hot
water with the United States government because of alleged
illegal U.S. ship purchases. Such friction with the U.S. invariably
led to differences with Joseph Kennedy's sons, John and Robert.

Onassis (left) and shipping rival Stavros Niarchos. Niarchos is charged in the *Key* with poisoning his wife Tina — Onassis' former spouse — to death, and beating to death his first wife, Eugenie.

Elliott Roosevelt (right), shown here testifying before a Senate subcommittee in August of 1947, is accused of criminal activity in the *Skeleton Key.* He was also accused in real life; at left is John Meyer, an attorney for Howard Hughes who was assisting Roosevelt in his defense on charges that the son of President Roosevelt allowed Hughes, through Meyer, to pay for hotel bills related to wild parties by Elliott Roosevelt and others. Elliott was also implicated in a murder of a Bahamas politician, and accused of seamy deals with the Soviet Union regarding acquisition of Fokker airplanes from Germany.

Eccentric billionaire Howard Hughes in a 1951 file photo. Hughes was never photographed after this. The *Skeleton Key* states that he was kidnapped and switched in 1957.

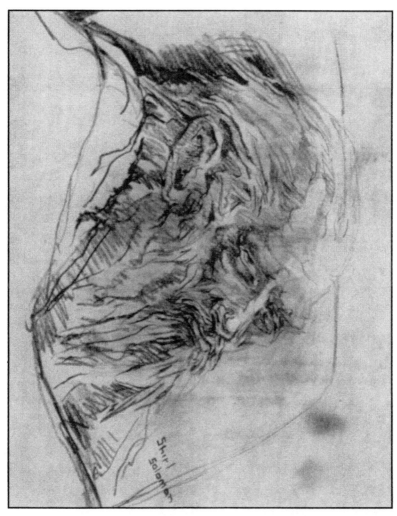

Billionaire Howard Hughes was sketched while aboard an airplane in April of 1976 just before he reportedly died. However, the *Key* states that this was actually a double for the real Hughes, who died in 1971 of a drug overdose on Onassis' Greek island of Skorpios.

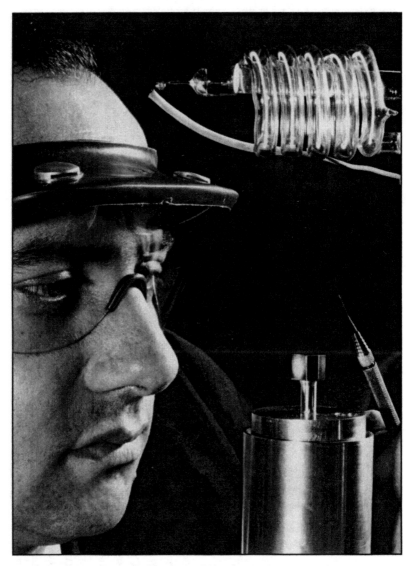

Dr. Theodore H. Maiman of Hughes Aircraft Co. works with a cube of synthetic ruby crystal during the development of the laser in 1960. Maiman told us he does not recall the source of rubies that finally worked in the experiment. Bruce Roberts, author of the Gemstone Files, claims his rubies were stolen and used for the experiment (Chapter 8).

This photograph shows a man named Bruce Roberts, an expert in synthetic jewel making,and actress Carmen Miranda, in 1952. Roberts, who died in 1976 at the age of 56, would have been in his 30s in this photo. Indications are this is the same Bruce Roberts who compiled the Gemstone files, with the involvement with Hollywood stars and synthetic gemstones a clear connection. Furthermore, this is right before the time that Roberts submitted synthetic rubies of high enough quality to Southern California-based Hughes Corp. for laser research, according to the *Skeleton Key.*

Howard Hughes is pictured at left in a 1947 file photo. The photo at right is allegedly of an elder Hughes in March of 1972 in Vancouver, British Columbia. However, the photo at right is actually of L. Wayne Rector, a Hughes double, according to the *Skeleton Key*. The giveaway is the positioning and shape of the ear in each photo. Rector was killed in London soon thereafter, in January of 1973, according to the *Key*. However, if that was the case, then the person who died in 1976 had to be yet another impostor.

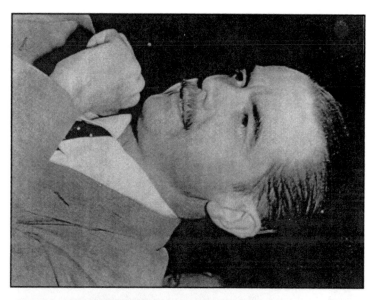

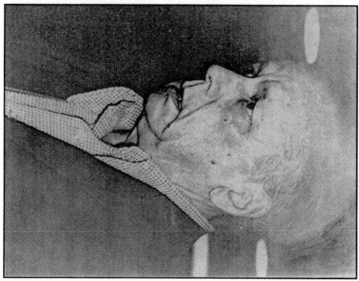

This photo sequence shows Dallas police officer Bobby W. Hargis (arrow), who was showered with the blood of President Kennedy at the moment of the assassination on Nov. 22, 1963. Hargis is shown in the bottom photo actually scaling the grassy knoll, from where he thought shots came. The photo surfaced in 1967 as part of a collection by assassination researcher Dr. Josiah Thompson.

This photo shows President Kennedy's limousine at left foreground and shows Kennedy's head reacting to the impact of a projectile. The arrow points to what appears to be a puff of smoke behind the fence atop the grassy knoll. Photo experts Jack White and Gary Mack independently computer-enhanced that portion of the Polaroid photo taken by Mary Ann Moorman and confirmed that a gunman wearing a uniform and an accomplice wearing a hardhat are positioned behind that puff of smoke. Another bystander is located to the left of the puff of smoke; he was a serviceman filming the motorcade at the time of the assassination and has since confirmed that he saw two men in that area, one with a gun and the other a "construction worker." The *Skeleton Key* states that expert Mafia gunman John Roselli was the grassy-knoll shooter; other theorists say it was a French assassin.

This is a photo of the Texas School Book Depository building from which Lee Harvey Oswald allegedly shot President Kennedy. The angle, however, was much too steep for the shooting to have taken place as the Warren Commission describes; instead, Oswald was aiming for and shot Gov. John Connally, according to the *Skeleton Key* and a 1980 account by James Reston Jr., who showed that Oswald had a long-standing grudge against the governor.

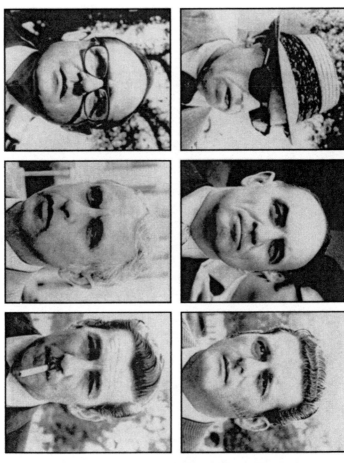

The Watergate conspirators. The *Skeleton Key* accurately traces their collective activities from the time of the Bay of Pigs and attempts to assassinate Fidel Castro to Watergate. They include, from left, (top row) E. Howard Hunt, James W. McCord Jr., Frank Sturgis, (bottom row) Bernard Barker, Eugenio Martinez and Virgilio Gonzales.

G. Gordon Liddy, a Watergate conspirator and the man credited with first coining the term "Gemstone" in reference to
political espionage. It is not known whether Liddy thought of
the term himself, referring to his own "Gemstone" plan that
featured Watergate as a key element, or if he borrowed the term
from Bruce Roberts' "Gemstone" files.

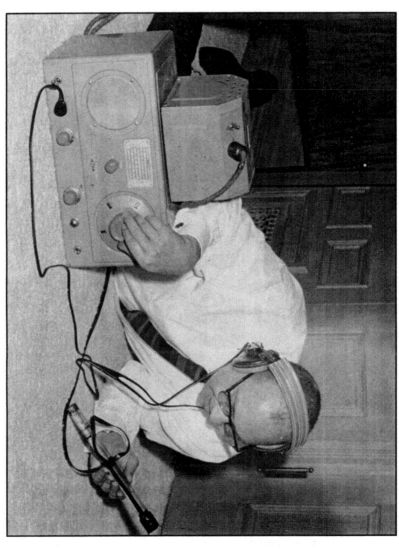

Hal Lipset, professional private investigator and alleged spy for *Washington Post* publisher Katharine Meyer Graham. The *Key* alleges that information acquired through Lipset's high-tech spying helped bag the Watergate burglars, but that he later switched allegiances to President Nixon's aide, John Dean III, and fed Nixon much of the "new information" used in White House press briefings pertaining to Watergate.

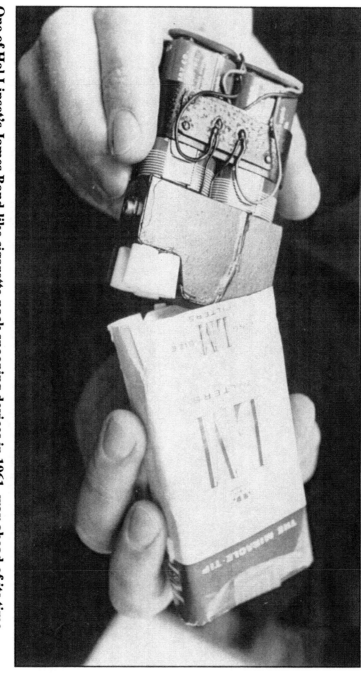

One of Hal Lipset's James Bond-like cigarette-pack snooping devices in 1961, way ahead of its time. Lipset was often steps ahead of even the CIA and FBI in his investigating techniques and equipment.

Hal Lipset (center) flanked by Sen. Thomas Hennings (right), D-Mo., and Sen. Alex Wiley (left), R-Wis. during a Senate Constitutional Rights Subcommittee meeting in December of 1959. Lipset was to become involved with the Watergate investigation in 1973, but backed out for "personal reasons."

Washington Post publisher Katharine Meyer Graham (right) and *Post* managing editor Ben Bradlee during the Watergate days.

Site of the old Drift Inn bar in San Francisco, where the *Skeleton Key* alleges that Watergate conspirators met prior to their work at the Democratic National Headquarters. The bar has since been converted into a Vietnamese restaurant and lounge.

CHAPTER 8

· · · · · · · · · · ·

Roberts, Rubies and Risky Business

Few researchers who have stumbled across the *Skeleton Key to the Gemstone Files* have bothered to look into the background of Bruce Roberts, around which the entire Gemstone scenario revolves. He is the declared author of the thesis, and the chilling candor with which the *Key* is written is perhaps reflective of the Gemstone papers themselves — papers which are perhaps lost forever, with only the *Key* surviving.

References to Roberts and his personal background are included in the *Key*, however, despite efforts to edit them from the *Hustler* version. These references clearly indicate that Bruce Roberts was in a position to learn the inside story behind the Onassis-Kennedy connections just after World War I and that he dutifully monitored the unfolding conflicts through the ensuing years until his death in 1976. Every reference made to Roberts in the *Key*, we have discovered, is corroborated by independent means — despite the U.S. government's efforts to cover up details of his life. And virtually every reference made by Roberts concerning his and his family's involvement in the Gemstone scenario has been confirmed by outside sources, we have learned. Indeed, we have little reason to believe that Roberts fabricated any of the information referred to in the *Key*. He might have been mistaken with a few facts, but honestly believed in what he was writing.

That is why we are including this segment here — to pull

together the Roberts references, add some background on him, and circumvent efforts to discredit his thesis on the basis that he was either insane or a crackpot. First, Roberts is identified as the Gemstone author in the first sentence of the *Key*. In the *Hustler* version, Roberts is given the by-line, but a lengthy disclaimer — before the edited *Key* text is presented — implies that Roberts was a nut case and that his thesis probably has no merit. That language clearly places the magazine in the role of messenger, not disciple, of the Roberts gospel, and clearly lets publisher Larry Flynt off the hook. With Flynt having been target of a brutal assassination attempt only a year prior to the 1979 publication of the *Key* — and been paralyzed as a result — it was easy to see why *Hustler* softened its position.

Hustler also declares that Roberts was dead at the time of publication of the *Key*, but claims not to have knowledge of how he died. Roberts' residence is also described as being in the Sunset District of San Francisco, without mentioning any of the early connections he and his family had in relationship to Onassis, Kennedy, the drug trade and U.S. intelligence community. Finally, most of the other references to Roberts and his background in crystallography and knowledge of foreign espionage operations are simply stricken from the *Hustler* version. Without this background, the only widespread published version of the *Skeleton Key to the Gemstone Files* is rendered confusing and worthless.

That will be examined in detail now, starting with the first mention of Roberts' background which is left out of the *Hustler* version:

(Gemstone 1:3) <u>Roberts, studying journalism at the University of Wisconsin, learned these things via personal contacts. His special interest was in crystallography — and the creation of synthetic rubies, the original Gemstone experiment.</u>

Was this true? Records at the University of Wisconsin indicate that Roberts did study at the Madison campus in the 1930s. He was enrolled in a Bachelor of Arts-track curriculum in 1936, although the university would not divulge the substance of his studies nor his transcript due to confidentiality policies. Roberts also studied in a BA track in 1938 — after apparently skipping the 1937 academic year — and was enrolled concurrently with his brother, Dayle L. Roberts, who was in a pre-med schedule. Roberts also was added as a late registrant in 1939. According to university records, Roberts never received a degree.

Perhaps the onset of World War II had something to do with that. In his obituary, published on Aug. 1, 1976, in the *San Francisco Examiner*, Roberts was mentioned as a World War II veteran, but the branch — Army, Air Force, Navy or Marines — was not specified. We feel it was the Navy, and that Roberts had occasion to mingle with the U.S. military intelligence community during the war. The branch in which Roberts served is obscured by the government's ability to censor or restrict access to records of military personnel who served within the last 75 years — a policy invoked for reasons of "national security."

This leads to the second reference to Roberts, which is also duly edited out of the *Hustler* rendition:

(Gemstone 2:7) Roberts brings his synthetic rubies — the original "Gemstones" — to Hughes Aircraft in Los Angeles. They steal his rubies, the basis for laser-beam research, laser bombs, etc., because of the optical quality of the rubies. One of eleven possible sources for one of the ingredients involved in the Gemstone experiment was the Golden Triangle area. Roberts was married to the daughter of the former French consul in Indochina. In that region, Onassis' involvement in the Golden Triangle dope trade was no secret. Roberts' investigation revealed the Onassis-Hughes connection, kidnap and switch.

(2:8) "Gemstones" — synthetic rubies and sapphires with accompanying "histories," otherwise known as Gemstone papers — were sold or given away to foreign consular officials in return for information. A worldwide information network was gradually developed, a trade of the intelligence activities of many countries. This intelligence network is the source for much of the information in the Gemstone files.

The above reference is potentially revealing. First, it refers to a marriage between Roberts and a foreign national whose father had connections with Indochina and the drug trade which has long infested that part of the world. The second major component, finally, is the mentioning of Roberts' making of rubies, some of sufficient quality to be used in laser research — the root inspiration behind the "Gemstone" nomenclature used in the *Key* and the original Gemstone writings. It is no surprise it was cautiously left out of the *Hustler* version.

Third, in Gemstone 2:8, the nature of Roberts' source development is revealed. Without this passage, most of the *Key* makes little sense. Without reference to sources, it is easy to discredit research efforts of any journalist. Again, it was left out of the *Hustler* version — sufficiently puzzling readers and leaving the remaining statements to stand with little support.

But did Roberts actually make rubies? Did he submit them to Hughes Corp., and were they used in laser-beam research? Why not ask the inventor of the laser himself, Dr. Theodore H. Maiman?

We did. In a rare interview by telephone on Feb. 2, 1990, Dr. Maiman revealed the following astonishing revelations:

- Howard Hughes and the Hughes Corp. in general *did not support the laser research program*, and Maiman was forced to pursuing the research *on his own*. Maiman remains embittered that Hughes would *still take credit* for the revolutionary invention.
- Maiman invented the laser during a nine-month break between government contracts. Funding came directly from the Hughes Corp.'s general research funds, an expenditure frowned upon by Hughes executives.

- Maiman bought all rubies for his experiments on his own, from independent sources. Primary source for rubies had always been reported as the Lindy Division of Union Carbide. Maiman says that although he used Lindy rubies, he also used some from other sources. Although vague on the exact source for the rubies that eventually worked, Maiman thought it was Griener, a small-scale company, but he is not sure. Right about that time, and all through the 1950s, a man named Bruce Roberts was making synthetic jewels for movie stars —jewels so real-looking and of such high quality, including rubies, that his talents were highly sought after all around Hollywood. Maiman implied that Roberts could well have been one of the independent contractors supplying rubies for the laser experiments.

Maiman outlines the laser scenario in his own words:

"...The (ruby-making) process is tricky. You have to heat the material to 2,300 degrees Centigrade, roughly 4,000 degrees... It's tricky to grow the crystals just right.

"...Hughes did not support the program. In fact, Hughes was *upset that I was working on it.* (emphasis ours). Myself and my masters candidate assistant, Irnee D'Haenens. Just us, no one else, from Hughes or anywhere else. Yet, they (Hughes) take credit for it.

"...You see, Hughes' interests were directed toward defense — military electronics, missile electronics... The idea of making a laser had never been done before, and it was a long-shot project. Plus, what would you do with it?

"...About funding, almost all work was done by Hughes was from government contracts. I happened to be between government contracts at the time. I had just gotten off a project for the U.S. Signal Corps and other things... At that time, I had 9-12 months to work on this (laser). I was not on contract.

"...Budget for the laser came from Hughes' General research Funds. They were very touchy about that because it was their own money, not the government's. See, they like to use government money, not their own... It was unfortunate that I was working on a project they didn't care about.

"...*The laser project was actually bootlegged* (emphasis ours).

"...By the way, we also worked with one other outfit for rubies, to get back to your question about the source for our rubies. The name was Griener...yes, I think that's it. If there ever was a person named Roberts, he would have worked for either Griener or Lindy... *But they did supply some synthetic crystals, not just rubies, but others as well. I think they made them for actresses...*(emphasis ours)

"Hughes didn't even file for a patent. That's the whole other story. The cost was ridiculously low for Hughes. Counting my salary, my assistant's, materials, everything, it came to $50,000. And it led to a huge discovery. They didn't file for a patent because they thought it wasn't any big deal."[1]

The presence of Roberts in Southern California during the 1950s is confirmed by a mysterious photograph that appeared in the newspaper supplement *American Weekly* on Oct. 12, 1952. A man named Bruce Roberts is shown adorning the neck of actress Carmen Miranda with synthetic jewels. It is a photo feature, with the following headline and copy block:

BUT...WOULD YOU WEAR THEM?
A designer creates some costume jewelry that might pass for jeweled costumes

"Bruce Roberts, former actor turned jewelry designer, can be thankful that Carmen Miranda got tired of her famous basket-of-fruit hat and sought something new. Her quest resulted in a new Miranda 'look' and a market for Roberts in costume

---

1. Telephone interview with Dr. Theodore H. Maiman, 1990, Gerald A. Carroll.

jewelry that is more costume than jewelry.

"When Carmen approached Roberts and outlined her dilemma, he realized one thing: Any accoutrements would have to
withstand her lively antics. So he strung his semi-precious
stones — synthetic pearls, *rubies* (emphasis ours), sapphires,
topazes on nylon parachute thread guaranteed to hold up under
360 pounds of weight."[2]

No further details were available in this account, but it was
enough to conclude that this could well have been the same Bruce
Roberts talked about in Gemstone 2:7-8. Not only does the
occupation and name fit the circumstances — and location, Southern
California — but so does the age: Roberts was born on Oct. 27,
1919, and he would have been 33 years old in 1952. The photo,
included in this book, looks like a man in his early to mid-30s.

If indeed this was the Bruce Roberts referred to in Gemstone
2:7-8, it would be quite easy to see how he would know so much
about the inner workings of the Hughes Corp., and how he
might have known about the disappearance of Howard Hughes
in 1957. It would go far in explaining how he would know about
the entire Hughes laser situation; in fact, the Carl Byoir public
relations firm wrote the promotional book on the laser — the
same group that allegedly provided L. Wayne Rector, the Hughes
double referred to in Gemstone 1:9. Carl Byoir himself died
mysteriously in 1957, during the period in which Hughes himself was allegedly kidnapped and switched.

The next mention of Roberts is in Gemstone 5:0, again
omitted from the *Hustler* version and in many other renditions
of the text. At least one compelling reason for the omission
looms clear:

(Gemstone 5:0a) <u>Sept. 16, 1968: Hit-and-run accident on
Roberts' car, parked in front of the Soviet consulate in San</u>

---

2. *American Weekly,* Oct. 12, 1952.

Francisco (the Soviets routinely take pictures of everything that goes on in front of the consulate). Their photos showed the license plate of the hit-and-run car: UKT-264, on a blue Cadillac belonging to Mia Angela Alioto, Joe's daughter, being driven by Tom Alioto, Joe's son, whose driver's license, and the car's license, were both fraudulent. To cover up the hit-and-run circumstances, the Presidio quickly staged a few more hit-and-runs on the same corner — all duly filmed by the Soviets. Kathryn Hollister, the Alioto family nurse, was "persuaded" to take the rap for the hit-and-run. Roberts threatened to spill the whole story in court with photos.

(5:0b) Next evening, Brading and Fratianno showed up in the Black Magic Bar — Brading wearing his X-marked hat from Dallas — to see whether Roberts recognized it, how much he knew, etc. A military policeman from the Presidio piped up from the end of the bar: "I heard they let everyone with an X-marked hatband through the police lines in Dallas."

(5:0c) Cover-up support for Alioto in the hit-and-run was complete.

(5:1) Mafia Joe Alioto had Presidential ambitions, shored up by his participation in the Dallas payoff. Everyone who helped kill JFK got a piece of the U.S. pie. But J. Edgar Hoover, FBI head, blew his cover by releasing some of the raw FBI files on Alioto at the Democratic National Convention. Joe was out of the running for V.P., and Hubert H. Humphrey had to settle for Edmund Muskie. Humphrey planned to come to S.F. for a final pre-election rally, sparked by Joe Alioto; Roberts threatened to blow the hit-and-run story plus its Mafia ramifications wide open if Humphrey came to S.F. Humphrey didn't come. Humphrey lost San Francisco, California and the election.

It is clear why this sensitive material was stricken from some published versions of the *Key*. Joseph L. Alioto is a formidable figure, one who put *Look* magazine out of business after the sensational 1969 story, *The Web That Links San Francisco's Mayor Alioto and the Mafia*, written by Richard Carlson and Lance Brisson, was published by the magazine. Alioto sued for libel and won the case after two stormy trials, which eventually led to the magazine issuing an apology, then folding. What is not often known about the episode was that the *Look* story, according to the *Key*, was an elaborate and expensive fake designed to deflect any direct connections between Alioto and the JFK assassination team (Gemstone 3:7b-d). But that is another story which will be detailed later.

With Alioto an attorney himself — and with his successful challenge of the *Look* magazine article, however fictitious it might have been — any mention of him in the *Skeleton Key* is risky. Not only is the former mayor of San Francisco accused of collaborating in the financing of the JFK assassination, he is also accused of knowing about a cover-up murder during the so-called "Zebra" killings which took place between 1970 and 1974 in San Francisco (Gemstone 11:7). That is another case we will investigate later in this book.

But regarding the case specified in 1968 in Gemstone 5:0a, any details about the alleged hit-and-run have been swept away. There is no official police report of the incident. One thing is certain, however — it would have been unwise to make a move on Roberts himself, because he was armed with photographs at the scene and could easily have had them distributed regardless if he was eliminated or not. Still, as evidenced in Gemstone 5:0c and 5:1, it was wise for the Mafia shooters to monitor Roberts, which they did. In any event, any political ambitions Alioto might have harbored were dashed when the FBI disclosed some information linking his family to early-century mob activity. Included in that release — but not widely publicized until the following year as the *Look* libel trials were raging — was the fact that Joe Alioto's uncle, a man named Mario Alioto, was shot to death in 1917 by a member of the so-called "Mano Nera," or "Black Hand," a criminal syndicate that would later be called the "Mafia."[3]

Roberts' claim that his handling of the Presidio hit-and-run evidence, drawn from his sources in the Soviet consulate, had an impact in the 1968 election (Gemstone 5:1) is not as far-fetched as it sounds. Certainly, Alioto had been pegged as one of the favorites for the vice presidential portion of the Democratic ticket under Hubert Humphrey until the mob controversies surfaced. However, once stigmatized by the negative FBI-related publicity coming out of the 1968 Democratic National Convention — which was newsworthy in many other violent and illogical ways — his chances at achieving the ticket were reduced to nil. Humphrey failing to show at the San Francisco pre-election rally as mentioned in Gemstone 5:1 was also a serious blow in the face of Richard Nixon's popularity gains in that state. In one of the closest elections in history, Nixon was elected and Humphrey was the loser. Losing California, as Gemstone 5:1 states, was a damaging blow. The next direct *Key* reference to Roberts follows:

(**Gemstone 7:7**) December, 1971: Roberts applied for a "Gemstone" visa from the Soviet consulate — on a tapped phone. Phone was tapped by Hal Lipset, S.F. private investigator, who worked for Katharine Meyer Graham, and others, and routinely monitored consulate phone calls.

(**7:8**) January, 1972: The Watergate team shows up at the S.F. Drift Inn, a CIA-FBI safe-house hangout bar [in San Francisco] where Roberts conducted a nightly Gemstone rap for benefit of any CIA, FBI or anyone who wandered in for a beer. James McCord, Martinez, Bernard Barker, Garcia and Frank Sturgis showed up — along with a San Francisco dentist named Fuller. James McCord remarked: "Sand and oil with hydrogen heat makes glass brick" — threat of war to Arab nations. The

---

3. *San Francisco Examiner,* Sept 6, 1969, "Alioto Slain Here in 1917," by Jane Eshelman Conant.

event, like any other nightly rap, is taped by [the] Drift Inn bartender Al Strom, who was paid to do so by his old friend, Katharine Meyer Graham — but [who[told [tells] his other friend, Roberts, about it. The bar was [is] also wired for sound by Arabs, Soviets [Russians] and Chinese.

Note that, in the above passage, very little was used in the *Hustler* version (the portion not underlined). Why would *Hustler's* editors omit these details? It would place the Watergate plumbers in San Francisco just prior to the twin break-ins and the start of the ensuing scandal that brought down the Nixon presidency. And what of the Drift Inn? Did it really exist? Was it the "CIA-FBI safehouse hangout bar" as the *Key* describes?

Indeed it was.

"The Drift Inn was a military hangout," said Randy Strom, son of Drift Inn bartender Al Strom described in Gemstone 7:8, during an exclusive telephone interview with us on Jan. 9, 1990. "The boys from the *(U.S.S.) Enterprise, Oriskany, Maine* were regulars. It was decorated in military style. Every branch of the service came through. *Heavy brass would show up from time to time* (emphasis ours).

"It was located on a hill, a pivotal spot. I was going to law school from 1970-74. Mom and myself helped Dad. I tended bar when not going to school... We constantly helped guys who came in to find places to stay. Dad was a happy-go-lucky guy, ex-military, small guy with a pot belly. he always had a cigar in his mouth that was never lit. That was his trademark."

Annie Strom, Al's wife, confirmed that a friend named "Bruce" would come in.

"Bruce," she said coldly during a telephone interview with us on Jan. 11, 1990. "Yeah, Bruce would come in... *We never knew anyone by their last names* (emphasis ours). Bruce would drive up in his station wagon. *He went to Vietnam, too, just like most of the other guys that came in. I think he had some family over there* (emphasis ours). But I barely knew him. He was Al's friend."

The site of the old Drift Inn still exists at 895 Bush St. in San Francisco. Randy Strom said it was purchased by Koreans soon after his father died on "July 9, 1973," confirming Gemstone 10:3's date (more on this later in this chapter), and it changed hands again. It is now a Vietnamese restaurant. "They completely changed everything," Randy Strom said.

"The Watergate guys? If they ever came in I didn't know about it," said Strom, who indicated that the *Hustler* version of the *Skeleton Key* caused quite a neighborhood stir because of its brief mention of the Drift Inn and of Al Strom, who allegedly taped conversations of patrons on a regular basis. "I'm not saying it would never happen because *plenty of colorful characters came through*... I only know that when the *Hustler* story came out everyone had some pretty good laughs about it."

Ha, ha.

Randy Strom also thinks that the *Hustler* story was a plant to deflect the media spotlight from a white supremacist tavern down the street from the Drift Inn. It was at that time that *Hustler* accelerated its coverage of extremist political splinter groups with neo-Nazi leanings. And Strom suggests that all the activity described by the *Key* involving the Watergate plumbers' presence in San Francisco was focused at this Nazi-leaning bar.

"You want to know what I really think about all this? That the article in *Hustler* appeared to take the heat off the *real place this stuff was all happening at* (emphasis ours)," Strom stated. "You know, there was this place down the street a block away, owned by a German guy...corner of Bush and Powell, I'm sure, but I don't recall the name of the place. It's not even there any more, but now there were some *real shenanigans going on at that place* (emphasis ours). Real shenanigans!

"It was racially oriented. Swaztikas, hard-hats, you name it... They openly did the 'Heil Hitlers' and stuff like that. The whole nine yards." And since the Stroms were Jewish — Annie

Strom was known as the "only Jewish Mother Theresa" in The City at that time — there was cause for alarm. The implication was that Randy Strom knew about the Watergate plumbers' presence, but was somehow uneasy discussing the subject and gave us the impression that he wanted to hint around about it; not exactly denying the *Key's* version of events, but not officially confirming it, either. He also implied that all the Watergate plumbers' visits actually happened, only down the street. Self-preservation might be a good enough motive to keep quiet on this topic from the Strom family's vantage point. Plus, it was evident that Randy Strom probably had no knowledge of the raw version of the *Key* we had in our possession and was therefore in no position to adequately comment on it.

But regardless of the location, military and intelligence operatives apparently crawled around San Francisco at that time, and according to Gemstone 7:7, private investigator Hal Lipset was monitoring all the activity with his ultra-sensitive snooping devices. Later, when the Watergate burglary is discussed in further detail, the crucial role Mr. Lipset played throughout the *Key* will be more carefully analyzed. Now, suffice it to say the activities of intelligence operatives were followed with great interest by powerful figures such as Katharine Meyer Graham, publisher of the *Washington Post.*

The plot continued to thicken for Roberts in this following sequence, also deleted from the *Hustler version:*

(**Gemstone 8:0**) February, 1972: Liddy and Hunt traveled around a lot, using "Hughes Tool Co." calling cards and aliases from Hunt's spy novels.

(**8:1a**) Liddy, Hunt and other Watergaters dropped by for a beer at the Drift Inn, where they were photographed while sitting on bar stools; the photos were for Katharine Graham and were later used in the *Washington Post* when Liddy, Hunt and the others were arrested at Watergate — because CIA men like

Liddy and Hunt aren't usually photographed.

(8:1b) Roberts quoted to Liddy the "Chinese stock market in ears" — the price on Onassis' head, by the ear — in retaliation for a few things Onassis had done; on Wayne Rector, the Hughes double; Eugene Wyman, California Democratic Party Chairman and Mafia JFK payoff bag man; and on Lyndon Johnson: "Four bodies twisting in the breeze."

(8:1c) Roberts: "Quoting the prices to Liddy at the Drift Inn made their deaths a mortal cinch. Liddy's like that — and that's why the murdering slob was picked by the Mafia… Gemstones rolling around the Drift Inn in February inspired Liddy's 'Gemstone Plan' that became Watergate."

This passage will make more sense as Watergate is analyzed later (Chapter 11), but it is included here to emphasize that Roberts was deeply on the inside of the entire U.S. domestic espionage system, and was not an easy person to simply rub out. Getting rid of him at this stage would have been much too flagrant an act and would have attracted far too much attention as the plumbers began to make their Watergate plans. As for Liddy, he wrote about his own "Gemstone" plans in his post-Watergate memoirs, *Will, the Autobiography of G. Gordon Liddy*. As we will soon discover, Liddy and the other Watergate conspirators who wrote book on their exploits might have carefully dodged out direct references to Roberts, Lipset and the Drift Inn, but their tracks would not be entirely covered.

****

(Gemstone 8:3a) In a Mafia-style effort to shut Roberts up, his father was murdered by "plumbers" team members Liz Dale (Francis L. Dale's ex-wife), Martinez, Gonzales and Barker; in Hahnemann's Hospital in San Francisco — where the senior Roberts had been taken after swallowing a sodium morphate "pill" slipped into his medicine bottle at home by Watergate locksmith Gonzales (from Miami's "Missing Link" locksmith shop). The pill didn't kill him; he had weak digestion and vomited up enough of the sodium morphate (it burned his lips and tongue on the way out). But the senior Roberts also had emphysema and went to the hospital.

(8:3b) In the hospital, "nurse" Liz Dale and "doctor" Martinez assisted the senior Roberts to sniff a quadruple-strength can of aerosol medicine — enough to kill him the next day.

When an insider like Roberts has the goods on an organization like the Mafia, and has rendered himself virtually untouchable because his death would trigger an unpleasant domino reaction through the media, his family becomes at risk. That is exactly what happened to Roberts' father, if the *Skeleton Key* is to be believed.

Intriguingly, this passage (note it is also underlined) is edited out of the *Hustler* version of the *Key*. Once again, it would have provided a mass audience some insight into the personal background of Bruce Roberts — background that could be checked through normal channels.

In this case, the death of Roberts' father poses an extraordinary opportunity to add enormous credibility to the *Skeleton Key* through hard medical evidence. The *Hustler* version's preamble does at least mention that Roberts claimed his father was killed by assassins, but that's as far as it would go. The questions about this incident are obvious: Who exactly was Bruce Roberts' father? Can he be identified by name? What is his background? Can it have anything to do with how son Bruce got inside of the U.S. intelligence network? Did it have anything to do with maritime interests? *Shipbuilding?*

Let's take each question one at a time, since we have uncovered most of these answers. The *Skeleton Key*, for reasons unknown, does not identify Bruce Roberts' father by name. But we searched obituaries for the time period described in the *Key* and discovered the obituary of one La Verne Dayle Roberts — father of Bruce Porter Roberts, who was author of the Gemstone papers and inspiration behind the *Skeleton Key to the Gemstone Files.*

A wealth of information is drawn from the death certificate of La Verne Roberts. The astonishing revelations include, but are not limited to:

- Cause of death. Despite his advanced age, 82 years, cause of death was *not from natural causes.* Immediate cause of death was listed as a "bleeding peptic ulcer (stress) due to or as a consequence of *cortisone ingestion* (emphasis ours)." La Verne Dayle Roberts was *poisoned by a caustic, reactive substance, just as described in Gemstone 8:3a!* Since sodium morphate is not a widely known poisonous substance, doctors treating Roberts evidently guessed it might have been a cortisone derivative, which would have had a similar effect on the body.

- The death certificate was signed *two days* after the death was recorded by the San Francisco coroner. There is no explaining this delay, since the elder Roberts was being treated at Hahnemann Hospital at the time; the place of death is listed as Hahnemann's, just as Gemstone 8:3a-b discloses.

- It was noted that La Verne Roberts suffered from "emphysema, chronic and acute," listed under "other significant conditions" — but emphysema was not listed as cause of death. This also confirmed a crucial detail in Gemstone 8:3a.

- There was a *13-day span* between the time the senior Roberts was admitted to Hahnemann's and his death. This would also match up with Gemstone 8:3a which describes a delay between the sodium morphate ("cortisone") poisoning and the actual killing in the hospital itself.

- Perhaps the most glaring bit of information gleaned on the death certificate was the elder Roberts' occupation — *retired shipyard worker from Bethlehem Steel Ship-*

yard. The death certificate states that the elder Roberts worked as a "shipbuilder" for over 30 years. He probably worked right up until retirement in the 1950s. Bethlehem's records indicate he worked for a time in a Bethlehem-run dry dock in Alameda, Calif., from 1947 until the mid-1950s, and that he had prior experience at Bethlehem's major shipyards in Sparrow's Point, Md., and Quincy, Mass., where Onassis' oil tankers were built in the late '30s.

That reveals one crucial fact: La Verne Dayle Roberts could well have worked in Quincy during the time Joseph Kennedy was head of Bethlehem Steel's shipyard there in 1917! This lends credence to Gemstone 1:3 when the *Skeleton Key* author states that Bruce Roberts "...learned these things through personal contacts."

This gives tremendous impetus to the *Key* and the Gemstone papers themselves. If the senior Roberts was connected with Bethlehem's shipbuilding operation during a career that spanned the better part of 40 years — during the time when Aristotle Socrates Onassis was amassing his international fleet of merchant vessels at mostly American taxpayer expense (see Chapter Four). This was especially the case in the late 1930s when Joe Kennedy, then head of the Maritime Commission, handed out plums to various shipping tycoons, including Onassis. And do not forget a young entrepreneur named Hank Greenspun who sold engines to Liberty ships, also in the late 1930s, when Onassis was busy either building his own fleet or illegally buying U.S. Liberties himself.

Shipyard workers talk. They are heavily networked with shipowners, and they collect and disseminate information about shipping in general from their co-workers and others. Drug trafficking plays a large role in the lives of these workers; if they do not directly participate in the transportation of this contraband, they look the other way while others do. This is taking place today just as it has for many hundreds of years.

And it most assuredly took place in the days when a young La Verne Dayle Roberts was working the Bethlehem Steel shipyards of both coasts.

(Gemstone 9:1) June 21, 1972: The 18-1/2-minutes of accidentally erased White House tape: [Eighteen-and-half minutes of White House tape is "accidentally" erased.] Nixon [is], furious over the Watergate plumbers' arrests, couldn't figure out who had [has] done it to him: Who taped the door at [the] Watergate that led to the arrests? Hal Lipset, whose primary employer at the time was Katharine Graham, couldn't tell him [The detective won't tell him]. Nixon figured [figures] that it had [has] to do somehow with Roberts' running around Vancouver tracing the "Hughes" Mormon Mafia nursemaid (Eckersley's) swindle of the Canadian Stock Exchange; and Trudeau. The 18-1/2 minutes was [is] of Nixon raving about Canada's "a--hole Trudeau," "a--hole Roberts," Onassis, "Hughes" and Francis L. Dale. It simply couldn't [can't] be released.

The preceding passage gives a crucial added reason why that particular Watergate tape had a lengthy erasure. It could well have been the only reference to Bruce Roberts made during the entire history of Watergate, and its discovery would have inevitably led to an expanded investigation — one aimed in the direction of Onassis. The incident of the double-taped door at Watergate (which will be addressed later in this book) has never been explained by anyone inside our outside the immediate Watergate circle (most of the Watergate conspirators' ensuing books seem to skip around that delicate question). Finally, as for the profanity used by Nixon in describing Trudeau, that was confirmed by a 1974 news report from United Press International which was circulated widely.

(Gemstone 9:8) March 18, 1973: Roberts called Hal Lipset,

discussing these matters publicly — over a tapped phone. Lipset reported to Dean, who had hired him away from Graham after they figured out who had taped the door at Watergate (Mitchell: "Katie Graham's liable to get her tit caught in a wringer.")

None of this Gemstone passage made the *Hustler* version, and the latter comment about Ms. Graham's anatomy has been edited to read "...Katie Graham's liable to get caught in a wringer" in most reproduced versions of the *Key*. This might be more palatable to a prudent readership, but masks the true contempt against Ms. Graham and the *Post* felt by Nixon administration officials.

It must also be pointed out that in no way does the *Hustler* version give away the name of Graham's spy, Hal Lipset. This is especially important in Gemstone 9:8 because Lipset shows no loyalties, instead choosing to sell his information to the highest bidder. Having done all the damage he could probably harp upon the beleaguered Nixon administration because of his timely Watergate disclosures (more on this later), he sold his talents to the administration itself and turned the espionage against his old employer. Again, this is left out of *Hustler's* version.

****

(Gemstone 10:3) July 9, 1973: Roberts had used Al Strom's Drift Inn bay as an "open lecture forum" for any and all — and Al Strom taped it, for his boss, Katharine Graham. But "Al was fair" — and told Roberts he was doing it — for which he was murdered on this date.

We have already covered some of this territory with the comments of Randy Strom, son of the Drift Inn bartender, and Annie Strom, his wife, the "Jewish Mother Theresa" of San Francisco. However, this Gemstone passage — again, left out of the *Hustler* version of the *Key* — keeps reminding the readers that Bruce Roberts maintains an inside position on the goings-on of the people around him, including key members of the covert unit known as the Watergate plumbers. However, his agenda became increasingly public, and this was giving some of these nefarious individuals a severe case of the jitters.

About the death of Al Strom: His death certificate confirms the exact day of death as outlined in Gemstone 10:3. Furthermore, the cause of death — listed as "cardiac failure due to or as a result of coronary arteriosclerosis" — also matches that of the passage. Sodium morphate poisoning leads to rapid deterioration of the coronary arteries; it is likely, if Strom did not die of natural causes, that poisoning was probably involved.

Randy Strom recalled that his father showed few signs of ill health before suddenly dying, and added that he had served admirably during World War II.

"Dad was a Lieutenant Colonel in the U.S. Submarine Service," Randy Strom said. This would have given Al Strom access to sensitive military intelligence during the war years; that, and an ongoing friendship with Bruce Roberts, would have fostered a free exchange of extraordinarily important information about Allied and Axis shipping during the war.

(Gemstone 10:4a) August, 1973: Murder of Chile, by "Group of 40:" Rockefeller and his man Kissinger, working with the CIA, and $8 million, accomplished this task. Allende's Chile had nationalized ITT. Rockefeller had copper mines in Chile. Admiral Noel Gayler, Naval Intelligence, told Roberts 1-1/2 years earlier that Chile would get it; Roberts warned the Chilean consul in advance: Allegria, who later "taught" at Stanford.

Roberts' inside connections with the U.S. intelligence network are clearly indicated here. As for the mention of a former Stanford instructor who was also Roberts' Chilean contact, it is well known that major U.S. universities are repositories for many personnel directly connected with U.S. intelligence operations all around the world. The Stanford Research Center is historically known as one of the most prominent sponsors of sociological terror in the name of "research."

(Gemstone 11:3a) Aug. 7, 1974: Roberts passed information to Pavlov at the S.F. Soviet consulate which led directly to Nixon's resignation: The *More* journalism review's story about Denny Walsh's "Reopening of the Alioto Mafia Web" story for the *New York Times*, a story killed in a panic; plus a long, taped discussion about who and what the Mafia is. Hal Lipset, listening to the conversation in the bugged consulate room, had phone lines open to Rockefeller and Kissinger, who listened, too. Rockefeller sent Kissinger running to the White House with Nixon's marching orders: "Resign. Right now."

The timing of Richard Nixon's resignation has always been something of an enigma, because up to that point, the only real evidence of his involvement in Watergate had been the one-sided and isolated articles by the *Washington Post*. The nation's media combines had also been preoccupied with the Patricia Hearst kidnapping (an alleged fake according to Gemstone 10:9), so media intensity regarding Watergate had subsided somewhat. If Bruce Roberts discovered information pertinent to Watergate, has was in position to use it in the most effective way — tapping into the bugging setup used for months at the Drift Inn and Soviet Consulate in San Francisco.

(Gemstone 11:8) Sept. 7, 1974: Roberts had made an agreement with a friend, Harp, of Kish Realty, over a bugged phone. Harp was to buy a Gemstone, with history, for $500 — the price of a trip to Canada for Roberts to check into the "Hughes" Mormon Mafia Canadian stock market swindle, and other matters. But Harp was sodium-morphate poisoned on this date, before the deal could go through.

This is another example of a passage that appears innocuous

on the surface, but has enormous importance once the death of "Harp" is analyzed. Gail Lawrence Harp was 62 years of age when he died unexpectedly. Date of death: Sept. 7, 1974, as recorded by the San Francisco coroner, which confirms the Gemstone date. Cause of death: "Severe arteriosclerotic heart disease," without going into specifics, which typically matches sodium morphate ingestion symptoms. Another astounding "coincidence:" According to his obituary, Harp served in the U.S. Marine Corps briefly before spending 28 years in the United States Navy, serving during World War II he was also a member of the Navy Fleet Reserve Association, which kept him in touch with naval intelligence operations at home and abroad. This simply means that Harp, Roberts and Al Strom, among others, probably served together during World War II on intelligence-sensitive operating units. Another intelligence operative by the name of Philip Graham also served during this time.

(Gemstone 13:0) March 15, 1975: Roberts got [gets] the "Brezhnev flu" and spent [spends] two weeks in [at] a U.C. [University of California] hospital [Hospital in San Francisco]. Doctors there, without the [Russian] Kirlian photography diagnostic technique, assumed [assume] the softball-sized lump over his heart was [is] cancer [and attempt to treat it with radiation]. It wasn't.

This is one of the final entries into the *Skeleton Key*, and with good reason: Bruce Porter Roberts died on July 30, 1976, as a result of "respiratory failure due to metastatic carcinoma of the lung," or lung cancer which had spread out of control, according to the San Francisco coroner's office. Whether it was really cancer, it will never be determined, because the body was cremated on Aug. 4. Since the death occurred eight months after the onset of the "disease," it would have provided sufficient time for medical teams at the University of California Medical Center to analyze exactly why he died. Instead, the mystery will remain.

One thing is certain: Bruce Porter Roberts may be dead, but his legacy as the author of the Gemstone thesis will never be forgotten.

****

With whom did Bruce Roberts associate? Reconstructing his past with the sketchy information available, it is clear he grew up in a cosmopolitan environment — his father a nomadic shipyard worker in coastal cities. That meant the younger Roberts had to be quite aware of international issues. He attended college at the University of Wisconsin in the 1930s, learning the rudiments of his first love, crystallography. Serving his country during World War II, more than likely in the U.S. Navy and probably associated with the intelligence community in the Pacific Theater, he met and married a French national with Southeast Asian connections.

After the war, he made gemstones for Hollywood's elite, eventually receiving unexpected attention from the Hughes Corp., which coveted the quality of his rubies. Cheated out of any credit for his role in the development of laser technology at Hughes, he vented his rage at the crooked establishment as a whole — going after his enemies with the only means at his disposal: His observational skills and analytical mind.

Those who knew Bruce Roberts cite the entire Hughes laser episode as outlined in Gemstone 2:7 as the major reason why he began his crusade into the darker depths of conspiracy research — starting with the unearthing of what he felt were the real reasons behind Howard Hughes' disappearance, and ending with exposing the Watergate scandal for what it truly was.

Stephanie Caruana, mentioned earlier as the author and distributor of the original *Skeleton Key to the Gemstone Files* we are using to construct this book, was already buried deeply in conspiracy lore when she apparently joined forces with California conspiracy theorist and Monterey Peninsula College "conspiracy" instructor Mae Brussell. Caruana claims authorship of the *Key* in a 1992 book, *The Gemstone File*, an anthology edited by Jim Keith and produced by an alternative press in Georgia. Brussell, in a late 1977 radio program on station KLRB-FM radio in Carmel, Calif., near Monterey, confirmed that Caruana was the original Gemstone editor, compressing the volumes of confusing papers allegedly written by Bruce Roberts and creating the disjointed *Skeleton Key to the Gemstone Files* which has circled the globe in its many variations since the mid-1970s. Caruana and Brussell combined their talents to write a controversial article, *Is Howard Hughes Dead and Buried Off a Greek Island?* that caused ripples of sensation when it appeared in the November, 1974 edition of *Playgirl* magazine (see Chapter 5). Caruana told Keith that an editor at *Playgirl* was fired after the story was published.

It was Brussell who possessed the "four hundred or so" pages of handwritten manuscript (Gemstone introduction) described in the *Key* as the original work of Bruce Roberts. Brussell claimed on radio that she obtained these writings directly from Roberts starting in 1972, after he contacted her, along with San Francisco magazine publisher Paul Krassner, about his research. Krassner, who voiced his own views often in his alternative magazine, *The Realist*, never took Roberts seriously, but Brussell gave the papers a hard look and analyzed them objectively. It was interesting that Roberts, according to Caruana's accounting to Keith in *The Gemstone File*, decided to give Brussell these papers soon after a tragic car accident in which one of Brussell's daughters was killed and another injured. In that same mishap, another girl lost her life and yet another was injured. This was mentioned on her radio show, *Dialogue: Conspiracy*, on which she mentioned the name of a man who showed up one day to express his regret about the accident and his sympathies. Bruce Roberts apparently listened to this broadcast, heard the name of the "comforter," and visited Brussell in Carmel to inform her that this "comforter" was in reality a man who "arranged" the "accident." He then gave her a copy of his Gemstone papers, and an intriguing relationship began. (It is interesting that *The Gemstone File* conveniently leaves out the name of this "comforter," although it would have been easy to include it).[4]

Brussell also was in a position to know more about the Gemstone files than almost anyone else. First, she associated directly with Bruce Roberts, or at least claimed she had. Second, she mentioned Caruana, confirming that she was indeed the editor of the *Skeleton Key*. Third, Brussell had actual Roberts papers in hand. And, finally, she was an insider to major league politics; she was related to retailing magnate and stalwart Democrat, Cyril Magnin (Gemstone 5:3b), a close associate of Joseph L. Alioto, who is also mentioned prominently in the *Key* (but not in the laundered *Hustler* version). Even more significant, perhaps, was her link to powerful forces in Hollywood through her father, Los Angeles Rabbi Edgar Magnin, whose grandfather, Isaac Magnin, founded the I. Magnin clothing-store chain. She was born wealthy in Beverly Hills and later attended Stanford University as a philosophy major — where she inexplicably left the school only *two weeks* shy of graduation to marry the first of two husbands.[5]

Intriguing, though, is that — despite the random, widespread dispersal of the *Skeleton Key* by Caruana in the mid-1970s — the mainstream press never followed up on *any* of the allegations, and Brussell espoused her numerous conspiracy theories in relative obscurity. It was only through Keith's narrative in *The Gemstone File* that the breakthrough was achieved — that the *Skeleton Key* editor at long last had been "found" and that some original Roberts scripture was suddenly extant.

However, this information has certain asterisks firmly attached. The entire chapter on Caruana in *The Gemstone File* is written in somewhat suspect style. Keith indicates that all corre-

---

4. *The Gemstone File*, by Jim Keith, ©1992 IllumiNet Press, p. 44-45.

5. *Mae Brussell, Conspiracy Theorist*, obituary, Oct. 5, 1988, United Press International.

spondence was conducted "through the mail" and that no telephone interviews or face-to-face meetings took place. These circumstances tend to reduce the credibility of what is being stated because: 1) There is no way to determine if "Stephanie Caruana" was actually writing this correspondence, and 2) we simply have to take it for granted that Keith is using normal journalistic procedures to make sure his information is genuine and from the proper sources. Yet, the material reads smoothly and here is no reason to question Keith's documentation so far.

In fact, when security is considered, there is nothing more secure, in this day and age of sophisticated electronic surveillance, than old-fashioned letter writing. Phone lines are easily tapped. Electronic "ears" and even satellites can be incorporated to follow the information flow between people. The massive Internet computer linkages are making practically all computer databases subject to "cracking" by experienced hackers. This is possibly one reason behind the "letters" disclaimer in the Keith-Caruana material in *The Gemstone File*.

Still, other critical facts are left out. Nowhere in *The Gemstone File* does editor Keith mention the fact that Mae Brussell died in 1988, and that her *archives and records have been sequestered* — including *all* of Bruce Roberts' original files. They are being warehoused at an unknown location, rumored to be in Santa Cruz, Calif., until "funding can be raised" to establish a Mae Brussell library of some sort. A more recent theory has it that the Gemstone papers have been "inherited" by conspiracy researcher John Judge.

"There certainly would be enough material for a library," said *Monterey Peninsula Herald* reporter Mac McDonald, who has for years monitored the Brussell conspiracy beat. "Her house was loaded, ceiling to floor, with files, books magazines...you name it. It was amazing. About five years ago or so, we were invited to a party over there, and it was astounding. I mean, Mae would spend hour after hour just clipping stories out of her magazines and newspapers. She must have subscribed to 100 or more magazines. I did notice she was taking *Soldier of Fortune* at one point. It was truly a 'conspiracy library.'"

However, Brussell was diagnosed with cancer soon thereafter, and she passed away on Oct. 3, 1988. It is unclear who the executor of her files might be at present, and McDonald said that it would have taken "truckload after truckload" to finally remove all the many files Brussell had collected over the years. One thing is certain — something terribly important remains hidden in those files, and the few people who know about it are not talking about it, especially about anything associated with the so-called Gemstone Files of Bruce Roberts.

In fact, it appears that Brussell's associates at the radio station are central to finding any of the original Gemstone papers from which Caruana claims to have pulled her *Skeleton Key*. But they are closing ranks while continuing to air Brussell's old tapes — and selling copies by mail.

The station has already undergone mysterious changes over the years since Brussell began broadcasting her conspiracy dogma. It was sold in the mid-1980s, and the call letters changed from KLRB to KMBY. McDonald says that the conspiracy broadcasts were stopped, and a satellite country-music format adopted. It bombed. Audiences demanded that Brussell be put back on the air, and the new owners sold the station back to its original owners, and renamed a third time to the call letters KAZU. But soon after Brussell started broadcasting again, she contracted her terminal illness.

That has not stopped her broadcasts, however. Radio personalities Al Kunzer and Marilyn Coleman are keeping the Brussell tapes alive and well, and still re-broadcasting her programs regularly on KAZU. The tapes are also for sale, and a catalog is available. However, Brussell's files remain off limits, and both Kunzer and Coleman try and skip around the apparently touchy topic of Bruce Roberts' Gemstone papers.

"Just what do you want those for, anyway?" Coleman asked

during a Dec. 7, 1993, telephone conversation with us, referring to the Gemstone writings. "They are just a *small* part of it all. You're better off reading the *Torbitt Document*. That says more about conspiracies than anything else. It's a much bigger picture than what you think.

"Besides, you probably know more about the Gemstone Files than I do. Why don't you go and talk to the *Key* authors? They might tell you where they are. I don't know where the Gemstone Files are. Even if I did know, I wouldn't tell you. I don't know anything about you, anyway." Agitated, it seemed, with the whole subject of Bruce Roberts and the Gemstone papers, Coleman became more and more angry over the phone.

"It's all on the tapes," Coleman said. "Mae talked about the Gemstones on her program. That's all we know about it."

You would figure that conspiracy researchers like Coleman and Kunzer might want to expand their own knowledge about something as crucial as this. We have already shown that the Gemstone papers exist, that Bruce Roberts wrote them, and that many of the allegations contained in them can be verified through simple cross-checks of other literature. Plus, if the Gemstone writings were valueless as Coleman asserts, why doesn't she simply share that information with other researchers, who might have already found some of the answers that Mae Brussell and others have been seeking for years?

"They (Brussell's talk shows) were very popular, and we have decided to stay with them," said Kunzer over the phone to us on Dec. 6, 1993. Kunzer goes by the name "Will Robinson" on his radio programs, and chooses to gloss over the subject of Brussell's files.

"They (the files) are in good hands," he said. But whose hands? What will they be used for? Will they be opened?

"I can't say right now," Kunzer said. "We're working on it."

He did not elaborate further, other than to mention in passing that he was one of the pallbearers at Mae Brussell's funeral.

Could it be that certain individuals or groups have a vested interest in keeping Brussell's research files under wraps for, say, another 10 to 20 years? It is a wonder these materials have, to this point, received very little public exposure outside the Monterey Bay area of California. Obviously, with the exception of Keith's work, these facts have eluded public notice.

****

Speculation about Roberts, however, has always been widespread in the underground "Gemstone" network. The scarcity of material has been paramount. Caruana told Keith that she was afraid of these "hot" allegations in Roberts' writings and decided to make copies, randomly mailing them to people — then wash her hands of the entire affair. She was afraid, and justly so, because Roberts himself had written about so many of his associates he claimed were killed because of their knowledge, or impending knowledge, of his Gemstone thesis. Roberts also claimed he had contracted an artificially induced cancer (Gemstone 13:0), and he was suffering the consequences of that inevitably fatal illness at the same time a young Stephanie Caruana was hastily throwing together a coherent outline of his massive conspiracy theory, the *Skeleton Key*.

Caruana claiming to be the *Key* author, and its corroboration by Brussell on the air, appears to be legitimate enough, but some gaping holes remain. For example, Caruana describes Roberts as an Indiana Jones-style swashbuckler "...more like Clint Eastwood/John Wayne if you want to go to Hollywood for images."[6] Brussell, meanwhile, perceived Roberts as a nondescript "Casper Milquetoast" who lived with his mother (Roberts, in fact, was living with his mother Eva R. Roberts in San Francisco at the time of his death). It is strange that the same person was seen in such divergent ways by two people.

Another suspicious facet of Caruana's and Brussell's "knowledge" of Roberts is a lack of physical description: Was he tall,

6. *Op. cit.*, Keith, P.45.

short, bald, fat, skinny? Both researchers were also dim about his exact of death, and when he died. Brussell says in a Dec. 25, 1977, radio broadcast that Roberts "died of a brain tumor about six months ago" when the cause of death was actually actually diagnosed as chest cancer. Later, on Jan. 1, 1978, Brussell said that Roberts "died of a brain tumor about a year ago."

This is mystifying, since Gemstone 13:0 specifically describes a *chest* tumor, and the cause of Roberts' death has been confirmed by his death certificate, which stated his death was caused by failure of his respiratory system due to the irrevocably spreading chest cancer. Any conspiracy researcher worth his or her salt would have combed the San Francisco government apparatus for that death certificate (Caruana's own *Skeleton Key* indicates that Roberts' health was failing at the outset of 1976). There is not much excuse for this poor accounting of Bruce Roberts and his eventual fate.

Perhaps the most important aspect of Brussell's work is that she stayed largely within the acceptable confines of the usual "Mafia-CIA-right wing-Castro" JFK assassination conspiracy parameters during her 17 years of broadcasting in the Monterey Bay Area. It is interesting that she attacked the *Skeleton Key* and the entire premise of the Gemstone Files, and disagreed with Bruce Roberts' assertion that Aristotle Onassis was the ultimate power of organized crime. She thought the scenario went much further; that Onassis was a relatively small player in a much larger scheme involving the most powerful families on earth. She was, to a large extent, correct on this premise, but she did not have the resources and connections to pull the entire story together. That is one purpose behind this particular work — perhaps more researchers, with vastly more resources and better connections, can add even more credence to the Gemstone thesis and related theories.

More crucial to the Gemstone thesis specifically is Caruana's confirmation that Roberts actually created and gave away gemstones in exchange for information (Gemstone 2:8), money, or both. She also claimed, in Keith's *The Gemstone File*, that Roberts actually showed her some of his stones. As we mentioned at the outset, Caruana confirms that Watergate conspirator G. Gordon Liddy probably borrowed the "Gemstone" label from Roberts when Liddy presented his package of espionage plans — including the proposed Watergate break-in — to President Nixon's Attorney General John Mitchell as described in Liddy's book, *Will*. The process was not vice-versa, as some would suggest; Roberts, according to Caruana's account, was the originator of the Gemstone label. This makes sense on an even larger scale, since Brussell claims that Roberts started writing the bulk of his papers in 1970 — *before* Liddy presented his "Gemstone Plan" to Mitchell and Nixon aides John Dean and Jeb Stuart Magruder on January 27, 1972.[7]

United Press International's widely circulated obituary on Mae Brussell (Oct. 5, 1988) included some interesting, but carefully edited, observations:

"...She (Brussell) said that, until the assassination of President Kennedy in 1963, she was 'just a housewife interested in tennis courts and dance lessons and orthodontia for my children.'

"The assassination changed her life.

"In 1964, she obtained a copy of the Warren Commission report and began what would become a career investigating political murders, Nazis, mind control, the Vatican, secret societies, espionage, organized crime, terrorism and hidden governments.

"She contended that United Nations was secretly controlled by an elite group of 5,000 powerful men who would stop at nothing to maintain that control.

"Brussell said the assassinations of Kennedy and Martin Luther King Jr., the Manson family murders, the Chappaquiddick affair and the Patricia Hearst kidnapping were all set into motion

---

7. *Will*, by G. Gordon Liddy, ©1980, St. Martin's Press, P. 196.

by the 'far right,' the CIA, the FBI and the Mafia under a massive conspiracy to discredit the left and establish a fascist state.

" 'After Watergate I found a lot more people were listening to me,' she said in a 1976 interview.

"Her radio program was syndicated to a half-dozen radio stations and hundreds of followers also bought tapes of her theories by mail.

" 'The irony is that if she were alive today, I'm sure she would find a conspiracy behind her own death,' noted Paul Krassner, editor and founder of *The Realist* and co-founder with Abbie Hoffman of the Yippie movement."

Notice that nothing about Bruce Roberts, or Brussell's possession of any original Gemstone papers is mentioned, nor is there any mention of Stephanie Caruana, co-writer with Brussell on the Howard Hughes expose in 1974 in *Playgirl* magazine and self-proclaimed writer and editor of the *Skeleton Key to the Gemstone Files*. Still, Caruana's general conspiracy knowledge as reported by Keith appears flawed on several fronts, making her blanket claim as sole author of the *Key* somewhat suspect. For example, she stated that *Hustler* publisher Larry Flynt was shot because of his magazine's publication of the *Skeleton Key*.[8] However, the *Hustler* version of the *Key* — carrying the by-line of Bruce Roberts and *not* Stephanie Caruana — did not appear until February of 1979, *almost a year after Flynt was shot in March of 1978*. It is more likely that Flynt was shot to *prevent* publication of the *Key*. As it was, the eventual *Hustler* version, as we have mentioned from the start, was heavily edited before its publication, and considerable material was added.

The lack of any insights regarding the fate of Roberts' associates whose deaths are mentioned in the *Skeleton Key* also presents serious questions as to Caruana's veracity. Surely, she would have developed these incidents in conversation with

8. *Op. cit.*, Keith, p. 46.

Keith in *The Gemstone File*, but chose not to (either that, or Keith has kept that information to himself). The only dead Roberts acquaintance mentioned at all was Gail Lawrence Harp (Gemstone 11:8), who actually did die on Sept. 7, 1974, as stated in the *Key* and described earlier in this chapter.

However, any details about Drift Inn bartender Al Strom's death — as we have chronicled — are not included in Keith's volume. Keith also keeps us in the dark about the alleged murder of Bruce Roberts' father by the Watergate plumbers (Gemstone 8:3), and fails to include the crucial background on the deceased La Verne Dayle Roberts, who worked for Joseph Kennedy and the Bethlehem Steel shipyard at the time Onassis was assembling his merchant fleet. These gaps are not clearly explained, unless Keith decided to self-censor his material for some future use.

(Keith also confuses the Drift Inn with the "Drift-In" Bar, another nightclub located on Broadway in San Francisco in the 1950s. The "Drift-In" Bar and the Drift Inn of Al Strom had no connection.)

We know what happened to Bruce Roberts, but what of Stephanie Caruana? In a *New York Times* story dated April 3, 1989, a "Stephanie Caruana" is quoted by a *Times* stringer concerning a proposed theme-park development in the Catskills region of New York state. The story mentions that Caruana is the "editor of *The Napanoch News*" which serviced the small town of Napanoch, near Ellenville, N.Y., the town used as the dateline for the story.[9] However, we learned from several area residents that a newspaper called *The Napanoch News* has "never existed here, to our knowledge."

****

---

9. *The New York Times*, April 3, 1989, "Sparks Fly in Catskills Over Fantasyland Plan."

When it comes to the *Skeleton Key*, Bruce Roberts or anything surrounding the Gemstone thesis, the mysteries continue. There is also evidence that the *Key* and the character of Bruce Roberts have been borrowed for several novels, even motion picture scripts, since its circulation started in the mid-1970s. *The Circle*, an espionage novel written by Steve Shagan, uses the *Key* as a central feature of his story, which fictionally attributes the Gemstone file to J. Edgar Hoover.

Movies like the *Romancing the Stone* series, which emphasize gemstones in their plot summaries, and the entire Indiana Jones series appear to have Gemstone and Roberts-related overtones. The latter films have some astonishing comparisons to the story of Bruce Roberts and the *Skeleton Key to the Gemstone Files*, and they were considered the blockbuster films of the 1980s in addition to the *Star Wars* trilogy.

Raiders of the Lost Ark, produced in 1981 by George Lucas and Steven Spielberg, is the story of an archaeologist named Indiana Jones, whose "passion for antiquities" and entanglements with Nazi Germany are curiously close to some of the Gemstone material — with the personality and mindset of the central character, Indiana Jones, remarkably similar to Stephanie Caruana's description of Bruce Roberts.

The second Indiana Jones film, *Indiana Jones and the Temple of Doom* (1984), has even more comparisons to the Bruce Roberts character and background. One, the opening sequence of that film places the hero in the middle of the Golden Triangle drug-trade financial center, pre-Communist Shanghai, battling the Asian organized-crime network. Again, in that opening sequence, a gemstone is used as *a trading item* for, in this case, money for Indiana Jones, who found the artifact for the villain, Lou-Che, who attempts unsuccessfully to kill Jones. This closely parallels Roberts' claim that he established an information network using gemstones as bargaining chips. Later in the *Temple of Doom*, Jones finds himself in yet another Golden Triangle-style situation, in India, seat of the British opium poppy business that the Crown milked for all it was worth in the 19th and early 20th centuries, as implied in the *Key*. His mission there? To reclaim yet another type of gemstone, this one with magical properties that kept alive a village of poor Indians, or so the plot goes. Jones then risks his life and those of his companions, in reclamation of this gemstone, which he succeeds in doing in the movie's conclusion.

The third Indiana Jones film, *Indiana Jones and the Last Crusade* (1989), again brings Nazi Germany back into the picture, and moves the background of the adventure to one of the centers of the European drug trade, Venice, Italy. The intrepid Jones has to solve an ancient riddle surrounding the search for the exalted Holy Grail in order to save the world from the Nazis, and save his father in the process. The early sequences of this film are somewhat remarkable in their similarities to Roberts-style characters. The young Jones — played by young actor River Phoenix who late in 1993 lost his life when he overdosed on dangerous illegal drugs in Hollywood — is portrayed early in the film as trying to steal an important artifact belonging to a shadowy figure which could easily have been modeled after Aristotle Onassis. This villain stays in the background while his henchman dig up the valued "Cross of Coronado," which the young Jones steals. In a wild chase scene, the cross is recovered by the henchmen. The film then shifts suddenly from 1912 to 1938, where an older Jones again challenges this villain aboard his ship in the Atlantic Ocean. Again, the object of contention is the cross, and this time Jones come out the winner — destroying the villain's ship in the process.

This is not to mention the Christian apologetics presented in *Indiana Jones and the Last Crusade*. There are plenty of those in addition to the central theme, that of finding the Holy Grail, the cup from which Jesus Christ and his disciples are said to have drunk during the Last Supper. It looks like Gemstone 8:4a through 8:4e might be receiving more than a gentle challenge through this plot summary. This is especially remarkable since

Spielberg is Jewish, and his films often carry spiritual overtones in their story lines.

These could well be only coincidences, but the similarities — especially when considering Caruana's descriptions in Keith's *The Gemstone File* — are inescapable. Perhaps the spirit of Bruce Roberts and those like him will never die in the world of heroes, fiction or otherwise, which have been dreamed up by our cultural and literary heritage.

CHAPTER 9

. . . .

Between Dealey Plaza and the Ambassador Hotel

In this exploration of the *Skeleton Key to the Gemstone Files* and in our determination to find out exactly how truthful Gemstone Files author Bruce Roberts actually was, it is interesting to make a few candid comparisons between the entire Gemstone scenario and other more widespread "conspiracy" theories surrounding the JFK assassination and resultant aftermath. It is intriguing, for example, that most conspiracy material is narrowly focused to the actual day of the assassination. Few, if any, conspiracy researchers venture far from the familiar confines of Dealey Plaza, the Texas School Book Depository, the grassy knoll and the six or seven seconds it took to take out President Kennedy. The *Skeleton Key* is a rare case of a truly historical grounding of the violent political period of upheaval, between 1957 and 1972, and its far-reaching consequences for the United States.

Few truly acceptable, compelling motives exist for the shooting of JFK aside from the tired theories already analyzed exhaustively by past and present waves of conspiracy researchers. Equally rare are bonafide suspects, with the exception of "Communist nut" Oswald. Plenty of historical events that transpired prior to the JFK assassination provide glimpses into the true motives behind that murder, and many of the events after JFK can also be tied to Dallas.

It is the content of these limited theories which has long been suspect. If we are to believe, as the *Skeleton Key* implies,

that the Warren Commission, and later the Watergate Committee, were cover-up schemes, evidence should exist to show this
could be true. The *Skeleton Key* does provide a blueprint for
chasing down and isolating some of this evidence.

Existing conspiracy theories which have gained widespread
acceptance appear to be preserved for posterity by seemingly
well-learned authors who claim to have "inside" information on
possible conspirators. But it is clear that any conspiratory theory
must first be legitimized, and its authors rewarded, in order for
those individuals ultimately behind such actions to count themselves among the legions of criminals who have effectively
beaten the system, especially in the crime-ridden, drug-infested
20th century. Aristotle Onassis had not only beaten the system,
he owned it; his maritime monopolies on transport of oil and
drugs, his de facto control of Howard Hughes' empire, his
gambling investments in Monaco and Cuba — and, finally,
control over the President of the United States, first through his
wife, then through his assassination.

The thousands of books and hundreds of video productions
spewed forth about the JFK assassination all seem to be variations on a basic theme. They imply there was a conspiracy, but
are slow to come forth with actual working hypotheses. One
reason for this is clear: They seek to capitalize on the story,
titillating the masses with speculation, but stop just short of
openly accusing individuals; this would not only pose legal
problems for the New York-dominated literary establishment,
but stop the spigot of money which pours forth with every JFK
assassination-related piece that comes out. *Keeping the American people in the dark over this situation is in the best interests
of the money-mongers who ride herd on the entire United States
media system.* In short: Keep up the suspense and tension, keep
the cash rolling in. A solution to the Kennedy enigma, such as
the thesis provided by the *Skeleton Key to the Gemstone Files*,
would pull the plug on a lot of conspiracy literature which is yet
to be generated.

People within the U.S. intelligence network have a term for written works that keep pumping new life into the CIA, Castro and Mafia conspiracy theories: "Cutouts." One such document that came into our possession points out the benefits of using such "cutouts" to repeatedly propagandize the nation, and the world for that matter, about what really happened to JFK and his brother Robert:

"...One of the CIA's operatives in the People's Temple cover-up is a long-time CIA asset by the name of Mark Lane. Mr. Lane is a writer and is known to the intelligence community as a 'Vac' or vacuum. His particular assignments deal with sucking up massive amounts of information from various concerned citizens and public researchers and then supplying these details to the particular intelligence agencies contracting him. Lane also disperses cover information and "cutouts," or *stories that parrot the basic conspiracy well enough to gain the confidence of the civilian community* (emphasis ours). The cutout is completed with the insertion of "skids" or elements which are completely fabricated in order to mislead those who seek the truth..."[1]

We will be hearing more on Mr. Lane a little later, since he was a key figure as the People's Temple attorney at the time Jim Jones and his band of religious followers reportedly committed suicide in Jonestown, Guyana, in 1978. He also represented James Earl Ray during the House Select Committee on Assassinations hearings (a.k.a. the Rockefeller Commission), and was in the middle of testimony along with Ray before the Committee when California Rep. Leo Ryan was assassinated at the Guyana airport, precipitating the alleged mass suicide (there is evidence it was not a mass cyanide poisoning as reported by the United States press, but that is another story).

But suffice it to say he was much more of a key player in the conspiracy business than simply his writings, which are very convincing and which seem to take an adversarial view to the

---

1. Intelligence Document No. 1 (title withheld), p. 41.

Warren Commission findings regarding JFK's death. His book, *Rush to Judgment*, typifies the "cutout" and "skid" technique; the primary cutout being a beating-the-chest tirade against the Warren Report, and the primary skid being the alleged "connections" Lee Harvey Oswald might have had with Communists and organized crime. As long as Lane takes this position, and steers his legions of followers away from any alternative explanations pertaining to the JFK assassination, he will remain richly rewarded and largely protected.

Hollywood's equivalent to Lane is movie director Oliver Stone, whose controversial film *JFK* puts forth the often-cited theory that war barons within the United States wanted to protract the Vietnam War to gain war-related profits. This is a tidy reason for the JFK assassination, but steers the nation and the world away from obvious connections the Vietnam conflict had with illegal drug trafficking, whose profits would dwarf any defense contractor's (with the possible exception of Howard Hughes, who apparently enjoyed both ends of that spectrum). One of our sources described *JFK* as a "monument to the stupidity of the human race."

Some journalists, however, have not fallen into the "cutout" mold, but their suppressed views are presented only in the alternative press, and their books are largely ignored by the bloated and arrogant New York-centered literary monopoly. One such writer is Anthony Summers, whose British Broadcasting Corp. (BBC) documentary work on the JFK assassination 15 years after the fact drew him into the conspiracy business. Just as the *Skeleton Key* indicates, Summers pointed out as recently as 1992 the obvious mob connections to the Kennedy situation:

"...The Kennedy family patriarch, Joseph, had *long-standing relationships with mobsters* (emphasis ours, Gemstone 1:1). The president (JFK) was indeed *helped on his way to power by the gangsters* (emphasis ours, Gemstone 2:2) and, FBI surveillance records suggest, (Mafia leader Sam) Giancana expected to get an easy ride from the Kennedy Justice Department as a result (Gemstone 2:5)."[2]

The only difference between this view — which is typical from a foreign correspondent's vantage point, since exposure to U.S. media propaganda is less pronounced — and the *Skeleton Key* is that Summers simply doesn't go far enough up the Mafia ladder. There is no way that Giancana and the other Mafioso most often mentioned in connection with JFK, Santos Trafficante, could have accessed the necessary international resources to pull off the most daring and astonishing assassination in history. Onassis was much more likely to possess the brains behind it all — he had extraordinary wealth, global power, and he even controlled Kennedy's *wife*, before and after the assassination.

And, as our *Skeleton Key* analysis proceeds further into these murky depths, do not forget some crucial facts that most media tend to ignore regarding the placement of JFK's assassination in proper political context. Not only was JFK and his brother-Attorney General Robert Kennedy winning their war on big-time organized crime, they were starting to achieve global acclaim. They were young, incredibly ambitious, treacherously tenacious, and charismatic beyond anything that had ever hit American politics. They were making legions of friends, and equally numerous enemies. Their friends were possessed of high public profiles, but their enemies chose to stay low and slowly build their ultimate revenge for the brothers' ravages of the old Mafia system.

Talk was beginning to build about the "Kennedy dynasty;" that JFK would serve out his two terms in office before setting up his brother Bobby for a run, possibly as early as 1968, and surely 1972. Brother Ted stood in the wings, too young to be much of a political firebrand, but ready to ascend with his

---

2. *The Independent*, Feb. 15, 1992, "Who Killed JFK?" by Anthony Summers.

brethren nonetheless.

It was only when the *international* media started getting hold of this "dynasty" concept did the international drug cartels start to take notice and realize that the Kennedy way of seducing the electorate could possibly stretch into the 21st century, and that organized crime's old grip on much of Western culture would be forever weakened. Unlike the insipid and dominant Rand Corp. "CIA did it" nonsense or the "Castro conspiracy" tomfoolery (Gemstone 6:9), this solid reasoning behind what happened to the Kennedy family — and eventually Onassis' clan as it turned out — cannot be swept away from the historical scene. It is there. The early segments of the *Skeleton Key* possess this one dominant feature, that of one powerful family battling another, and their allies clashing as well. It is a story of epic proportions and, until the advent of huge intelligence leaks like the *Skeleton Key to the Gemstone Files*, was largely untold and unappreciated for what it really was. That is essentially why the JFK assassination is so horribly misunderstood. It is something that *had to happen*. History demanded that a breaking point be reached. Frankly, it is of little consequence who actually pulled the trigger; rather, the bigger question should be: Why did this take place, and what forces were in place to assure the unprecedented violence?

Summers was not the only reporter on the other side of the Atlantic who had a more accurate picture of this situation. Godfrey Hodgson of the *London Observer* put it this way in April of 1963 as the JFK political freight train was picking up steam and accelerating into uncharted territory:

"...The strength of the Kennedy family is somehow far more than the sum of the offices held by its members. It is, as a liberal columnist put it the other day, *'a fighting gang,'* bound *together by fierce ties of blood, loyalty, interest and affection* (emphasis ours). It would be hard for the President to stand against the legitimate ambitions of his younger brothers, particularly against Bobby's, given this code of loyalty and Bobby's extraordinary services as a lieutenant... It is hard to feel that the *dynasty can hurt the President himself* (emphasis ours)."[3]

How prevalent, and how wrong, this myth turned out to be. The Kennedy mystique had gained tremendous momentum, but one man — John F. Kennedy — held the whole structure together. Organized crime realized this Achilles heel, and took advantage of it under sunny skies, in late November of 1963 — in Dallas.

Some American researchers had the right, idea, too, but their theories were not reaching a wide audience. Peter Dale Scott authored a story entitled *From Dallas to Watergate — the Longest Cover-Up*, which is frighteningly close to the *Skeleton Key's* central thesis. The only problem with this story was that it was presented in the November 1973 edition of *Ramparts* magazine, considered a fringe publication at that time, brash and flamboyant, but not mainstream media during that period, which happened to be right as Watergate was blowing up in the face of President Richard Nixon. One of Scott's views again mirrors the *Skeleton Key* thesis to a large extent:

"...On the contrary, I believe that a full exposure of the Watergate conspiracy will help us to understand what happened in Dallas, and also to understand the covert forces which later mired America in a criminal war in Southeast Asia. Conversely, an analysis of the cover-up in Dallas will do much to illuminate Watergate and its ramifications, including that Miami demimonde of (Cuban) exiles, Teamster investments, and Syndicate real estate deals with which Nixon and his friend Bebe Rebozo have been involved..."[4]

Still, Scott, in most of his material related to the JFK assassination and other political intrigues, falls prey to the irresistible

---

3. *San Francisco Examiner*, April 1, 1963, "A Kennedy Dynasty?" by Godfrey Hodgson, London Observer.

4. *Ramparts* magazine, November 1973, "From Dallas to Watergate — the Longest Cover-Up," by Peter Dale Scott.

Cuban snare — tracing the Bay of Pigs operatives all the way from 1961 to the Watergate Hotel in 1972, then unloading more and more crud atop the flawed Castro-as-the-force-behind-the-assassination nonsense.

But modern media coverage has mastered these masking techniques, and even the most horribly obvious scandals are easily left alone by a skittish press corps. President Ronald Reagan's atrocious Iran-Contra affair was rife with media censorship and suppression, with criminal Lt. Col. Oliver North declared a national hero, with best-selling books, speaking tours and a possible U.S. Senate run instead of the prison sentence he deserved.

Another example was the brutal Persian Gulf War of early 1991, when Ted Turner's Cable News Network (CNN) provided the most astonishingly massive "cutout" in history — live, satellite-driven news "coverage" controlled by U.S. military intelligence. Nothing compares to live television. "Vacuums" like Mark Lane were never necessary in the aftermath of the Persian Gulf War atrocities ordered by former CIA chieftain and U.S. "President" George Bush; the electronic media took care of an entire culture in a very tidy and convenient fashion. This kind of power cannot be underestimated.

And now, we will zero in on the *Skeleton Key's* followup material on the JFK assassination, and with cross-checks, try to verify much of what is being stated. Keep in mind that the U.S. press really dropped the ball in focusing only on the aftermath of the JFK assassination itself, restricting its "investigations" to mostly the actual day of the shooting (and some limited material on Oswald's past, most of it useless, but still good copy for American consumption), and neglecting to check what major socio-political forces might have wrought this disaster in the first place — and what happened in the weeks and months that followed.

****

(Gemstone 3:6b) [Unwitting] Cover-up participants include,

among many: Gerald Ford, on the Warren Commission (a Nixon recommendation); <u>CIA attorney</u> Leon Jaworski, <u>of the CIA-front Anderson Foundation, representing Texas before the Commission to see that the fair name of Texas was not besmirched by the investigation</u> [(just off the Texas assassination commission, who keeps the fact that Oswald had operative status with the FBI secret from the Warren Commission)]; CIA <u>Dallas</u> chief John McCone; his assistant [CIA Deputy Director] Richard Helms; and a passel of police, FBI, news media, etc.

Gerald Ford was an unusual member of the Warren Commission. He was far younger than most of the Commission members, all of whom are now dead with the exception of Ford, and Ford has never been hesitant to defend in the most rigorous terms the conclusion of the Commission — that Lee Harvey Oswald fired the fatal shots from the Texas School Book Depository and that he acted on his own. Ford can speak from a position of enormous power, because he's right about the evidence. There really is very little evidence, hard or otherwise, of an actual conspiracy that led to the JFK shooting. Gemstone 3:6 explains why: Most witnesses found themselves dead soon after the assassination, and others were discredited. Lies and disinformation were spread by U.S. intelligence operations. The doctors who attended the President were young and incompetent to start with, and were caught up in the bedlam that was swirling around them; no coherent autopsy would have been possible under those confounding circumstances. That trashes once and for all any "information" that could have been useful from those well-publicized autopsy photos obtained by researcher Robert Groden. All the volumes written about how the autopsy was handled are just about good enough for the nearest garbage heap.

The same goes for ballistic evidence: The utter stupidity of the Secret Service coming up with all the "bullets" and "bullet fragments" from the presidential limousine, the bodies of Kennedy and Gov. Connally (who survived the attack), and the *stretcher* afterward (how absurd can such material be?). The only source for this "evidence" was the Secret Service, and the FBI personnel who hovered over the President's body while doctors struggled with their flawed autopsy proceedings. And what of the military? It was reported by some doctors that a military general prevented a fair autopsy from being performed on the body, which was mangled anyway from the hopeless efforts of doctors to "save" the President.

Note the careful edit from the *Hustler* version: Leon Jaworski's relationship with the CIA as mentioned in Gemstone 3:6a is stricken from the original *Key* by *Hustler.* The connection with the Anderson Foundation is also left out, along with the angle about the state of Texas trying to save some face from this terrible incident. *Hustler* , though, to its credit, mentioned that Jaworski was involved with the Texas end of the assassination investigation, a fact left out of most assassination conspiracy literature, and blames him for the suppression of information that connected Oswald with the FBI. Jaworski's skills would later be used to cover for the floundering Richard Nixon as a hastily appointed successor to fired Watergate prosecutor Archibald Cox (Gemstone 4:1). This is yet another significant connection between key information-controlling people involved with both JFK and Watergate probes. The press is mentioned here as an accessory to the cover-up because it immediately jumped on the Oswald bandwagon, especially when it was revealed he was a "Communist sympathizer" within hours after his arrest. Remember, the Cold War was still raging, and between Oswald and the Soviet Union, the American people had their short-term answer to the JFK killing and their long-term scapegoat in one neat package.

(**Gemstone 3:7a**) Where are they now? Johnny Roselli received [receives] part of his payoff for the head shot on JFK [shooting at JFK] in the form of a $250,000 "finder's fee" for bringing "Hughes" (Onassis) to Las Vegas in 1967 [when the

Desert Inn is sold to Hughes in 1966]. **When Roselli fails to collect mob money from a Las Vegas casino owner, he is asphyxiated in 1976.**

We have already touched upon Roselli's untimely and untidy end, as reiterated by *Hustler* at the end of this passage, but what of this large sum of Hughes-related cash? It is never explained thoroughly, but a close investigation into this reference in Gemstone 3:7a will reveal a host of familiar characters to the Gemstone thesis:

"...The inspiration to bring Hughes to Las Vegas originated with Johnny Roselli, who secretly arranged for Hughes to take over the penthouse floor of the Desert Inn. But the task itself was accomplished by (Robert) Maheu and two close friends: *Las Vegas Sun* publisher Hank Greenspun, who had started his newspaper career in that gambling city as Bugsy Siegel's press agent, and Washington attorney Edward P. Morgan. Maheu and Morgan were former FBI agents, both having served between 1940 and 1947, Morgan as the expert on Communism and Maheu as a 'brick agent' on espionage. *Roselli, Morgan, Maheu and Greenspun were close friends* (emphasis ours), and all four would make money during Howard Hughes' brief stay in Nevada."[5]

As momentum built toward Roselli's big score with the Desert Inn deal, it is interesting to note that Greenspun used the weapon of his newspaper column, "Where I Stand," to rigorously defend Hughes and his privacy in Las Vegas. The reasoning was clear: Through his old maritime business connections (see Chapter 4), Greenspun knew the terrible secret behind "Hughes" (Gemstone 7:9).

In 1966, when "Hughes" first moved into Las Vegas, the entire world wondered why. This was the last place a reclusive billionaire like Howard Hughes would want to find himself. Yet,

---

5. *The Last Mafioso*, by Ovid Demaris, N.Y. Times Books, 1981, p. 184.

this is where he reportedly stayed for a short time. It is easier in this context to believe the *Skeleton Key's* reasoning for Hughes' presence in Las Vegas to begin with: That he was not Hughes at all, but a double, having been kidnapped and "switched" nine years earlier in the Bahamas. This would go far in explaining why "Hughes" wanted to even come near a wild and open place like Las Vegas — and why he would even think of associating with gangsters, and letting them spend his vast fortune for him.

Like a leech siphoning blood from a host, organized crime siphoned money from "Hughes" during his brief Vegas visit. The Desert Inn transaction was a tremendous heist, and since Hughes was the only individual capable of coming up with enough cash to satisfy the needs of the JFK conspirators, or so the *Key* implies, it would only be natural to make Las Vegas a prime payoff point. Roselli bragged about his role in the Desert Inn purchase by Hughes, and brought another name into the picture — a name inexplicably left out of Gemstone 3:7a, the name of *Sam Giancana, one of the Mafia kingpins most closely linked to a mob assassination plot to kill President Kennedy!* This linkage is a definite support of the Gemstone thesis compared to other conspiracy advocates who fail to bring the Vegas connection into the JFK picture:

"The deal for the Desert Inn was finalized at $13.6 million. On the surface, it appeared as an ordinary transaction, but, as Roselli would explain to Jimmy (Fratianno), it was anything but ordinary.

"Throughout this period, Roselli and Jimmy had few opportunities for any lengthy conversations, for each was tied up with his own affairs (like separate payoffs for their respective roles in the JFK murder, if the *Key* is any indicator). But on this evening, it was a time for celebration. They met in a hotel room at the Desert Inn and both men removed their jackets and ties, slipped off their shoes, and with drinks and cigars, settled down for a long evening of catch-up talk.

"Roselli puffed on the cigar and grinned at Jimmy. *'I just split four hundred big ones with Sam (Giancana),'* he said (emphasis ours), his blue eyes watching for Jimmy's reaction.

"Jimmy gasped.

"'Let me lay this one out for you,' Roselli said with a proud smile. 'We've roped Hughes into buying the D.I. Now it looks like he wants to buy out the whole town, if we let him...

"'...What's even better, Sam and I get to split a finder's fee...of $800,000 — under the fucking table.'

"Jimmy did a double-take. 'I thought you said it was four hundred.'

"'Right, but that's only half,' Roselli said. 'We get the rest later...'"[6]

Despite the smokescreen thrown up with this "conversation," it is obvious that Roselli is receiving a large sum of money for doing apparently little. Either it was part of a payoff for his part in the JFK assassination, as the *Skeleton Key* asserts, or it was a giveaway — and the Mafia never does anything for free.

And the connection with Giancana on this deal is something overlooked for years by the conspiracy crowd, and with good reason. Anyone mentioning this would start the rumor mill going on alternate conspiracy theories which would depart from the "skids" provided by Castro and lesser Mafia entities. It would start people talking about the real reasons behind the JFK assassination as the *Skeleton Key* has outlined them. Such information would never receive widespread attention or dissemination by the New York publishing oligarchy. It would forever be shoved into underground status — until now.

****

Before we touch upon the alleged JFK-related payments to Fratianno and other post-assassination circumstances the *Skeleton Key* dutifully describes, it might be a good idea to study the veracity of having Roselli and Fratianno involved in the assassi-

---

6. *Ibid.*

nation in the first place. For one, both men carried high rankings in organized crime's hierarchy at the time, and some researchers doubt they would "dirty their hands" by attempting to assassinate the President of the United States. It has also not been proven they were in Dallas that day (although it has not been proven they *weren't* in Dallas that day), and other factors might have prevented their participation as outlined in the *Skeleton Key*. Still, Roselli has always admitted his role in the CIA-supported attempts on the life of Cuban leader Fidel Castro, so it is obvious he was still in the shooting business. As for Fratianno, he could still pack a pistol with the best of them.

The skepticism of a Roselli-Fratianno involvement dissipates even further when it was apparent that the Mafia had already botched the Castro job, and that more industrial-strength talent was needed to get to JFK. There is ample evidence pointing to *multiple conspiracies* involving plots to murder Kennedy, and we will outline a few of those here — as documented by news reports. It is interesting that assassination theorists tend to ignore these prior attempts on Kennedy's life, which date back to his status as the Democratic nominee:

Grab 2 Gunmen
KENNEDY DEATH PLOT?

CHICAGO, Nov. 4 (1960) — Police tonight seized a man who they said was chasing the car of Sen. John Kennedy with a .25 caliber automatic loaded and cocked in his pocket.

An hour earlier, before the Democratic presidential candidate's motorcade drove into view, another man was apprehended carrying a revolver in a brown paper bag at the entrance of the Chicago stadium.

Both men, questioned separately, said they were carrying the arms for their own protection. Both men were held without charge for further questioning.

The second man, who identified himself as Jaime Cruz, 30,

of Puerto Rican descent, was pinned down by police after a furious struggle. Patrolman Vincent Moretti told the story:

Kennedy's motorcade was inching through the jammed streets approaching the stadium when Moretti said he brushed against a man and felt the bulge of a pistol. Cruz, Moretti said, was chasing the Kennedy car and was about *20 feet behind trying to "close in"* (emphasis ours).

"When he saw me, he put his hand in his pocket and then started to run. I had to tackle him and then about 20 officers jumped in.

"I hollered, 'he's got a gun in his pocket.' I had to rip the pocket to get the gun out.

"He put up a helluva struggle. *It took the 20 of us to take him* (emphasis ours)."

The weapon contained a shell in the chamber and the safety was removed.

...The man with the revolver in the paper bag was identified as Israel Dabney, 61, a Negro. He told officers he was carrying the weapon for his own protection as he "lived in a bad neighborhood." He insisted he had no designs on Kennedy's life.[7]

This astonishing incident was not widely reported by the media; the above account was rendered by a combination of Associated Press and United Press International wire copy that was rewritten for the *San Francisco Examiner*. It was clear that JFK was a target even before he was elected President of the United States.

More incidents were to follow, such as in this report dated Aug. 28, 1961:

---

7. *San Francisco Examiner*, Nov. 5, 1960, "Kennedy Death Plot?" by the Associated Press and United Press International.

Old Man's Confession
PLOT TO KILL JFK REVEALED

(A mentally deranged old man set out to kill President-elect Kennedy last winter, but changed his mind. Details of the episode, as the old man related them to the Secret Service, came to light today.)

WASHINGTON, Aug. 27 — (UPI) — A desire to spare the lives of President Kennedy's wife and two children caused a 73-year-old man to abandon his "human bomb" attempt on the life of the Chief Executive.

Richard P. Pavlick was parked in front of the Joseph P. Kennedy home in Palm Beach, Fla., last Dec. 11, a Sunday. He was waiting for the then-President-elect to leave his father's house to attend mass at St. Edward's Roman Catholic Church.

Inside Pavlick's 1950 green Buick with New Hampshire tags were seven sticks of dynamite and detonating equipment. Pavlick planned to smash his car into Kennedy's and set off the explosives.

"I intended to die at the same time," Pavlick said later.

Although the Secret Service had been tipped off about Pavlick and was looking for him, *agents apparently failed to spot him as he sat in his car in front of the Kennedy house* (emphasis ours).

...After his arrest, he told John A. Marshall, agent-in-charge of the service's Miami office, that he did not carry out his "human bomb" plan because he did not wish to kill Jacqueline Kennedy, the President's wife, and their two children, Caroline, 3, and John Jr., then a month old.

...Pavlick was arrested *four days later* (emphasis ours).[8]

The above account is a glaring example of the lax protection offered Kennedy by his own Secret Service crew. Clearly, the

---

8. *San Francisco Examiner*, Aug. 28, 1961, "Plot to Kill JFK Revealed," United Press International.

security breakdown in Dealey Plaza on Nov. 22, 1963, was not an isolated occurrence. Note that, in the above situation, that the Secret Service did not detect the bomb's danger, and that they were slow in finally arresting the suspect.

Only a few days later in 1961, another incident was reported, this one closer to the Kennedy family's so-called summer White House in Hyannis Port, Mass.:

COP ALERT ON THREAT TO JFK

QUINCY (Mass.), Sept. 2 (1961) — Search for a two-gun (?) escaped mental patient who allegedly threatened the life of President Kennedy centered here today.

A motorist told police he was *shot twice by a man resembling the suspect* (emphasis ours). The shooting was at Quincy within 30 miles of the summer White House.

At Hyannis Port, Kennedy's Secret Service detail, however, *expressed no special concern* (emphasis ours).

Massachusetts state police, in their search for the mental patient, ordered an all-out alert of all state and local police in the Cape Cod-South Shore area. Roadblocks established earlier on entrances to the Cape were manned by double forces and additional roadblocks were ordered.

Maine state police broadcast a general alert that former mental patient Howard Cooper, 48, of the Boston suburb of Brookline was reported to have been living in the state (of Massachusetts) in recent weeks.[9]

Note that, once again, Kennedy's indifferent Secret Service people appeared to be slow in reacting to a possible threat. This incident is significant because local and state police saw fit to take the extreme measure of blocking entrances to the Cape Cod

---

9. *San Francisco Examiner*, Sept. 3, 1961, "Cop Alert on Threat to JFK," United Press International.

area and deploy plenty of manpower to insure the protection of the Kennedy family even when the Secret Service saw no apparent need.

In 1962, another report surfaced:

A THREAT TO KILL KENNEDY

WASHINGTON, June 9 (1962) — (UPI) — The Secret Service disclosed Saturday that it is investigating a reported threat to kill President Kennedy by a man who claimed he lost money in the recent stock market.

A Secret Service spokesman said the service *felt there was "no significant danger" to Kennedy* (emphasis ours).

Agents stationed in New York are looking into the incident. The man is thought to be in that city.

The Secret Service spokesman said the man's identity was known but he declined to give the name or any description.

The spokesman said the service was told that the man mentioned a specific method for killing the President but this information was also withheld...[10]

Again, a lack of enthusiasm on the Secret Service's part is reported, and it is apparent that these three reports probably represent only a small fraction of the actual death threats Kennedy received during his stormy presidency. This illustrates, too, why the lack of protection for JFK in Dallas on the day of his assassination was even more incredulous, given the atmosphere. In short, it is clear that more than one conspiracy to assassinate Kennedy was in the works at any given time during his tenure as President.

When the assassination of JFK actually occurred, it was equally astonishing just how fast the media jumped on the

---

10. *San Francisco Examiner*, June 10, 1962, "A Threat to Kill Kennedy," United Press International.

Oswald angle. The Associated Press account presented in the Nov. 23, 1963, edition of the *San Francisco Examiner* typified the national tone:

PRESIDENT KENNEDY ASSASSINATED

DALLAS — (AP) —President John F. Kennedy was assassinated yesterday.

He was shot by a sniper while riding through the streets in what had been a triumphant motorcade.

Nearly 12 hours later, Lee H. Oswald, a 24-year-old man who *professed love for Russia*, was charged with the murder.

Officers said he was the man *who hid on the fifth floor of a textbook warehouse and snapped off three quick shots that killed the President and wounded Governor John B. Connally of Texas* (emphasis ours).

As the shots reverberated, blood flowed from the President's face. He fell *face downward* (emphasis ours) in the back seat of his car. His wife grasped his head and tried to lift it, crying, "Oh, no!"

The assassin *used a telescopic rifle from 100 yards* (emphasis ours) to kill the 35th President of the United States. Kennedy was shot at 12:31 p.m. CST (10:31 a.m. PST).[11]

This account is riddled with clear violations of virtually every basic journalistic axiom. Errors of fact abound. The presumed circumstances of the shooting are presented as *facts*, not possibilities. And this report was published in less than 24 hours after the assassination. How could Associated Press's reporters and editors nail down the exact sequence of events (fourth paragraph) in so short a period of time? How could they emphasize, in the fifth paragraph, that Kennedy's body fell "face

---

11. *San Francisco Examiner*, Nov. 23, 1963, "President Kennedy Assassinated," Associated Press.

downward" when he actually was forced backward? How could they already determine the murder weapon in the sixth paragraph, when the Italian rifle had just been "found" in the Texas School Book Depository?

And how could they have gotten the wrong floor (fifth paragraph) in the story? The *sixth* floor of the Texas School Book Depository was eventually isolated as the site of the sniper's nest. Granted, in the emotion of such moments, it would be easy for facts to become garbled. But this report was published almost a day after the fact. It would be difficult to blame all the inaccuracies (and incredible presumptions of fact) on simple emotion. Obviously, Associated Press was fed this version by outside sources who wanted to isolate Oswald very early in the process.

Even more amazing is the editorial comment that accompanied the lead story:

<u>JOHN F. KENNEDY</u>
<u>An Editorial</u>

The assassination of President Kennedy has overwhelmed the Nation with grief. In Dallas, Texas, that grief must be almost intolerably compounded with shame.

As (sic) now (it) is clear the assassination was committed by a Communist fanatic unaware of the depth of evil to which such dogma could lead him. In so doing he served the Communist cause (sic) its worst setback in the 46 years since its baneful inception (emphasis ours).

And certainly the President was the victim of insensate hatred — so depraved and vicious as to be beyond normal understanding...[12]

---

12. *San Francisco Examiner*, Nov. 23, 1963, "John F. Kennedy, an Editorial."

So, only 24 hours after the assassination, the assassin has been found, convicted, and his Communist leanings exposed. Clearly, the U.S. press was used as a mouthpiece to establish a "motive" for the assassination, and none of the facts were even in yet surrounding the stunning events at Dealey Plaza. All this in less than a day; it took years for the Watergate scandal to be fully reported and make any sense.

The single-assassin scenario in the JFK murder was propped up by the U.S. media for years, and it was astonishing that the Warren Commission Report was accepted as gospel without so much as a whimper. The assumption was that the Warren Commission was made up of people who were genuinely seeking the truth. As history has taught us, this was simply not true. The Warren Commission went out of its way to ignore many important pieces of evidence brought before it, and to bar many potentially important witnesses from testifying in the first place. Whatever the truth of the JFK assassination, the news media in America can never be excused from its full endorsement of the Warren Report.

Mark Lane, mentioned earlier as author of so-called "cut-out" versions of the JFK assassination that take a "conspiracy" tone but fail to develop specifics, has had to modify his research in order to be published in the first place. Lane's book on the Warren Report, *Rush to Judgment*, was purposely delayed from being published in a timely manner by the New York-centered literary establishment. As Lane was struggling to get his version of events in print, the *New York Times* blocked at least one leading scholar's critical analysis of the Warren Report from being published, saying simply "the case is closed." This attitude permeates the public consciousness even today, with Gerald Posner's pro-Warren Commission book, *Case Closed*, systematically discrediting the still-surviving witnesses to the JFK assassination while fully supporting the flawed Warren Report conclusions. Posner's book received immediate and generous backing from the New York literary barons.

Lane finally did get *Rush to Judgment* published, but it took almost 18 months to accomplish the feat after the Warren Report was issued, and only after the U.S. media establishment decided the issue was "acceptable" as a valid "controversy." Lane also wrote a second book, *Citizen's Dissent*, which was published in early 1968. However, the book was never mentioned in the U.S. press, because in it Lane describes his rejection by such major publications as *Saturday Evening Post, Life, Look* and other major magazines whose editors refused to even consider evidence that contradicted the Warren Report.

Clearly, the media in this country has staged a "conspiracy" of its own by letting arguments against the Warren Report be shunted aside, and attacking them with a vengeance as soon as they begin to achieve even marginal public acceptance. The most striking example to date is Oliver Stone's movie *JFK*, which was blasted by the establishment press to such a degree that Stone had to hire internationally recognized public relations experts from Hill & Knowlton to counteract the vehement assaults.

Even the Abraham Zapruder film of the actual assassination has been treated with scorn, despite its shocking testament to the monstrous falsehood of the Warren Report. The small strip of 8mm color film was censored for 12 years until it was finally aired on the *Tomorrow* show, with Tom Snyder as host, in 1975. Versions of the film have since been floating around the world in various edited states. Time-Life Co. originally purchased rights to the film before selling them back to Zapruder, and only recently have several "missing" frames been restored to fully disclose how flawed the Warren Report's version of the assassination really is. The most recent use of these missing frames was incorporated in *High Treason*, a controversial book by Robert J. Groden and Harrison Edward Livingstone. The book not only restores the Zapruder film, but uses that evidence to point out that the JFK autopsy photographs recently released by the Kennedy family are fakes designed to misinform and confuse the American public.

****

(**Gemstone 3:7b**) Jimmy Fratianno's payoff included [includes] $109,000 in "non-repayable loans" from the San Francisco National Bank (President: Joe Alioto). Credit authorization for the series of loans, from 1964 to 1965, came from Joe Alioto and a high Teamster official. Dunn & Bradstreet noted this transaction in amazement, listing the loans in their 1964-65 monthly reports, and wondering how Fratianno could obtain so much "credit," as his only known title (listed in D&B) was "Mafia Executioner." Fratianno went around for years bragging about it: "Hi there. I'm Jimmy Fratianno, Mafia Executioner..." A bank V.P. told the whole story to the California Crime Commission, where Al Harris heard it, and it was hidden in a file folder there. Al Harris, who later shot off his mouth a little too much, "heart attacked."

(**6:3**) "Gemstone" papers rolling around the world here and aboard kept the situation hot. Everyone was nervous. Rockefeller gave Kissinger $50,000 for Carlson and Brisson to write their "expose" for *Look* magazine entitled *The Alioto Mafia Web*. Their mission: Find out everything that was public record about Alioto's connection with the JFK murder (his payoffs to Fratianno, listed in D&B) and explain it away — in any way that didn't lead back to Dallas. The idea was to get Alioto to quickly go away but still keep the lid on everything.

These passages, mostly censored in the *Hustler* version of the Skeleton Key, deal with sensitive information pertaining to former San Francisco Mayor Joseph L. Alioto. It is our conclusion that Alioto was never part of the Mafia-related plot to assassinate President Kennedy, mainly because he was doing very well in the legal profession and had been the top antitrust attorney in America. The cases in which he was most successful included the antitrust lawsuit brought against the National Football League by Oakland Raiders owner Al Davis, who moved his football franchise to Los Angeles against the wishes of the NFL in the early 1980s. After crushing the NFL's case in court, Alioto received a reported $3 million fee from Davis.

Alioto was also noted for the case against *Look* magazine, in which he sued the magazine for libel, won the case after two trials, and forced the magazine to fold (Gemstone 7:5). In that case, he was victimized by the lengthy story, *The Web That Links San Francisco's Mayor Alioto and the Mafia*, published in the Sept. 23, 1969, issue of *Look*, and authored by Richard Carlson and Lance Brisson. The *Skeleton Key's* insistence that this story was designed to discredit Alioto has merit (Gemstone 6:3), because carefully planted "skids" keep the Mafioso in the story safely separated from the JFK assassination. And, although some facts in the story appear to be correct, many of the alleged "associations" Alioto had with alleged mobsters simply do not ring true.

In our view, more direct references to any association Alioto might have had with Jimmy "The Weasel" Fratianno can be found in the Ovid Demaris text, *The Last Mafioso*, against which Alioto never filed a suit, despite the references to his links with Mafioso which could be construed as much more serious than those in the *Look* story. The book, as described earlier, is written in a curious conversational style, as if Demaris had access to actual tapes of conversations, or he was in the same room when they took place. Nevertheless, Demaris records several conversations between Alioto and Fratianno, and lays out a loan deal similar to the one described in Gemstone 3:7b. The book also confirms Alioto's somewhat liberal lifestyle, confirming what Gemstone 4:6 says about Alioto's alleged "philandering." This opens the door to even more serious allegations against Alioto, but none, in our view, have nearly as much merit as Bruce Roberts would like everyone to believe.

Regarding a loan, or loans, to Fratianno, Demaris states:

"...Alioto quickly placed a call to Nick Rizzo at the First San Francisco Bank and told him that Jimmy (Fratianno) would be in for a loan. The loan was for $60,500, discounted at four percent simple interest. *It was the first of five loans Jimmy would receive from Alioto's bank....Jimmy was not asked to furnish a financial statement...*(emphasis ours)"[13]

Look magazine further describes these loans, detailing how they came about and specifically when they were made and for what amounts. The most glaring information, though, which could conceivably connect Alioto to the JFK assassination payoff scenario as outlined in the *Skeleton Key* involved descriptions of a meeting (or meetings) at the Nut Tree restaurant in Vacaville, Calif. (Gemstone 4:6), between Alioto, Fratianno and alleged Mafioso in 1964 — meetings which set the stage for Fratianno's loans as described in Gemstone 3:7b. These meetings were described in extraordinary detail by the *Look* story — detail which would not be available unless the individual supplying this information were covertly observing the meetings in process.

Confusing this issue is the fact that the *Skeleton Key* scatters references to Alioto, Fratianno, the alleged meetings and loans throughout its text — making it tough to reconstruct the premise. Following are the other references:

(Gemstone 4:6) Silva, a San Francisco private detective hired by Angelina Alioto to get the goods on philandering Joe, followed Joe Alioto to Vacaville to the Nut Tree Restaurant, where Joe held a private meeting with other Mafioso to arrange the details of the JFK assassination payoff to Fratianno.

(6:3) "Gemstone" papers rolling around the world here and aboard kept the situation hot. Everyone was nervous. Rockefeller gave Kissinger $50,000 for Carlson and Brisson to write their "expose" for *Look* magazine entitled *The Alioto Mafia Web.* Their mission: Find out everything that was public record about

---

13. *The Last Mafioso*, by Ovid Demaris, ©1981 Times Books, p. 142.

Alioto's connection with the JFK murder (his payoffs to Fratianno, listed in D&B) and explain it away — in any way that didn't lead back to Dallas. The idea was to get Alioto to quickly go away but still keep the lid on everything.

(7:5) October, 1971: *Look* magazine apologized to Alioto for their "Alioto Mafia Webb" article — and folded. The sticking point: They couldn't prove Alioto's Nut Tree meeting back in 1963 related to the JFK murder.

We will walk through these statements one at a time, and then it will be clear why Alioto felt compelled to sue *Look* with the goal of putting the magazine out of business. We must emphasize that we feel Alioto was justified in his actions, and the courts agreed with his reasoning, but it is not altogether clear *why* Alioto concluded the *Look* magazine story was more damaging, say, than the Demaris book. It must also be pointed out at this juncture that we are simply tracing through *allegations* and that none of this material referring to Alioto can in any way be construed as being confirmed by hard evidence. This is why *Hustler* simply omitted any mention of Joe Alioto in its version of the *Skeleton Key*; at that time, in February of 1979, it was clear that Alioto would go after anyone who pulled his name into juxtaposition with mobsters.

First, regarding Gemstone 4:6, the *Skeleton Key* agrees with Demaris that Alioto was accused of "philandering" by his wife, Angelina Alioto. In fact, Demaris describes an incident where Angelina waited for Joe at home, greeting him with the barrel of a shotgun, after he arrived home late one night.[14] However, there is no mention by Demaris that Angelina put a private investigator on his tail, as Gemstone 4:6 states. The private eye is identified as a man named Silva, who was later allegedly shot to death (Gemstone 11:7). We have reason to believe that this

14. *Ibid.*, p. 138.

"Silva" actually existed, and that he was the source for Richard Carlson and Lance Brisson's detailed descriptions of the alleged Nut Tree meetings for *Look* magazine. "Silva" is a crucial element here, because as mentioned in Gemstone 7:5, lack of confirmation of the Nut Tree meetings was critical in nailing *Look* as guilty in the libel trial.

(**Gemstone 11:7**) San Francisco "Zebra" Murders: A series of "random" killings, dubbed "Zebra Murders" by the police because, supposedly, blacks were killing whites. The real target was Silva, the witness to Alioto's Mafia Nut Tree meeting. Silva was shot to death in an alley. Careful Mafia planning went into this series, to kill several birds with one stone: 1. Get witness Silva out of the way, without being "obvious" about it; 2. Spread fear of "black terrorists" and convince people that the police department needed more money and more repressive power; 3. Blame — and frame — Black Muslims, knocking off leaders of the opposition.

Three questions need attention here: 1) Who was Silva? 2) Did he meet his fate as described above? 3) Were the Zebra killings a cover for this entire episode? Timing is crucial, because Mr. Silva would have had to be "eliminated" before the *Look* libel trial for Gemstone 11:7 to be seriously considered.

First, consider that the *Look* story appeared in the Sept. 23, 1969, edition of the magazine. Controversy was already raging before it went to press, and Alioto tried to get the story suppressed. He blasted it as a "wanton disregard for the truth" and filed a $12.5 million libel suit on Sept. 5, 17 days before the story was actually published (news of it leaked early).[15] However, *Look* thought it had an airtight story. Editor William B. Arthur stated that he thought the story was both "justified and accurate" and

---

15. *San Francisco Chronicle*, Sept. 6, 1969, "Alioto Angrily Denies Look's Charges...," by Charles Raudebaugh.

that "we are prepared to defend our article in a court of law." [16]

The first trial, in May 1970, ended in a hung jury, and a second trial was planned but did not take place until 1976, after *Look* had already folded. It was in the second trial that Lawrence Alioto, attorney representing Joe Alioto, took solid aim at the Nut Tree meetings.[17] If any testimony from the private investigator named "Silva," the person pegged by the *Skeleton Key* as the lone witness to the Nut Tree meeting(s), was to do the most damage, it would be in this second trial. Does the timetable fit? And what of the Zebra connection, if any?

We have uncovered documentation that a man named "Silva" was indeed among those named by Alioto as one of the Zebra (also known as "Death Angel") victims, and that circumstances indicate that this "Silva" shooting was mysterious in more ways than one. On May 2, 1974, the following report was published in the *San Francisco Examiner*:

THE RANDOM VICTIMS
A Startling Pattern of Senseless Attacks
Dating Back Almost Four Years Surfaces
By Lynn Ludlow

At least 36 murders in Northern California appear on the list of incidents attributed by Mayor Alioto to the Death Angels. Only two had been solved earlier.

Previously, 12 deaths had been blamed on the "Zebra" killers in San Francisco.

In most cases, so far as police reports indicate, victims were on foot when abducted, shot in the back or hacked to death. Of the 36, nine were women.

The list from Alioto's office includes 57 cases in Northern

---

16. *San Francisco Chronicle*, Sept. 12, 1969, "Look Editor Says Alioto Article Was Justified," by Charles Raudebaugh.

17. *San Francisco Examiner*, Oct. 4, 1972, "Pat Brown to Testify in Look Trial."

California. Alameda County had 29 incidents, *but details were skimpy on No. 11, Arthur E. Silva* (emphasis ours). Of the other 28, 16 were murders.[18]

Another critical item on "Silva" as it related to the Arthur E. Silva mentioned above: *The death certificate on Arthur E. Silva is missing* from the Alameda County coroner's office. Of all the Alameda County victims of the so-called Zebra and Death Angel killings, only Arthur E. Silva's death certificate is unaccounted for. The certificate would confirm that "Silva" was "shot to death in an alley," as Gemstone 11:7 describes.

The death of Arthur E. Silva occurred on Sept. 2, 1971. It would have happened in time for this "Silva," if he were indeed the private investigator mentioned in the *Key*, to be prevented from testifying in the second *Look* trial as the source for Carlson and Brisson's story pertaining to the Nut Tree meetings. Further, the death of Arthur E. Silva is buried in a list of 73 victims released by the mayor's office on May 1, 1974, reaffirming Gemstone 11:7 as mixing the Silva death with many others linked to Zebra or the Death Angels in order to "get witness Silva out of the way, without being 'obvious' about it."

Plus, why would the *San Francisco Examiner* make special mention of information being "skimpy" regarding the Arthur E. Silva death? Reporter Lynn Ludlow, who wrote the story, offered no comment when asked about it by us in 1990. "It's been too long," Ludlow said. "I can't recall why I wrote that into the story." In any event, such information gives credence to the *Skeleton Key's* references to the Nut Tree "cover-up" and the alleged murder that took place to keep a lid on it.

Why would Alioto consider this material to be that sensitive? The detail provided by Carlson and Brisson concerning the Nut Tree meetings speaks for itself:

---

18. *San Francisco Examiner*, May 2, 1974, "The Random Victims," by Lynn Ludlow.

"...Those (Alioto's business) obligations apparently included a series of nighttime meetings (in early 1964) at the Nut Tree, a restaurant along the highway between San Francisco and Sacramento. Among those present at one or more of the conferences, in addition to Alioto, were Fratianno, (Frank 'The Bump') Bompensiero, Angelo Marino, (Frank) LaPorte and one of Jimmy Hoffa's top Teamster representatives on the West Coast. Alioto's plan to organize a bank was a subject of intense discussion.

"After one meeting, Fratianno said he was 'excited' about the possibilities for the future because 'my man (Alioto)' would control the bank's board of directors. Fratianno also expressed the belief that he would be able to buy a piece of the bank's stock. Later, after another meeting at the Nut Tree, Fratianno said Alioto was excluding him because of his hoodlum reputation but had assured him he would be able to obtain loans from the bank."[19]

The Nut Tree was a perfect location for such meetings. Nowadays a multipurpose entertainment and shopping complex, the Nut Tree in the mid-1960s was a simple family restaurant, located in the Sacramento Valley city of Vacaville on Interstate 80 about halfway between San Francisco and the state capital of Sacramento, making access easy by car from the more populous San Francisco Bay Area cities. A small airport is also located almost next to the restaurant (it is a county facility, but carries the name "Nut Tree Airport"), making it easy for executives to fly their private airplanes in from all around the country, and escape from their busy urban environments to a more pastoral, peaceful setting. Coincidentally, Vacaville is also the location of the California Medical Facility (CMF), a prison where some of the more infamous inmates include mass murderers Charles Manson and Edmund Kemper, and a man named

---

19. *Look*, Sept. 23, 1969, "The Web That San Francisco's Mayor Alioto and the Mafia," by Richard Carlson and Lance Brisson.

Donald "Cinque" DeFreeze, alleged kidnapper of newspaper heiress Patricia Hearst in 1974 (we will delve more into that area — which is also mentioned in the *Skeleton Key* — a little later).

And although no solid evidence exists for the "Nut Tree meetings" as described by Carlson and Brisson, the meetings are legendary among the employees there. One former busboy at the nearby Coffee Tree restaurant — a subsidiary of the Nut Tree — recalled that during his three months on the job there during the winter of 1972-73, the "meetings," as mentioned in the *Skeleton Key* and outlined in more detail by Carlson and Brisson, provided plenty of material for gossip and hearsay. Some table servers at the Nut Tree would jokingly place patrons at the "Mafia table" or the "chair where Mafia Executioner Jimmy 'The Weasel' Fratianno sat." That busboy, who inquired a little too often about such matters, was fired without apparent cause in January of 1973. He felt he was let go because of his intense interest in these "meetings," which became a forbidden subject among executives and employees of the Nut Tree.

Regardless of Joe Alioto's role in all this, it was amazing to observe the tenacity by which he attacked the *Look* story. It represents a rare example of a libel suit being carried all the way through the court system, and a plaintiff with a dogged enough attitude to see the process to its conclusion. But this suit took a lot of Alioto's time and energy, and was directed straight at a magazine story which, as Gemstone 6:3 points out, carried very little new information about Alioto and his alleged "web" of Mafioso acquaintances. Further, these links have been mentioned in other sources without Alioto flinching. The main problem with the *Look* story was the Nut Tree meetings information; Alioto apparently perceived that as the most critical portion of that document, as did his attorneys.

That is why the "Silva" story remains the one breaking point for the entire episode, and that is probably why Bruce Roberts pounded away at it throughout the *Skeleton Key*. But there was one more sensitive issue: Alioto fought with equal energy the alleged "connections" he had with James "Jimmy" Lanza, a known figure at the Apalachin (New York) meeting of mob figures mentioned in Gemstone 2:1. Such a connection would have serious implications, conceivably linking Alioto to Aristotle Onassis, if Bruce Robert's assertion in Gemstone 2:1 was correct — that of Onassis briefing the dons on his kidnap and switch of Howard Hughes. The fact that Roberts also mentions the "message" Onassis sent to the Apalachin group was intercepted by the FBI, "on the basis of a tip-off from some Army intelligence guys who weren't in on the plan," gives some indication that such a message could well have been part of that meeting (the actual purpose of the Apalachin gathering mystified law enforcement groups for many years afterward; nobody could really figure out why these mobsters would meet in such an overtly public forum to discuss such pivotal business).

Concerning Lanza and Alioto, Carlson and Brisson write:

"...Lanza, who was in the vicinity of the convention of Mafia dons at Apalachin, NY, in 1957, has been friendly with members of the Alioto family for more than 30 years. In fact, Lanza's father, a San Francisco Cosa Nostra chieftain until his death in 1937, was in business with Alioto's father in a Fisherman's Wharf restaurant.

"A police stakeout on Lanza, after the Apalachin trip, revealed numerous instances of Alioto-Lanza contact. One day in 1958, agents observed Joseph Alioto and his father meeting with Lanza at the latter's office. Joseph was the first to leave and was later interrogated by Federal agents. He stated he was planning to accompany Lanza to Los Angeles the next day to represent him before a grand jury investigating the Apalachin affair..."[20]

Demaris also includes several conversations Fratianno allegedly had with Alioto, including an interesting get-acquainted

---

20 . *Ibid.*

session in 1964 that had to do with Fratianno's alleged "loans" from Alioto's newly founded San Francisco National Bank. The conversation is related as follows, with Fratianno speaking first as the two met in Alioto's San Francisco office:

"...By the way, Joe, Angelo (Marino) tells me you've got a new bank."

"Yes. It's been open just a few months, and doing quite nicely, I might add."

"Angelo just sprung that one on me this morning, but I'm going to talk to my wife about it and see about *transferring our business to your bank* (emphasis ours). He was telling me I could get a *pretty good interest rate on loans.*"

"Yes, that's true. We're a new bank and naturally we're looking for business. The competition is pretty fierce out there."

"I would think so," Jimmy said. "There's a bank on every corner in this town."

"Well, Jimmy, we enjoy a good challenge, and we've got come competent people at the bank. Nick Rizzo, our president, and Joe Demers, one of our vice presidents, are both excellent men. *When you're ready to do business with us, let me know and I'll personally call both men and advise them of your intentions. I assure you they will take excellent care of you* (emphasis ours). By the way," Alioto said, standing up and offering his hand to Jimmy, a definite cue that the final curtain was coming down, "our bank is just around the corner. If you have a moment, take a look at it."

Jimmy firmly gripped Alioto's hand. "I think we can do business together."[21]

It is evident that these outside sources of information tend to back the *Skeleton Key's* assertion that Jimmy "The Weasel" Fratianno received loans from Joe Alioto's bank. However, the

---

21. *Op. cit.*, Demaris, pp. 140-141.

jury is still out as to the purpose of those loans, and why Fratianno "defaulted" on them at a later date. *Look* magazine tried to make sense out of this, and paid a high price. Plus, if Gemstone 6:3 is any indication, the Carlson and Brisson story contained much disinformation designed to confuse people more than anything else.

****

(**Gemstone 3:8a**) [Eugene] Brading was [is] questioned by the FBI two months after his arrest [interrogation] — and release — in Dallas, as part of the Warren Commission's determination to "leave no stone unturned" in its quest for the truth about the JFK assassination. In spite of the fact that Brading was [is] a known criminal with an arrest record dating back about 20 years [a long arrest record], the FBI reported [reports] that Brading knew [knows] nothing whatsoever [whatever] about the assassination, **and Brading is not called to testify before the Warren Commission.**

(**3:8b**) Brading became [becomes] a charter member of the La Costa Country Club, Mafia heaven [a country club] down near San Clemente [, a reputed Mafia haven]. He also became a runner for the skim money from the Onassis-"Hughes" Las Vegas casinos to Onassis' Swiss banks.

Of the four gunmen allegedly on the JFK assassination squad — Fratianno, Roselli, Oswald and Eugene Brading — Brading is the gunman most likely to have actually participated in the assassination. He was photographed in Dallas, but the photos were reportedly confiscated by the FBI that day (Gemstone 4:4). However, they surfaced years later, and one of those photos was published in the recent Groden and Livingstone work, *High Treason* (photo section between pages 209 and 211). The book was published in 1989, and it marked the first time the Brading photo received widespread attention.

This lends some tremendous impetus to the *Skeleton Key,*

because it must now be determined how Bruce Roberts might have known about the Brading photograph, particularly the description of the "big leather hat, its hatband marked with large, conspicuous X's" (Gemstone 3:4e). In looking at the Groden-Livingstone photo, the X marks are clearly visible, and the hat — a large, wide-brimmed variety — has a sheen that makes it appear to be leather. Clearly, Roberts had the photo pegged in the early 1970s, but it was not made public until 1989.

"That is what convinced me," said Donald Neuhaus, the former member of Howard Hughes' personal staff who talked with us earlier. "I saw that photo in *High Treason* and it hit me that at least this part of the Gemstone abstract I had received was true."

CHAPTER 10

. . . .

Robert Dies, Ted Lies

R obert F. Kennedy began his face-to-face battle with Aristotle Onassis exactly two days after his brother was shot to death. It is recorded by several journalists, usually without comment, but the circumstances surrounding the Onassis involvement in the hours immediately after the assassination of President John F. Kennedy are strange ones, indeed. Nagging questions remain unanswered as to why he was present at the Kennedy enclave at JFK's funeral, how he got there in time for it, and if he had prior knowledge the assassination was going to take place. Capping the mystery was his almost surreal meeting with Bobby Kennedy.

In *The Death of a President*, the landmark account of the assassination by William Manchester, the Onassis presence at the JFK funeral is described as follows:

"...Rose Kennedy dined upstairs with Stas Radziwill; Jacqueline Kennedy, her sister, and Robert Kennedy were served in the sitting room. The rest of the Kennedys ate in the family dining room with their house guests, (Defense Secretary Robert) McNamara, Phyllis Dillon, Dave Powers, and Aristotle Socrates Onassis, the shipowner, who provided *comic relief of sorts* (emphasis ours). They badgered him mercilessly about his yacht and his Man of Mystery aura. During coffee the Attorney General (Robert Kennedy) came down and *drew up a formal docu-*

ment stipulating that Onassis give half his wealth to help the poor in Latin America (emphasis ours). It was preposterous (and obviously unenforceable), and the Greek millionaire signed it in Greek.[1]

There is no further mention of Onassis in Manchester's book. Another version of the scene was also included in *Onassis: Aristotle and Christina*, by L.J. Davis:

"...Onassis was in Germany when he heard of the assassination in Dallas. Apparently on impulse (?), he immediately flew to Washington, *presented his passport at the gate of the White House, and — rather astonishingly — was admitted* (emphasis ours). No less astonishing was the sight that met his eyes when he encountered the party of mourners: Ted Kennedy, drunk and doing imitations, Robert McNamara, the secretary of defense, in one of Ethel Kennedy's wigs. At some point, they all piled into cars for a wild ride out to Arlington National Cemetery and back. After dinner, Attorney General Robert F. Kennedy drew up a document in which Onassis agreed to *give half his fortune to the poor of Latin America* (emphasis ours). Onassis, joining into what, to him (on most occasions when his obsessions were not involved, he had a highly developed sense of appropriate behavior) must have been the perplexing spirit of the occasion, signed it in Greek. Jackie remained upstairs, in seclusion.[2]

Manchester and Davis were describing the same scene, and more than a few remarkable issues are raised. The first question is why would Robert Kennedy decide to conduct foreign policy on the day of his brother's funeral? It had been less than 48

---

1. *The Death of a President*, ©1963, Harper & Row, by William Manchester, p. 641.

2. *Onassis: Aristotle and Christina*, ©1986 St. Martin's Press, by L.J. Davis, p. 126.

hours after the President of the United States was assassinated. It is amazing the this kind of haggling diplomacy would be taking place. And a written document? What were its details? If Onassis was going to give away half his wealth to the poor nations of Latin America, would that not merit some mention and analysis from the national press? Something in this scene is missing; it does not make sense. Yet, it is an example of the adversarial attitude Robert Kennedy had toward Aristotle Onassis. That animosity would not soften, and tension had already built to a high pitch because of John and Robert Kennedy's crusade to clean up organized crime in the United States, reduce the role of U.S. intelligence agencies — to the disdain of the FBI's J. Edgar Hoover and Allen Dulles of the CIA — and begin a military withdrawal from South Vietnam.

None of those approaches helped Onassis' shipping business, and if he was involved in the omnipresent drug trade, he certainly would not have approved of this approach, and might have even welcomed the death of JFK. The *Skeleton Key* asserts that Onassis played a large role in setting up the assassination team that ended up killing the President, but regardless of that assertion, Onassis would be in a prime position to benefit most from the eventual steep escalation of the Vietnam War under President Lyndon B. Johnson. His ships would once again carry important war-related cargo to and from the Far East, and the defense industries anchored by the Onassis-controlled Hughes companies — according to the *Key* — would prosper. The slowdown of the Kennedys' war against the Mafia would also take the heat off alleged associates of Onassis. Happy days, it seemed, would return.

The adversarial atmosphere between RFK and Onassis was nothing new. It started as early as the early 1950s, when Onassis' illegal purchase of American ships (Gemstone 1:6) through his dummy company, Victory Carriers, was coming under fire in the United States to the point that a grand jury was looking into the allegations. It was also at that time that Sen. Joseph R.

McCarthy was rising to power as a phobic anti-Communist and was assembling the infamous "witch hunts" that would characterize the McCarthy era.

In this hostile environment, a young and hawkish Robert F. Kennedy got his start. He was a staffer for McCarthy in the early 1950s, and picked on the Greek shippers, especially Onassis, on the topic of using U.S. ships to aid America's enemies. According to McCarthy, at least 96 ships which the United States had sold to foreigners were engaged in a "blood trade," carrying strategic material to the Iron Curtain, where it was being used to "kill Yanks in Korea." Onassis was targeted despite his supposed lack of trade contacts with Communist nations.

But RFK would not let up. He met with some Greek shippers — Onassis was not one of them — in 1953 and accused some Greeks of trading with China. He was not specific, but it was clear the opium trade was part and parcel of the "trade" referred to by RFK, who added that the McCarthy Committee had some "other dirt" on the shipowners.[3] Again, the specifics were not revealed, but it was also at that time that the U.S. government was cranking up its offensive against organized crime. Any citizens who dealt with either Communist block countries or Mafia dons would be targeted for immediate prosecution and harsh penalties.

McCarthy ended up wanting to cut a special deal with the Greek shippers, since most of them, including Onassis, appeared to be technically within legal boundaries. After all, 51 percent of Victory Carriers was "owned" by American interests, despite being "controlled" by Onassis. It was this control, though, that would continually be challenged by the Americans, and Bobby Kennedy was right in the middle of it.

The harassment of Onassis' ships increased later in 1953:

---

3. *Op. cit.,* Fraser, Jacobson, Ottaway, Chester, pp. 108-109.

"...By the fall of 1953 Onassis was in the curious situation of knowing that the U.S. government had instituted some form of legal proceedings against him, but being uncertain of their precise nature... Each time an Onassis ship docked in the United States, a customs official would inform its master by letter that the ship was 'under seizure.' A few hours later a federal marshal would appear on the scene to post a 'letter of attachment' on the ship's bridge... *The captain was sworn in as a deputy marshal and allowed to continue with his duties... In effect, the government was operating Onassis' fleet on his behalf.*"[4]

All this was happening under the able eye of Robert F. Kennedy. He would never let Onassis forget that he was able to watch his every move, and shut down Onassis' entire merchant fleet whenever he wanted. This was one trait that distinguished Robert Kennedy from his brother John — that of relentless harassment of enemies. It was a trait Onassis would resent for years.

After JFK was killed, Onassis started moving in on Jacqueline Kennedy, and RFK deeply resented the entire affair. It was another reason for Onassis to want the truculent younger brother of JFK out of the picture. In the days prior to the RFK assassination, Robert would ruefully describe the Onassis-Jackie "romance" in the following manner: "It's a family illness."[5] Soon after that comment was spread about, Robert F. Kennedy was dead, victim of a sudden multiple-gun assault (despite "evidence" to the contrary) near the kitchen area of the Ambassador Hotel in Los Angeles on June 5, 1968, the night he won the California Democratic primary vote as a suddenly viable candidate for President of the United States.

The *Skeleton Key* briefly describes the RFK assassination in the following manner:

---

4. *Ibid.*, p. 110.
5. *IBid.*, p. 128.

(**Gemstone 4:9a**) June 17, 1968: Bobby Kennedy knew [knows] who killed his brother; he wrote about it in his unpublished book, *The Enemy Within*. When he foolishly tried [tries] to run for President, Onassis had him offed, using a sophisticated new technique: Hypnotizing Sirhan Sirhan shooting from the front, "security guard" Thane Cesar (from Lockheed Aircraft) shooting from two or three inches away from Bobby's head — from the rear. Sirhan's shots all missed; Cesar's couldn't possibly miss. Evelle Younger, then the Los Angeles D.A., covered it all up, including the squawks of L.A. coroner Thomas Noguchi. Younger was rewarded with the post of California Attorney General later. His son, Eric Younger, got a second-generation Mafia reward: A judge-ship at age 30 (see Ted Charach, L.A., author and director of *The Second Gun*, a documentary film on the RFK murder, bought and suppressed by Warner Brothers, for more details).

(**4:9b**) After Bobby's death, Teddy knew who did it, he ran to Onassis, afraid for his life, and swore total obedience. In return, Onassis granted him his life and said he could be President, too, just like his big brother, if he would just behave himself and follow orders

In typical *Key* fashion, the above statements include a tangle of information that needs clarification. It is not known why the *Key* has Gemstone 4:9a dated "June 17" when the RFK assassination occurred the night of June 5, 1968. This is strange because the *Key* is shown to be extraordinarily accurate in many of its times and dates. There is also concern that Stephanie Caruana, who claims to have authored the originally circulated version of the *Skeleton Key* (see Chapter 8), might have used some dated information concerning RFK.

First, the book mentioned in Gemstone 4:9a, *The Enemy Within*, was published in 1960 by Harper & Row. However, the book never achieved widespread acceptance, and of course it was in print before JFK was shot, so RFK could not have included information about the JFK assassination in it. But it was rumored throughout the New York literary establishment that Robert would update *The Enemy Within* to include his brother's assassination, hopefully tying it into some type of conspiracy (or multiple conspiracies) linked to the explosive growth of organized crime that both brothers had committed themselves to fighting. In 1990, Greenwood Press published the book once again — with no changes from 1960. Either Robert Kennedy's revisions never made the new edition, or the *Skeleton Key* is just plain wrong. Second, the Ted Charach film mentioned was indeed suppressed for a period of time, but due to Charach's persistence, it was shown to a limited audience, mostly on college campuses, and PBS later used some of his material for a later documentary which clearly showed how bluntly wrong the RFK assassination investigators were in pinning the entire RFK killing on a "lone nut assassin," the same erroneous "conclusion" reached by the Warren Commission concerning JFK. Sound familiar?

The topic of convicted RFK assassin Sirhan B. Sirhan being hypnotized was certainly on the minds of investigators of the RFK assassination — a topic we will probe in detail, especially as it relates to similar and carefully researched mind control techniques used by U.S. intelligence agencies since 1940s. Unlike JFK, the shooting of RFK took place in a crowded room, with literally hundreds of people present. Bystanders were also shot, and up to 17 bullet holes were initially spotted in the ceiling tiles and door jambs in the area of the shooting.[5]

Granted, Sirhan was the most likely suspect, as he approached Sen. Kennedy as his post-primary press conference broke up and aimed a .22-caliber H&R handgun at the candidate. He got off some wild shots before being subdued by people in the area, including track star Rafer Johnson, who wrested the weapon from Sirhan and presented it to police on the scene.

---

5. *Op. Cit.*, Davis, p. 128

Sealing off the area, police began a thorough sweep of the shooting scene, and collected the kind of information that was simply impossible to collect at the scene of the JFK assassination. The autopsy on RFK would not be botched as was the JFK autopsy, but it would be a clean effort, meticulously executed by Los Angeles Coroner Thomas Noguchi, who would later come under severe character attack after his conclusions failed to match the single-gun-Sirhan "explanation" for the assassination. There could be no mistaking Noguchi's technique; the autopsy on RFK's body took place on June 6, 1968, only hours after the shooting, in early morning. Two assistants aided Noguchi, and at least a dozen other people witnessed the procedure. U.S. government pathologists from Washington were hastily flown to Los Angeles to scrutinize every detail. Nobody present argued the startling results.

Assassination witnesses stated that Sirhan never came closer than a few feet of Kennedy, and approached the senator from the front. Kennedy used his hands to cover his face as Sirhan opened fire, and retreated as the firing continued. But Noguchi's autopsy showed clearly that the nature of Robert Kennedy's wounds precluded Sirhan being a lone assassin. The autopsy clearly showed that RFK died of a wound in the head, the trajectory being back to front, right to left, and *upward.* Two other bullets had struck the senator. One entered the *back* of the right armpit and exited out the front of the right shoulder. The third bullet entered within half an inch of the second one, traveled along the muscle structure of the back and lodged in the base of the neck. It was this third bullet that was extracted and used as ballistics evidence in the case.

In the area of the head shot, Noguchi spotted a "very distinct paper-like stapling, as we call it, powder tattooing on the surface of the right ear," according to the autopsy report, and "there was no powder in the front of the ear, no powder on the side." This was conclusive proof the shots were fired at close range, and from the rear, not the front. At the grand jury hearing, Noguchi stated that the position of the "tattooing" indicated that the muzzle of the weapon used was "very, very close" to Sen. Kennedy's head at the time it was fired.

"Allowing a variation, I don't think it (the gun's position) will be more than two or three inches from the right ear," Noguchi replied when asked about his thoughts on the muzzle's distance. The test-firing of a similar .22-caliber weapon to Sirhan's gun on a hog's head showed a similar tattooing pattern on the hog's ear. That test, and the autopsy itself, substantiates Noguchi's conclusion that the shots were almost "contact wounds."

During Sirhan's trial, this information was available, but somehow did not affect the outcome, for it was "obvious" Sirhan was the shooter. Plus, ballistics evidence was screwed up by the LAPD when one of its experts, DeWayne Wolfer, got bullets test-shot from Sirhan's weapon mixed up and mislabeled with bullets from a test-fired gun similar to Sirhan's.

As for the many bullet holes in the pantry area of the shooting, there is quite a body of evidence to show that the crime scene was altered by certain members of the LAPD, and this is where Gemstone 4:9a's assertion that Los Angeles District Attorney Evelle Younger and his staff probably had something to do with it. We have learned through several sources that two members of the LAPD's "Special Unit: Senator" (SUS) unit task force the combed the assassination scene were Manny Pena and Enrique "Hank" Hernandez, who had previously worked for the CIA in South America. They along with other SUS personnel removed and burned wooden door jambs and ceiling panels which had multiple bullet holes in them. A broadcast videotape shot at the scene also had important acoustic evidence which would show that many more shots were fired than the nine maximum Sirhan would have gotten off with his weapon.

The *Skeleton Key* also mentions "security guard" Thane Eugene Cesar, who was close to Kennedy — and behind him — when the shots rang out. The *Key* mentions he worked for Lockheed; what the *Key* did not mention was that he worked at

Lockheed's Burbank facility, which was heavily involved in the U-2 spyplane project. The most well-known photograph of the assassination shows Robert Kennedy lying on the floor, the back of his head bleeding, and a small black clip-on tie lying on the floor by his right hand. Other photos show a young security guard, Cesar, with his tie missing. Interestingly, a CBS reporter on the scene reported seeing a "security guard" firing his weapon during the melee, presumably in the direction of Sirhan.

The "hypnotism" of Sirhan became a major issue, and was used against him during his trial. When investigators searched Sirhan's living quarters, they found a large spiral notebook in which bizarre notes were scribbled. Among the notes, on a page dated "May 18, 9:45 a.m. 1968," was the following scrawled message: "My determination to eliminate RFK is becoming more of an unshakable obsession. RFK must die, RFK must be killed, RFK must be assassinated, RFK must die, RFK must be killed, RFK must be assassinated, RFK must die, RFK must be killed, RFK must be assassinated, RFK must die, RFK must be killed, RFK must be assassinated...Robert F. Kennedy must be assassinated before 5 June 68, Robert Kennedy must be assassinated..."

In the process of his conviction and ensuing incarceration, Sirhan has been exhaustively tested by experts in the field of psychoanalysis. Dr. Bernard L. Diamond, who worked for the University of California at Los Angeles and was a leading authority on law, hypnosis and psychiatry, analyzed Sirhan for his trial defense. In the process, he hypnotized him on at least a half-dozen other occasions.

Another battery of tests was administered by Dr. Eric Marcus, a court-appointed psychiatrist for the defense who put Sirhan through the Minnesota Multi-Phasic Personality Inventory (MMPI), which involves more than 500 questions answered in true-false fashion by the person being examined. Sirhan would not answer two of those questions: No. 291, which read: "At one or more times of my life, I felt that someone was making me do things by hypnotizing me," and question No. 293, which read: "Someone has been trying to influence my mind." These are indications that Sirhan might have been hypnotized many times *before* the assassination of RFK. Dr. Edward Simpson, who later would recommend the case be re-opened after pointing out "numerous factual errors" in the trial that convicted Sirhan, also argued that Sirhan was not handled properly by the court-appointed mental health professionals. It was Simpson who also concluded that Sirhan was not a "paranoid schizophrenic" as some doctors were pushing.

This vagueness about Sirhan's mental capacity at the time he entered the Ambassador Hotel and sprayed the pantry area with gunfire, and allegedly assassinated Robert F. Kennedy in the process, has lingered since. On June 2, 1977, for instance, Sirhan stated from Soledad Prison that he "remembered nothing" of the assassination. The press was speculating at that time that Sirhan might have been hypnotized into assassinating RFK, saying that author Richard Condon's book, *The Manchurian Candidate*, had sparked the rumors about Sirhan. In that book, an American prisoner of war is brainwashed into killing a presidential candidate in the United States. Sirhan responded to reporters' questions by reaffirming the statements he made during his 3½-month trial in which he said he went into a "trance" shortly before the killing and recalled nothing of the event.

The "Manchurian Candidate-type" assassin profile has cropped up elsewhere, including the recently distributed *Wilcher Transcripts* (more on them in Chapter 13), which use that term on pages 19, 26 and 29 to describe various assassination scenarios which called for "robot-like" assassins that would commit the murder — then either be killed themselves or imprisoned for life. Wilcher cites Sirhan, David Hinckley (who attempted to assassinate President Reagan), and Mark David Chapman (who was successful in assassinating former Beatle John Lennon). On page 19, the late Paul Wilcher, a Washington D.C. attorney who researched conspiracy theories, states:

"...The CIA has apparently been able to produce 'Manchurian-Candidate-type' robot assassins ever since the late 1940s, using methods reminiscent of the 'brainwashing' we have all heard about in Soviet (and American) prisoner of war camps and prisons — as well as far more sophisticated and sinister techniques which have been developed and perfected over the intervening years.

"One of the most important features of this kind of mind control programming or 'brainwashing' is the fact that critical segments of the subject's memory — including most or all of the programming experience itself — are erased (or at least suppressed and deeply buried), with new false 'memories' implanted into the subject's unconscious mind in their place. Indeed, all of this mind, behavior and memory alteration is done at the subconscious or unconscious level."

And Sirhan has had so many psychological handlers before and after his trial that anything could happen regarding his memory. There is also indications he dabbled in hypnosis *before* the assassination, and therefore the idea to assassinate Robert Kennedy might have been planted as well. The opportunities were many beforehand, according to information we have received on some irregularities with Sirhan's treatment, and some evidence at the time of his arrest that was either ignored or forgotten as the case unfolded.

First, it has long been rumored that Dr. Diamond could well have "implanted" into Sirhan's mind he and he alone had killed RFK. During the trial, Diamond argued that the trauma Sirhan had suffered during the bombing of his homeland during the Arab-Israeli War had impaired his mental faculties. Diamond then stated that he thought Sirhan had placed himself in a trance during the time of RFK's assassination and should be judged outside the parameters used for "normal" murderers. Still, Sirhan was convicted of the murder and is serving a life sentence.

In an interview with the *Los Angeles Times* in June of 1985,

17 years after the shooting, Sirhan lucidly denies he was aware of what he was doing, although he does admit to shooting Kennedy and that he regretfully must be held responsible. Still, he says:

"...That whole evening is fuzzy. I remember some things but I honestly *have no recollection to this day of firing at Kennedy or shouting 'you son of a bitch' at him* (emphasis ours). That part is a total blank...

"This is a funny thing. What I remember, in my confused state, was a typewriter typing without anybody doing the typing. Now I know that I was in the press room and what I was looking at was a teletype machine. There was a lady there who saw me and *told police that I seemed to be in a trance* (emphasis ours). That report, by the way, couldn't be found at the time of my trial but I understand they found it later...

"They claim I was lying in wait. How could that be? I did not know what way he was coming out. In fact, only a *last-minute decision by a Secret Service man prompted Kennedy to leave through the kitchen. There is another 'if.' If the Secret Service man had not suddenly changed the route, our paths would not have crossed. Kennedy would not be dead and I would not be in prison* (emphasis ours)."[6]

Stories continue to echo around L.A. about what transpired that night. It was claimed the SUS found a book in Sirhan's car at the time of the arrest, *Healing, the Divine Art*, by Manly Palmer Hall, a locally popular hypnotist and founder of the Philosophical Research Society. Sirhan allegedly attended Hall's Institute of Reflection from time to time, our sources tell us. Among Hall's clients was Los Angeles Mayor Sam Yorty. It was interesting that Yorty, the morning after the assassination, sug-

---

6. *Los Angeles Times*, June 24, 1985, "After 17 Years, 'Ifs' Still Haunt Sirhan," by Bill Farr.

gested Sirhan was a Communist and had many Communist leanings, before any real facts about Sirhan had surfaced. This was a chilling reminder of how Lee Harvey Oswald was branded a "Communist" almost immediately after he was apprehended in Dallas after the JFK assassination.

But no matter how many stories are circulated about Sirhan and the RFK assassination, some basic facts cannot go unchallenged. How could it possibly be that, five years after his presidential brother was assassinated in Dallas, the same thing could happen to Robert Kennedy? How could it be that, as Sirhan pointed out himself, the Secret Service crew on the night at the Ambassador Hotel dropped their guard in much the same way they did in Dallas with JFK? How could it be that a "lone nut assassin" was again responsible? How could it be that some physical evidence at the scene was drastically altered (i.e., bullet holes covered up or eliminated), just as evidence was clearly altered in Dallas?

And how could the results of a *good, honest autopsy done right after the killing* be so much in doubt? If RFK was killed by a point-blank range pistol shot behind his right ear, why was that not considered in Sirhan's trial or in any other commentary about this assassination? Unfortunately, Gemstone 4:9a is probably correct when it suggests a highly polished and successful cover-up managed to creep itself into yet another Kennedy assassination.

****

(**Gemstone 5:2**) October, 1968: Jackie Kennedy was now "free" to marry Onassis. [According to] An old Mafia rule: If someone welches on a deal, kill him and take his girl and his gun; in this case, Jackie and the Pentagon.

(**5:3a**) July, 1969: Mary Jo Kopechne, devoted JFK girl and later one of Bobby's trusted aides [a former secretary of Robert Kennedy], was [is] in charge of packing up his [Bobby's] files after his assassination in L.A. She read [reads] too much —

learned [learns] of the [about] the Kennedy-Mafia involvement and [among] other things. She said to friends: "This isn't Camelot, this is murder." She was an idealistic American Catholic. She didn't like murdering hypocrites. She died [dies] trying to get off Chappaquiddick Island[.] ,where she had overheard (along with everyone else in the cottage) Teddy Kennedy's end of the D.H. Lawrence cottage telephone calls from John Tunney, and to Joe Alioto and Democratic bigwigs Swig, Shorenstein, Schumann and Bechtel.

(5:3b) Teddy's good friend Tunney called to complain that Alioto's friend Cyril Magnin and others had tried to bribe Jess Unruh to switch from the Governor's race to run for the Senate — for the seat Tunney wanted — so that Alioto would have an easier run for Governor. Teddy called Alioto, who told him to go to hell; then Teddy called the rest to arrange for yet another Mafia murder.

(5:3c) Mary Jo, suddenly up to there in Mafia s---, ran screaming out of the cottage on her way to see Nader. Drunken Teddy offered [offers] to drive her to the ferry. Trying to get away from the curious Sheriff Look, Teddy sped [speeds] off toward the bridge, busted Mary Jo's nose when she tried to grab his arm while sitting in the back seat, and bailed [bails] out of the car as it went [goes] off the bridge. Mary Jo, with a busted nose, breathed in an air bubble in the car for more than two hours, waiting for help [waits for help — her nose is badly broken —] while Teddy, Assuming she was [is] dead, ran [runs] off to set up an alibi. Mary Jo finally suffocated [suffocates] in the air bubble, which was [is] diluted with carbon dioxide from her exhalations. It took her two hours, 37 minutes to suffocate while Teddy had Joseph Kennedy II steal a boat and ferry him across to Edgartown.

(5:3d) Mary Jo was still pounding on the upturned floorboards of Teddy's car while Teddy called Jackie and Onassis on the *Christina*. Teddy also called Katharine Meyer Graham, lawyers, etc. On Teddy's behalf, Jackie called [calls] the Pope, who assigned [assigns] Cardinal Cushing to help. [The Cardinal assigns priests, who appear before the Kopechnes "direct from God," with personal instructions from Him that Mary Jo's broken nose is patched up.] The next morning, the first person Teddy tried to call after deciding he'd have to take the rap himself was lawyer Burke Marshall, Onassis' friend in the U.S. Liberty Ships deal back in the '40s, also the designated custodian of JFK's brains after Dallas (the brains have since disappeared). [He (Teddy) also calls Ted Sorenson.]

(5:3e) Cover-up of the Chappaquiddick murder required the help of the following:

- The Massachusetts Highway Patrol, which "confiscated" the plates from Teddy's car after it was fished out of the pond.
- The Massachusetts Legislature, which changed a 150-year-old law requiring an autopsy (which would have revealed the suffocation and broken nose).
- Coroner Mills, who let Kennedy's aide, K. Dun Gifford, supply him with a death certificate, already prepared, for Mills' signature, listing the cause of death as "drowning."
- Police Chief Arenas, and Cardinal Cushing's priests, who appeared before the Kopechnes "direct from God" with personal instructions from Him that Mary Jo was not to be disturbed.
- A Pennsylvania mortuary where Mary Jo's broken nose was patched up.
- East and West Coast phone companies, which clamped maximum security on records of calls to and from the cottage (S.F. Police Chief Cahill was reassigned to a new job: Security Chief for Pacific Telephone).
- And the rest: The U.S. Senate, which never said a word about Teddy's (required equipment) plug-in phone; the judge who presided over the mock hearing; James Reston, editor of Martha's Vineyard's only newspaper, who never heard a word about Teddy's phone at the cottage, though residents called in to tell the newspaper; the *New York*

Times, Washington Post, etc., etc.

The entire July 18, 1969, episode at Chappaquiddick, we feel, was a set-up to ruin Ted Kennedy's political career without having to kill him. And, as self-proclaimed *Skeleton Key* author Stephanie Caruana states rather bluntly in Jim Keith's *The Gemstone File,* "...Teddy Kennedy...allowed Mary Jo to die to cover his own sickening ass, and of those battalions of folks who helped him in the cover-up."[7] In the same book, conspiracy researcher John Judge states we have been made to think that Ted Kennedy "jumped out of the car" as Gemstone 5:3c states, but some circumstances seem to place that entire picture in doubt. Judge thinks that Kopechne was dead, and that she was placed in the car before it was pushed into the water, and that Ted Kennedy was not driving it at the time. That would mean a direct frame-up, which would put Kennedy out of commission without having to go through a third assassination and third cover-up.[8]

However, when the *Skeleton Key* talks about the asphyxiation of Mary Jo inside an air bubble, there certainly might be some truth to that, at least according to Jack Olsen's landmark and well-researched work on the case, *The Bridge at Chappaquiddick.* The following sequence describes the position of the vehicle, which would indeed have formed an air pocket, and finally the position of Miss Kopechne:

"...Then he (police diver John Farrar, immersed in the water) saw that the car had apparently executed a complex maneuver before settling to the bottom. It had rolled completely over, and the front end had turned through 180 degrees, so that it was facing almost exactly opposite to its initial path of travel...

"Both windows on the passenger's side were blown in, and only tiny fragments remained around the edges. Farrar stuck his head in the rear window and saw a young blond woman. He

---

7. *The Gemstone File,* edited by Jim Keith, ©1992 IllimiNet Press, p. 50.
8. *Ibid.,* p. 196.

reached out and touched the thigh and realized that she had been dead for hours. The leg was like iron; rigor mortis had set in. *Apparently she had lived for a time before the water had risen over her head* (emphasis ours). Farrar noted that her head was cocked back as though to *reach the last available oxygen in the car* (emphasis ours)...

"It seemed to the diver that the position could not have been assumed unconsciously, that she must have been holding the edge of the seat and craning her neck upward in the last seconds of her life..."[9]

The *Skeleton Key's* reference to Kopechne having a broken nose is also backed by Olsen's account, especially with regard to coroner Donald Mills. The description of Kopechne's body after it was extracted from the submerged car carried with it some embellishments that appear to be designed to cover for the fact that Mary Jo's nose was indeed injured: "...There was white foam about the woman's nose and throat. Dr. Mills knew that the foam and the *tiny web of blood at the corner of her nose* were signs of death by drowning."[10] It is worth noting that writer Olsen even appears to be putting a "spin" on his own observations. Why concede that the blood around the nose automatically had to do with drowning? An autopsy would have shown that.

Gemstone 5:4 refers to Ted Kennedy aide Dun Gifford rushing a death certificate, already filled out, listing the cause of death as "drowning." This arm-twisting is confirmed in Olsen's account, who adds that Gifford was insistent on also rushing Kopechne's body out to be buried without an autopsy.

It is Judge who has also pushed the theory that Kopechne was a spy inserted into the Kennedy family political machine to keep track of developments. One thing Ted Kennedy endeavored to do after his brother Robert was killed was to keep *all* of

---

9. *The Bridge at Chappaquiddick*, by Jack Olsen, ©1970, p. 125-126.

10. *Ibid.*, p. 144.

RFK's staffers on the Kennedy payroll by absorbing them into his political operation.[11] One lingering factor, too, was that Kopechne, while she attended Caldwell College for Women in Caldwell, NJ., had worked for John Kennedy in New Jersey during the 1960 campaign. After graduating from Caldwell as a government major, she took a job working for Sen. George Smathers of Florida — who reportedly was on shaky footing when it came to his opinion of Lyndon B. Johnson, John Kennedy's vice president. John Kennedy had been rumored to be leaning toward dumping Johnson off the ticket for the 1964 election, and Smathers would be the replacement. Smathers shared the same ominous views that Kennedy exhibited toward the growing power of the U.S. intelligence network, particularly the CIA. Her positions with John Kennedy, Smathers and Robert Kennedy certainly provided enough opportunities for Kopechne to be exposed to much sensitive information about a variety of topics.

The rest of the *Skeleton Key's* tirade over Chappaquiddick appears to agree, for the most part, with elements of the extensive cover that Ted Kennedy's associates provided during this tragic and embarrassing episode. As for the *Key's* characterization of Kopchne's attitude just before her death ("'This isn't Camelot, this is murder.' She was in idealistic American Catholic. She didn't like murdering hypocrites." — Gemstone 5:3a), that characterization of the entire Kennedy political machine was shared by a lot of people at the time, they just kept it under wraps. Families in Massachusetts even today bitterly dislike the Kennedy legacy which has tarnished their proud state's history.

This viewpoint achieved widespread notoriety when attorney William Kunstler publicly announced what many Americans had been feeling in a Jan. 28, 1976, news conference. The

---

11. *San Francisco Examiner*, July 20, 1969, "Mary Joe Worked for JFK, RFK," by United Press International.

San Francisco Examiner reported the episode as follows:

"Not Entirely Upset" By Deaths
KUNSTLER: JFK AND BOBBY
2 OF THE MOST DANGEROUS

DALLAS — Attorney William Kunstler called John and Robert Kennedy two of the "most dangerous men in America" and said he was "not entirely upset" by their assassinations.

"Although I couldn't pull the trigger myself, *I don't disagree with murder sometimes, especially political assassinations, which have been a part of political life since the beginning of recorded history,*" he told a news conference Tuesday.

"In many ways, two of the most dangerous men in the country were eliminated," he said.

"It is hard to tell what the glamour of Kennedy could have done," he observed. "Kennedy excited adulation. And adulation is the *first step toward dictatorship.*"[12]

Ted Kennedy was also siding closer with Aristotle Onassis; the statement in Gemstone 4:9b that Kennedy "ran to Onassis" after Robert's death certainly has merit. He and Jackie were observed making the pilgrimage to the *Christina* soon after the RFK assassination, and it was widely reported by major wire services.

The rest of the *Skeleton Key's* tirade pertaining to the developments at Chappaquiddick has elements of truth in it, especially how friends of the Kennedy family closed ranks around Ted during he aftermath of the tragedy. But the most amazing material in the *Key* account is that of connecting phone calls Kennedy made from the D.H. Lawrence cottage to political

---

12. *San Francisco Examiner*, Jan. 29, 1976, "Kunstler: JFK and Bobby 2 of the Most Dangerous."

figures discussing crucial political matters within the Democratic Party, and the almost incredulous connection to what happened to Rep. John Tunney's sister.

(Gemstone 5:5a) John Tunney's sister Joan heard her brother's end of the phone call, made from her house in Tiburon to the Chappaquiddick cottage. The next day, after Mary Jo died, Joan ran away to Norway, where she was kidnapped by Mafia hoods Mari and Adamo. They locked her up in a Marseilles heroin factory for 60 days, where the heroin fumes turned her into a junkie (no needle marks). Then they turned her loose outside the factory.

(5:5b) Joan's husband complained, so she chopped his head off with an ax and was subsequently locked up in a nuthouse belonging to the Marquess of Blandford, then Tina Livanos Onassis' husband.

(5:5c) Mari and Adamo got pressed into scrap metal in a New Jersey auto junkyard.

(5:6) In the panic of trying to cover up Teddy's guilt at Chappaquiddick, many things became unglued. The JFK murder threatened to come out of the woodwork again. Black Panthers Hampton and Clark were murdered (the Chicago cops fired over attorney Charles Garry's [unreadable garble]) because of what they knew about the JFK murder squad's presence in Chicago on Nov. 1, 1963.

Indeed, our research has revealed that something terrible did happen to Tunney's sister. Whether it had to do with an overheard phone call from Ted Kennedy to her brother John is quite another matter. This much is known for sure: John Tunney was a respected Democratic congressman from California and a friend of the Kennedys. In fact, Tunney and Ted Sorenson, mentioned in the *Key* as people Ted Kennedy called right around the time Kopechne died, flew out to Massachusetts immediately after the tragedy to offer assistance. Burke Marshall, as the *Key* states, was also on the scene.[13]

And only three months before, Tunney — son of boxer Gene Tunney — had unwisely taken on the CIA in a public condemnation of the Vietnam War, in particular fingering the Agency's involvement a Laotian tribal war over the opium trade in the region:

<u>TUNNEY SAYS LAOS</u>
<u>WAR OVER OPIUM</u>

LOS ANGELES — (UPI) — Rep. John V. Tunney charged the Nixon administration today with involving American troops in a Laotian tribal war being fought over one of the world's largest opium-growing regions — with opium as the prize.

"The CIA has committed the United States to support a faction of Meo tribesmen, led by Vang Pao, whose sole objective is to dominate other factions of this opium-producing tribe throughout northern Laos," he said.

The area can produce four to 10 tons of marketable opium annually, he said, which refined as heroin would bring nearly $900 million on the American market.[14]

Did drug traffickers want to teach Tunney a lesson? Three months after the Chappaquiddick incident, six months after the statements Tunney made exposing the CIA's interest in the drug trade and its mountains of money, Joan Tunney Wilkinson disappeared from her comfortable suburban home in Tiburon, a quaint Marin County community just north of San Francisco's Golden Gate Bridge. She vanished in Bergen, Norway, on Aug. 28, a few days before a prearranged rendezvous in Hamburg,

---

13. *Op. Cit.*, Olsen, p. 242.

14. *San Francisco Examiner*, March 24, 1970, "Tunney Says Laos War Over Opium," by United Press International.

Germany, with her two children and her husband, Lynn Carter Wilkinson Jr. The Wilkinsons had rented their home at 2290 Paradise Drive in Tiburon and departed last spring for a year-long tour of Europe.[15]

Wilkinson, 30, was characterized as an absolutely normal "housewife," not prone to any errant behavior whatsoever. Gemstone 5:5a states that Joan "ran away to Norway" the day after Kopechne died, which is somewhat contradicted by news reports as to why the family had hightailed it to Europe to begin with. It could well have been that Wilkinson indeed did flee, with her husband and children in pursuit, and that the story of a "year-long European vacation" was fabricated as a cover.

In any case, the story began changing shape almost immediately. On Oct. 1, 1969, it was reported that Wilkinson was "last seen in Cuxhaven, northern Germany, which she reached on the West German passenger ship *Vikingfjord* from Stavanger, Norway."[16]

Her husband, who went by the name Carter Wilkinson, was in frantic pursuit. He personally checked German youth hostels because "he thinks his wife ought to be in one of them."[17] Such hostels often housed drug-addicted German youth, so it was curious as to why Mr. Wilkinson would seek out his wife in those areas. She was later traced to Hamburg, where a fellow passenger allegedly saw her taking a bus from Stavenger, Norway, to Hamburg.[18] It is interesting that she appeared to be in flight at this stage, which would strengthen Gemstone 5:5a's premise that Wilkinson "ran away."

---

15. *San Francisco Examiner*, Sept. 30, 1969, "Europe Hunts Marin Woman."

16. *San Francisco Examiner*, Oct. 1, 1969, "Schmeling Reward for Tunney Kin."

17. *San Francisco Examiner*, Oct. 3, 1969, "Still No Trace of Gene Tunney's Lost Daughter."

18. *San Francisco Examiner*, Oct. 9, 1969, "Tunney's Daughter Traced."

There were no further reports of Joan Wilkinson's whereabouts until Oct. 27, 1969, when the following news was reported:

"Loss of Memory"
TUNNEY KIN IN MARSEILLES

MARSEILLES, France — (AP) — Joan Tunney Wilkinson, daughter of former heavyweight boxing champion Gene Tunney, is in a Marseilles hospital after being missing for two months... Officials refused to say whether she was seriously ill.

...Reached by the *Examiner* at the hospital, (husband Carter) Wilkinson refused to say anything about his wife's disappearance or her condition. But relatives in the United States got word that *Mrs. Wilkinson was very emaciated and sick and had suffered a complete loss of memory* (emphasis ours).[19]

The staggering point here is that the *Skeleton Key* could well be accurate regarding this entire episode, which was not reported widely, nor was there any real followup on Joan Wilkinson's reappearance. First, it would appear she was in flight earlier in the sequence. Second, she was missing and not seen by anyone for over two weeks. Third, her husband sought her out in areas she would not normally be seen. Fourth, she was found in Marseilles, France, seat of the European heroin-shipping empire and exactly where the *Skeleton Key* said she was found. Fifth, symptoms of emaciation and loss of memory are indicative of being drugged for a lengthy period of time. Too many pieces of this puzzle make sense for the *Key* to have fabricated the story.

And that was not all. Joan Wilkinson could not recall what happened to her, and was unable to explain her disappearance to her family, who ended up telling the press that "she was robbed." But the theft occurred only as she wandered the Mediterranean seacoast of France — after her "captivity," if the Gemstone

---

19. *San Francisco Examiner*, Oct. 27, 1969, "Tunney Kin in Marseilles."

account is to be believed. She told a local resident in Marseilles, Lucien Canal, that she had "worked in vineyards on the Riviera" after the theft of her belongings.[20]

A woman named Leonie Rolling was reported to have found Joan Wilkinson. saying she had come to her door at a campground outside Marseilles asking for water.

"She was only skin and bones," Rolling was quoted as saying. "'Aren't you hungry?' I asked." She said Mrs. Wilkinson replied: "Thank you, but I don't accept charity." In order to make sure she would take some nourishment, Rolling offered some tuna fish and ales in exchange for a promise that Wilkinson would be able to do some work in exchange. It was at that point that Wilkinson explained that she had come to Europe with her husband *but did not know how she had lost him.*[21] Clearly, the family was mystified at the entire experience.

As for the terrible conclusion to all this, Joan Tunney Wilkinson was committed to the mental hospital in Chesham, England, just as Gemstone 5:5b states, after being convicted of killing her husband Carter with a hatchet. The only discrepancy is that, instead of "chopping his head off" as the *Key* states, the mother of Carter Wilkinson stated in court that she had discovered her son's body with "his head *almost* chopped off."[22]

If no other passages in the *Skeleton Key* deserve any credit for accuracy, it would be this material on John Tunney's sister. It remains to be seen if any of this was connected in any way to Chappaquiddick, however, despite the circumstances.

---

20. *San Francisco Examiner*, Oct. 28, 1969, "She Was Robbed, Said Tunney Kin."

21. *Ibid.*

22. *San Francisco Examiner*, March 30, 1970, "Mrs. Wilkinson Jailed Pending Trial Ruling."

CHAPTER 11

. . . .

Water Under the Gate

Could it be that the *Skeleton Key to the Gemstone Files* has by far the most accurate rendering of the two Watergate burglaries, the capture of the so-called Plumbers, and the ultimate reason why no other news organization on earth could touch the story except for the *Washington Post*? If that question were asked in 1975 when the *Skeleton Key* started floating around, laughs would greet the inquirer. But in 1993, with all the original Watergate conspirators writing their testimonies about that fateful time for public consumption, it is not wise to dismiss the *Skeleton Key's* version of events, for it is a rare case of making some common sense out of the most sensational political scandal in American history.

However, with the eventual resignation of President Richard M. Nixon on Aug. 8, 1974, the entire nation realized that aggressive press coverage that digs for and prints the truth could successfully bring down a corrupt state of affairs. But the journalistic shoe can just as easily fit the other foot — those vested interests who were crushed by Watergate learned their lessons well, and the American media establishment has played the role of passive coward ever since, especially when it comes to getting a handle on a runaway intelligence community.

Briefly, in 1975, soon after Nixon resigned, the *New York Times* made a mediocre splash by publishing revelations that the CIA had performed illegal domestic spying on dissident organizations and American citizens in general. It was that same year that columnist Jack Anderson "broke" (or was fed) the story about the Hughes Corp.'s supersecret ship, the *Glomar Explorer*, mentioned in Gemstone 13:2, one of Gemstone Files author Bruce Roberts' final entries. During the Jimmy Carter administration, the Georgia peanut farmer's alleged connections with the dark and mysterious Trilateral Commission (an organization described in detail in the *Kiwi Gemstone*, Chapter 13) and the Iranian hostage crisis brought down the Democrat in much the same way Nixon was swallowed by Watergate.

The way the Watergate case was investigated and reported raises questions which have yet to be answered (or will never be answered). These include:

- **Why the Washington press corps failed to pick up on the story:** In the early stages of the scandal, immediately after the Watergate burglars were nabbed the night of June 17, 1972, the mainstream press simply ignored major developments. The only newspaper pursuing the story was the *Washington Post*, and even that paper was trusting the story to a pair of relatively inexperienced reporters, Bob Woodward and Carl Bernstein. Only when the scandal spread sufficiently did other media jump into the story, and then only tentatively. There has never been a suitable explanation as to why this happened; the *Post* had proprietary access to almost all Watergate-related tips, detailed information and documentation. How? The *Skeleton Key* provides a workable answer — successful counterintelligence by *Post* publisher Katharine Meyer Graham. We will look more closely into that possibility later this chapter.
- **What the Watergate burglars were searching for:** The Watergate "plumbers unit" was captured during a *second* burglary attempt into the Democratic National Committee headquarters. This second entry, its timing and purpose, drew heavy criticism from Watergate conspirators

E. Howard Hunt and Gordon Liddy. Further, the burglars, as outlined in several books by former Watergate conspirators including Liddy and James McCord, ran into some severe difficulties entering the hotel a second time. Despite these difficulties, they refused to abort the mission. *There was no reason to rush into that place a second time*, unless the Nixon administration and Attorney General John Mitchell suddenly learned the DNC might have nabbed new, very sensitive information about the Republicans. Even so, the exact nature of this "information" was never disclosed; it was apparent in the end the DNC did not harbor that information, and that the second entry was never necessary to begin with.

• **The identity of "Deep Throat" which has never been revealed:** Since Bob Woodward worked for Naval Intelligence as a lieutenant from 1965-70 after his graduation from Yale, he knows how to keep a secret. He has never revealed the identity of a key source throughout coverage of the Watergate scandal, referred to as "Deep Throat." Some researchers have concluded that Gen. Alexander Haig, who new Woodward in his Navy days, was Deep Throat. The *Skeleton Key* points to Katharine Meyer Graham, through her counterintelligence source, as her own Deep Throat. We feel a combination of sources combined to become a collective "Deep Throat," and that Graham remains a key in this scenario. There is no other explanation why she decided to put the entire *Washington Post* company on the line with the serious Watergate allegations as they unfolded — without having airtight information in hand, and *without leaking that information to other news organizations.*

****

(Gemstone 7:0a) Nixon had gotten a copy of the first Gemstone papers circulated in the U.S. back in 1969. He was now wondering how much information Democratic Chairman Larry O'Brien had received about Hughes, Onassis, JFK, RFK, et al, and how much of the dirt the Democrats planned to use.

(7:0b) Nixon set [sets] up the "plumbers" unit[.] to "stop security leaks, investigate other security matters." Ehrlichman, Krogh, Liddy, Hunt, Young, etc. were the core members. [E. Howard] Hunt, as "White House consultant," worked [works] for the [CIA-front] Mullen Corp., a CIA cover [— after he resigns from the CIA]. Mullen's chief client was [is] "Howard Hughes." Robert Bennett was head of the Mullen Corp.

(7:1) June 28, 1971 [Dec. 29, 1971]: Ellsberg indicted for leaking the Pentagon Papers.

(7:2) Sept. 3, 1971: The Watergate team broke into Ellsberg's doctor's (Fielding's) office [into the office of Ellsberg's doctor (Lewis Fielding)] to get Ellsberg's psychiatric records. Team members: CIA [CIA's] Hunt, and [G. Gordon] Liddy [plan it]; Cuban "freedom fighters" [Felipe] DeDiego, [Eugenio] Martinez, and [Bernard] Barker take part. All except Liddy had worked together at the Bay of Pigs.

(7:4) Sept. 23, 1971: E. Howard Hunt spliced up the phony cables implicating JFK's administration in the Diem assassination.

Gemstone 6:9 is a crucial passage because it hints at when Bruce Roberts first started circulating his Gemstone papers. This would go against reputed *Skeleton Key* author Stephanie Caruana's assertion in Jim Keith's *The Gemstone File* that Roberts never intended to circulate his research; that he was compiling these writings as a personal diary. If 1969 is the year the Gemstone ideas began their circulation, it would behoove Nixon to pay attention to developments — and to establish a special group of trusted aides (i.e. the Plumbers), many of whom he knew from the Bay of Pigs days, to keep a lid on the Gemstone thesis.

(Gemstone 7:9) January 27, 1972: Liddy and Dean met in

Mitchell's office, with Liddy's charts of his $1 million "plan" of spying, kidnapping, etc. The plans included breaking into Hank Greenspun's Las Vegas office safe in hopes of recovering Greenspun's files on the Hughes kidnapping and Onassis' Vegas operations, which Greenspun had successfully used to blackmail Onassis out of $4 million or so. A "Hughes" getaway plane would stand by to take the White House burglars to Mexico.

The meeting where Liddy's so-called Gemstone plan came together is outlined in detail in *Will*, in Liddy's own words, and confirms that Attorney General John Mitchell was in on the entire plan. Liddy claims the "Gemstone" meeting took place on January 27, 1972. Mitchell's primary concern was then high monetary cost for Liddy's ambitious plan, which was designed to destabilize any challenges to the Nixon re-election. What is never explained, though, is why all these measures were needed. Nixon had enjoyed a heady first four years of his administration; he was effectively bringing the United States military involvement in Vietnam to an end, he was helping warm the Cold War relationship between the United States and Soviet Union, and he was opening the long-shut door of open diplomacy between the United States and China. Because of these measures, Nixon was enjoying unparalleled popularity. The Democrats were struggling to even come up with a candidate who would offer even token opposition in he November election. Gemstone 6:1c indicates that the Gemstone papers were being used as leverage by foreign governments to extract "deals" such as Nixon's controversial dealing with China, as well as the equally shady "Russian wheat deals" which gave the Soviets tremendous volume discounts on American grain. Despite the outlandish nature of this view, few other explanations have been offered to explain he "success" by which Nixon dealt with these otherwise hostile governments.

(Gemstone 8:0) February, 1972: Liddy and Hunt traveled

around a lot, using "Hughes Tool Co." calling cards and aliases from Hunt's spy novels.

(8:1a) Liddy, Hunt and other Watergaters dropped by for a beer at the Drift Inn, where they were photographed while sitting on bar stools; the photos were for Katharine Graham and were later used in the *Washington Post* when Liddy, Hunt and the others were arrested at Watergate — because CIA men like Liddy and Hunt aren't usually photographed.

It is true that photos of the Watergate burglars were not easily available, and that the *Washington Post* appeared to be the first newspaper to acquire them. It was only after the Watergate allegations achieved more notoriety that photos of all the conspirators were made widely available to media other than the *Post*. Note also that the *Skeleton Key* passages above were edited out of the *Hustler* version — further blocking opportunities of research in the more gray areas of the Watergate probe and helping to further discredit the "investigation" (Gemstone 12:3).

(Gemstone 8:2) February, 1972: Francis L. Dale, head of CREEP and ITT board of directors member, pushed Magruder to push Liddy into Watergate.

(8:6) April, 1972: Money pours into CREEP: "Gulf Resources and Chemicals Corp., Houston, Texas" [Gulf Oil Corporation] contributes $100,000. [Ashland Oil, $100,000; Braniff Airways, $40,000; American Airlines, $55,000. Financier] Robert Vesco gives Maurice Stans [and John Mitchell a] $200,000 "campaign contribution," etc., etc. Liddy gives McCord $76,000 [, etc.] McCord buys $58,000 worth of bugging equipment, cameras, etc.

Finances of the Committee to Re-Elect the President — unflatteringly referred to as CREEP by the *Skeleton Key* — have long been targets of controversy, as were the finances of Nixon himself throughout his political career. The late conspiracy theorist Mae Brussell places Howard Hughes's financial "investment" in Nixon back to 1946, when Nixon ran for Congress in California against Jerry Voorhis, and when he was still technically serving in the U.S. Navy (he was a "supply officer" serving in the South Pacific during World War II, and left the service as a lieutenant commander). Backed by Hughes, Nixon went on to ruin Voorhis in a brutal public-relations attack and win that election by 16,000 votes, launching his political career. He also helped Sen. Joseph McCarthy lay groundwork to harass any number of political "enemies" through the Committee on Un-American Activities.

Gemstone 5:7 simply refers to Nixon as "Mafia" himself, a blunt statement and seemingly without foundation unless Nixon's finances are examined closely. First, Nixon was apparently bankrolled to a large extent by Aristotle Onassis himself, although this information is not common knowledge. In a book entitled *The Empire of Howard Hughes*, by Davenport and Lawson, an alleged deal involving Onassis and John Mitchell, who later served as Nixon's attorney general and who had advance knowledge of the Watergate plans, was described as being worth "$900 million," and that Martha Mitchell had some knowledge of "her husband's and Nixon's relations with the Onassis shipping industry."[1]

Other widely documented contributions from mob figures to Nixon include $5,000 from Mickey Cohen during Nixon's '46 campaign against Voorhis; an additional $75,000 from Cohen during the 1950 Senate campaign, Carlos Marcello's $500,000 delivered to Nixon in 1960, and $1 million backing for Nixon supplied by Teamsters power brokers Frank Fitzsimmons and Tony Provenzano.[2]

---

1. *The Gemstone File*, ©1992 IllumiNet Press, edited by Jim Keith, pp. 127-128.

2. *Ibid.*

(**Gemstone 8:7**) May, 1972: J. Edgar Hoover had [has] the Gemstone file [File]; [and] threatened [threatens] to expose Dallas-JFK in an "anonymous" book, *The Texas Mafia*. Instead, someone put sodium morphate in his apple pie. The corpse was carted away from his home in the back seat of a Volkswagen — [and] his files were burned, but some of them got away [although some are retrieved].

(**8:8a**) May 28, 1972: First break-in at [the] Watergate. McCord, Barker, Martinez, Garcia, Gonzales and Sturgis were involved. DeDiego and Pico stood guard outside. Hunt and Liddy directed the operation from a (safe?) distance — across the street. The object was [is] to check on Onassis' two men at the Democratic Party headquarters: Larry O'Brien and [R.] Spencer Oliver. (O'Brien's chief "public relations" client had [has] been "Hughes;" Oliver's father worked for Onassis). [James W.] McCord wiretapped [wiretaps] their [the Democratic National Committee's] phones. [Oliver's phone is tapped.]

(**8:8b**) But! Little did [does] McCord know [that] the "plumbers" were [are] being observed by Hal Lipset, Katharine Graham's S.F. detective, who had followed two of the plumbers from Liz Dale's side in San Francisco to Watergate. [a detective, who reports his operations by radio-phone.] Lipset "watched in amazement" as the plumbers broke in and bugged the phones; then he reported back to his boss, Graham. Lipset and Graham set the trap [and the trap is set] for the Watergaters when they returned [return] to remove their bugs and equipment.

(**8:9a**) June 17, 1972: Bernard Barker was wearing his Sears, Roebuck deliveryman costume — the same one he wore at the Dr. Fielding break-in and at the Hahnemann's Hospital murder of the senior Roberts.

(**8:9b**) Hal Lipset, Graham's spy, was dressed as a mailman. He left his mailsack behind when he taped the door at Watergate [The detective tapes the door lock at the Watergate], watched [watches as] security guard Frank Wills remove [removes the tape] it and walks on, retaped the door [; he *retapes* the lock,

Wills sees the door taped again] and, as a result, Frank Wills went [goes] across the street and called [to call] the police — and McCord, Martinez, Sturgis, Barker and Gonzales were [are] caught in the act. Graham had them on tape and film, too, every minute of the time. Liddy and Hunt, across the street supervising via walkie-talkie, were not [are not caught].

Rumors of the alleged involvement of Hal Lipset as Katharine Graham's spy have been banging around the city of San Francisco for years. In a telephone interview with us on Nov. 23, 1993, Lipset stated, without being prompted: "I didn't have anything to do with Topaz, or whatever it was called (he avoided the use of the term 'Gemstone'). People were saying I spied for Kay Graham, but that's a bunch of baloney."

Lipset's unprompted use of the term "Topaz" is interesting, since that was one of Liddy's "Gemstone" options listed in *Will*: "...I presented a plan for four black-bag jobs, OPALS I through IV. These were clandestine entries at which *microphone surveillances* could be placed, as well as TOPAZ: photographs taken of any documents available, including those under lock."[3] Crucial point: Watergate's first burglary was an *OPAL operation*. The second break-in was a *TOPAZ operation*, because Nixon aide Jeb Stuart Magruder wanted the burglars to "...photograph *everything*...in those files," a task termed too risky by both Liddy and Hunt. Liddy also adds, in italics, what the purpose of that second break-in was: "...*The purpose of the second Watergate break-in was to find out what (DNC chief Larry) O'Brien had of a derogatory nature about us, not for us to get something on him or the Democrats.*"[4] This is consistent with Gemstone 7:0 and provides a desperately needed motive for the second burglary. Again, there was no need to find any more dirt

---

3. *Will*, ©1980, St. Martin's Press, by G. Gordon Liddy, p. 199.

4. *Ibid.*, p. 237

on the Democrats; the "dirty tricks" campaign was already well under way to discredit Sen. Edmund Muskie, which would force ultra-liberal Sen. George McGovern into becoming the Democratic "nominee" who would be crushed, in turn, in the November general election.

Still, Lipset, due to his extraordinary state-of-the-art knowledge of electronic surveillance that transcended even the abilities of U.S. intelligence organizations, was appointed briefly to the Watergate Committee as support staff by his good friend Samuel Dash, "independent counsel" for the Senate committee investigating the Watergate scandal. Gemstones 7:7, 8:8b, 8:9a, 8:9b, 9:8 and 10:0 indicate that Lipset worked both sides of the fence during the Watergate period, and would therefore be a valuable tool to *either side* in the case of a more detailed probe.

Because of this brief involvement with the Watergate Committee — he backed out on April 13, 1973, because charges of wrongdoing on an unrelated "snooping" job in 1966 surfaced — circumstances indicate that Lipset was a major source of intelligence information for the *Washington Post* during the Watergate controversy, which would back the basic premises of the *Skeleton Key*. For example, this short story appearing in the *Washington Times* reveals more than it probably should:

THE WOODWARD MANEUVER REVEALED
By Tom Kelly

Among those with whom private eye Hal Lipset has had a professional fling over the years is Bob Woodward, golden boy of the *Washington Post*.

The two got acquainted when Mr. Woodward was a reporter and Mr. Lipset was working for Samuel Dash, independent counsel for the Senate committee investigating the Watergate scandal that Mr. Woodward helped create.

"Hal had lunch every day with Bob Woodward," says Lipset biographer Patricia Holt, "and Woodward *would give him leads — all the people who had refused to talk to him* (emphasis ours).

And Hal and Dash would then *subpoena them and then report to the (Watergate) committee everything they had* (emphasis ours).

"The people on the committee would then *leak it all back to Woodward,*" (emphasis ours) Miss Holt says. "Woodward manipulated the committee and Dash knew just what was happening. Hal figured that was just the way things were done in Washington."

Mr. Woodward, asked to comment on this story from his glory days, says his recollection is that Mr. Lipset's tenure as committee imvestigator was relatively brief. Though he met and talked to Lipset several times, the *Post* editor says, they certainly didn't do lunch daily.

He did have confidential exchanges with other committee staffers, Mr. Woodward says, but not with Mr. Lipset. He declines comment on the question of leaks on the Watergate committee.[5]

This entire episode reeks of falsehood. If indeed Lipset had regular contact with Woodward during the Watergate period, including the time the committee was piecing its case against the Nixon administration, then it is certainly very possible that Lipset was supplying Woodward with leads — *not the other way around.* Clearly, Lipset's biographer is admitting here that Lipset was a virtual treasury of Watergate information that Woodward — and, indirectly, Katharine Graham — was tapping into. This places a firm foundation of truth to the idea that the *Post* and Mr. Lipset enjoyed a symbiotic relationship.

As for Lipset actually being the mailman on the scene at the Watergate hotel (Gemstone 8:9b) — and the person who taped the door a second time which led to the burglars' capture — he did not deny that openly, saying simply it was part of the "baloney" stated in the *Skeleton Key*. He did say, though that he

---

5. *Washington Times*, Nov. 20, 1991, "The Woodward Maneuver Revealed," by Tom Kelly.

and Dash — and James McCord's attorney Bernard Fensterwald — met a few days after March 16, 1973, when Judge John Sirica read the bombshell letter from McCord that placed the scandal as high as Mitchell.

"Soon after that, on a Saturday, myself, Dash, Fensterwald and McCord got together and we interviewed McCord," Lipset tells us. "That's when it all started to come out — the first brick was laid on the structure that was to eventually bring down the Nixon White House."

McCord was always tortured by the "second taping" of the door. In fact, his book on Watergate is entitled *A Piece of Tape*. Neither he nor Liddy can figure out who taped the door a second time at the Watergate Hotel. During the first burglary, taping the doors enabled the burglars easy access to the hotel — but the tape was *always removed after the burglars gained entrance*. Otherwise, it would send up a red flag to any security guard who sauntered past and saw the door, or doors, taped.

McCord was the person responsible for gaining entrance into the hotel in advance, and taping the appropriate doors open. he would then return to the hotel's lobby and signal the others to enter the hotel and proceed with the burglary. This plan was carried out without incident in the first entry on May 28 (Gemstone 8:8). However, during the second attempt, there was a major snag. According to McCord, he taped the doors as usual the night of June 17, then returned to the lobby to notify the rest of the crew that it was clear to enter. However, the men returned, saying that someone had removed the tape and the door was locked. This led to a lengthy delay in getting into the hotel; the conspirators ended up having to take that door off its hinges. They almost aborted the mission, but proceeded anyway, and they were caught after security guard Frank Wills spotted the *retaped* door and called police.[6]

---

6. *A Piece of Tape*, ©1974 Washington Media Services Ltd., by James W. McCord, p. 29.

While describing this delicate sequence, McCord does not mention the presence of a mailman — a mailman who could have removed that tape. But in Liddy's version of that same incident, he states the following:

"...Within a few minutes, McCord, (Bernard) Barker, and (Eugenio) Martinez were back wearing troubled expressions. McCord said that when they had gotten down to the garage-level doors they found the tape had been removed. McCord said he thought it *might have been a mailman who did it* (emphasis ours) because there were some mail sacks in evidence. Hunt was sure it was a guard. He wanted to abort. McCord didn't think it necessary to abort and said (Virgilio) Gonzales was unlocking the doors from the garage side, protected by Sturgis, so we could go forward or not, however it was decided... The tape had not popped off, someone had removed it. *Some mail sacks were nearby* (emphasis ours)...

"I had *no idea that McCord was going to retape the locks...once in, the tape was supposed to be removed behind the team...*[7]

Lipset was very evasive when we asked him if the issue of the tape had come up when he, Fensterwald and Dash had interviewed McCord.

"That (the tape issue) is *minutia!*" shouted Lipset over the phone. "Who the hell *cares* about if the door was taped once or twice? That leads everyone off on a tangent that goes absolutely *nowhere!*" Clearly, Lipset preferred to, as almost all journalists, concentrate on the cover-up that followed the break-in, instead of the capture itself. The *Skeleton Key* deals, appropriately in our view, with the capture, since without that happening, the entire Watergate scandal might never have been unearthed. Lipset's reaction also indicates there is something to hide in what happened that night.

---

7. *Op. Cit.*, Liddy, p. 243.

McCord's position of pushing the second break-in, despite the snags with the tapes door, has raised concerns that he might have taped the door a second time himself, purposely, to push the burglars into a situation where they might be detected and captured. Jim Hougan, a Washington editor of *Harper's Magazine*, made that assertion in a December, 1979, article in the magazine. Of particular note is a reference to how the door was taped a second time. Normally, the article pointed out, such taping was done with the tape fastened in a vertical manner so its edges would not show. But the second tape was positioned *horizontally*, so its extended edges would easily have been detected by the security guard.[8]

(Gemstone 8:9c) Time to burn files. Liddy shredded [has his secretary, Sally Harmony, shred] the Gemstone files [File] at CREEP headquarters.

(8:9d) [John] Dean cleaned [cleans] out Hunt's safe at the White House and gave Hunt's copy of the Gemstone file (File) to L. Patrick Gray, acting FBI head, saying: "Deep-six this — in the interest of national security. This should never see the light of day." Gray burned the file.

(9:0) June 20, 1972: DNC Chairman Larry O'Brien filed [files] a $1 million suit against CREEP — naming Francis L. Dale, the head of CREEP. This was [is] a big Mafia mistake — for Dale led directly back to Onassis.

(9:1) June 21, 1972: The 18 1/2-minutes of accidentally erased White House tape: [Eighteen-and-half minutes of White House tape is "accidentally" erased.] Nixon [is], furious over the Watergate plumbers' arrests, couldn't figure out who had [has] done it to him: Who taped the door at [the] Watergate that led to the arrests? Hal Lipset, whose primary employer at the time was Katharine Graham, couldn't tell him [The detective

---

8. *San Francisco Examiner*, Dec. 17, 1979, "Watergate: Did McCord Set a Trap?" by United Press International.

won't tell him]. Nixon figured [figures] that it had [has] to do somehow with Roberts' running around Vancouver tracing the "Hughes" Mormon Mafia nursemaid's (Eckersley's) Mafia swindle of the Canadian Stock Exchange; and Trudeau. The 18 1/2 minutes was [is] of Nixon raving about Canada's "a--hole Trudeau," "a--hole Roberts," Onassis, "Hughes" and Francis L. Dale. It simply couldn't [can't] be released.

(9:2) Stephen Bull's secretary, Beverly Kaye, later heard the "erased" tape, stored in a locked room in the White House. She was horrified. She sent out some depressed Christmas cards and notes to friends, and sodium-morphate "heart-attacked" at age 40 in a White House elevator outside the locked room where the tapes were stored.

****

(Gemstone 10:9) February, 1974: Mafia Hearst's daughter Patty "kidnapped" by Lipset's SLA — in a fake terrorist action.

Hal Lipset has simply denied any connection with the so-called Symbionese Liberation Army (SLA), which we feel staged a series of events — including the Patricia Hearst "kidnapping" — which were designed to do nothing more than take media pressure off the red-hot, ongoing Watergate revelations. The time frame for the Hearst kidnapping brings it within the meat of the Watergate turmoil, and only after Patricia Hearst was reunited with her family did the media spotlight again turn to Nixon, who resigned soon thereafter.

Patricia Hearst was reported kidnapped on Feb. 4, 1974, right as the Watergate Committee was bearing down on Nixon's key aides. Without exception, all major newspapers jumped on the Hearst story wholesale, and the Watergate proceedings clearly took second billing for quite some time. Patricia Hearst, after all, was a newspaper empire heiress. William Randolph Hearst, Jr., Patty's uncle, and her father Randolph A. Hearst kept the flames fanned regularly, keeping up the "intensity" right until Patty was "captured" in San Francisco soon after the May 19, 1974 shootout in Los Angeles — with police knowing Patty was not in the building that was eventually destroyed.

And the developments surrounding the SLA situation cropped up at regular intervals. The "food distribution" demand met by the Hearsts took place on Feb. 29. The "Tanya" tape from Patty Hearst was released on April 4. The Hibernia bank robbery, with Patty participating, was on April 15. It is our view that the Hearst family was fed information from an undisclosed intelligence source — it could have been Lipset — that kept them fully informed about Patty's situation, with assurances that she would not be harmed throughout her "imprisonment." Patty and her father, at that time publisher of the *San Francisco Examiner*, would frequent the *Examiner* library periodically, purging the paper's text and photo files from any inside information that would contradict the carefully controlled version of events that the mainstream media publicized. Famed attorney F. Lee Bailey was hired not only to defend Patty Hearst in the ensuing bank-robbery trial, but to keep the underlying truth about the escapade from leaking.

It is interesting that conspiracy researcher Carl Oglesby points out that the infamous "Special Unit: Senator" (SUS) was so effective in erasing physical bullet-hole evidence at the Robert Kennedy assassination at the Ambassador Hotel in 1968 that it was retooled by California Attorney General Evelle Younger — accused in Gemstone 4:9a of covering up the RFK assassination conspiracy as the district attorney for Los Angeles — into the Criminal Conspiracy Section (CCS). Under Younger, the CCS was responsible for taking over the war against Communist sympathizers in the state, as well as organized black groups. It was deeply involved in the California prison system, most notably at the California Medical Facility (CMF) in Vacaville, where the likes of Donald "Cinque" DeFreeze (accused kidnapper of Patty Hearst) were "treated" and released upon an unsuspecting public.[9]

****

(**Gemstone 11:1**) <u>April 4, 1974: Mary McCarthy, a writer who had been given a copy of the Gemstone file, said in an article in the *New York Review of Books* that the key to the formation of Liddy's Gemstone plan lay in the whereabouts and activities of the plumbers between December, 1971, and February, 1972. Answer: They were at the Drift Inn, watching Gemstones rolling around on the bar top.</u>

We obtained a copy of McCarthy's story, and the *Skeleton Key* rightfully points out the time gap as being mysterious; as for the alleged activity at the Drift Inn, we can only imagine that might have happened, although young bartender Randy Strom — son of late Drift Inn owner Al Strom and assistant to Hal Lipset and Katharine Graham in the alleged taping of conversations in that establishment as the *Key* stipulates — has implied to us that the Plumbers did frequent an area tavern, not the Drift Inn (Chapter 8). Specifically, we feel that Gemstone 11:1 relates to the following passage in McCarthy's opus:

"...Several times in his (Watergate Committee) testimony, (Nixon aide John) Dean returned to the incredible transformation that, in the space of a month and a half, had overtaken a project with which he thought he was familiar.

"'That has always been one of the great mysteries to me, between the time be (Liddy) went over there...what happened *between December 10 and January 27* (emphasis ours) and my conception of what his responsibilities were and possibly his own and others' conception (sic) dramatically changed.'

"His mystification continued and embraced the whole sequence of events right up to June 17. He had thought the plan

---

9. *Op. Cit.,* Keith, pp. 209-210

was dead after January 27. When it resurfaced on February 4, he was alarmed enough to inform (H.R.) Haldeman."[10]

Clearly, plans had been made outside the confines of Washington D.C. But where? The *Skeleton Key's* rendition about where the Gemstone plan of G. Gordon Liddy was originally cooked up is as good as any explanation.

(Gemstone 11:2) Aug. 6, 1974: Nixon and Ford signed [sign] a paper [an agreement] at the White House. It was an agreement: Ford could be President; Nixon got to burn his tapes and files and murder anyone he needed in order to cover it all up.

(11:3a) Aug. 7, 1974: Roberts passed information to Pavlov at the S.F. Soviet consulate which led directly to Nixon's resignation: The *More* journalism review's story about Denny Walsh's "Reopening of the Alioto Mafia Web" story for the *New York Times*, a story killed in a panic; plus a long, taped discussion about who and what the Mafia is. Hal Lipset, listening to the conversation in the bugged consulate room, had phone lines open to Rockefeller and Kissinger, who listened, too. Rockefeller sent Kissinger running to the White House with Nixon's marching orders: "Resign. Right now."

(11:3b) Nixon and Julie cried. But there was still some hope, if Nixon resigned immediately, of drawing the line somewhere — before it got back to the King of the Mountain himself: Onassis. Nixon, on trial, would blurt out those names to save himself: Onassis, Dale, "Hughes," even "JFK."

(11:4) Aug. 8, 1974: Nixon stepped [steps] down and Ford stepped [steps] up, to keep the cover-up going.

---

10. *The New York Review of Books*, April 4, 1974, "The Watergate Solution," by Mary McCarthy.

CHAPTER 12

· · · · · · · · · · · · ·

A More Realistic View of History

It is clear that humanity has been victimized by its own historians, and the *Skeleton Key to the Gemstone Files* gives us but a glimpse of this phenomenon. Bruce Roberts not only touches upon the preconceptions we all have pertaining to 20th-century history — he reminds us that a sweeping reassessment of our own written records is very much in order. We must also admit to ourselves that we have dug ourselves into a nasty socioeconomic hole when it comes to commodities such as drugs and oil, which now stand as the currency by which the global economy is structured, whether we like it or not.

The Bruce Roberts version of Western civilization's history might go something like this:

Humanity overcame its primitive beginnings and started to meld into civilized groups, mostly through the cultivation of crops for food, and the domestication of animals for both food and labor. In the process, opium was discovered, and opium poppies cultivated for the express purpose of producing opium for human consumption. Opium became currency in early civilizations, and the economic leverage it produced was readily apparent. Merchants, most of them Europeans, took advantage of this. By the Middle Ages, opium trade was a regular part of everyday life. Because of the increasing demand for opium, the price rose relative to other commodities, and the merchants who dealt in opium became wealthy and powerful.

Opium-producing cultures began to convert their crops into profits, and gold was a favorite medium of exchange. Ancient civilizations either mined gold, or traded for it with opium. Wars were fought over opium markets and territory. Opium-producing cultures, most of them agrarian, found themselves overrun by outside colonial powers. These colonialists were able to exert their power by way of the sea. It became obvious that those nations who controlled the ocean shipping lanes — the only existing international transportation network of that day — would become the richest and most powerful nations on earth. That opened the door for the Europeans to dominate trade and, hence, the world for centuries.

With opium and gold the major focal points of trade, the various monarchies of Europe sought to acquire the most dominant market share possible. This led to enormous friction between the Europeans. England, Spain, Portugal and France were the major players. Most of the wars in the last 400 years have been fought to preserve or expand the gold and opium trades. More recently, in the 20th century, these wars have grown more fierce as populations have increased and more potent opiates have been developed, expanding the markets for them, and the accompanying economic rewards.

With all due respect to the "traditional" history texts available, the "spice trade" was little more than the opium trade as the demand for opium grew worldwide. Granted, other spices were shipped, but opium was without question the biggest seller, and the market for opium never seemed to slump. In fact, the market would keep growing. The Europeans, masters of the sea, were also masters of the opium trade.

That was why a faster route to the Far East was desperately sought by the Europeans as the 15th century came to a close. Commerce between the East and West was increasing, but transportation overland was extraordinarily slow. The Portuguese did discover a water route to the East around the southern tip of Africa, but even that route took years. There had to be a better way. Christopher Columbus found it, and discovered the New World in the process.

The New World became a huge white elephant in the minds of the Europeans, who were greedily seeking to increase their lucrative opium and gold trade. North and South America just got in the way — until the fledgling American colonies in North America began to develop a sophisticated economy, and began importing modest amounts of opium. This was slow in developing, since many of the colonists moved to the New World, in part, to escape the drug culture of Europe. "Religious freedom" also meant casting aside the bondage of the opium pipe. However, as the colonies grew, so did the inevitable appetite for such consumables as tobacco, tea, liquor and opium. This drew the attention of Great Britain, which had already subjugated the population of Mainland China and exploited them by pushing opium through Chinese ports.

It was opium, not furs, that made the British East India Company the wealthiest group of merchants on earth, with China by far the largest "customer" for opium. However, despite the comparatively minuscule market for opium in the American colonies compared to China, the British could readily foresee an extraordinary chance to grow a massive new market for opium, and keep that market in almost total bondage to the mother country. If the colonies for some reason began to get restless or want to split from the British Empire, the British would simply withhold opium shipments. After all, this is what the British were doing to China; it should be much easier to subjugate a rough, agrarian society like the American colonies without so much as a whimper. The South was already playing along — enslaving millions of blacks to accelerate the production of cotton, which was being shipped to British mills, from which finished cloth would be shipped to India in exchange for opium. The chain of trade would conclude in China, where the opium would be sold to the masses for consumption and enormous profit. Hong Kong would become the gold exchange capital of planet Earth, which it still is today.

But where it would take the Chinese another 100 years or so to challenge the British opium chokehold on their continent, the Americans would not be so easily seduced. The mid-1700s were marked by periods of turmoil, where the American colonists were militantly opposing the British trade abuses relating to opium. Excessive prices would be challenged. The American Revolution would be the final breaking point starting in 1776. The Revolution was a raw, protracted struggle bankrolled by Americans who could see for themselves the profitability of the expanding opium trade, and wanted to see more of those dollars stay in the colonies instead of being shipped overseas to Britain. The British ruled the seas, and hence the opium trade, by crushing France and Spain in brutal wars. But the pesky Americans, driven by new tactics of guerrilla warfare, held out long enough to draw France into the war. France's economy was spiraling downward, mainly because of its insignificant share of the opium trade which was virtually monopolized by the British fleet. It was the promise of opium and the endless stream of gold it would provide the French monarchy that motivated the French to enter the Revolution on the side of the United States.

Do not forget the settlement of inland areas of the future United States, settlement accompanied by extraordinary drug production and use that continues today. Marijuana was the drug of choice for Native Americans, who wooed the invading white man and cushioned the cultural clash with the symbolic "peace pipe." Daniel Boone and his descendants cultivated marijuana in Kentucky as a hardy alternative to tobacco, and highly marketable to transient trappers and hunters, along with its extensive use as a currency to placate the Cherokee and Shawnee tribes who would otherwise rampage through white settlements. The crop was also known as "hemp," and almost the entire central portion of Kentucky was a major hemp producer for decades before the federal government put a stop to growing the crop because of its side-use as a smoked sedative.

The lower Cumberland River valley is even today an ideal marijuana cultivating area, and illegal growing and marketing of the marijuana crop — using tobacco largely as a front — provides a sizable underground economy for residents there. Law enforcement personnel are often in on the trade, and demand payoffs for "protection" from prosecution. If such payoffs are not made, the marijuana cultivators are quickly arrested and punished according to existing law.

By 1783, the Revolution was over, and the combined forces of the United States and France finally drove the British out of North America. It wasn't that King George III could not overwhelm the Americans and French had he wanted to, it was just that the struggle was getting too expensive. Instead of trying to force the issue with the Americans, the British instead turned their attention toward locking up the opium fields of India, and controlling the distribution of the drug in China. The British had already quietly poured money and resources into the American South, where the constant production of high-quality cotton from the slave-driven plantations was providing more than enough raw material for eventual conversion into Indian opium. The insistent British connection with the South helped precipitate the American Civil War in the mid-1800s.

First, however, the Chinese began to see the swath of destruction opium was causing its population. It was draining the Chinese economy of badly needed domestic capital. The Chinese work force languished, choosing opium addiction to productive enterprise. But there was hope. The American Revolution set an important example for the rest of the world, that opium monopolies — even one as monstrous and complete as that of Great Britain and its armada of merchant vessels — could be broken by persistence and will. That inspired the Chinese to take back their nation from the British opium overlords. However, the British were far superior in military technology and crushed the Chinese in the two so-called "Opium Wars," one which played out its slaughter from 1839-1847, and the other from 1856-1860. In each war, the British easily defeated the Chinese and forced stringent trade agreements on the helpless Chinese — including the *permanent* opening of Chinese ports to unrestricted opium shipments, and the establishment of Hong Kong as a British colony until 1997. Hong Kong became the richest city in the world, swollen with the incredible gold of the opium trade — the final resting point of British wealth and power.

As soon as the British locked up the Chinese opium market by winning the second and final Opium War, the American Civil War broke out. The Southern states, seceding from the United States to create their own nation known as the Confederacy, raised their own army, ejected U.S. troops out of Fort Sumter and precipitated what turned out to be a holocaust that lasted four years. Great Britain came very close to entering the war on the side of the Confederacy, but could foresee that the United States would never again give the British a toehold on the American continent, and would render moot any possible British gains from the war. However, many wealthy British families gave generously to the South's war effort and propped up the fading Confederacy in order to keep the flow of ever-crucial cotton steady.

The eventual military defeat of the South did nothing to hurt the British, however. For one, the protracted length of the war provided a springboard for a new opiate recently invented and marketed — morphine, which was shipped in vast quantities to treat U.S. war wounded on both sides. Morphine was invented by the German scientist F.W.A. Seturner between 1805 and 1817, and it is the chemical essence of opium. Where opium had to be smoked and carried with it an noxious odor, morphine was simply ingested. With medical technology beginning to develop, the syringe was invented during the American Civil War.

The syringe revolutionized battlefield treatment, which had to be dramatically speeded up during the Civil War because of the astonishing casualty rate. Battlefield weaponry was highly developed, and such technology was way ahead of the old Napoleonic infantry tactics still in use at that time. This led to enormous numbers of killed and wounded soldiers, mass on-site amputations of shattered limbs and dreadful understaffing of the few available medical facilities.

Compounding the morphine addiction wave about to be perpetrated on an already divided and demoralized United States was a lack of knowledge of opiates and their addictive traits. It was first thought that injecting morphine by syringe would prevent patients from becoming addicted to opium and its derivatives. However, injection proved *much more* addicting, and by the time the war ended, it was impossible to prevent thousands of troops from developing severe morphine addictions which they carried home with them after the shooting stopped.

After the war, the push westward increased in earnest. Chinese "coolies" — imported Asian slaves who were, in reality, opium-addicted rejects of Chinese society — were used extensively to build railroads and levees all across the western territories. The California Gold Rush, which began in 1849, quickly ushered in a new wave of profiteering by drug lords, who used the "coolies" to prime a money pump that would gush forth profits long after the gold supply drained out of California. The presence of gold only further stimulated opium imports and sales; the "coolies" simply brought along their own supply from the Far East.

The turn of the century brought on an even more potent opiate, heroin. It was developed in 1898 by the I.G. Farben company in Germany, where morphine had been invented less than 100 years earlier. Heroin is up to three times more potent than morphine as a pain-killer, and therefore far more addictive. Some newer synthetic compounds are 1,000 to 10,000 times more potent than morphine.[1]

---

1. *Funk & Wagnalls New Encyclopedia*, ©1982, Vol. 18, p. 263.

As preparations for World War I began, a new kind of drug from the coca plant in South America, cocaine, was developed. For centuries, the Inca Indians and their descendants chewed on coca leaves because they seemed to make a workday go a little faster, the crushed leaves acting as a mild stimulant. Eventually, methods were developed to concentrate that stimulant into a white powder, which is highly addictive. Beverage manufacturers in the United States saw a ready opportunity to use the new discovery in a concoction called "Coca-Cola," which would combine the pleasant effects of cocaine with the flavor of the cola nut. Consumers flocked to the new drink, but the government stepped in and made the company discontinue the use of cocaine in the product. Instead, "Coca-Cola" now contains caffeine, which was used as a substitute stimulant to cocaine. Present-day cola drinks often contain caffeine, as does coffee, tea and other beverages.

As profitable as the drug trade — legal and otherwise — had been over the centuries, the 20th century would take the industry to incredible new heights, mainly because opiates were made largely illegal in the United States at the outset of the century. The opium trade, including cultivation of the poppies and the processing of morphine and heroin, would continue to be legal in many countries in the world until 1963, when an agreement would finally be reached controlling the cultivation of opium poppies. Still, even to this day, such directives are rarely enforced, and opium production continues virtually unabated.

But the illegalization of drugs is what made drug lords wealthy beyond comprehension at the beginning of the 20th century, particularly those individuals with extensive maritime interests — the transportation network to take advantage of the so-called Golden Triangle (Southeast Asia) and Golden Crescent (Middle East) opium trade routes.

World War I was a catastrophe which was unimaginable at the time, leading to millions of dead and wounded troops, and a virtual flood of morphine — and even heroin — use and inevitable addiction. Once again, the theory was flawed behind the newer substance, heroin; it was predicted it would alleviate addiction to morphine and opium. Instead, it *increased* the addiction.[2] But it was too late to do much about it; by 1918, when the Armistice was signed and the war brought to an end, opiate addiction was rampant, both among the wounded veterans returning from the war, and the people who sought the refuge or drugs to alleviate the extreme stress brought about by the condition of war.

The extreme profitability of the drug trade during and immediately after a raging war would not go unnoticed later in the 20th century by opportunists such as Aristotle Onassis, Howard Hughes, Nelson Rockefeller and other powerful individuals. Even the grandfather of Franklin D. Roosevelt, on the Delano side, was reputed to have become enriched by the Chinese opium trade. These opportunistic people knew the value of opiates, weapons of war, and petroleum — a rich and lethal combination that would that would adequately fuel any conflict. As another World War approached, preparations could be made to profit from it; the lessons of World War I were still fresh.

Between wars, the "Roaring '20s" roared for more reasons than simply illegal booze. Heroin use and addiction was kicking in among the elite of America, as was extensively stepped-up use of the latest "recreational" drug, cocaine. Without the trapping of syringes and other inconveniences, cocaine could easily be snorted. It was considered "fun." Marijuana, meanwhile, was cursed as the "killer weed" and drew the same fate as Prohibition alcohol. An argument could be made that erratic flows of drug money helped destabilize the stock market, overstate the available money supply and eventually precipitate the Great Depression. Only another major war would allow the world to crawl out from under the economic hardships of the Depression.

---

2. *Ibid.*

World War II, as the early portions of the *Skeleton Key* describe, created money machines for those individuals who were well-positioned. In the context of this chapter, it is not difficult to imagine that what the *Skeleton Key* states is probably closer to the truth than we would like it admit. The Korean War did the same, as did the Vietnam War:

(**Gemstone 6:5a**) May, 1971: "Folk hero" Daniel Ellsberg, a well-known hawk from the Rand Corporation who had designed the missile ring around the "Iron Curtain" countries (how many missiles to aim at which cities), [releases] was told to release the faked-up "Pentagon Papers" to help [which helps] distract people from Hughes, JFK, RFK, MLK [King], etc. The papers were carefully designed by Ellsberg and his boss, Rand chief and later World Bank chief Robert McNamara to make the Vietnam War look like "just one of those incredibly dumb mistakes." This helped [helps] to cover up the real purpose of the war: Continued control, for Onassis and his friends, of the Golden Triangle dope trade (Vietnam, Laos, Cambodia); and the same kind of control [and for] Onassis and the oil people, [control] of Eastern oil sources. The war also had the effect of controlling [— to say nothing of control over] huge Federal [federal] monies [sums], which could [can] be siphoned off in profitable arms contracts, or [made to] conveniently "disappear" in the war effort.

The late Mae Brussell, like most conspiracy researchers, did not agree with Roberts' view on the Pentagon Papers as stated in Gemstone 6:5. Instead, Brussels argued during her radio broadcasts that Ellsberg precipitated a lot more criticism of the unjust nature of the Vietnam War, but in the context of the all-consuming drug trade, it is not wise to completely dismiss the idea that the Pentagon papers were carefully designed as a "cutout" to cloud the drug-related issues connected to the CIA's alleged drug-running activities between Laos, Cambodia and Vietnam. After all, it was the *New York Times* that is the mouthpiece of the CIA, conspiracy researchers say. But it was also the *Times* that broke the Pentagon Papers story, and won a court battle to get them into print.

****

(**Gemstone 6:7a**) Notes in passing: The dope routes are: Golden Triangle to Taiwan to San Francisco. Heroin coming from the Golden Triangle was sometimes smuggled into S.F. inside the bodies of American GIs who died in battle in Vietnam. One body can hold up to 40 pounds of heroin, crammed in where the organs would normally be.

(**6:7b**) Some dope gets pressed into dinner plates, and painted with pretty patterns. One dope bust in San Francisco alone yielded $6 billion in heroin "China plates" — the largest dope bust in history — quickly and completely hushed up by the S.F. press Mafia. The dope sat in S.F.P.D. for a while, then was removed by FBI men and probably sent on its way — to American veins. All this dope processing and shipping is controlled and supervised by the Mafia for the Mafia. Dope arrests and murders are aimed at independent pushers and maverick peddlers and smugglers who are competing with, or holding out on, the Mafia. While Nixon was conducting his noisy campaign against dope smuggling across the Mexican border, his dope officer in charge of protecting the Mafia dope trade was E. Howard Hunt.

(**6:7c**) Lots of heroin gets processed in a Pepsi Cola factory in Laos. So far, it hasn't produced a single bottle of Pepsi Cola.

(**6:7d**) Some dope gets processed in heroin factories in Marseilles (see the movie, *The French Connection*).

(**6:7e**) Still more dope comes from South America — cocaine, and now heroin. U.S. aid went to build a highway across Paraguay (Uruguay?). Useless to the natives, who have no cars; they use it for sunbathing during the day. All night, airplanes loaded with cocaine take off from the longest landing strip in the world — financed by U.S. tax money for the benefit of international Mafia dope pushers. And then there is opium from Turkey — morphine, the starting point of Onassis' fortune.

(6:8) In case one is still wondering whether the Mafia can actually get away with such things, consider the benefits derived from controlling the stock market, the courts, the police, etc., in one swindle alone: The 1970 "acquisition" by "Hughes" of "Air West," which involved swindling Air West stockholders of $45 million. Indicted for this swindle by the S.E.C. (in a civil suit) were "Howard Hughes" and Jimmy "The Greek" Snyder (not usually associated with the Hughes crowd) and others.

Note that almost the entire preceding passage is underlined, meaning that the *Hustler* left it out of its version of the *Skeleton Key*. It is interesting that a magazine can couch itself in language about the "first amendment" and "freedom of speech" regarding the pornographic content of its pages — but sidestep the common decency of pointing out the treacheries of the illegal drug trade and the organized crime it supports.

Regarding Gemstone 6:7, it is interesting to note that some of Onassis' Victory Carriers ships that were "seized" by the U.S. government during their feud in the 1950s carried home the bodies of American soldiers killed in the Korean War. It was not disclosed whether these bodies were hollowed out as described and used as depositories for drugs.

But clearly, modern taboos on drugs have only increased the demand for the substances, and organized crime has grown dramatically. The Mafia was not always the omnipresent evil as described by Gemstone 6:7b and the *Skeleton Key* overall. It started as a small group of Sicilian and Corsican families who skimmed profits from some legitimate businesses, dodged taxes, made modest sums from illegal gambling and sold some narcotics. Large-scale drug dealing was not considered "proper" work for the mob; besides, it was too risky when other easier business activities such as prostitution and numbers rackets (which were the predecessors to present-day legal lotteries in most states — draining the illegal profits from mob coffers and instead channeling them into useful areas). The combination of illegal opiates and illegal alcoholic beverages during the Prohibition era simply made the Mafia grow at a cancerous rate.

Now, it is difficult to distinguish legal activities from illegal ones when it comes to business and commerce. Most banks, whether they realize it or not, launder illegal drug money to some degree. They can't help it. Drug money serves to undergird our entire economy, especially when economic recession strikes. *The drug business never sees bad times.* If all the illegal drug money were to vanish tomorrow, our nation would be plunged into a deep economic depression, as would most of the Western world. And now that Communism no longer carries ideological clout, there is simply no protection from the exploiters of these controlled substances, other than conscious efforts from good people to abstain from using them.

Laws making street drugs illegal today serve only to make the cost of drugs 200 to 400 times greater than they would be if they were legal, taxable commodities. Then, drug use and addiction could be attacked as the social problem that it is, instead of a full-blown criminal offense. Under current laws, drug-selling "territories" in large urban areas become war zones, because the local drug dealers want to keep their market share up, and their competition down. It is an old-fashioned economic truth: Once a substance is "illegal," the price rockets upward, well beyond the normal price for the substance if it were "legal." Current law benefits the criminal and no one else.

In the final analysis, it is not the monolithic British crown or the all-powerful Mafia that is to blame for the central thesis of the *Skeleton Key*. We are to blame. Our young people are drawn to and use illegal drugs. Our young women then turn to such extremes as prostitution to pay for the inflated price of the illegal substances; such activity only enhances the incomes of criminals and further encourages even more intense illegal activity as part of a vicious circle. We are feeding the beast. It is time to stop.

CHAPTER 13

· · · · · · · · · · · · ·

Shiny New Gemstones

Perhaps the strongest argument favoring the basic legitimacy of the Gemstone thesis, and the *Skeleton Key to the Gemstone Files,* is the groundwork they have provided for a modern-day, technology-driven worldwide information network that presently sidesteps mainstream media and provides an independent forum for healthy discussion of unsolved mysteries, covert government intelligence activities and unexplained world events. Such diverse topics as the Balkan civil war in the former Yugoslavian republics, the collapse of Communism and the Soviet Union, and the spread of AIDS on a genocidal scale in Africa are now taking on new perspectives, in much the same way Bruce Roberts attempted to see world events of his time by way of the Gemstone Files.

For that matter, the way news is reported has changed drastically since the days of Watergate, when "leaks" from top government officials kept getting into print, eventually leading to a breakdown in administrative cohesiveness and the resignation of a President of the United States. Since Watergate, the mainstream media has been subdued. Politicians and major companies treat their information as strictly proprietary, and media professionals are hired to disseminate it through proper channels, and with prior approval. Sophisticated public relations groups are prospering, while major newspapers are dying. Reporters are more cautious than ever. Editors are slow to hit the streets with a "major" story, especially if it is about political corruption. The teeth have been knocked out of the mainstream press in uncovering and honestly reporting when powerful people make mistakes that can affect peoples' lives around the world. This suffocating caution has pushed disillusioned readers from the mainstream press, and into alternative forms of communication. Radio and television talk shows have been major vendors of controversial material, almost replacing newspapers. Alternative newspapers are prospering. Small, alternative presses are churning out the controversial books that analyze the stories the mainstream media have failed to cover effectively. The New York literary monopoly has been slowly crumbling as the years have gone by. Desktop publishing technology and interconnected electronic databases that encircle the globe have empowered individuals to speak out against the evils of this world. Instead of international satellite communications being used as a control mechanism for the powers elite as envisioned in the 1960s, the tables are turned. The small voice in the crowd can become a roaring lion with the flick of a switch, or the turn of a dial.

In this "information age" transition, where control of information flow is increasingly impossible, risks to reporters and their sources are inevitable. Just as some of Roberts' associates in the *Skeleton Key* met their doom, allegedly as a result of knowledge garnered from his original Gemstones with "histories" he scattered around the world, some individuals in the present worldwide network have, in recent years, died mysteriously — right as they were assembling evidence that backed their elaborate theories. Some of these theories dovetail the Gemstone thesis; that is, they are essentially extensions of that thesis, detailing the post-Onassis era in which activities such as drug trafficking, arms sales and petroleum-market manipulation. We will be looking at three post-Gemstone documents here which have strong ties to the original Bruce Roberts theories, and which provide extended circumstances that not only reaffirm their own separate theses, but give more backing to the

Skeleton Key's underlying points. The three documents are:

- The *Kiwi Gemstone*, which is topped by the original *Skeleton Key* up to Gemstone 2:2 (mentioning Joseph Kennedy's introduction of son John to Onassis). Then, the *Kiwi Gemstone* jumps across the Pacific to New Zealand, where it describes an extensive financial network established for the primary purposes of monopolizing a big Great South Basin petroleum discovery, and to launder illegal drug money. Where the *Skeleton Key* cuts off in 1975, the *Kiwi Gemstone* has updates through 1987.

- The "Octopus" thesis put together by investigative reporter Joseph Daniel Casolaro, who was collecting material on a variety of scandalous intelligence operations when he was found dead in a West Virginia hotel room on Aug. 10, 1991. Casolaro never produced a formal document on his thesis, which characterized all-powerful U.S. intelligence operations as an "octopus" whose conspiratorial arms wound themselves around virtually every aspect of American life, domestically and overseas as well. His proposed book, *Behold a Pale Horse*, was partially written but never published. His notes vanished after his death, which was ruled a suicide. Many of Casolaro's projects looked like offshoots of the original *Skeleton Key.*

- A lengthy document referred to as the *Wilcher Transcripts*, which were copied and distributed Gemstone-style in mid-1993. They were assembled by Washington attorney Paul D. Wilcher, who allegedly mailed a condensed version to U.S. Attorney General Janet Reno on May 21, 1993, only a month after a Waco, Texas, religious cult compound burned to the ground as an apparent result of a botched Department of Justice-approved operation. Wilcher connected the Waco fiasco to other intelligence operations, and detailed a 30-year series of events — including the assassinations of John and Robert Kennedy — which he felt were interconnected, the same conclusion the *Skeleton Key* outlines. Perhaps the most significant material in the *Wilcher Transcripts* is detail on the so-called "October Surprise" in 1980, when the Reagan-Bush campaign allegedly cut a deal with Iran to withhold the release of 52 U.S. hostages until after the 1980 election. Soon after this document was released, Wilcher's decomposed body was found in his Washington D.C. apartment on June 23, 1993, by police who were nudged into action by close friend and freelance broadcast reporter Sarah McClendon, and attorney Marion Kindig, our sources say. Police are still investigating the circumstances surrounding Wilcher's death.

****

THE KIWI GEMSTONE

This document was published by an alternate newspaper in New Zealand, *The State Adversary*, whose agenda is anarchy. Curiously, its contents are being challenged in court in New Zealand, mainly because many prominent people are mentioned as taking part in illegal or questionable activities. The most important aspect of the *Kiwi Gemstone* with regard to the *Skeleton Key* is that Onassis is tagged with the label "crowned head of the Mafia" in one early reference, and the force behind most of the financial and political upheaval described in the *Kiwi Gemstone*. We present the following portions of the *Kiwi Gemstone* with the understanding that we have not been able to check their veracity. And we have selected those passages in the *Kiwi Gemstone* which have some connection to the *Skeleton Key*. Our comments are bracketed, and the most significant passages pertaining to the *Skeleton Key* are italicized:

(18th May 1967) Texas oil billionaire Nelson Bunker Hunt, using a sophisticated satellite technique to detect global deposits, discovers a huge oil source near Aotearoa (New Zealand) in the Great South Basin.

(**10th May 1968**) *Hawaiian meeting between Onassis and top lieutenants, William Colby [CIA director after George Bush] and Gerald Parsky [hotshot young Nixon administration attorney whose specialty was international finance involving Middle East and Pacific Rim nations, and who was a key person in oil czar William Simon's operations during the Arab oil embargo of 1973], to discuss establishment of a new front company in Australia* — Australian & Pacific Holdings Limited — to be managed by Michael Hand [It is our position that Parsky simply helped to set up this financial network and had no direct knowledge of its real purpose. Colby's role is also probably exaggerated here]. Using Onassis-Rockefeller banks, Chase Manhattan and Schroders' Travelodge Management Ltd. sets up another front to link the operation to the U.S. Onassis now crowned head of the Mafia; Colby (head of CIA covert operations in S.E. Asia) ran the Onassis heroin operations in the Golden Triangle (Laos, Burma, Thailand) with 200 Green Beret mercenaries — i.e. the Phoenix Progamme. *Gerald Parsky, deputy to ex-CIA/ FBI Robert Maheu in the Howard Hughes organization,* took orders from Onassis and was made responsible for laundering skim money from Onassis' casino operations in Las Vegas and the Bahamas.

(**24th February 1969**) Onassis calls Council meeting in Washington to discuss strategy to monopolize the Great South Basin discovery. Council members included Nelson Rockefeller and John McCloy [earlier on the Warren Commission], who managed the Seven Sisters, and David Rockefeller, managing the Mafia's banking operations. McCloy outlines the plan to capture all oil and mineral resources in Australia and Aotearoa (New Zealand).

(**April 1970**) *Onassis, Rockefeller and the Seven Sisters begin setting up the Shadow World Government using the Illuminati-controlled banks and the transnational corporations.* In Melbourne, they set up the Australian International Finance

Corp., using:

- Irving Trust Co., N.Y. — linked to Shell Oil, Continental Oil and Phillips Petroleum.
- Crocker Citizens National — linked to Atlantic Richfield (ARCO) and Standard Oil of California, which is Rockefeller-controlled.
- Bank of Montreal — Petro Canada, Penarctic Oils, Alberta Gas, Gulf Oil.
- Australia and New Zealand banks.

(**Early 1971**) *Onassis and Rockefeller begin global operation to buy influence for the One World Government concept.* They use Lockheed, Northrup and Litton Industries' agent, Adnan Khashoggi, to organize operations in the Middle East, Iran and Indonesia.

(**February 1972**) Onassis and Rockefeller help their associate Adnan Khashoggi buy the Security Pacific National Bank in California and take control of the United California Bank through CIA-linked Lockheed Aircraft Corp. Both banks used by Onassis and Khashoggi to funnel bribes and payoffs to captive Japanese and other crooked politicians, via the CIA's Deal Bank. Security Pacific also used to launder over $2 million for Nixon's re-election campaign, Khashoggi buys 21 percent of Southern Pacific Properties, which is the majority stockholder in Travelodge (Aust.).

(**26th May 1972**) Gerald Parsky installs Michele Sindona as "owner" of Franklin National Bank, helped by the Gambino Mafia family and David Kennedy, chairman of Continental Illinois Bank and Nixon's Secretary of the Treasury... Sindona, acting as go-between for the Mafia and CIA, was the conduit between U.S. and European banks. Sindona's Vatican Bank and associates Calvi's Ambrosiano Bank were used to finance CIA neo-fascist Italian/Latin-American operations through Licio Gelli's P2 Lodge [the investigation of which might have led to the death of TV journalist Jessica Savitch in a Mary Jo Kopechne-style car crash into water in 1983], which helped organize the "death squads" in Argentina, Uruguay and Chile. They were aided by P2 members such as Klaus Barbie (the Butcher of Lyons) and Jose Rega, organizer of the AAA in Argentina.

(February 1973) Gerald Parsky, William Colby, Michael Hand, Frank Nugan and Bob Seldon move on to further consolidate the Mafia banking operations... In Australia, Nugan Hand Bank begins operations, with 30 percent of the stock held by A'asian and Pacific Holdings (100 percent Chase Manhattan Bank), 25 percent *by CIA's Air America (known as Air Opium) [see Gemstone 2:9b]*, 25 percent by South Pacific Properties, and 20 percent held by Seldon, Nugan and Hand. The Irving Trust Bank's New York branch establishes U.S. links between the CIA and Nugan Hand Bank — a worldwide network of 22 banks set up to:

- Launder money from Onassis heroin operations in the Golden Triangle and Iran.
- As a CIA funnel (sic) to pro-U.S. political parties in Europe and Latin America, including P2.
- A spying conduit (sic) for information from Cambodia, Laos, Vietnam and Thailand.
- Finance arms smuggled to Libya, Indonesia, South America, Middle East and Rhodesia, using the CIA's Edwin Wilson.

Heroin flown into Australia by CIA's Air America and transshipped to Onassis lieutenant in Florida, Santos Trafficante Jr., assisted by Australian Federal Bureau of Narcotics officials and coordinated by CIA's Ray Cline.

(14th June 1973) *Inauguration of the Onassis shadow world government — the Trilateral Commission.* Includes over 200 members from the U.S., Europe and Japan... Trilateralist strategy: Monopolization of the world's resources, production facilities, labor technology, markets, transport and finance. These aims backed up by the U.S. military and industrial complexes hat are already controlled and backed up by the CIA.

(Mid-1974) Gough Whitlam (Australian prime minister)

and Norman Kirk (New Zealand prime minister) begin a series of moves absolutely against the Mafia Trilateralists. Whitlam refuses to waive restrictions on overseas borrowing to finance Alwest Aluminum Consortium of Rupert Murdoch, BHP and R.J. Reynolds. *Whitlam had also ended Vietnam War support, blocked uranium mining, and wanted more control over U.S. secret spy bases — e.g. Pine Gap, Northwest Cape.* Kirk had introduced a new, tough, anti-monopoly bill and had tried to redistribute income from big companies to the labor force through price regulation and a wages policy... Kirk had found out that Hunt Petroleum, drilling in the Great South Basin, had discovered a huge resource of oil, comparable in size to the North Sea or Alaskan North Slope... Oil companies completely hushed up these facts. To have announced a vast new oil source would probably have meant a decline in world oil prices, which would not have allowed OPEC's and Onassis' plans for the Arabs to eventuate... Kirk was the last to hold out.

(September 1974) Death of Norman Kirk [heart failure at age 51]. According to CIA sources, *Kirk was killed by the Trilateralists using sodium morphate.* [Successor Wallace Edward] Rowling's first act as prime minister was to withdraw Kirk's anti-monopoly bill and the petroleum amendment bill. Later, Rowling was to be rewarded with ambassadorship to Washington. *Incidentally, the Shah of Iran was murdered the same way as Kirk on his arrival in the USA.*

(6th October 1974) Ray Cline implements William Colby's plan to oust Australian Prime Minister Whitlam. Nugan Hand Bank finances payoffs to [future prime minister] Malcolm Fraser and other pro-U.S. politicians. A joint bugging operation commences between the CIA and ASIO [Australian intelligence]. Rupert Murdoch, playing his part, uses his newspapers and TV network to spread lies and misinformation [attacked Whitlam's liberal social agenda, similar to the type of plans U.S. President Bill Clinton is now advocating and pushing through the U.S. Congress].

(**December 1974**) Australian Governor-General John Kerr joins Ray Cline's payroll, and received his first payoff of $200,000 (U.S.) credited to his account number 767748 at the Singapore branch of the Nugan Hand Bank.

(**18th February**) Governor Kerr sacks the Whitlam government [Fraser takes over as prime minister and reverses Whitlam's moves which had blocked Trilateralist activity].

(**December 1975**) Election battle [in New Zealand] between Rowling and [Robert] Muldoon. Oil companies pour thousands of dollars into Muldoon's campaign via National Bank (NZ)... Muldoon wins.

(**Late 1977**) Muldoon travels to the U.S. to meet top Rockefeller officials, including Trilateralists' Deputy Secretary of State, Warren Christopher [under the administration of U.S. President Jimmy Carter, now Secretary of State under Clinton], and Richard Holbrooke, who were in charge of the new South Pacific Desk at the State Department established by Rockefeller to target exploitation of both Aotearoa (New Zealand) and Australia.

(**May 1979**) Trilateral Commission secretary Zbigniew Brzezinski appoints Muldoon as chairman of Board of Governors of IMF/World Bank, on orders from David Rockefeller.

(**27th November 1979**) Gerald Parsky's lieutenant, David Kennedy, meets Muldoon to deliver $100,000 (U.S.) cash to Muldoon for implementing Mafia "Think Big" plans.

(**May 1980**) Mafia's Nugan Hand banking operation crashes after Frank Nugan killed. Death ruled as a suicide, even though no fingerprints found on the rifle [Colby's business card was found on body.]... CIA helps Hand and bank president Donald Beasley escape to the U.S. The CIA and ASIO cover everything up... There is a possibility that Michael Hand killed Frank Nugan because of his involvement with Hand's fiancee.

[Important note: A crucial cross-reference surfaced independently of the *Kiwi Gemstone* which deals with the Nugan Hand bank failure. We received it as part of a larger document generally outlining U.S. intelligence operations. The entry reads as follows: "The Black Rose Organization originally funded the 'Black World Order' with proceeds from two areas. One, in Southeast Asia, is known as the Golden Triangle. The other area lies on the border of Iran and Iraq, and between Iran and Afghanistan and is known as the Golden Crescent. The drug proceeds from these two areas wound up deposited in the Nugenhun (sic, actually Nugan Hand) Bank in Australia after *Dr. Earl Brian (connected with the Inslaw software scandal of the mid- and late-1980s; more on that later this chapter)* carried the bank codes out of Southeast Asia using formal diplomatic immunity. In Australia, countless banks and persons were ruined when two operatives by the names of *Frank Nugan and Michael Hand* went into action. Frank Nugan was later "terminated" (listed as suicide). Michael Hand fled Australia with all the money from the so-called Black Fund. Hand is currently the most-wanted individual the Australian government has its sights on. He is living in the Middle East under the protection of an Islamic group..."]

(**27th September 1984**) Plans outlined for an expanded (money) laundering operation which will coincide with the launch of "crack" [cocaine] — a new addictive product developed by CIA chemists for the world market.

(**10th March 1987**) Parsky, Colby, Cline and others meet in the Gibbs safe house in Auckland. Parsky outlines the expansion of the European banking operation with 12 new subsidiaries to be set up in South America to replace the United Fruit Co. front and which will:

• Launder heroin dollars from the Rockefeller operations in the Golden triangle and Pakistan.
• Launder coke and crack dollars from Colombia, Peru, Bolivia, Ecuador and Venezuela.
• [Provide] CIA funnel to pro-U.S. political parties in Europe and Latin America,
• [Provide] financial conduit to Colby's P2 neo-fascists in Panama, Argentina, Chile and Uruguay.

- [Provide] spying conduit for information from Middle East, Latin and South America.
- Finance arms smuggling to Central and South America and the Middle East, including the Christian Militia in Lebanon.
- [Provide] financial conduit to mercenary army in Kuwait (standing by to conduct CIA invasion of Iran) via CIA's Vinell Corp.

The preceding excerpt is but a small portion of a much larger document, but the selections are the most relevant, we feel, to a logical extension of the Gemstone thesis beyond the Watergate period. The *Kiwi Gemstone* also credits Bruce Roberts with authorship. That could be difficult, though, since Roberts died in 1976, and the *Kiwi* thesis extends far beyond that point. Despite this confusion, it is interesting to pick through the *Kiwi Gemstone* and ascertain whether any of the points are worth considering.

Since most of the *Kiwi* information is centered around New Zealand and Australian politics and economics, most of the names are unfamiliar, as are the companies. But it is interesting that Onassis is linked to the oil interests in the area, and that he is also linked to key Americans who are involved in Southern Hemisphere banking. The most striking name to be liberally bandied about is that of Gerald Parsky, the talented attorney who is accused by the *Kiwi Gemstone* of being the point man for most of the money-laundering schemes set up in that part of the world.

We do not agree with the *Kiwi Gemstone* on Parsky's active role in illegal activities. For one, he was busy making a fortune on legal deals, mainly through the oil-rich Saudis he hooked up with while serving as an assistant treasury secretary under Treasury Secretary William Simon, who doubled as oil czar during the Arab oil embargo of the early 1970s. Parsky later teamed up with Simon after the Nixon administration fell apart and engineered profitable deals overseas. Parsky was a skilled financial wizard and handled extraordinarily large sums of money with responsibility and integrity. However, it was not his position to question where these large sums of money came from, or where they went. He was a very sophisticated traffic cop regarding movements of international currency.

And although Parsky did do business in virtually every major Asian and European financial center, there is no evidence he was ever involved in Australian or New Zealand-based transactions as the *Kiwi Gemstone* suggests. His alleged involvement in the Italian P2 situation is also suspect, although in his European dealings, he would have occasion to possibly contact Italian financiers from time to time.

Even so, as we pointed out in the last chapter, almost every bank in the world has recycled drug money flowing through it. That does not necessarily mean that every bank is crooked regarding the laundering of illicit drug profits, it simply means that there is no way to avoid sums of money that huge. For example, when Colombian drug lord Pablo Escobar was hunted down and shot to death on Dec. 2, 1993, his personal fortune was estimated to have been $4 billion through cocaine trafficking.[1] Estimates vary on the exact amount of annual income is derived from illegal drug sales, but most experts place that amount in the neighborhood of *$500 billion.*

That money has to be kept somewhere, and most drug barons usually start banks of their own to launder the profits, then arrange for massive financial transactions where these funds are transferred to several banks in succession. For the *Kiwi Gemstone* to finger Parsky as a major player in this laundering chain is very dubious, and the names of people like David Rockefeller are also thrown about as participating in this activity. Again, most major banks would probably admit to their cash flows being at least partially polluted by drug money.

---

1. *New York Times*, Dec. 3, 1993, "Head of Medellin Cocaine Cartel Is Killed by Troops in Colombia," by Robert D. McFadden.

Where the *Kiwi Gemstone* strikes home, however, is nailing the CIA as a prime influence in drug trafficking and money laundering in that part of the world. Gemstone 2:9b mentions that the CIA's air transportation arm was nicknamed "Air Opium," and the *Kiwi* concurs. Although Bruce Roberts was considerably ahead of his time in the early 1970s when making such naked accusations against the CIA's long-cherished involvement in the international drug trade as a cornerstone of his Gemstone writings, investigative reporters — mainly former CIA types who were fed up with the way in which the organization's operating capital was raised — have blown the whistle more than a few times. The ongoing scandal regarding the Bank of Credit and Commerce International (BCCI) — dubbed the "Bank of Crooks and Criminals International" as early as 1986 by CIA Director-designate Robert Gates, according to former U.S. Customs Service commissioner William Von Rabb — is the biggest chink yet in the previously impervious armor surrounding the world of drug-money laundering. The CIA has had a lengthy history of money mismanagement, mainly finding a place for these extraordinary sums without raising suspicion.

Burton Hersh, author of *The Old Boys*, an authoritative account of the origins of the CIA, writes bluntly:

"...With BCCI debris increasingly scattered throughout world capitals, any number of questions on just this point are now bouncing around. Charges are already circulating that CIA representatives 'collaborated with the (BCCI's) *black network* (emphasis ours) in several operations that, preoccupied with Afghanistan, CIA officers turned a blind eye...to the heroin trafficking in Pakistan,' and that BCCI money bankrolled the 'covert sales of American arms to Iran in 1986.'

"...Financially, the CIA was conceived in sin. Before there was a CIA, there was an OSS, the Office of Strategic Services. The OSS's parent, the Coordinator of Intelligence, was authorized by Franklin D. Roosevelt in 1941, in good part to *permit the Roosevelt administration to support its friends around the world no matter what the laggard and frequently isolationist Congress might prefer* (emphasis ours).

"...The renegade ex-CIA arms merchant, Edwin Wilson [mentioned prominently in the *Kiwi Gemstone*], financed his catastrophic weaponry empire through *Nugan Hand, including, by the end, the transfer of tons of plastique [explosive] to Moammar Kadafi* (emphasis ours). According to a galvanizing 1982 series in the *Wall Street Journal* by Jonathan Kwitny, the bank not only financed, but arranged for the trans-shipment of, *millions of dollars worth of heroin — often by the contract pilots who flew for Air America, the CIA's huge proprietary fleet* (emphasis ours). 'Air America was a Vietnam War-era airline,' Kwitny wrote, 'with close connections with the CIA. U.S. drug officials now acknowledge that the airline also occasionally *ran heroin out of Southeast Asia's famed 'Golden Triangle' poppy-growing areas* (emphasis ours).' A Joint Task Force study by Australian officials confirmed the extensive use of the Nugan Hand Bank as a blind repository by CIA leaders."[2]

This is an astonishing confirmation of not only the heart of the *Kiwi Gemstone* but of Bruce Roberts' assessment in the *Skeleton Key.* It was Roberts who was on to this early, but whose voice was drowned by the overcautious — and by those acquaintances who stumbled across this information, only to pay for it with their lives. In context with the preceding material concerning our efforts to confirm, corroborate or otherwise document *The Skeleton Key to the Gemstone Files*, it is clear that the *Skeleton Key* author is passionately committed to "getting the truth out," no matter what the price.

****

---

2. *The Old Boys,* Burton Hersh.

"THE OCTOPUS"

As the "information age" closes in, it is not surprising that the first major computer software scandal was to dominate the middle 1980s — but you would not know this through the established channels of the mainstream press.

When Joseph Daniel Casolaro was found dead in his West Virginia hotel room in August of 1991, his arms sliced up and blood pooled inside his room's bathtub, he was hot on the heels of what some reporters have called "the unified field of conspiracy theories." He was about to chop the arms off his "octopus" — the all-powerful "force" behind many of the troubles which have beset the United States and the world at large throughout most of the war-torn 20th century. The story Casolaro was chasing was so complex, most mainstream reporters simply stayed away from it. For those publications willing to take on the story, it was a challenge to simplify the high-tech plot line enough to make apparent the story's extreme importance.

We have pieced together the story as follows:

It started innocently enough, with a seemingly small software scandal unfolding between a fledgling company named Inslaw and the U.S. Department of Justice. Inslaw (Institute for Law and Social Research), developed a software package called PROMIS (Prosecutor's Management Information System) during the late 1970s. By 1980, PROMIS was installed in many district attorney's offices, a division of the Department of Justice and two large U.S. Attorney's offices. Inslaw founders Bill and Nancy Hamilton felt that PROMIS was just the tool that would bring law enforcement into the computer age — cutting down on the mountains of paperwork that even routine cases would build up. PROMIS was designed to follow criminal cases through the court system, monitoring each stage and keeping accurate records as the cases unfolded.

With Congress eliminating the grant funding that Inslaw enjoyed since its inception in 1973, the Hamiltons prepared to convert the company from non-profit to for-profit status, using PROMIS as the anchor program for marketing and distribution. Demand for PROMIS was growing, and the Hamiltons had developed an enhanced version of it. As Inslaw converted into a private enterprise, the Department of Justice entered into a $10 million contract in March of 1982. The deal called for PROMIS to be installed in 94 U.S. Attorney's offices nationwide.

This was the break the Hamiltons were waiting for, since many other federal branches of government — the Bureau of Prisons, U.S. Customs, U.S. Marshal's offices, the Immigration and Naturalization Service, Drug Enforcement Administration and (DEA) even the FBI would probably want the flexibility that PROMIS offered.

But the Department of Justice contract started running into difficulty almost immediately. Officials claimed that Inslaw was not fulfilling its contract and started holding back payments. This led to severe cash-flow troubles for Inslaw. However, the department said it would continue working within the agreement — pending a settlement of "differences" — *if Inslaw would let the department use the enhanced version of PROMIS.* Seeing that it would be the only way to keep the contract going, the Hamiltons handed over the enhanced version on April 11, 1983.

Three months later, with the enhanced version in hand, Justice officials announced they were cutting off payments to Inslaw anyway — violating federal statutes that prevented such action. Soon after, they canceled the bulk of Inslaw's contract. The Hamiltons, stunned by this development, asked Elliot Richardson, the former attorney general in the Nixon Administration, to take the case and hired him as their attorney. Richardson, famous for resigning as attorney general after he refused to fire Archibald Cox as special prosecutor in the Watergate scandal, clearly sensed a Watergate-style scenario with Inslaw, but realized the paper trail would not be as easy to follow in the high-tech world of the 1980s. Richardson's first step was to meet with Department of Justice officials and find out the real reason for the contract cancellation.

He got nowhere. And Inslaw was going broke. Richardson recommended that the Hamiltons file for bankruptcy under Chapter 11, which would allow the company to reorganize. Strangely, Justice attorneys then pressured bankruptcy officials to convert the Chapter 11 proceeding into a Chapter 7, which would mean liquidation of Inslaw's assets. Anthony Pasciuto, a deputy director for the Department of Justice, was the person who alerted the Hamiltons to this — and was fired by the department after 21 years' service. It was at this time that department officials *secretly expanded the use of the enhanced PROMIS software*, without any compensation to Inslaw.

Evidence mounted that the illegal use of the enhanced PROMIS was taking place, and the Hamiltons sued the Justice Department. In January of 1988, bankruptcy court Judge George Bason, Jr. ruled in favor of Inslaw, bluntly saying in his decision that the department had stolen the software through "trickery, fraud and deceit." He ordered the Hamiltons be paid more than $7 million in damages. The department then tried to starve out Inslaw through the appeals process.

Justice attorneys were helped dramatically when Judge Bason was denied reppointment to bankruptcy court a few weeks later when his term expired, despite four years' experience as a federal judge and 12 years as a bankruptcy attorney before that. The Department of Justice's replacement for Bason just happened to be the attorney who argued the department's case, and lost. But it was too late to prevent Inslaw from continuing its winning streak, as U.S. District Judge William Bryant Jr. *upheld Bason's decision* in 1989. Again, the department stonewalled, filing yet another appeal.

Because of its commanding position as overseer of "law and order" at the federal level, the Department of Justice appointed a retired judge, Nicholas Bua, to conduct a lengthy "independent" investigation of he Inslaw matter. Finally, on June 17, 1993, the department "rejected without foundation" that high-level department officials used "fraud, trickery and deceit" to steal software from Inslaw — *despite overwhelming evidence to the contrary, and two court decisions in favor of Inslaw.* Attorney General Janet Reno, however, is not buying Bua's report just yet, and she announced to an Oct. 28, 1993, press briefing that she is personally looking into the Inslaw case and has appointed assistant attorney general Webb Hubbell to "coordinate all Inslaw matters." A Senate bill has also been introduced by Sens. Carl Levin (D-Mich.) and William S. Cohen (D-Maine) and an accompanying House bill — introduced by Rep. Jack Brooks (D-Texas) — to allow Reno to ask for an independent counsel to settle the Inslaw case once and for all.

Bua's credibility has been blasted by more than one attorney in Washington. In a written statement to Reno, the late attorney Paul D. Wilcher — who had also informed Reno of much more alleged corruption within the federal government as we have mentioned earlier — detailed his views on Bua. We have acquired a copy of that letter, part of the *Wilcher Transcripts* which will be discussed in detail later in this chapter. It reads, in part, as follows:

"...Attorney General Reno, I strongly suspect that he report you received not long ago on the Inslaw case from former Chicago Federal District Judge Nicholas Bua (who was appointed by former President Bush and former Attorney General Barr to conduct a so-called independent 'investigation' — as a way around their having to appoint an independent counsel) is highly unreliable, if not outright false and fraudulent. I know Judge Bua personally, and can testify from bitter first-hand personal experience that he is a *first-rate crook and thief — the very embodiment of a thoroughly corrupt Judge* (emphasis ours)... Therefore, I strongly suspect that Judge Bua's report to you is nothing more than a further chapter in the ongoing saga of the official cover-up, obfuscation, and obstruction of justice which have characterized the history of the Inslaw case from its inception."[3]

Wilcher and others have long suspected that the Inslaw case extends far beyond the simple theft of a software program. And it appears as the Justice Department continues to stonewall on telling the truth about this issue, it will give reporters more time to track down these leads, exposing the government to an even wider scandal.

One potentially explosive angle is that the Inslaw case is connected to the so-called "October Surprise," mentioned earlier as a plan by which the Reagan-Bush campaign derailed President Jimmy Carter's efforts to negotiate the release of 52 U.S. hostages being held by Islamic fundamentalists in Iran. The alleged deal between the Reagan-Bush forces and the Iranians called for some $40 million in outright bribes and a clandestine multibillion-dollar weapons deal for Iran in exchange for hanging on to the hostages until after the 1980 election. William Casey, a co-founder of the CIA in 1947 and CIA chief in the Bush administration, was Reagan's campaign manager in 1980 and allegedly masterminded the "October Surprise" with assistance from a man named Dr. Earl Brian.

In 1990, Brian was fingered by a Stanford computer whiz, Michael Riconosciuto, as a key figure in the Inslaw affair and told Bill Hamilton that over the phone. Riconosciuto's credibility, however, has been laced in doubt, since he has since been imprisoned on drug trafficking charges. Riconosciuto told Hamilton that Brian had been given the stolen, enhanced version of PROMIS to sell to foreign intelligence interests as a "reward" for his part in the "October Surprise." Riconosciuto filed a sworn affifdavit on March 25, 1991, outlining these charges, and adding that he helped Brian to modify PROMIS to make it more marketable overseas.

Indications are that PROMIS, or variations of it, are in use in Israel, where Israeli intelligence chief Rafi Eitan admitted that he not only met with Brian, but acquired PROMIS for use by the

---

3. *Wilcher Transcripts*, p. 49.

Israeli Defense Signals Unit. This information came from former Israeli intelligence operative Ari Ben-Menashe, whose credibility has also been challenged by the Justice Department. Ben-Menashe had recently been acquitted of illegal arms dealing and was planning to write a book about his experiences.

Other PROMIS users allegedly fed the software by Brian include Iraqi military intelligence, according to Ben-Menashe, and this claim is confirmed by arms trader Richard Babayan in a separate sworn statement. Not only did Babayan claim that PROMIS had been sold to the Iraqis, he added that Korean and Libyan intelligence groups were in possession of it.

Bill Hamilton has been developing his own sources within the CIA, who have leaked information to him revealing hat the CIA has indeed acquired PROMIS — a claim substantiated by at least two other reporters — and incorporated it into other software that has been sold to "friendly" foreign intelligence agencies. Hamilton has also learned that PROMIS is being used on nuclear submarines' tracking systems. Canadian television has reported, with the Canadian government denying, that PROMIS has found its way into the databases of the Royal Canadian Mounted Police.

This tangled web of accusations and associations is what reporter Danny Casolaro was tracking down when he was found dead in his Martinsburg, West Virginia, hotel room on Aug. 10, 1991. The death has been ruled a suicide by the local Martinsburg police, who saw to it that the body was embalmed quickly, without an autopsy, and the hotel room cleaned thoroughly before a full probe could take place. Further, all of Casolaro's notes — a briefcase full of them — were missing from his room.

We have learned from a separate source that Casolaro was supplied much of his information on alleged high-level government corruption from a man named Alan David Standorf, who was a civilian employee at the National Security Agency (NSA) facility at the Vint Hill Farm military reservation near Manassas, Va. Vint Hill is a top-secret NSA signal-processing station that gathers electronic intelligence data from spy satellites and other sources from around the globe. The NSA itself is a super-secret organization based at Fort Meade, Md., and its specialty is spying on foreign governments with an array of eavesdropping equipment, including satellites, ground stations and ships.

If anyone could access these databases and provide Casolaro with sensitive documents, it would be Standorf. A U.S. Army official at Vint Hill said that Standorf served in an administrative capacity and oversaw the repair and distribution of electronic equipment.[4] Standorf also had resigned from this position on Dec. 19, 1990, effective Jan. 14, because his U.S. Army reserve unit had been activated in preparation for duty in the upcoming Persian Gulf War. Standorf was a first lieutenant with the 450th Civil Affairs Co. at Fort Bragg, N.C.

Our source indicated that Casolaro and Standorf agreed to set up a "nerve center" for operations involving duplication of sensitive documents. High-speed Xerox commercial duplicating and collating equipment was installed in "Room No. 900 of the Hilton Hotel in West Virginia to provide Casolaro copies of all documents and to allow Standorf a location and time to return the documents back to their original storage files."

If Casolaro's investigation hinged upon this information provided by Standorf, that investigation received a serious setback on Jan. 30, 1991, when Standorf was found dead in his parked car at Washington National Airport, the victim of an apparent blow to the head. Investigators at the scene reported that luggage was inside the car, which alerted airport security to check inside the vehicle that morning.

Curiously, both major Washington newspapers, the *Post* and the *Times*, reported the incident quite differently. The *Post* ran a routine police-blotter brief of four paragraphs, and did not mention Standorf's connection to the NSA. The *Times* ran a much

---

4. *Washington Times*, Jan. 31, 1991, "Slain Man in Car at National Worked for Top Security Agency," by Jim Keary.

more extensive report, detailing not only Standorf's sensitive position with the NSA, but the fact that Standorf was probably killed elsewhere and transported to the airport parking lot and deposited into his car.[5] Police and airport security speculated that a possible motive in the killing was robbery. It remains unsolved.

Casolaro, at the time he died, was looking into connections between Michael Riconosciuto and the Cabazon Indian tribe in California, whose 1,700-acre reservation was home base for a variety of U.S. military and intelligence operations, according to a three-part investigative report by the *San Francisco Chronicle* in September of 1991.[6] Riconosciuto had also participated in an aborted Nicaraguan contra arms deal on that same Cabazon reservation in 1987 where the CIA, FBI and elements of organized crime were also operating, according to investigative reporters Mary Fricker and Stephen Pizzo. After the arms deal went sour, four people connected to it were murdered. One was Riconosciuto's partner, Paul Morasca, whose hog-tied body was found next to his computer, from which the hard disk had been removed. All the murders remain unsolved.[7]

Casolaro reported receiving death threats as he pursued his investigation despite the death of Standorf. One caller told Casolaro's housekeeper, "I will cut his body and throw it to the sharks." Another said, "You son of a bitch — you're dead." Casolaro told his brother to be suspicious if he should suddenly die in an "accident." As it was, both arms of Casolaro's dead body had deep cuts; presumably, to help in his suicide attempt (slashing of wrists), according to the Martinsburg police.

At present, Casolaro's "octopus" is still at large — but others are closing in on all the facts.

---

5. *Ibid.*

6. *San Francisco Chronicle*, Sept. 4, 1991, "Tiny California Tribe's Huge Clout," by Jonathan Littman.

7. *This World, San Francisco Chronicle Sunday Edition*, June 14, 1992, "Outlaws at Justice," by Mary Fricker and Stephen Pizzo.

****

THE WILCHER TRANSCRIPTS

Washington attorney Paul David Wilcher mentions Casolaro in his May 21, 1993, letter to U.S. Attorney General Janet Reno — a 101-page document that is part of the *Wilcher Transcripts*. This material was duplicated and privately circulated, *Skeleton Key*-style, through an underground network before Wilcher was found dead in his apartment on June 23, 1993. Wilcher had already contacted the Justice Department and delivered the transcripts to Reno's office before his death.

Before we detail the *Transcripts* and their astonishing revelations, the circumstances surrounding Wilcher's death need to be addressed. The *Washington Times* reported in its June 15, 1993, edition that Wilcher's brother Bob was kept waiting in Wooster, Ohio, almost a month while investigators in Washington D.C. were trying to determine Paul Wilcher's death.

"We'd like to put it to rest," Bob Wilcher was quoted as saying after a memorial service in Ohio that was held without the body. "We've decided to go ahead and grieve the death. When we learn, we learn and we'll take it from there."[8]

The Wilchers are probably still waiting, and for good reason. Paul Wilcher's death remains mysterious and, as yet, unsolved. One of our sources indicated that Wilcher's body was found on June 23 after a lengthy effort from colleague and independent broadcast journalist Sarah McClendon to get police to open Wilcher's apartment to see if he was there. Police, who were reluctant to become involved in the case according to our source, discovered the body, which was sitting on a toilet seat in the bathroom. McClendon and Washington attorney Marion Kindig, who also knew Wilcher, were asked to view the body to make a positive identification. The two women were allowed to

---

8. *Washington Times*, July 15, 1993, "Autopsies Delayed as Body Count Rises," by Brian Reilly.

view only the body's face, which was badly decomposed, swollen and purple. Both women said that face looked badly beaten. *Neither woman, even though they knew Wilcher well, could make a positive identification.* If the body was not the 49-year-old Wilcher, then who was it? And where was Paul Wilcher if he was still alive?

Confusion surrounds Wilcher's death at the Metropolitan Police Department's homicide office in Washington, where the designation "natural causes" has been stamped next to Wilcher's name in the department log book.[9] The *Washington Times*, in following up on the Wilcher story (something the *Washington Post* chose not to do), observed: "...When Mr. Wilcher's body was found on June 23, he was investigating the theory of an 'October Surprise' conspiracy during the 1980 federal election campaign. He had been interviewing an inmate who claimed to have piloted George Bush to Paris so he could secretly seek to delay the release of 52 American hostages in Iran."[10]

That is certainly what the *Wilcher Transcripts* reveal. Unlike the *Skeleton Key to the Gemstone Files* or Danny Casolaro's "octopus" theory, the *Transcripts* are very meticulous. Most of the material is boiled down from a series of interviews Wilcher had with imprisoned pilot Gunther Russbacher in the Jefferson City (Mo.) Correctional Center from early April through mid-June, 1992. Wilcher writes in the *Transcripts* (p. 82) that he taped 90 hours' worth of interviews with Russbacher, using "attorney-client" privilege to protect the secrecy of the material. He claims to have processed "2,000 pages of single-spaced transcripts of these tapes" which he proceeded to cull several long communiqués, one sent to Rep. Lee Hamilton, head of the "October Surprise" fact-finding committee which, on Jan. 13, 1993, announced that it could find "no evidence" that such an

---

9. *Ibid.*
10. *Ibid.*

event had taken place. Another lengthy letter of over 100 pages was sent to Attorney General Janet Reno, and not only offered details about the "October Surprise," but blamed everything from the John F. Kennedy assassination in 1963 to the Inslaw software scandal of the 1980s and '90s on a "secret government," a similar thesis to the "octopus" of Danny Casolaro, who is mentioned in the *Wilcher Transcripts* but only as a "murdered witness" and not an investigative reporter (p. 49).

Clearly, the bulk of this information was drawn from Russbacher himself, and all the government has to do to quell the disturbance the *Wilcher Transcripts* might cause is to discredit Russbacher. That media campaign is already in high gear, but it might be tougher to put Russbacher out of commission than the "secret government" might think.

As we went to press, Russbacher was recuperating from quadruple-bypass heart surgery somewhere near the home of his first wife, whom he divorced some years ago, according to a reliable source. Russbacher's current wife, Rayelan Russbacher, was living in Carmel, Calif., and is now reportedly at her husband's side. It is strange that when it was clear the *Wilcher Transcripts* were leaked to the public, Russbacher was suddenly released from prison in Missouri, where he had been held on theft charges. With the *Transcripts* now out, and being freely discussed on radio talk shows, there is no sense in keeping Russbacher in prison any longer. Now, several scenaros are possible:

- Russbacher could be paid off by the government for his silence and shipped out of the country for his own protection.
- He could blow the lid off the "October Surprise" and a bundle of other CIA-related covert operations that have taken place over the past 30 years.
- He could die of "complications" related to his recent heart surgery.

Many reasons exist to discount the current media onslaught on Russbacher's credibility and to believe him when he states he is a long-term CIA operative, and that he indeed did fly George Bush back from Paris on Oct. 19, 1980, in a supersonic SR-71 aircraft to get the vice-presidential running mate of Ronald Reagan back to the United States before it was discovered he was missing. First, Russbacher has had many aliases. Second, he has been allowed free access to military bases, housing and equipment, and has been observed wearing several different types of uniforms and "impersonated" several types of officers. This information was made public when he was arrested by the FBI in 1990 while living in visiting officers' quarters at Castle AFB in California. That was about the time the "October Surprise" information was breaking loose.

Wilcher (p. 67) characterizes Russbacher, now 49 years old, as a "life-long covert operative for the CIA and the Office of Naval Intelligence (ONI) who has operated at the highest levels of both of these super-secret organizations over the past 30 and 25 years, respectively.

"Because of his extremely high intelligence, his exceptional physical skills, his extensive training, his fluency in eight languages, his proficiency as one of the CIA's top pilots and marksmen, and the fact that his father was one of the *original founders (along with William Casey, 'Wild Bill' Donovan, and others) of the Central Intelligence Agency, back in 1947* (emphasis ours), Gunther has always operated at the highest level of these 'intelligence' organizations..."

The real kicker in the "October Surprise" situation is that Russbacher's associates have in their possession a "smoking gun" cockpit videotape that shows George Bush being flown back to the United States from Paris. Wilcher states (p. 74) that "a complete video is *always* made of the entire experience," in this case a one-hour, 45-minute SR-71 blast straight from Paris to McGuire Air Force Base in New Jersey, including an air refueling session via a KC-135 over the Atlantic Ocean (p. 73).

The videotape recorder is built into the cockpit, and is removed after every flight and the tape extracted. However, an *exact duplicate of the video is transmitted to the nearest Key-hole spy satellite and the signal is bounced down to Fort Meade, Md., where it is recorded as an exact replica of the cockpit tape.* This satellite transmission (p. 76) carries with it a "satellite signature" that displays the Greenwich Mean Time and date in the form of "a constant stream of numbers running across the bottom of the film for its entire duration (p. 76)."

When things started to unravel with regard to leaks of information about the "October Surprise," Wilcher writes, "Russbacher tipped associates who then 'liberated' (the tape) from NSA headquarters in Fort Meade, Md., later that same evening, and put it into safekeeping."

Wilcher compares that video to the "smoking gun" audio tape that helped sink the Nixon administration in the Watergate scandal.

The *Transcripts* also contain a bundle of information, prob-ably from Russbacher as well, detailing the "real" set of circum-stances surrounding the Waco religious cult compound and its fiery destruction on April 19, 1993. Wilcher proposes that a CIA "wet" team entered the compound and either gassed or mur-dered most of the 86 people who died in the holocaust (pp. 37-43) prior to the flames erupting. He also claims that Branch Davidian leader David Koresh and his six closest followers were "sleepers," or "persons whom the Agency (CIA) had per-formed mind control experiments on (p. 18)." When the Bureau of Alcohol, Tobacco and Firearms (BATF) raided the compound on Feb. 28, they ran into an astonishing array of firepower the Branch Davidians had assembled, and it was totally unexpected; that is, the "sleepers" were not operating as programmed. The only other option was total annihilation of the group, but only after they were bombarded with "20 gigahertz microwave trans-missions, designed to be as stressful and destructive to the human physiology, inner ear, psyche and mental stability as possible (p. 35)." Loud music was also played to cover for he fact that these microwave transmissions were bombarding the people in the compound.

Wilcher also claims that, as a direct result of this operation, some 16 members of the FBI who participated in the Waco operation stand ready to come forward and testify against the CIA elements who actually destroyed the compound and everyone in it. This element of the story contains a memo from the 16 members to former FBI Director William Sessions which outlined how the assault was handled, and why it actually took place.

This faxed memo, dated July 9, 1993, and attached as an addendum to the *Wilcher Transcripts*, has the following shocking disclosure:

"...5. Waco compound members had almost completed assembly of a nerve-gas toxin device massive/large enough in quantity to *target and destroy all organic life in 432-square-mile area* (emphasis ours). A city the size of Oklahoma City was intended [as the target?]. However, Houston, Tx., was designated as the principal (sic) target. Denver had been considered along with Salt Lake City, but the mountainous area precludes accurate dispersion...

"6. The device in Waco was in very few hours of completion. *Order to go in was not made by Executive Branch (i.e. Attorney General Reno's office)!!!* (emphasis ours). Orders assumed 'Code Actual' when the infiltrator agent residing within the complex stated 'Code Blue'...

"7....Reno acted as if she knew nothing about the real problem — the device!"

It was known that Koresh and his followers had enormous firepower at their disposal, but a secret nerve-gas weapon? It is almost impossible to consider this as a viable reason behind the sudden attack on the compound and its eventual destruction, but Reno certainly gave no reason other than the agents "were tired."

****

Clearly, these latest "Gemstones" shine with a luster all their own. Bruce Roberts would have been proud.

CHAPTER 14

As We Went to Press

- **Opium and Onassis:** There is one Aristotle Onassis biography, *Onassis: Aristotle and Christina*, by L.J. Davis, that refers to the opium trade (p. 13) as it relates to Onassis (Gemstone 1:1): "He had made his first real money there, in South America (Argentina), but the fact was that *almost no one but Onassis knew just how* (emphasis ours). The stories, some of them of which he told himself, were various and conflicting; at least one tale had him running a string of prostitutes *that included the future Eva Peron* (emphasis ours). Despite his later protestations to the contrary, his family had been prosperous in Turkey, exporting the produce, *opium* (emphasis ours), and tobacco to the Anatolian interior."

****

- **Byoir, Hughes and the Nazis:** Howard Hughes publicist Carl Byoir leads us to more possible connections to Onassis. Throughout World War II, the Byoir agency not only represented the Howard Hughes interests but those of Nazi bankers and industrialists. Even the infamous I.G. Farben company — including member Ernest Schmitz — was a client of Byoir's. Still another Byoir customer was the German American Board of Trade, which monitored, among other things, the maritime traffic between Nazi Germany and the United States. The Frederick Flick Group, also represented by Byoir, was beneficiary of not only of Byoir's public relations skills, but of a timely pardon by attorney John McCloy after the Nuremberg trials. McCloy later served with the Warren Commission in the investigation of the JFK assassination. These connections could well have led to some connection with Onassis, who dealt with the Nazis during the war as prime customers of his shipping services, according to the *Skeleton Key*. Nazis were well-known Onassis customers, and some, like Hjalmar Schacht, president of Adolf Hitler's Reichsbank, were hired as consultants after the war. Such associations were the linchpins behind Mae Brussell's elaborate conspiracy scenarios — many of which credit expatriate Nazis for planning the assassination of President Kennedy.

****

• **Peron, Onassis and Nazi Germany:** Many influential Nazis bailed out of Germany before the curtain came down on Adolf Hitler , and many of them found a haven in South America, including Josef Mengele, Heinrich Dorge, Rudolf Freude, Dr. Fritz Thyssen, Dr. Gustav Krupp, and Schacht's son-in-law, Otto Skorzeny, according to conspiracy researcher John Judge in an article entitled *Good Americans*. Eva Peron, the Argentine leader who was allegedly sexually involved with Onassis, provided help for these criminals through money she obtained through Martin Bormann, Hitler's Deputy Fuhrer who looted the Nazi treasury right before the end of the conflict. It was also reported in an episode of *In Search Of* with Leonard Nimoy that the ancient golden treasures of Troy, discovered near the turn of the century and later placed on display at the Berlin Museum, were included in the loot. As partially described in Chapter 8, such tales of Nazis stealing these archaeological treasures — accompanied by a largely accurate profile of American Bruce Roberts, author of the Gemstone Files and inspiration for the *Skeleton Key* — could well have inspired the entire Indiana Jones trilogy of motion pictures in the 1980s.

****

• **The death of Al Harris:** Gemstone 3:7b mentions, in passing, that a man named Al Harris "heart attacked" after hearing testimony before the California Crime Commission concerning loans from Joseph L. Alioto's bank to Jimmy Fratianno, a mobster implicated in the *Skeleton Key* as a member of the JFK assassination team. Albert W. Harris Jr. is listed as dying Dec. 4, 1974, in a San Rafael, Calif., hospital. Cause of death was reported as "pneumonia" by the Dec. 5 edition of the *San Francisco Examiner* (Obituary labeled, "Al Harris, prosecutor of Angela Davis"). The story went on to say that "Mr. Harris, who headed the (state) attorney general's organized crime unit, had been ill with the flu since Thanksgiving, but *continued working through last week* (emphasis ours), an associate said. Harris, though, was declared dead of pneumonia 10 hours after he was admitted to Kaiser Hospital in San Rafael on Dec. 4. Harris was the prosecutor for the trial of Angela Davis in 1972; Davis was a militant black activist who was accused of masterminding a "kidnap raid at the Marin County Hall of Justice on Aug. 7, 1970, which ended in the deaths of a judge and three of the abductors." This was also the time when the so-called Zebra and Death Angel killing sprees began. Although Harris was unsuccessful at getting a guilty verdict on Davis — she was acquitted — he probably earned the scorn of organized crime, in whose best interests the entire Zebra and Death Angel series of killings was engineered, according to the *Skeleton Key*.

****

• **Black Muslims and the Zebra deaths:** The tail-end of Gemstone 11:7 mentions that Black Muslims were to be "blamed and framed" for the Zebra killings. A story that ran on the United Press International wire service on April 17, 1989, gave some misleading information about the Zebra killings in a story about "cult killings:" "The Zebra killings that terrorized California in the early 1970s involved normal people inspired by a charismatic leader. A Black Muslim leader persuaded his followers — 'death angels,' he called them — to slaughter whites, 'evil blue-eyed devils.' Fourteen died. '(Charles) Manson and the Zebra leader gave their followers a cause,' Jack Levin, sociology professor at Northeastern University, said. 'That justified their staying together and staying silent. *Nobody was hypnotized into joining the groups* (emphasis ours). They joined because it gave them a chance to be important, to put their mark on the world.'" It is interesting that Levin makes it a point to stress that the Zebra killers were *not* "hypnotized" into joining the death squad, but there was never any evidence gathered that they *weren't* hypnotized, either.

****

• **Onassis and J. Edgar Hoover:** Aristotle Onassis drew the attention of J. Edgar Hoover and the FBI in the late 1930s because of an association with Austrian arms tycoon Fritz Mandl as preparations for World War II were pervading the European continent. This is outlined in *Aristotle Onassis*, by Nicholas Fraser, Philip Jacobson, Mark Ottaway and Lewis Chester: "...Onassis' contact with Mendl and, possibly, with others out of favor with the U.S. authorities (there were more Argentines on the blacklist than any other nationality) may explain one of the most intriguing episodes of his (Onassis') early career — a recommendation by J. Edgar Hoover that Onassis should be spied on while he was in the United States." This recommendation came in the form of a letter to Admiral Emory S. Land, head of the War Shipping Administration. It would appear the FBI knew everything there was to know about Onassis, including the Gemstone files, according to the *Skeleton Key* (Gemstone 8:7), and it cost Hoover his life.

****

- **Vatican conspiracy:** The *Skeleton Key* talks at length about a Catholic cardinal "Tisseront" (sic) being murdered (Gemstone 8:4) as a cover-up to his research on the early Christian church — research which overturns much of what is now accepted as true Christianity as presented in the Bible, specifically the four Gospels of Matthew, Mark, Luke and John. Apparently, Bruce Roberts was referring to Eugene Cardinal Tisserant, who died at the age of 87 of a "heart attack" on Feb. 21, 1972 in a clinic in Albano, Italy, according to an obituary in the *New York Times*. Tisserant apparently had a personal diary, and Roberts might have acquired some entries from that diary to lay the groundwork for is tirade against Christianity. The most significant aspect of this is the very start of Gemstone 8:4, when Roberts says Tisserant's death occurred "the day before" his father was allegedly murdered by the Watergate plumbers in San Francisco (Chapter 8). The date of La Verne Dayle Roberts' death was Feb. 22, 1972, according to the death certificate, so Bruce Roberts is accurate here.

****

- **Sunol scandal:** Gemstone 3:8c mentions the "Sunol Golf Course swindle" which cost the city of San Francisco between $100,000 and $500,000 and involved East Coast Mafia figure Tony Romano and San Francisco Mayor Joe Alioto. This scandal was followed very closely by *San Francisco Examiner* columnist Dick Nolan, who wrote in a July 13, 1976, column that "...Joe Alioto was our mayor at the time, and it was his public utilities lads who dealt Tony (Romano) the golf course. In subsequent proceedings, involving a rubber check of imposing dimensions, Alioto has denied he gave Romano assurance of any kind..." Nolan details the repeated mob beatings of Joe Madeiros, a Bay Area culinary union leader who apparently stood in the way of the golf course deal. Nolan also states: "...A lot of people wanted that golf course concession, and wanted it badly enough to lay out important wads of money. One group, a Chinese syndicate based in Taiwan, *got swindled out of $300,000 or so in its efforts to get the golf course lease* (emphasis ours). The Chinese entrepreneurs want their money back, if anybody can find it, and they are suing everyone in sight..."

****

- **Media control:** Gemstone 1:4 that "news censorship of all other major news media goes into effect" after Eugene Meyer bought the *Washington Post*, and that this censorship reflected news stories that would place the Mafia and the U.S. intelligence community in a bad light. There is plenty of circumstantial evidence that strengthens this view. For example, in November, 1960, *The Nation* magazine — a fringe publication, not considered part of the media mainstream — tried to interest major news media in a story that outlined pending U.S. plans to invade Cuba. However, the *New York Times* blasted the story as "shrill...anti-American propaganda" at the same time it was putting a clamp on the story at the request of President Kennedy in the interest of "national security." However, after the ill-fated Bay of Pigs fiasco, JFK admitted that had the *Times* run the story, public pressure would have likely led to cancellation of the operation. He told the *Times*: "If you had printed more about the operation, you could have saved us from a colossal mistake."

****

- **The death of Alexander Onassis:** Onassis' only son was killed in an airplane crash on Jan. 22, 1973. Gemstone 9:5 blames the crash on a "fixed altimeter." The *Skeleton Key* had the right idea, but the wrong method. Alexander and pilot Donald McCusker were in the Piaggio seaplane when it crashed just after takeoff; Alexander was mortally injured,

McCusker survived, but was mystified as to the cause of the crash. Aristotle Onassis hired Alan Hunter, a British aviation expert, to undertake a thorough investigation. Hunter discovered that someone had *reversed the Piaggio's aileron controls.* When McCusker, who was piloting the plane, tried to obey the air controller's order for a left turn when airborne, presumably to escape the wake of a French Boeing 727 jet that had taken off moments earlier, the seaplane instead banked to the right. McCusker reacted by applying more left wheel, which only succeeded in driving the Piaggio into the ground. Clearly, some kind of sabotage was evident, but Onassis would never find the perpetrator. According to biographer L.J. Davis, Onassis suspected almost everyone — his rival, Stavros Niarchos; the American CIA; even his wife Jackie was rumored to be a suspect. His son's death destroyed Onassis, and he himself was dead of respiratory failure two years later.

****

• **Christina Onassis' death:** Completing the legacy of death, daughter Christina's passing was the most mysterious of the three. Christina was only 37 years old when she collapsed and died suddenly in Buenas Aires, Argentina, on Nov. 20, 1989. An Argentine judge, Juan Carlos Cardinalli, said the day after that an autopsy showed that Christina died of "a lung disorder" described as "pulmonary edema," caused by "an accumulation of blood in the lung," according to wire reports as rewritten in the Nov. 21, 1989, editions of the *San Francisco Examiner.* Chemical poisoning, such as the effects caused by the feared sodium morphate, could have caused similar symptoms; after all, Christina was healthy at the time, and she was in fact becoming quite the businesswoman and took a hands-on approach to the running of her late father's shipping company. Cardinalli was quoted in that same story that the possible presence of any drugs in Christina's system would be ascertained by ensuing blood analysis, the "results of which would be available in a few days." Those test results were never released. In fact, there was a conflicting report out of Buenos Aires that stated Christina suffered a "heart attack" and died as she prepared to go swimming in a country-club pool some 25 northwest of Buenos Aires, according to Dr. Herman Bunge.

****

* **The Illuminati conspiracy:** A popular theory that conspiracy advocates have pushed for years involves the so-called "Illuminati," a powerful secret society that is supposed to be answerable to no earthly laws. One of the latest backers of the thesis is television evangelist Pat Robertson, who blames the Illuminati for attempting to overthrow "Christian culture" and replace it with an occult-driven, anarchist Illuminati leadership in his recent book, *The New World Order*. Robertson states that "for the past 200 years the term 'new world order' has been the code phrase of those who desired to destroy the Christian faith and 'the Christian social order.' They wish to replace it with an occult-inspired dictatorship. At the central core is a belief in the superiority of their own skill to form a world system in which enlightened monopolistic capitalism can bring all of the diverse currencies, banking systems, credit, manufacturing and raw materials into one government-supervised whole, policed of course by their own world army." The conspiracy allegedly began in 1776, when "a Bavarian professor named Adam Weishaupt launched a small secret society called the Order of the Illuminati. Weishaupt's aims were to establish a new world order based on the overthrow of civilian government, the church, and private property and the elevation of world leadership of a group of hand-picked 'adepts' or 'illumined' ones. Weishaupt chose as his vehicle for infiltration and takeover the established Continental Order of Freemasons." The only trouble with this thesis is that it's too easy an explanation for the current world situation. Granted,

some Freemasons are in positions of power. But some people, like Onassis, were members of no such group.

****

- **The invention of AIDS:** Is Acquired Immune Deficiency Syndrome (AIDS) a plot to kill off undesirable elements in our society? At least one document we acquired insisted that it was, saying simply: "AIDS was invented by the U.S. Army Germ Warfare Laboratory at Fort Detrick, Md. House of Representatives Appropriations Committee allocated $10 million to the Army labs to 'develop a virus capable of destroying the human immune system.' (Ref.: U.S. Senate Library — House Appropriation Committee HB 15090, 1970, Vol. VI, page 129). The World Health Organization contaminated the smallpox vaccine with AIDS virus (HIV) to purposely spread AIDS all through Africa. The New York blood bank put AIDS virus in the hepatitis vaccine soon after the smallpox introduction. (Refs.: Dr. Robert Strecker, Dr. William Campbell Douglass, *London Times*, May 11, 1987.) A U.S. Ambassador (Ted Maino), who lived for several years in Africa, may have further information on this subject." You decide.

****

- **The deaths of Tower, Heinz, Weiss:** The *Wilcher Transcripts* claim (p. 47) that the airplane-crash deaths of Sens. John Tower (April 5, 1991) and John Heinz (April 4, 1991) were not accidental; that these airplanes were "blown out of the sky" to silence Tower and Heinz regarding the "October Surprise." The *Transcripts* also say that the death of Rep. Ted Weiss (Sept. 14, 1992), determined to be "heart failure," was also not a natural death; that he was poisoned because he threatened to blow the lid off "October Surprise" allegations. Tower and Heinz (p. 69) were part of the U.S. delegation — along with CIA chief and vice-presidential candidate George Bush — that were allegedly flown to Paris to participate in the

"October Surprise" negotiations. The plane used was a BAC-111 provided by the Saudi royal family and piloted by Gunther Russbacher (p. 68). Taking these incidents one at a time:

- **Tower:** A Brazilian-made Embraer 120, reportedly in perfect mechanical shape before takeoff, is what crashed and killed Tower and 22 others. Space shuttle astronaut Manley Lanier Carter was also killed. The *Washington Post* reported on April 7, 1991, quoted witnesses as saying that the plane was seen to "pitch suddenly to one side and descend abruptly," and one witness reported a "squealing noise." This could indicate an explosion of some kind. The National Transportation Safety Board later blamed the crash on "a faulty part in a propeller control system." The *Wilcher Transcripts* state (p. 69) that Tower was about to revise some chapters in his book, *Consequences: A Personal and Political Memoir*, which would expose the "October Surprise" flight of which he was a part, the *Transcripts* say. The *Post*, in that same April 7, 1991, account, did state that "...Tower, 65, and his daughter Marian, 35 (also killed in the crash), were to spend the weekend at the home of his literary agent, Margaret McBride..."

- **Heinz:** The *Wilcher Transcripts* version of this mishap follows (p. 69): "...Like Sen. Tower, Sen. Heinz's death resulted from his private plane being blown out of the sky. News reports at the time indicated that Sen. Heinz's plane had collided with a helicopter, What actually happened, however, is that the helicopter fired a missile at Heinz's plane causing it to explode. But because the helicopter pilot was inexperienced and did not get out of the way in time, the exploding debris from the plane fell onto the helicopter, causing it to crash also." The *Atlanta Journal and Constitution* reported on April 5, 1991, facts that would tend to back Wilcher's assessment: "...As the helicopter hovered below the airplane, witnesses said, the two aircraft collided. The plane *exploded in a fireball, while the helicopter fell largely intact* (emphasis ours)." Heinz and six other people, including two first-grade school children on the ground, were killed in the "accident."

****

• **Gander, Newfoundland, crash:** The *Wilcher Transcripts* also blame the Dec. 12, 1985, crash of an Arrow Air jet over Gander, Newfoundland, that killed 248 U.S. servicemen returning from duty in the Middle East, plus a crew of eight (p. 48). Reuters news service reported on Dec. 13, 1985, that an anonymous caller phones the Reuters news bureau in Beirut, Lebanon, immediately after the plane went down, saying that they "bombed a charter airliner out of the sky." Wilcher states the plane was "blown out of the sky." Another point: In a 1993 book, *The Outlaw Bank*, an account of the BCCI failure and ensuing scandal written by Jonathan Beaty and S.C. Gwynne, the BCCI mess is connected to the Gander crash. In a *Cleveland Plain Dealer* book review published on July 3, 1993: "...Beaty and Gwynne have added fascinating tales to BCCI lore. One involves the 1985 crash of an Arrow Air jet in Gander, Newfoundland, killing 248 American soldiers returning from the Middle East. It was linked to BCCI through *crates the military hustled away and a duffel bag stuffed full of hundred-dollar bills* (emphasis ours). A German arms dealer told Beaty and Gwynne that after the crash, high-level BCCI contacts complained about losing a lot of money in the Gander crash; the same man reportedly went into the Soviet space program's offices and photographed U.S. satellite documents, which the Russians bragged had been procured by BCCI."

****

• **The Jonestown "mass suicide":** Like the "Ranch Apocalypse" in Waco, Texas, the *Wilcher Transcripts* say that the "mass suicide" of 914 people in Jonestown, Guyana, was the result of a government mind-control experiment gone awry

(p. 48) and an entire settlement of people had to be destroyed to cover it up. We have an additional account of he Jonestown situation acquired independently of Wilcher which gives the following synopsis of what happened that day after Rep. Leo Ryan and his party were ambushed by gunmen at the Guyana airport (Ryan and others were shot to death): "...On Nov. 18, 1978, more than 900 people allegedly committed suicide in Jonestown, Guyana, leaving over 200 more people unaccounted for to this day as 1,100 passports had been issued to (People's) Temple members to travel to Guyana. Officials later stated to the press that only 900 passports had been issued. Of those 900 individuals, over two-thirds of them were either shot, strangled or showed injection or puncture marks on heir bodies. Contrary to what all established media said at the time, very few actually died from self-administered, cyanide-laced Kool-Aid." Ryan had been on the CIA's tail about such matters, co-sponsoring the Hughes-Ryan Act of 1974 which ordered that all CIA covert activities must be reported in advance to congressional oversight committees. Also stated from our source: "...(There was) a contingency plan to help eliminate those who would not cooperate in ingesting the cyanide-laced Kool-Aid. The (so-called Agency) Clean Teams used two small, specially equipped helicopters as "dusters" to deliver sleeping gas to put the settlement under as quickly and quietly as possible. Clean Team squads were then sent in to administer lethal injections of, if necessary, to eliminate any individuals attempting to escape by the use of snipers and general small-arms elimination." The report added that, unlike media videotape that showed bodies piled on top of each other, bodies were recovered in a "three-square-mile area" around the compound.

The Rev. Jim Jones, leader of the People's Temple "cult" that settled Jonestown, was fearful of just such a scenario. One of the followers, Deborah Layton Blakey, stated in a sworn affidavit on June 15, 1978, in San Francisco that Jones actually held rehearsals for an attack from the outside: "...At least once a week, Rev. Jones would declare a "white night," or state of emergency. The entire population of Jonestown would be awakened by blaring sirens. Designated persons, approximately 50 in number, would *arm themselves with rifles, move from cabin to cabin, and make certain that all members were responding* (emphasis ours). A mass meeting would ensue. Frequently during these crises, we would be told that the jungle was *swarming with mercenaries and that death could be expected any minute* (emphasis ours)."

****

• **Did Wilcher get greedy?** Washington D.C. freelance reporter Sarah McClendon told us by telephone Dec. 29, 1993, that attorney Paul Wilcher might have become enraptured in his abilities to interview, at length, purported "October Surprise" pilot Gunther Russbacher, and pushed for a little more than Justice Department higher-ups would care to grant. "My understanding is that Wilcher presented all this information from his many interviews with Russbacher to the Justice people — I think even (Attorney General Janet) Reno knows about most of this — but that he added one stipulation in exchange for his information," said McClendon. "He wanted to be granted a high position in the Department. That's what really sank him, and hurt his credibility." McClendon, a veteran independent correspondent who fearlessly tracks down every conspiracy theory in Washington, added that "everyone made fun of Wilcher" for the most part, but that when he turned up dead, "apparently murdered," McClendon said, many reporters ran for cover. "The atmosphere is very fearful around here these days," said McClendon, who said that Wilcher was attracted to researching Washington conspiracy lore after his Chicago-area family's fortune was lost as a result of the savings and loan debacle in the 1980s under the aloof Reagan administration. "Paul was very bitter about this, because he saw plenty of corruption in the Chicago-area judges, and in fact traced plenty of corruption in the judges around here as well."

****

- **Russbacher was for real:** We have also acquired an interesting memo, dated May 20, 1986, written on "United States Government Memorandum" stationery and reading as follows:

Date: 20 May 1986.
Reply to the Attn. of: Bill Casey HQ, CIA.
Subject: *Russbacher Karl Gunther ONI* (emphasis ours), Segal Robert John CIA.
To: John Poindexter NSA.
Re: Operation MAGG PIE.

Please be advised these men will meet with agents Robert Hunt ONI, Bud McFarlane NSA, Oliver North NSA, George Cavo CIA, and Howard Teicher also CIA. They will give complete briefing at Tel Aviv Ben Gurion Airport. *Pilot selection is now finale* (sic, emphasis ours). If you have any questions please call me soon. We leave Sunday the 25 (sic). Im (sic) keeping my fingers crossed.

Good Luck,
(Signed) Bill Casey CIA.

CC
VP, Bush (emphasis ours)

The significant thing here is that Gunther Russbacher was apparently flying airplanes for the CIA until at least 1986 (Wilcher has stated Russbacher was let out of jail in Missouri briefly to fly yet another mission during his recent incarceration on "theft" and "impersonating an officer" charges) and that a copy of this memo was shipped straight to George Bush. Of course, we have no way of determining if this memo was genuine, although Bill Casey's signature looks authentic enough to us.

****

- **Brussell death threat:** Conspiracy expert Mae Brussell (see Chapter 8) might have died of "natural" causes in October of 1988, but it must be noted that she received a death threat earlier that year, and suspended her Monterey, Calif., area radio broadcasts on KAZU as a result. The *Monterey Peninsula Herald* reported on March 10, 1988, that Brussell was quite shaken by the phoned-in threat. "In 17 years (of broadcasting) I've never had anything like that," she told the *Herald.* "I really know he meant it." The call allegedly came in to Brussell's home on Feb. 25, 1988, and the caller reportedly said: "I'm coming up (to the Monterey Peninsula area) and you are never going to be on the radio again. I'm coming up there fully armed and I'm going to blow your head off and nobody will ever find a trace of you. You're going to be like those missing people that you talk about." Brussell's further reaction: "If you get a call like that, you would take it seriously," she said. "I really know he meant it. I put about $3,000 worth of security (monitoring equipment) in at the house...I'm taking it seriously enough to go off the air after 17 years." She ended up staying on the air until she died.

****

- **More Hughes evidence:** Donald Neuhaus, our source for much of the Howard Hughes material in Chapter 5, has recalled even more evidence that the real Hughes was switched in 1957 as the *Skeleton Key* maintains. For one, Neuhaus maintains that actress Jean Peters did not accompany Hughes to Montreal, then Nassau, as some Hughes biographers maintain. In fact, Neuhaus recalls that a young 16-year-old daughter of a Southern California dairy farmer and Canadian national, named "Yvonne," was the woman who accompanied Hughes to Montreal, then to Nassau. That would mean the woman that pilot Bill Bushey thought was Jean Peters was actually "Yvonne." Interestingly, Yvonne's father, when he caught wind of his 16-year-old daughter having audience with Howard Hughes, angrily decided to "bring the world down on Howard," as Neuhaus put it. Those emotions were changed radically when the dairy farmer was suddenly awarded a fat contract to supply all the milk consumed by the Hughes Corporation. Other long-time Hughes aides, meanwhile, were pushed aside. Bill Gay, for example, dropped out of sight for a long time, and Hughes issued the directive that Gay was not to be disturbed at all since he had contracted mononucleosis, Neuhaus says. Other personnel were issued walking papers after years of service in the Hughes company — confirming the portion of Gemstone 1:9 that refers to Hughes' men "either quit, get fired or stay on in the new Onassis organization."

****

• **Hughes' habits:** Gemstone 1:9 comments that the Jean Peters "marriage" was arranged to "explain Hughes's sudden loss of interest in chasing movie stars." Having to make most of those arrangements, Neuhaus can vouch for the truth of that statement. An example of Hughes's treatment of Hollywood starlets, Neuhaus told us, was when he invited actress Julie Newmar for a visit. Newmar had just starred in film musicals like *L'il Abner* and Hughes wanted to see her. He had her flown in to Beverly Hills, where Neuhaus picked her up at the airport. The Hughes associates would then take Newmar out to dinner before taking her to a doctor for a complete physical examination. "Hughes would not touch these women without the checkup," said Neuhaus. Then, Newmar was taken to a dentist to "make sure her mouth was clean," then to a classy hotel, most of the time the Chateau

Marmont in Hollywood. Hughes entertained Newmar and sent a photographer to do a set of photos, which were developed and printed immediately and set to Hughes's suite, where he would make the decision if she was worth any further attention. All this was done, Neuhaus explained, to screen actresses for contract work in Hughes-backed motion picture projects. But after mid-1957, *all this type of screening activity ceased abruptly*, backing Gemstone 1:9's remark.

****

• **Roberts' father and the Plumbers:** Gemstone 8:3 alleges that the Watergate plumbers assassinated Bruce Roberts' father, whom we have identified as La Verne Dayle Roberts, a long-time Bethlehem Steel shipbuilder in the days of Onassis' oil-tanker heights in the 1920s and '30s. As described in Chapter 8, we have determined the cause of death could well have been poisoning of some kind, but any connection with the Plumbers is sheer speculation. Or is it? Note the following passage from Gordon Liddy's biography, *Will*, page 208: "...Other methods (of assassination) were discussed and discarded. *'Aspirin Roulette,' for example: the placing of a poisoned replica of the appropriate brand of headache tablet into the bottle usually found in the target's medicine cabinet* (emphasis ours). That method was rejected because it would gratuitously endanger innocent members of his family and might take months before it worked." Compare this to Gemstone 8:3.

****

• **Bush, Lipset and surveillance:** Indications are that George Bush knew all about Hal Lipset and his connections with any intelligence information collected during Watergate. In a July 25, 1973, story in the *San Francisco Examiner* ("Stoffman Under Fire From GOP"), Bush is said to have produced three affidavits "he said strongly indicate (Carmine) Bellino used electronic surveillance to monitor conversations in the hotel space in which Nixon prepared for his televised debates with John F. Kennedy." Bush served as the GOP National Chairman at the time, and it is interesting that he "produced" these affidavits just as the noose was closing around the Nixon administration's neck regarding the Watergate tapes. Bellino, well known for his own forms of electronic snooping, was hired along with Lipset by Samuel Dash of the Watergate committee as "investigators." It is intriguing that Kennedy might have benefited from the same tactics allegedly used by Nixon's Watergate "plumbers," but Bellino never had to answer for it. It appears that Bush, at a very early age, knew the benefits of information extracted by such covert means.

****

- **BCCI in a nutshell:** The massive scandal involving the Bank of Credit and Commerce International (BCCI) might end up being *too* big to do much about. For those who remain in the dark about this entire episode (we have touched upon it off and on throughout this volume), a summary follows, garnered from a plethora of international press on this issue:

  - The BCCI scandal, according to the latest evidence, is emerging as the largest bank fraud in history.

  - Until it shut down in 1991, BCCI was a Pakistani-run empire with more than a million depositors and $20 billion in assets in 73 countries.

  - BCCI secretly bought the biggest bank in Washington D.C., First American Bankshares Inc., whose chairman was distinguished American Clark Clifford.

  - BCCI moved money for arms dealers, drug traffickers, terrorists, bribers of politicians and tax dodgers. It acted as Manuel Noriega's personal banker.

  - BCCI concealed massive losses, and some Third World

countries whose central banks deposited money — including Jamaica, Nigeria, the Philippines, Cameroon, Trinidad, Syria, Hungary, Sri Lanka, Iraq, the former Soviet Union, Mexico, Cuba, Bangladesh and Sierra Leone — lost everything.

• BCCI financed Pakistan's efforts to acquired nuclear-weapons technology — as well as shipments of Scud missiles from North Korea (where, according to U.S. intelligence agencies, the North Koreans have already developed at least one functional nuclear bomb) to Syria, and Chinese Silkworm missiles to the Middle East. Pakistanis used BCCI accounts to intercept U.S. funds intended for the Afghan rebels in their struggle against the Soviet Union.

• BCCI was linked to money-laundering rackets involving aides of India's Rajiv Gandhi (since assassinated), and bribed two Peruvian central bankers when Peru placed $270 million with the bank in 1986-87.

• BCCI was used as a front company in Poland to help Abu Nidel, the Palestinian terrorist mastermind, buy weapons.

Reporters who were closing in on even more disclosures about BCCI have died under mysterious circumstances. Danny Casolaro was found dead in his West Virginia hotel room on Aug. 10, 1991, and Anson Ng — a stringer for *Financial Times* who was based in Guatemala — died of what officials first said was a suicide. However, a suspect was arrested in Guatemala, David Eduardo Lanza Marroquin, in January of 1992 and charged with killing Ng. Both Casolaro and Ng had apparently acquired BCCI-related information prior to their deaths.

Investigation of BCCI has been hampered because its main offices were located in Luxembourg and the Grand Cayman Islands, countries that have stiff secrecy laws relating to banking.

One of our sources frequents Islamabad, capital of Pakistan, and has told us that crews of so-called "narcs" roam the streets of the city, making sure the Pakistani drug trade flows smoothly. These "narcs," our source said, have ties with the CIA, who knew about BCCI's excesses in the 1980s but refused to blow the whistle on the bank because the Agency used bank connections to monitor the activities of international terrorist organizations.

Nobody really knows the scope of the BCCI disaster, and nobody knows where the money is.

****

- **Roberts, UCSF and MK-ULTRA:** Bruce Roberts implies (Gemstone 12:6, 13:1) that he contracted a "cancer" that was purposely inflicted upon him by U.S. intelligence operatives, allegedly using the same technique he says was used to give Soviet leader Leonid Brezhnev a cancer-like illness. An important discrepancy exists between the *Hustler* account and the original *Skeleton Key.* In the *Hustler* version, it is stated that a speck of "nickel dust" caused the Soviet leader's "cancer." In our copy, it simply states that a "speck of metal" caused the ailment. Did *Hustler* know more than Bruce Roberts (or purported *Key* author Stephanie Caruana) about exactly how this type of illness was inflicted? Bruce Roberts' death certificate indicates that he was "treated" for his "cancer" from Nov. 17, 1975, until he time he died on July 30, 1976. The doctor who signed the certificate also wrote that the last time he saw the patient before he died was July 23, 1976 — a full week. It is hard to fathom why a doctor attending a dying patient would not see that patient the final week he (or she) was alive. Further, it is curious why Roberts used the UCSF Oncology Clinic, part of the university's Medical Center, which would have been enormously expensive. He was self-employed "construction contractor," according to his death certificate, and that matches Caruana's statements to Jim Keith in *The Gemstone File* (p. 49) that he roofed buildings. If so, he would not have had medical insurance to pay for such treatments. Plus, according to his obituary (*San Francisco Examiner*, Aug. 1, 1976) Roberts was a "veteran of World War II." Why not just use the nearest Veterans Hospital? UCSF has been the site of many government medical testing programs, including so-called MK-ULTRA tests in the 1940s. At least eight patients underwent "radiation experiments" at USCF Medical Center, according to a story by Lisa Kreiger of the *San Francisco Examiner* (Dec. 29, 1993), and this number could increase as the facts continue to unfold in this story. If U.S. intelligence wanted to infect Bruce Roberts with an artificially induced cancer, UCSF would have been the place to do it.

****

• **"Sodium Morphate:"** Many conspiracy researchers cannot get past the term "sodium morphate" that the *Skeleton Key* used to describe the slow-acting "heart-attack" poison mentioned several times in the *Key*. Nobody really has a ready explanation for the chemical composition of such a substance, if it indeed did exist. We have a possible solution to this: At the turn of the century, the full name of the drug "morphine" was "morphine sulphate." Shortened, that would produce the word "morphate." So, simply put, "sodium morphate" is morphine with a caustic, sodium-based chemical added. Pure sodium metal actually explodes when combined with water; a carefully mixed sodium-based compound, in turn mixed with some potent "morphine sulfate," could well cause the "arteriosclerosis" described on many a Gemstone-related death certificate (and, believe us, we've got them all).

****

- **Casolaro's brother wants answers:** Tony Casolaro, brother of deceased journalist Danny Casolaro, told writer David Corn of *The Nation* magazine that the belated autopsy of Danny Casolaro showed the presence of an antidepressant drug in his bloodstream at the time he died. Tony says Danny was not taking any prescription medicine of any kind at the time. An X-Acto knife apparently used to slice up Danny's arms was not sold locally. Plus, the 12 cuts on his arms — eight of them on the right arm (Casolaro was right-handed) cut all the way through muscles, tendons and right to the bone — rendering the limbs useless. It would have been impossible for Danny to have self-inflicted all of the cuts. Corn also reported that *Village Voice* editor Dan Bischoff received an anonymous phone call the day Casolaro's body was discovered. The caller stated that a journalist named Casolaro was found dead in West Virginia, that he had been working on the October Surprise story and that this should be scrutinized. But Casolaro's death did not become widely known *until the day after* the call when Martinsburg police actually announced it. Investigative Reporters and Editors (IRE), we have learned, acquired at least four file cabinets of Danny Casolaro's documents and notes — contributed by Tony Casolaro and kept under tight security at IRE headquarters at the University of Missouri in Columbia, Mo.

CONCLUSION

· · · · · · · · · · · · · · · · ·

The Next American Revolution

President Bill Clinton is the first person since John F. Kennedy to bring real power back to the office. He is smart enough not to make the mistakes of his predecessors, but he is never far away from the real sources of power in this country.

For example, Clinton "vacationed" for 10 days during the last week of August, 1993. The mainstream media reported, for the most part, that it was a time of relative calm for the President and his family. Clinton was shown playing miniature golf and enjoying the many pleasantries of the Martha's Vineyard area of Massachusetts, near Edgartown — which is also Kennedy country.

What the media failed to bring out in any meaningful way was the time Clinton was spending *away* from his family. Some newspapers did manage to report that he met with Jacqueline Kennedy Onassis during the 10-day period, and others cited some discussion with *Washington Post* publisher Katharine Meyer Graham. These are easily two of the world's most powerful media figures; Graham controls not only the *Post* but a large segment of United States print media in general, and Jacqueline Onassis has the New York literary establishment tap-dancing to her tunes. Neither woman would like the U.S. print media to be any more "truthful" than it now is, and both women are in positions to maintain that information control.

But what the mainstream media did not report, in general, was that Clinton met with Jacqueline Onassis for *six hours* aboard the yacht (sound familiar?) of long-time Onassis associate — diamond magnate Maurice Tempelsman — and a variety of critical issues were discussed, in particular Mr. Clinton's role in the world power structure. If there is any single person who could bring down a President, it would be Jackie Onassis. All she would have to do, for instance, is commission an investigative team to report in detail all of Clinton's past extramarital affairs, particularly the 10-year relationship with Gennifer Flowers. Such a book would be fully sanctioned by Jackie Onassis, embraced by a wealthy publishing house, and promoted without restriction. It would sell millions of copies, enrich some fortunate writer or team of writers, and potentially be a death blow to Clinton's credibility.

The mainstream media also did not treat with any distinction that *two separate dinner meetings* took place between Clinton and Graham — again, with substantial issues covered, mostly having to do with Clinton staying in line, or a Watergate-style roasting could certainly begin in earnest. Bob Woodward, with deep contacts within the U.S. intelligence establishment, also remains to this day one of the premier news reporters in the world. If it serves his purposes, and those of Graham and the *Post*, then the Presidency could again be held hostage.

Finally, a personality was introduced during that fateful 10 days, a personality not reported by any news organization — that of Henry Kissinger, easily one of the world's most powerful persons. It is a near-certainty that Kissinger made it clear to Clinton what his marching orders would be as the year 1994 starts.

****

The *Skeleton Key* clearly points to the positions of power these individuals have achieved, and although the *Key's* accuracy in describing the details of how this structure came to be can be challenged on a line-by-line basis, the thesis holds firm, in our view.

But with Clinton and his able Vice President Al Gore, this

power structure stands threatened. Already, Clinton has pushed through two enormously important pieces of legislation — a substantial tax increase and deficit-cutting measure, and the North American Free Trade Agreement (NAFTA) — through Congress in only his first year in office, and medical-care reform is around the corner. All these measures render shaky many established power structures. The tax hike and budget-cutting will stabilize the nation economically, something the real power brokers do not want to see. Destabilization of America would enhance the sales of arms and illegal street drugs, the bread-and-butter of our current "shadow government." This will not be tolerated for any length of time.

Medical-care reform threatens the power base established by private medical practitioners, many of whom have become astonishingly rich by way of the socialized medical programs, such as Medicare and Medicaid, which are already in place. Any further government control of medicine will place top-secret intelligence mind-control experiments at risk of exposure. Many of these experiments, fully sanctioned by the "shadow government," are not too easily pushed past the American people. The currently unfolding revelations about nuclear radiation experiments conducted on captive individuals and populations, without their knowledge, are just now coming to the forefront as a precursor to government overhaul of the medical establishment. Too many sensitive issues are at risk; the health crusade of Hillary Clinton will not be allowed to run its course.

And regardless of what people might think of the *Skeleton Key to the Gemstone Files*, the *Kiwi Gemstone*, the *Wilcher Transcripts* or other privately circulated conspiracy scenarios, the facts are clearly these: The American Presidency has been powerless since JFK was assassinated. Following JFK were:

- Lyndon B. Johnson, who could not live with the contradictions of his office and simply gave up.
- Richard M. Nixon, who was hounded from office by a pariah media establishment and forced to resign in disgrace.

- Gerald R. Ford, an "appointed" president who simply did what he was told.
- And Jimmy Carter, who genuinely tried to change the course of the nation, only to be handcuffed by the Iranian hostage crisis. Whether or not the "October Surprise" took place, clearly the hostage issue doomed the Carter administration.

And then we get to the Ronald Reagan-George Bush years. We feel that history will show that the years 1980 through 1992 were dominated by a de facto three-term presidency. George Herbert Walker Bush was the duly elected President of the United States from 1988 to 1992, but also ran the country covertly with Reagan as figurehead. Nothing else makes sense, especially when the Iran-Contra, savings and loan collapse and BCCI issues are analyzed thoroughly. Indeed, Reagan had no idea what was going on, but Bush clearly knew what was happening. As a career intelligence operative and former chief of the CIA, Bush also knew how to handle these sensitive operations and avoid the pitfalls which created such monstrous problems with the patched-together cover-up of the JFK-RFK-Martin Luther King Jr. assassination cover-ups.

One thing the *Skeleton Key* and associated conspiracy theories are truthful about is that organized crime and the U.S. intelligence community has enjoyed a fruitful relationship which is now visibly fragmenting. The *Wilcher Transcripts*, when all the high-pitched emotion is stripped from them, is accurate when it states that botched operations—like the Manson family slayings, the Jonestown disaster and the Waco religious cult holocaust — have precipitated breakaway factions within the U.S. intelligence establishment that are now willing to step forth and tell all. Wilcher describes at least "16 agents" who took part in the Waco "massacre," fed up with such activity, who will offer sworn testimony in exchange for immunity from prosecution, having been sickened by the mindless violence associated with that atrocity.

Another major breaking point is with the cockpit videotape that purported "October Surprise" pilot Gunther Russbacher is soon to supply authorities, if he has not already done so. This tape, which shows George Bush flying back from the "October Surprise" meeting with the Iranians in October of 1980, was procured from the high-security archives of the National Security Agency (NSA) with help from insiders loyal to Russbacher, according to the *Wilcher Transcripts*. Russbacher was one of the nation's top intelligence talents and is now prepared to turn on the "shadow government" and expose it for what it is.

Yet another schism in the intelligence community is the increasing presence of private security and espionage services which are spreading at an alarming rate. These services are not answerable to the government, and are often staffed by former CIA, FBI and State Department intelligence operatives. These services are also global in scope and control such sensitive areas as the nuclear power and computer industries. They are headed for a direct confrontation with the government intelligence agencies.

This was never more apparent than with the Inslaw software scandal, which started off as a juvenile rip-off and has mushroomed into a major league intelligence feud. The stolen software and its variations now dominate surveillance of virtually anyone the government wants to follow, not only domestically but on a global basis as well. The biggest obstacle here is the federal Department of Justice, which we feel is corrupt to the core and needs a complete overhaul. But current Attorney General Janet Reno is simply uninformed as to the extent of the DOJ problem. She has possessed the *Wilcher Transcripts* since May of 1993 and has chosen not to take immediate, aggressive action to investigate the charges contained therein, despite evidence that some of them might actually have substance.

The control that used to be exerted by people like Aristotle Onassis is a thing of the past. Technology is the main culprit at present and needs to be reined in before it gets so out of control that Americans will lose control of their nation as established by the Constitution.

Of course, the print and broadcast media have made it a

point to keep any discussion of these crucial issues at an absolute minimum. Watergate was an important lesson, and the very forces that revealed the Watergate cover-up revelations are now stamping out opposition to what is going on right now. The *Washington Post* and the *New York Times* have a chokehold on most other print media, and the four major television networks and satellite cable services are easily controlled by central authorities. The actual free press as envisioned and protected by the Constitution is a thing of the past, except for scattered alternative newspapers and book presses which are undercapitalized and easily squeezed out of existence by the dominant media. With the GATT treaty, American entertainment conglomerates are muscling their way into international markets and will soon monopolize artistic expression worldwide.

And look what is pushed onto populations: Excessive violent programming across the board, "gangster" rap which glorifies criminal behavior, obvious cover-ups and "investigations" that seek to prevent the public from knowing the truth.

Even glimmers of hope are disappearing. Bobby Ray Inman, the retired admiral who had been appointed the new Secretary of Defense by Clinton, before backing out, happens to side with a reformist wing of the U.S. intelligence community. Inman monitored the dangerous William Casey and made sure Congress knew about him. We know from documented sources that Inman is very close to Gunther Russbacher and would have made sure nothing happened to the aviator. In fact, under some operational procedures, Russbacher actually served as Inman's *double* since they look so much alike, according to recent media reports. But Clinton could not get away with the appointment.

It could be that the long-time grip on power that the "shadow government" has held since the JFK assassination might never be loosened. The only way to reverse this is to keep the fires burning, and the information flowing. Bruce Roberts and others like him have championed the cause as pioneers of revisionist history. We must all follow that lead.

Figure 2 347

Conspiracy Network

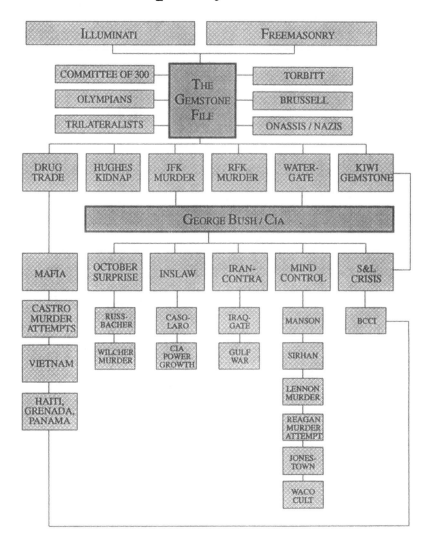

Fig. 2, ©1994 by Gerald A. Carroll

INDEX

. . . .

(Names Index in bold-face; Regular Index in light-face)

J _____

K _____

THE IMMACULATE DECEPTION
THE BUSH CRIME FAMILY EXPOSED
By Russell S. Bowen
$12.95 + SHIPPING...210pgs...Trade Paper
ISBN: 0-922356-80-7

This is perhaps the most shocking book written this century about **TREASON** committed by the highest leaders within the U.S. Government. This disturbing and thought-provoking exposé, which few Americans know anything about, is written by **Ret. Brigadier General Russell S. Bowen**, who has courageously come forward with the truth about his association with the **Office of Security Services** (OSS), and his "drug running" activities in behalf of the "secret" government. You will learn about the unsavory past of **George Bush** and his family, as well as the unscrupulous and treasonous activities in which he has been and is currently involved. Knowing the truth will arm you as a citizen of our country against the tyranny of our "leadership." We the people must unite with the sword of truth and knowledge for the enemy has infiltrated within our very government!

WHERE WAS GEORGE:

When during World WAR II his shipmates were drowning after the
    bomber plane **George Bush** was piloting was shot down?
When the Bay of Pigs fiasco was planned and executed?
When **President John F. Kennedy** was assassinated?
When a "deal" was made to hold the hostages in Iran until after
    the inauguration of Reagan?
When **Ronald Reagan** was nearly assassinated in Washington
    by a known Bush family associate?
When the truth about his association with Iraq should have been
    made clear to the American people?

Says Bowen, *"Don't ask George Bush to answer the above questions. He's more acquainted with deniability than tell the truth."*

KNOWING THE TRUTH WILL ARM YOU AS A CITIZEN OF OUR COUNTRY AGAINST THE TYRANNY OF OUR "LEADERSHIP." WE THE PEOPLE MUST UNITE WITH THE SWORD OF TRUTH AND KNOWLEDGE FOR THE ENEMY HAS INFILTRATED WITHIN OUR VERY GOVERNMENT! IT IS TIME TO WAKE-UP AMERICA BEFORE THE SOVEREIGNTY GUARANTEED UNDER OUR U.S. CONSTITUTION IS ABOLISHED!

ABOUT THE AUTHOR

Gerald A. Carroll is a Program Assistant and Adjunct Assistant Professor for the University of Iowa School of Journalism and Mass Communication. Prior to that appointment, he spent 20 years as a newspaper reporter, columnist and editor with Gannett, Copley, Thomson, Hearst and McNaughton companies, the bulk of that at the Hearst-owned *San Francisco Examiner.* He is a graduate of California State University-Sacramento. Carroll is married with two children and resides in Iowa City, Iowa.

For other titles
or a free catalog
call 800-729-4131
or visit www.nohoax.com

CPSIA information can be obtained at www.ICGtesting.com

263700BV00006B/1/P

9 780964 010406